VANCOUVER
& BRITISH COLUMBIA

Signpost
Guides

Titles in this series include:

- **Andalucía and the Costa del Sol**, with the cities of Granada, Cordoba and Seville
- **Australia**, the whole continent in one volume, with all major sights and attractions, including Tasmania
- **Bavaria and the Austrian Tyrol**, with guides to Salzburg and Munich
- **Brittany and Normandy**, with scenic routes from the Channel ports
- **California**, with Las Vegas and the Grand Canyon
- **Catalonia and the Spanish Pyrenees**, including Bilbao, Barcelona and the Costa Brava
- **Dordogne and Western France**, including Bordeaux and the Atlantic coast
- **Florida**, with a full guide to theme parks
- **Ireland**, with Eire and Northern Ireland
- **Languedoc and South-west France**, including Cathar country, the Cévennes, and the Tarn and Gard regions
- **New England**, with Boston and Cape Cod
- **New Zealand**, including outdoor activities and national parks
- **Portugal**, from the sunny Algarve, via Lisbon and Oporto to the magnificent mountains of the north
- **Provence and the Côte d'Azur**, from the glittering Mediterranean to the inland villages of the Alpes de Haute Provence
- **Scotland**, including the Highlands and Islands, Royal Deeside and the Whisky Routes
- **Vancouver and British Columbia**, including Victoria, river-raft expeditions, railway journeys and the Rockies
- **Selected Hotels and Inns in North America**, the definitive guide for the independent traveller

and

- **Bed and Breakfast in France 2000**, the Guide to friendly B&B accommodation throughout France

For further information about these and other Thomas Cook publications, write to Thomas Cook Publishing, PO Box 227, Thorpe Wood, Peterborough PE3 6PU, United Kingdom

Signpost
Guides

VANCOUVER
& BRITISH COLUMBIA

The best of Vancouver's big city
attractions plus Victoria's heritage
buildings and the magnificent scenery
of British Columbia's mountains,
forests and rivers

Fred Gebhart and Maxine Cass

The
Globe
Pequot
Press

Guilford, Connecticut

Thomas
Cook
Publishing

Published by Thomas Cook Publishing
The Thomas Cook Group Ltd
PO Box 227
Thorpe Wood
Peterborough PE3 6PU
United Kingdom

Telephone 01733 503571
E-Mail: books@thomascook.com
Advertising sales: 01733 503568

The Globe Pequot Press, PO Box 480, Guilford, Connecticut, USA, 06437

Text: © 2000 The Thomas Cook Group Ltd
Maps and diagrams:
Road maps supplied and designed by Lovell Johns Ltd., OX8 8LH
Road map data © Map Quest.com Inc., Mountville PA 17554
City maps prepared by RJS Associates, © Thomas Cook Group Ltd.

ISBN 0 7627 0692 9

Library of Congress Cataloging-in-Publication Data is available.

Publisher: Stephen York
Commissioning Editor: Deborah Parker
Map Editor: Bernard Horton

Series Editor: Christopher Catling
Copy Editor: Karen Pieringer
Proofreader: Merle Read
Written and researched by: Fred Gebhart and Maxine Cass

Although every care has been taken in compiling this publication, and the contents
are believed to be correct at the time of printing, The Thomas Cook Group Ltd cannot
accept responsibility for errors or omissions, however caused, or for the changes in
detail given in the guide book, or for the consequences of any reliance on the
information provided.

The opinions and assessments expressed in this book do not necessarily represent
those of The Thomas Cook Group Ltd.

Readers are asked to remember that attractions and establishments may open, close
or change owners or circumstances during the lifetime of this edition. Descriptions
and assessments are given in good faith but are based on the authors views and
experience at the time of writing and therefore contain an element of subjective
opinion which may not accord with the readers subsequent experience.

We would be grateful to be told of any changes and inaccuracies in order to update
future editions. Please notify them to the commissioning Editor at the above address.

About the authors

Fred Gebhart has lived in the West for more than 40 years, interrupted by extended sojourns in Europe and West Africa. He has travelled BC as a teenager as well as an adult, exploring by bicycle, kayak, rail, horseback, helicopter, sailboat and cruise ship, as well as by car. A freelance photojournalist for two decades, Fred covers the western side of North America for publications in Asia and Europe, and Australasia for North American readers. Fred has written eight Thomas Cook titles with his wife, Maxine Cass, including *Signpost Guide: California, Discover Guide: California* and *Discover Guide: Florida*. Fred's passion is scuba diving, a love that is more happily consummated in tropical climes than in the vivid but chilly waters off British Columbia.

In the 40-some years since **Maxine Cass** was born on the Stanford University campus in Palo Alto, California, she has studied Medieval European History at the University of California, Santa Barbara, lived in Greece and Senegal and become a widely published photojournalist and writer. Maxine is the author of the *AAA Photo Journey to San Francisco* and contributes to travel and business publications in Europe, the US, Canada and Asia, as well as collaborating with other authors on the *Signpost Guides, On the Road Around* and *Discover Guides* series. Between research trips around the world and exploring every corner of the West, Maxine gardens and shares the indulgences of two pampered cats with her husband and series co-author, Fred Gebhart, at their home in San Francisco.

Acknowledgements

The authors and publishers would like to thank the following people and organisations for their assistance during the preparation of this book: John Bateman, Super, Natural British Columbia; BC Ferries; BC Rail; Monica Campbell-Hoppé, Canadian Tourism Commission; Heather Day, Tourism Victoria; Lou Gebhart; Michael & Manon Hobbis and the *Duen*; Laurel Point Inn, Victoria; Paul & Virginia McCarthy; Mendo; Mary Ellen Quesada; Panther; Julia Retallack, Vancouver, Coast & Mountains Tourism Region; Miranda Richter & Dick Griffith, Air Canada; The Rocky Mountaineer; Laura Serena, Tourism Vancouver and VIA Rail.

Contents

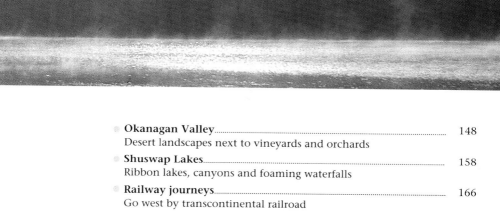

About Signpost Guides

Thomas Cook's Signpost Guides are designed to provide you with a comprehensive but flexible reference source to guide you as you tour a country or region by car. This guide divides Vancouver and British Columbia into touring areas – one per chapter. Major cultural centres o cities form chapters in their own right. Each chapter contains enough attractions to provide at least a day's worth of activities – often more.

Star ratings
To make it easier for you to plan your time and decide what to see, the principal sights and attractions are given a star rating. A three-star rating indicates an outstanding sight or major attraction. Often these can be worth at least half a day of your time. A two-star attraction i worth an hour or so of your time, and a one-star attraction indicates a site that is good but often of specialist interest.

Chapter contents
Every chapter has an introduction summing up the main attraction of the area, and a ratings box, which will highlight the area's strength and weaknesses – some areas may be more attractive to familie travelling with children, others to wine-lovers visiting vineyards, and others to people interested in finding castles, churches, nature reserve or good beaches.

Each chapter is then divided into an alphabetical gazetteer, and a suggested tour. You can select whether you just want to visit a particular sight or attraction, choosing from those described in the gazetteer, or whether you want to tour the area comprehensively. I the latter, you can construct your own itinerary, or follow the authors suggested tour, which comes at the end of every area chapter.

The gazetteer
The gazetteer section describes all the major attractions in the area - the villages, towns, historic sites, nature reserves, parks or museum that you are most likely to want to see. Maps of the area highlight al the places mentioned in the text. Using this comprehensive overview of the area, you may choose just to visit one or two sights.

One way to use the guide is simply to find individual sights that interest you, using the index, overview map or star ratings, and read what our authors have to say about them. This will help you decide whether to visit the sight. If you do, you will find plenty of practical information, such as the street address, the telephone number for enquiries and opening times.

Alternatively, you can choose a hotel, perhaps with the help of the accommodation recommendations contained in this guide. You can

Symbol Key

❶ Tourist Information Centre

⇄ Advice on arriving or departing

❷ Parking locations

❸ Advice on getting around

⊃ Directions

❹ Sights and attractions

❺ Accommodation

❻ Eating

❼ Shopping

❽ Sport

❾ Entertainment

Practical information

The practical information in the page margins, or sidebar, will help you locate the services you need as an independent traveller – including the tourist information centre, car parks and public transport facilities. You will also find the opening times of sights, museums, churches and other attractions, as well as useful tips on shopping, market days, cultural events, entertainment, festivals and sports facilities.

then turn to the overall map on page 10 to help you work out which chapters in the book describe those cities and regions that lie closest to your chosen touring base.

Driving tours

The suggested tour is just that – a suggestion, with plenty of optional detours and one or two ideas for making your own discoveries, under the heading *Also worth exploring*. The routes are designed to link the attractions described in the gazetteer section, and to cover outstandingly scenic coastal, mountain and rural landscapes. The total distance is given for each tour, as is the time it will take you to drive the complete route, but bear in mind that this indication is just for the driving time: you will need to add on extra time for visiting attractions along the way.

Many of the routes are circular, so that you can join them at any point. Where the nature of the terrain dictates that the route has to be linear, the route can either be followed out and back, or you can use it as a link route, to get from one area in the book to another.

As you follow the route descriptions, you will find names picked out in bold capital letters – this means that the place is described fully in the gazetteer. Other names picked out in bold indicate additional villages or attractions worth a brief stop along the route.

Accommodation and food

In every chapter you will find lodging and eating recommendations for individual towns, or for the area as a whole. These are designed to cover a range of price brackets and concentrate on more characterful small or individualistic hotels and restaurants. In addition, you will find information in the *Travel facts* chapter on chain hotels, with an address to which you can write for a guide, map or directory. The price indications used in the guide have the following meanings:

$	budget level
$$	typical/average prices
$$$	de luxe

Page 206

Prince Rupert

Page 116

Hazelton

Page 106

Terrace

Page 214

Page 166

M

Houston

Fraser Lake

Kitimat

P

P

Wistaria

Hartley Bay

Quesnel

Kiemtu

Page 198

Bella Coola

Williams La

Bella Bella

Kleena Kleene

Page 96

Port Hardy

Alert Bay

Kelsey Bay

Page

Campbell River

Page 86

Squam

Courtenay

Parksville

P

Tofino

Port Alberni

Page 56

Ucluelet

Nanaimo

Page 76

Port Renfrew

V

Sydney

P

Victoria

Page 6

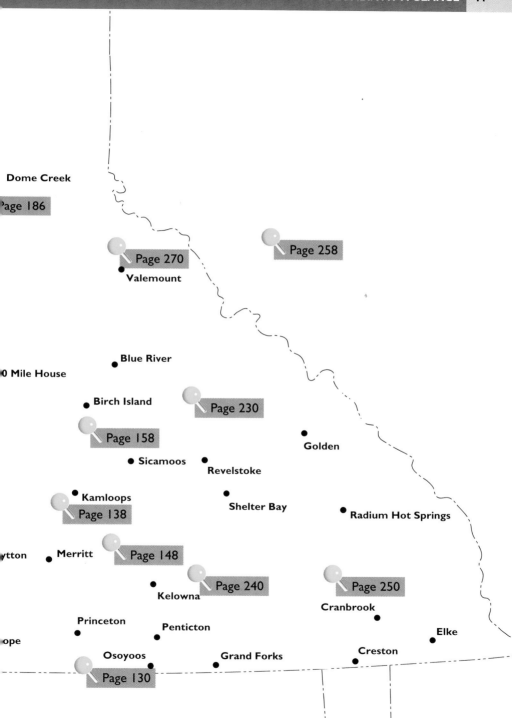

Dome Creek

age 186

Page 270

Valemount

Page 258

Blue River

0 Mile House

Birch Island

Page 230

Page 158

Golden

Sicamoos

Revelstoke

Kamloops

Shelter Bay

Page 138

Radium Hot Springs

ytton   Merritt   Page 148

Page 240

Page 250

Kelowna

Cranbrook

Princeton   Penticton

Elke

ope

Osoyoos   Grand Forks   Creston

Page 130

Introduction

Above
Fraser River

Even if you've been to British Columbia before, you may have missed the best the province has to offer. If this is your first visit, chances are that you'll still miss some of the most amazing country to be found in North America. BC is simply too big, too grand and too empty to take in at one visit. It's not that the province doesn't try. The provincial tourist authority calls itself Super, Natural British Columbia, trying to convey the immense variety bursting from within its boundaries. But the grand sense of space and discovery that comes from so few people scattered across such an immense territory is also BC's biggest stumbling block. Beyond Vancouver, BC's economic heartland, Victoria, its political capital, and a handful of smaller population centres, the province is almost empty.

British Columbians are justifiably proud of the rolling grasslands of the Chilcotin Plateau stretching westward from Williams Lake, but few have actually *seen* the vast prairies and the occasional rough-hewn fence snaking along the only road for 200km in any direction. The magnificently decaying totem poles that still dot the Queen Charlotte Islands a century after smallpox decimated the population are famous around the globe. But more Americans, Britons, Germans, Italians and Japanese actually visit Gwaii Haanas National Park each year than Canadians.

That's not to deny BC's obvious urban allure. Vancouver is one of the cleanest, most scenic and most walkable big cities in North America, a combination of late 19th-century urban planning and late 20th-century affluence, surrounded by snow-capped mountains and sparkling ocean inlets. Victoria is a classic capital that has adapted to the modern era without sacrificing its grand façades, open views or British style.

BC is schizophrenic. Greenpeace was born of ecological angst in Vancouver, yet both city and province remain heavily dependent on the continuing exploitation of forest, fish and mineral resources that are rapidly disappearing. The sea otters and fur seals that first lured outsiders to the BC coast have been hunted to extinction. Coastal and interior rain forests that once stretched for days in any direction are being systematically reduced to scattered holdings in isolated parklands.

Seemingly endless shoals of silvery salmon that gave coastal and interior First Nation groups the wealth and leisure to produce some of the finest art the world has seen have been reduced to annual trickles by overfishing at sea and clearcutting (the practice of cutting down every tree, leaving the landscape barren) on land. Toxic run-off from mining operations in the Kootenays and other regions that have been closed for three generations continues to poison the land.

The unrelenting and very public battle between preservation and continued exploitation gives BC a sense of tension and endless struggle. Look carefully from viewpoints such as Meadows in the Sky, vast wildflower fields at the top of Mount Revelstoke, and it's easy to believe that nature reigns supreme and serene. Turn your gaze beyond park boundaries and entire mountainsides have been shorn of trees and riven with erosion scars.

It seems a miracle that any sense whatsoever of the natural grandeur of forest, lake and mountains, the isolation and unabashed awe recorded by travellers less than 150 years ago, can still be found. It's more a testament to commercial and political avarice than to any far-sighted policy of preservation.

Early businessmen and politicians contrived to turn immense tracts of crown lands into semi-private playgrounds along railways and roadways and called them National Parks. Banff, Glacier, Jasper and Yoho may have been created for the enjoyment of the rich and the enrichment of the Canadian Pacific Railway, but all have become spiritual and physical refuges for the public.

It's not the first time that private enrichment schemes have backfired. BC's original First Nation inhabitants were systematically deprived of land, liberty and tradition by government policies designed to open the land to White settlers, loggers and miners. But the traditions and peoples that generations of government agents worked so hard to suppress have re-emerged as potent political, economic and cultural forces – fuelled in large part by modern angst over those not-so-long-ago transgressions.

Change has become a permanent part of the BC landscape. The First Nations were overtaken by fur traders and explorers in the 18th century, who were themselves displaced by lumbermen, then by farmers, in the 19th century, only to be overtaken by First Nations claims in the 20th century.

Nature continues a tug-of-war, with points won and lost on all sides. The once-mighty Columbia River has long-since been banished into a series of placid lakes behind a series of dams extending south into the United States. At Rogers Pass, railway builders abandoned the surface to unrelenting snowfall and endless avalanches and drove tunnels nearly 400m beneath the inhospitable pass. Faced with similar problems in the Cascades, the Kettle Valley Railway simply gave up and closed.

Whether resource industries simply give up or find new routes in the 21st century remains to be seen. The battle between exhausting natural resources or preserving them for future uses is already straining BC's social and economic fabric. Either way, the outcome will mean the passing of traditional ways of life that someone holds dear. If BC finally breaks with tradition to favour conservation, the awe-inspiring scenery that has been creating legends for the last 100 centuries will still be around for another visit.

Travel facts

Accommodation

Chain hotels and motels provide the most reliable accommodation, while bed and breakfast may be good value outside major cities. Expect to pay $100–200 per night in major cities, $40–100 in smaller towns, single or double occupancy.

To book accommodation, including some national park camping pitches, contact **Super, Natural British Columbia**, *tel: (800) 435-5622* or *(250) 800-HELLOBC; web: www.hellobc.com/*

Travel Alberta, *tel: (800) 661-8888* or *(780) 427-4321*, has lodging information but does not make bookings. Local tourist offices have lists of area accommodations.

Prices vary as much as 60 per cent from value season to high season (about mid-May to early September, and winter at ski resorts), when cities and tourism areas are booked out months in advance.

Airports

Most international visitors arrive at Vancouver International Airport (YVR). Calgary International Airport (YYC) provides access to the Rocky Mountain National Parks from Alberta. For flight information and bookings, contact individual airlines, not the airport. Luggage trolleys are free for international arrivals; expect to pay $1–2 at local airports. Major airports have foreign exchange and banking services as well as car hire/rental facilities. Airport Improvement Tax of $5–15 is levied unless passengers have same-day flight connections.

Children

Most attractions offer reduced prices for children (or students). Major hotels and motels can arrange for baby-sitters, a pricey service. Children stay free in their parents' room with many motel chains.

Picnics offer mealtime flexibility, so does a small cooler filled with cold drinks and snacks. Most towns have roadside restaurants with long hours, cheap children's menus and familiar names.

Climate

Western Canadians are proud of the damp coastal weather that nurtures lush forests and the dramatic climate that transforms the interior with a snowy winter blanket or sizzling summer temperatures. Weather and temperature can vary widely along the coast, fog one

Thomas Cook Foreign Exchange Bureaux

Thomas Cook Foreign
Exchange
Pan Pacific Hotel
999 Canada Place Suite 130
Vancouver VC6 3D5
Tel: 1 604 6411229

Thomas Cook Foreign
Exchange
Park Royal Shopping
Centre
2009 South Park Royal
West Vancouver V7T IAI
Tel: 1 604 913 0034

Thomas Cook Travel
Eatons
Brentwood Shopping
Centre
2193A, 4700 Kingsway
Burnaby V5H 4MI
Tel: 1 604 430 3990

Thomas Cook Foreign
Exchange
IIII Guildford Town
Centre
Guildford Mall
Surrey V3R INI
Tel: 1 604 584 3338

hour, drizzle the next, crisp blue sky followed by scudding clouds. Prepare for rain and snow from October to April, and plunging temperatures and heavy snow any month in the Canadian Rockies. Coastal BC climate is moderated by the Pacific Ocean. Victoria and the Gulf Islands are famed as Canadian sun spots, sheltered by Vancouver Island's mountains and Washington's Olympic Mountains.

Currency

Canadian dollars come in denominations of $1 and $2 coins, and $5, $10, $20, $50 and $100 notes (bills). Bills vary in colour, but are the same size. There are 100 cents to the dollar. Coins are: 1 cent (penny), 5 cents (nickel), 10 cents (dime), 25 cents (quarter), 1 dollar (loonie) and 2 dollars (toonie).

The safest forms of money are travellers' cheques and credit or debit cards. Carry at least one, preferably two, major credit cards, such as **American Express, MasterCard (Access)** or **Visa**. Car hire companies, hotels and motels require a credit card or a substantial cash deposit, even if the bill has been prepaid or will be settled in cash. Some shops, motels, restaurants and petrol (gas) stations will accept only cash.

Thomas Cook Travellers' Cheques free you from the hazards of carrying large amounts of cash. Thomas Cook foreign exchange bureaux are listed in the side column. They all provide full foreign exchange facilities and will change currency and travellers' cheques (free of commission in the case of Thomas Cook Travellers' Cheques). They can also provide emergency assistance in the event of loss or theft of Thomas Cook Travellers' Cheques.

Banks can exchange foreign currency or travellers' cheques, but expect delays at small town branches. Travellers' cheques from well-known issuers such as Thomas Cook are acceptable everywhere. To report Thomas Cook Travellers' Cheque losses and thefts; *tel: (800) 223-7373* (freephone, 24-hour service).

Customs allowances

Visitors to Canada may bring 1.14 litres of spirits or wine or 8.5 litres of beer or ale, 200 cigarettes, 50 cigars and 200g of loose tobacco.

Check with customs officials at home for returning duty-free allowances. Because of taxes, alcohol is cheaper at duty-free shops. Tobacco and perfume are cheaper at supermarkets and department stores than at airport and duty-free shops.

Drinking laws

The minimum drinking age is 19 in British Columbia and 18 in Alberta and it is strictly enforced. Beer, wine and spirits can be purchased in BC-owned Liquor Stores; beer and wine are also available in privately owned beer and wine stores. Look for beer, wine and

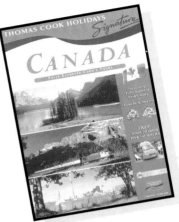
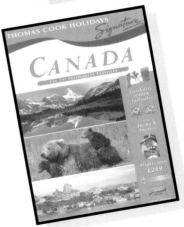

Electricity

Canada uses 110 volt, 60 Hertz current with two- or three-prong plugs. Power and plug converters are seldom available.

Beware of buying electrical equipment – it probably won't operate on the 220v 50 Hz power the rest of the world uses. Exceptions are battery-operated items such as radios, cameras and portable computers.

Be equally wary of pre-recorded videotapes. Canada uses the NTSC format while most other countries use PAL or SECAM. When buying pre-recorded videos, check the box for compatibility. If no system is listed, it's probably NTSC.

spirits in provincially licensed Liquor Stores in Alberta. Licensed establishments, bars, lounges, saloons, taverns or pubs may open between 0800 and varying times after midnight.

Laws against drinking and driving are severe and strictly enforced *(see Drinking and driving laws, page 26)*.

Eating out

Canadians enjoy eating out as an occasion, a chance for social mixing and to see how the rest of the world lives. Even in casual spots, smart-casual clothing and footwear are required.

Salmon and berry dishes have been part of the Western Canadian diet for generations, and are dependable. Very few things from Canada on any menu are expensive, though imported foodstuffs or exotic game such as caribou will reflect availability and cost of transportation. Portions are hearty, in keeping with pioneer traditions of serving without stint.

Breakfast often includes rashers of Canadian bacon or sausages with hash browns (shredded fried potatoes), eggs, pancakes and toast. Bagels, fruit or bran muffins, scones or English muffins (crumpets), porridge or cereal are other possibilities. A 'Continental breakfast' is juice, coffee or tea and bread or pastry.

Lunch and dinner menus feature appetisers (starters), salads, soups, pastas, entrées (main courses) and deserts. Salads come at the beginning of the meal. Sunday brunch (usually 1100–1400), self-service buffets piled high with hot and cold dishes, can be good value for hearty eaters. Many fast-food outlets have drive-up windows. Look for A&W, Burger King, KFC (Kentucky Fried Chicken), Little Caesar's, McDonald's, Pizza Hut and Taco Bell.

Coffee and tea are widely available and, except when served at coffee shops or coffee houses in major cities, often weaker than that served in Europe. Iced tea may be sweet; ask if you prefer it plain, without sugar and unflavoured. Plain water is served free of charge upon request.

Entry formalities

Except for US citizens whose proof of citizenship can be a birth certificate, voter registration, baptismal certificate or a passport, non-Canadian citizens generally need a passport. Check with the Canadian Embassy or Consulate for passport, visa and proof of return travel requirements before departing for Canada.

Canada prohibits revolvers, pistols, fully automatic firearms and other weapons and self-defence sprays such as mace and pepper spray. Firearms such as hunting rifles and shotguns must be declared at entry. Narcotics and certain pharmaceutical products may not be imported. Carry documentation such as a doctor's prescription to prove that medications are legitimate.

Festivals

Western Canada's events are the mirror of the community, from wine festivals (Okanagan Spring (May) and Fall (mid-Oct) Wine Festivals) and fruit (Peach Festival, Penticton – Aug), to boating events (Classic Boat Festival, Victoria Inner Harbour – Sep), rodeos (Clinton Rodeo – May) and First Nations pow-wows (Squilax Pow Wow, Squilax, North Shuswap – July; Kamploopa Pow Wow, Kamloops – Aug) and sophisticated music, film and theatre festivals in Vancouver (DuMaurier International Jazz Festival Vancouver – late Jun–early Jul; Vancouver Folk Music Festival – mid-Jul; Benson and Hedges Symphony of Fire(works) – late Jul–early Aug; Vancouver International Film Festival – late Sep–early Oct) and Victoria (Shakespeare Festival – Jul; Fringe Theatre Festival – Aug; Vancouver Island Blues Bash – Sep).

Food

Rich, delicate salmon is king on any Western Canadian menu, from raw to grilled, broiled, poached, creamed, sauced or doused with Eastern Canada's contribution, maple syrup. Fish is delicious whether farmed or wild. Alberta contributes lean beef and buffalo for meat eaters; autumn brings caribou, venison and elk (wapiti) to the menu.

The Okanagan Valley's fruitbasket grows peaches, pears, apples, cherries, plums, nectarines, grapes and vegetables, while the Lower Fraser Valley produces berries – blueberries, raspberries, blackberries, gooseberries and huckleberries.

Health

In the event of a life-threatening emergency, telephone 911 for an ambulance. If a life is at stake, treatment will be swift and professional as government-run health programmes cover everyone. Non Canadians pay for treatment, and non-emergency care cost is reasonable, though emergency care can be exorbitant. Most travel agents selling international travel offer travel insurance policies covering Canadian medical costs.

Bring prescription medication for the entire trip, plus a few extra days. Carry a copy of the prescription showing the generic (chemical name and formulation, not just a brand name.

Canada is basically a healthy place. No inoculations are required and common sense is enough to avoid most health problems. Eat sensibly and don't drink water that hasn't come from the tap or a bottle. Most ground water is contaminated with *Giardia lamblia* which results in a severe bacterial infection of the gut.

Sunglasses, broad-brimmed hats and sun-screen help prevent sunburn, sunstroke and heat prostration. Drink plenty of non alcoholic liquids, especially in warm weather.

Information

Tourism British Columbia PO Box 9830, tn Prov Govt, Victoria, BC 8W 9W5; tel: (800) 435-622 or (250) 387-1642; or 3 Regent St, London, England SW1Y 4NS; tel: 0171) 930 6857; web: www.travel.bc.ca

Travel Alberta PO Box 500, Edmonton, AB T5J Z4; tel: (800) 661-8888 or 780) 427-4321; fax: (780) 27-0867; web: www.discoveralberta.com

(National) **Parks Canada: British Columbia** Box 29, 23433 Mavis Ave, Fort angley, BC V1M 2R5; tel: 604) 666-1280; fax: (604) 13-4798; **Alberta** Room 52, 220-4th Ave SE, Calgary, AB T2G 4X3; tel: 800) 748-7275 or (403) 92-4401; fax: (403) 292-408; eb: www.parkscanada. ch.gc.ca

(Provincial) **BC Parks** 800 ohnson St, Victoria, BC V8V X4; tel: (250) 387-4550; web: www.elp.gov.bc. a/bcparks

Insurance

Travel insurance should over your body, your elongings and your oliday investment. Buy over for delayed or ancelled flights, as well as weather problems and vacuation in case of medical emergencies.

Language

Canada is officially bi-ngual in English and French; all public signage and documents will be in oth languages (see also age 282).

Maps

The **Canadian Automobile Association** (CAA) prints useful road maps in conjunction with the **American Automobile Association** (AAA), free to members at CAA offices. The RAC and other automobile clubs have reciprocal agreements with the CAA. **MapArt** *70 Bloor St E, Oshawa, ON L1H 3M2; tel: (905) 436-2525*, produce easy-to-use regional and city maps. Detailed, 3-dimensional maps of Rocky Mountain National Parks are designed by **Gem Trek Publishing** *Box 1618, Cochrane, AB T0L 0W0; tel: (403) 266-2523*.

Museums

Most museums charge an entry fee, and are closed one day a week. Rural museums sometimes open only on weekends or in summer.

National and Provincial Parks

National Parks and Historic Heritage Sites charge daily entry fees per person. Camping fees are extra. Save money and purchase the personal **Great Western Annual Pass** ($35) for entry to 11 parks (excluding Gwaii Haanas National Park). BC Provincial Parks fees vary, and differ seasonally.

Opening times

Standard office and business hours are 0830/0900–1630/1700 Mon–Fri. Most banks are open Mon–Fri 1000–1600, and Sat mornings. ATMs are open 24 hours. Shops are open Mon–Wed and Sat 0900/1000–1800, and Thur and Fri until 2100. Sun hours are 1100/1200–1700.

Tourist offices outside Vancouver and Victoria have limited hours or are closed from mid-Sept–mid-May. Petrol (gas) stations are open long hours, but may close between 2200 and 0630. Pub, saloon and restaurant hours vary greatly between areas, but are likely to close earlier in winter. Call churches, synagogues, temples or mosques in advance for services and open hours.

Packing

Outside a handful of restaurants in the major cities and resorts that require business attire, dress is casual and practical. Take rainwear and at least one change of warm clothing (sweater/pullover and jacket) and sturdy shoes, or consider buying them at one of Canada's fine-quality outdoor outfitters.

Dress in layers as temperatures can change dramatically during the day, especially in the mountains and near the ocean. A backpack can be pre-packed or stocked upon arrival with a hat, sun-screen cream,

Public holidays

The following public holidays are observed in British Columbia and Alberta:

New Year's (1 Jan);
Good Friday (Mar/Apr);
Easter Monday (Mar/Apr);
Victoria Day (Mon on
   or prior to 24 May);
Canada Day (1 Jul);
BC Day and Alberta
   Heritage Day (first Mon
   in Aug);
Labour Day
   (first Mon in Sep);
Thanksgiving Day
   (second Mon in Oct);
Remembrance Day
   (11 Nov);
Christmas (25 Dec)
   and Boxing Day (26 Dec).

Post offices and government offices close on public holidays.

insect repellent, sunglasses, prescription medicine, contraceptives, an umbrella, raincoat, electricity adaptor, alarm clock and a camera.

Postal services

Every town has at least one **Canada Post/Postes Canada** office, listed in the phone directory blue pages. Most are open Mon–Fri 0900–1700. Hotel concierges, drug stores and tourist shops often sell stamps.

Letters or parcels sent abroad (even to the USA) should go airmail to avoid delays. Domestic letters generally arrive in three to seven days.

Public transport

• **BC Transit** have extensive systems throughout the province, including Vancouver, *tel: (604) 521-0400*, and Victoria, *tel: (250) 382-6161; web: www.transitbc.com.*
• **BC Ferries**, *tel: (250) 386-3431* or *(888) 223-3779; web: www.bcferries.bc.ca*, serve Victoria, Vancouver Island, the Gulf Islands and Queen Charlotte Islands, Prince Rupert and Bella Coola, with stops along Inside Passage, and other BC coastal areas.

Reading

• *Backroading Vancouver Island,* by Rosemary Neering, 1996, Whitecap Books, Vancouver.
• *The BC Fact Book,* by Mark Zuehlke, 1995, Whitecap Books, Vancouver.
• *The Big New Beautiful British Columbia BC Travel Guide,* by Bryan McGill *et al*, 1999, Beautiful British Columbia, Victoria.
• *The Greater Vancouver Book,* by Chuck Davis et al, 1997, the Linkman Press, Surrey, BC.
• *Haida Gwaii: Journeys Through the Queen Charlotte Islands,* by Ian Gill, 1997, Raincoast Books, Vancouver.
• *Handbook of the Canadian Rockies,* by Ben Gadd, 1995, Corax Press, Jasper.
• *Looking at Indian Art of the Northwest Coast,* by Hilary Stewart, 1979, Douglas & McIntyre, Vancouver/Toronto.
• *More English than the English: A Social History of Victoria*, by Terry Reksten, 1986, Orca Book Publishers, Victoria.
• *Native Peoples and Cultures of Canada,* by Alan D McMillan, 1997, Douglas & McIntyre, Vancouver.
• *Native Sites in Western Canada,* by Pat Kramer, 1994, Altitude Publishing Canada Ltd, Canmore, Alberta.
• *Official Guide to Pacific Rim National Park Reserve,* by JM MacFarlane *et al*, 1996, Blackbird Naturgraphics, Inc, Calgary.
• *Raven Steals the Light,* by Bill Reid and Robert Bringhurst, 1996, Douglas & McIntyre Ltd, Vancouver.

• *Totem Poles*, by Pat Kramer, 1998, Altitude Publishing Canada Ltd, Canmore, Alberta.
• *Touring the Canadian Rockies*, by Fred Gebhart and Maxine Cass, 1998, Thomas Cook Publishing, Peterborough, UK.
• *A Traveller's Guide to Aboriginal BC*, by Cheryl Coull, 1996, Whitecap Books, Vancouver.
• *A Traveller's Guide to Historic British Columbia*, by Rosemary Neering, 1993, Whitecap Books, Vancouver.
• *The West Beyond the West: A History of British Columbia*, by Jean Barman, Revised Edition 1996, University of Toronto Press, Toronto.

Safety and security

• Dial 911 on any telephone for free emergency assistance from police, fire and medical authorities.
• Never discuss travel plans or valuables in public. Walk with assurance in well-lit places and give the impression that you are not worth robbing (eg don't wear expensive jewellery). A wallet in a back pocket or an open handbag is an invitation to theft. Report incidents to local police immediately, and get a report for your insurance company.
• Unwatched luggage can vanish in an instant. Most airports and bus or train stations have lockers; guard the key and memorise the locker number. Hotel bell staff may keep guest luggage for a few days, but always get receipts.
• If your car breaks down, turn on the flashing emergency lights, raise the bonnet and wait inside the vehicle. Have your keys out to unlock car doors before entering a car park on foot, and check around and inside the vehicle before entering. Don't pick up hitchhikers and never leave the car with the engine running.
• Lock room doors, windows and sliding glass doors from the inside. Ground-floor rooms are convenient but easier to break into. When leaving the room at night, leave a light on. When someone knocks at the door, use the peephole to see who it is. If someone claims to be on the hotel staff, check with the front desk. Money, cheques, credit cards, passports and keys should be with you or in the hotel safe deposit box. Photocopy the important pages of your passport and visas. Carry the copies and extra passport photos separately from the documents themselves.

Stores

Major department store chains include The Bay Company and Eaton's. Discount chains are Kmart and Wal-Mart.

Shopping

Food souvenirs include smoked or tinned salmon; local Okanagan Valley wines; dried cherries, berries, and apples; berry conserves and syrups.

Canadian-made clothing and footwear are well made, attractive and practical. Outdoor outfitters and discount stores carry a wide range of goods, many sport-specific. Mountie (RCMP) souvenirs come in wood, tea towels or as stuffed bears or beavers.

First Nations artwork is usually pricey; ask for the artist's certificate of authentication when you purchase an artefact. Aboriginal peoples produce masks; baskets; stone, wooden and soapstone carvings, jewellery; paintings; and hand-made grey or white Cowichan sweaters.

Sport

Vancouver offers several professional sports: NBA Vancouver Grizzlies basketball; NHL Vancouver Canucks hockey; CFL BC Lions football; and Vancouver 86ers soccer. Victoria anticipates hosting IHL Spiders hockey when Victoria Centre is completed after 2000. Playing fields abound throughout British Columbia. Golf, marathons, bicycling, fishing, alpine and Nordic skiing, sailing, windsurfing and the very Canadian sport of curling are popular for individual recreation.

Time

Most of British Columbia is on Pacific Standard Time (PST), GMT -8. Alberta and roughly the Rocky Mountain section of BC are on Mountain Standard Time (MST), GMT -7. Both provinces jump ahead to Daylight Time (PDT) GMT -7/(MDT) GST -6, from the first Sunday in April until the last Sunday in October.

Tipping

Tipping is standard except in the very rare restaurant where a service charge is added. Servers expect 15 per cent of the food and drink charge; bartenders at least 50¢ per drink.

Hotel porters get $1 per bag and the bellperson who shows you your room several dollars more. Expect to pay $1–5 for valet parking each time your car is delivered. Don't tip ushers in cinemas, theatres and similar establishments.

Toilets

Canadians know them as washrooms. Restrooms, bathrooms and toilet are terms imported from the USA. Men and Women are also common designations. Ultra-trendy bars, parks and recreational areas may have unisex washrooms.

Taxes

British Columbia's sales tax is 7 per cent; Alberta has none. Most services are subject to a Canadian Goods and Services Tax, or GST, of 7 per cent, though purchases of goods, including accommodation, of over $50 per transaction can have the GST rebated upon application to *Revenue Canada Visitor Rebate Programme, Summerside Tax Centre, Summerside, PE C1N 6C6; tel: (800) 668-4748 or (902) 432-5608.* Both provinces charge a room tax.

Telephones

Public telephones (pay phones) are marked by a white telephone on a blue background. Dialling instructions are posted on the telephone or in the telephone directory white pages. Local calls cost 25¢; toll-free (800, 877 and 888 area codes) and 911 (emergency) calls are free. To talk to an operator, dial 0. To locate local numbers, dial 411. For long-distance information, dial 1 + area code + 555-1212. There is a charge for all information calls.

Talking Yellow Pages, *tel: (local area code) 299-9000* in both provinces, has free information on time, road conditions, weather, news and entertainment.

Many hotels and motels add steep surcharges to the cost of phone calls, even calling toll-free numbers from rooms; use a pay phone in the lobby. Prepaid phone cards are widely available.

For international enquires or assistance, dial 00. For international calls, dial 011 (access code) + country code + city code (omit the first zero if there is one) + local number. To call inner London, for example, dial 011-44-171 + local number.

Travellers with disabilities

While Federal and provincial laws require that public business and services be readily accessible by handicapped persons, not all are. For specific information, contact **SATH** (Society for the Advancement of Travel for the Handicapped), *347 5th Ave, Suite 610, New York, NY 10016; tel: (212) 447-7284.* **RADAR**, *12 City Forum, 250 City Rd, London EC1V 8AF; tel: (0171) 250 3222,* publishes a useful annual guide, *Holidays and Travel Abroad,* with details of facilities for the disabled in different countries.

Wheelchair accessibility information is free from the **Canadian Paraplegic Association** *780 SW Marine Dr, Vancouver, BC V6P 5Y7; tel: (604) 324-3611; fax (604) 326-1227.* **Access Canada** *Tourism BC, Box 9830, Stn Prov Govt 300–1803 Douglas St, Victoria, BC V8W 9W5,* certifies agility, mobility, vision and hearing-impaired, disabled-designated accommodations, Canada-wide. **SPARC** *106-2182 W 12th Ave, Vancouver, BC V6K 2N4; tel: (604) 736-4367,* provide disabled parking permits.

Driver's guide

Accidents

Canadians drive on the right-hand side of the road. If involved in collision, stop immediately and call the local police or RCMP. Britis Columbia and Alberta require you to produce your driving licence vehicle licence number, vehicle registration number, insurance carrie and policy number along with your contact information. Exchang the same information with the other driver(s) involved in the acciden and get the names and addresses of any witnesses, includin passengers in the other vehicles.

Accidents must also be reported to your car-hire company an insurance company. Vehicle accidents registered in British Columbi must be reported to the province's **Insurance Corporation of Britis Columbia (ICBC)**; *tel: (800) 663-3051* or *(604) 520-8222.*

Automobile clubs

The RAC and other touring clubs have reciprocal agreements with th **Canadian Automobile Association (CAA)**, which in turn ha reciprocal agreements with the **American Automobile Association (AAA)** in the USA. Ask for **CAA** discounts on accommodation, car hir and attraction/museum admission. Road maps are free.

Right
Kabuki Kabs, Victoria

Breakdowns

Pull as far off the road as possible, turn on the flashing hazard lights and raise the bonnet. Use flares at night. Change tyres only when out of traffic. Dial 911 from any telephone for police/RCMP or medical assistance, but not for a breakdown lorry ('tow truck').

CAA or other auto club membership usually includes a free towing service to the nearest garage for repairs. Most car-hire companies either pay for repairs directly or reimburse the cost shown on repair receipts. If a hire car will be out of service for more than a few hours, ask the hire company for a replacement vehicle.

Camper vans, caravans and recreational vehicles

Recreational vehicles or RVs (camper vans and caravans) are a popular way to travel in Western Canada, though hire companies restrict access to some highways and may limit cross-border travel to the USA. Hire options include a choice of daily mileage limits and seasons; high season is July–August.

The higher cost of hiring and operating an RV is offset by savings on accommodation and meals and the convenience of not packing and unpacking at every stop. RVs *are* cramped, and savings evaporate if you give in to the temptation of high-priced hotels and fancy restaurant meals.

Get operating manuals and a full demonstration for *all* systems before leaving with the RV. Shopping, cooking and cleaning take extra time. Buy a pair of sturdy rubber washing gloves to handle daily sewer chores. Pack old clothes to wear while crawling beneath the vehicle to hook up and disconnect at each stop.

RVs drive more like lorries than cars and are generally treated as lorries by traffic laws. They are blown about by the wind more than cars, are more subject to rollover and are also taller and wider than cars, which can create hazards at petrol stations and car parks with low-hanging trees or signs.

To book a camping pitch in **BC Parks**, call **Discover Camping** *tel: (800) 689-9025; web: www.discovercamping.ca/* from March to 15 September.

Car hire

Car categories vary, but most hire companies offer subcompact, compact, economy, mid-sized, full-sized, luxury and sport utility (SUV) vehicles. Book well in advance to ensure getting the type and size vehicle you need. Standard features usually include automatic transmission, air-conditioning and unlimited mileage. Some hire companies restrict travel east of Saskatchewan or into the USA, and/or charge for outside-the-area kilometres; ensure that the hire agreement indicates any restrictions.

It's usually cheaper to pick up a vehicle at an airport than in the city centre. A surcharge, or drop fee, may be levied for dropping the vehicle off somewhere other than the place of hire. Ask about RV one-way rates if you aren't planning to arrive and leave from the same place.

All drivers must be listed on the hire contract. If an unlisted driver has an accident, you will likely be required to pay for repairs yourself.

Most car-hire companies require a credit card deposit, even if the hire has been prepaid. Before leaving, be sure you have all necessary registration and insurance documents and that you know how to operate the vehicle.

Documents

Your home-country driving licence or an International Driver's Licence is valid in British Columbia and Alberta. Always carry it while driving. The minimum legal driving age is 16, but most car-hire companies require that all drivers be at least 21, usually 25. For RVs there may be a maximum age limit, 70 or 75. Be sure to have the vehicle registration and proof of liability insurance at all times.

Drinking and driving laws

DUI, driving under the influence of alcohol or any other drug, is illegal. The criminal blood alcohol limit is 0.08mg. Strict enforcement permits a breath sample to be taken by a police officer. Police establish random checkpoints and frequent roads near winery tasting rooms, popular roadside restaurants and entertainment venues.

Driving conditions

The greatest challenge is that pedestrians always have the right of way at zebra crossings and intersections. Be sure that air-conditioner and heater are both in good order. Carry extra water, food, warm clothing and a torch in case of trouble.

In winter away from the coast, blowing snow can reduce visibility to zero and slow or halt traffic for hours. Highways require mandatory use of chains or other traction devices between 1 November and 30 April, and the speed limit becomes 40–50kph. If you're planning mountain driving in winter, ask the car-hire company to include chains or buy your own (under $50). When chains are required, gas station attendants and roadside workers will install them for about $20. Carry warm clothing and food in case of traffic delays and always keep the petrol tank at least half-full. Useful items include an ice scraper and a small shovel. Snow-bound cars should be equipped with a front engine compartment plug, plugged into an electrical source and the engine block heater turned on when temperatures fall to -10°C.

When cars arrive at an intersection at the same moment, the vehicle to the right proceeds first. Oncoming traffic on narrow roads is required to let the uphill driver proceed. If stuck in mud or snow, gently rock the vehicle by changing from forward to reverse gears.

Stop when a school bus lowers its red and white Stop sign or flashes its lights – and do not pass.

Fuel

Petrol and diesel are sold at gas stations in litres. Most vehicles take unleaded petrol, which comes in regular, premium and super grades. Buy regular unless the car-hire company specifies otherwise. Most stations are self-service, although some offer a higher priced full-serve alternative. Pump prices include all taxes. Gas stations generally accept credit cards and $20 travellers' cheques but will not take $50 or $100 bills because of counterfeiting concerns.

Information

British Columbia **Ministry of Transport and Highways InfoLine** *tel (900) 451-4997 (75 cents)* and the **Alberta Motoring Association (AMA)** *tel: (800) 642-3810,* have recorded road conditions. Local radio stations also broadcast weather and driving information. In urban areas, most stations have regular traffic reports during morning and evening rush hours. **Government of Canada Weather Information** is in the phone directory blue pages. Weather for **British Columbia** is online at *www.weatherwise.com/free/regional/bc/bcmap.htm* and for **Alberta** at *www.weather.total.net/english/ab.shtml*

our perfect
getaway vehicle

iday autos is the world's leading leisure car rental company
h more than 4,000 locations worldwide. with an award
ining service, top quality vehicles and fully inclusive prices
ı can be sure to drive away with a great deal. to hire your
fect getaway vehicle, call:

870 400 0011

w.holidayautos.com

holiday
autos

Lights

Leave headlights on at all times for safety; modern car headlights come on automatically when the car is started.

Insurance

Canadian and US drivers may be covered by their own insurance, but other renters are strongly advised to take out their own coverage or purchase the collision damage waiver (CDW), sometimes called loss damage waiver (LDW), offered by hire companies. Without the waiver, renters are personally liable for the full value of the vehicle CDW is often required as part of fly-drive packages or for RV hire.

Parking

Parking garages, parking lots and parkades (car parks) are indicated by a white P on a blue background. Prices are posted at the entrance, and some urban parkades accept credit cards.

Kerbside parking time is usually limited, either by posted signs or by coin-operated parking meters, where the per-hour rate may be higher than that in lots and parkades.

Kerbs may be colour-coded: *red* is no stopping or parking at any time; *white* is for passenger loading/unloading only; *green* is limited

Below
Banff National Park

ed limits

highway speed limit is
ally 80–100kph for cars,
:ed for less for trucks
RVs. Slow down in
ins and cities where the
: is 50kph or lower. If
ing conditions are
:r, drivers are required
eep to a safe speed, no
:er how slow. Police
radar and aeroplanes
rack, stop and ticket
:ders, but be alert even
n traffic normally flows
ast 10kph above the
:ed limit.

time parking (usually 10 minutes); *yellow* is a commercial loading zone; *blue* is special permit handicapped parking. Parking is not allowed within 5m of a fire hydrant, near a disabled kerb ramp, at bus stops, intersections or zebra crossings (crosswalks), sidewalks (pavements) or on freeways. Fines levied against hired cars are charged against the hirer's credit card.

Police

Local police or the RCMP (Royal Canadian Mounted Police) signal drivers with flashing red and blue lights, sirens and loudhailers. Pull off the roadway as quickly as possible, turn off the engine and roll down the driver's side window. Stay inside the vehicle unless asked to step out. Have your driving licence and vehicle registration ready for inspection and be prepared to give a breath sample to test your blood alcohol level.

Road signs

European-style road signs are widely used. A black chequerboard surrounding a number on a yellow sign indicates a speed limit change in non-urban areas. Signs reflect Canada's official metric usage, and give directions in both English and French.

Seat belts

The driver and all passengers must wear seat belts. Children under the age of 6 or weighing less than 18kg (Alberta) must ride in approved child-safety restraint seats. Safety seats can be hired with a car, or purchased for under $100 at a discount store. In an RV, passengers riding behind the driver's seat need not wear belts, but should be safely seated.

Security

Try not to accept a vehicle with a hire company decal or logo visible – it's an advertisement for theft. You probably can't hide the hire company advert on an RV, but the rolling homes are obvious targets already.

Whether it's an RV or a car, lock your vehicle when you're in it as well as when you leave it. Check for intruders before getting in, especially at night and in RVs any time. Never leave the engine running when the driver isn't behind the wheel and always park in well-lit areas.

Tolls

Except for the 210km Coquihalla Highway, Hwy 5 from Kamloops to Hope *(see pages 127–8)*, which has a $10 toll, there are no other toll roads in British Columbia.

Getting to Vancouver and British Columbia

Unless you already live within driving distance of British Columbia, flying is the most practical way to get there, with rail a close second. **VIA Rail** operates a popular transcontinental railway service to Vancouver and Prince Rupert. Summer schedules are timed for daylight transit through the Rocky Mountains and through the Skeena River Valley to Prince Rupert. **BC Rail** operates popular tourist orientated services between Vancouver and Prince George.

There is also a ferry service from Seattle and other cities in Washington State to Vancouver and Victoria, as well as a rail service from the US via **AMTRAK**.

Motor coach travel is possible, though slow and cramped. Air travel is even more cramped, but travel time is counted in hours rather than days.

If your primary interest is the Rocky Mountains, consider flying into Calgary, Alberta, rather than Vancouver. Banff is two hours by car from Calgary compared to 12 to 14 hours of driving from Vancouver via Hwy 1, the TransCanada Highway. If you *are* driving from Vancouver, consider overnighting in Revelstoke, about halfway to Banff National Park.

No matter where you're flying into, don't let airline flight schedules mislead you into a full first day of touring. Vancouver may be only 10–12 air hours from much of Europe or Asia, but jet lag intensifies the effects of long distance air travel. Expect to arrive fatigued, disoriented, short-tempered and otherwise *not* ready to drive.

Night-time flights are attractive because they seem to offer an extra day of sightseeing upon arrival. Resist the temptation. Most travellers do better by timing their flights to arrive in the late afternoon or early evening, then getting a good night's sleep before tackling the sights. Since many airport area hotels and motels offer a free shuttle service to and from the airport, you can take a shuttle to the hotel, sleep off the flight, shuttle back to the airport the next morning and pick up the rental car at no additional cost.

One of the best 'cures' for jet lag is simply spending lots of time in the outdoors and letting the sun help you adjust to the new time zone. Drinking lots of water during the flight and going easy on the alcohol also help.

Many fly-drive programmes offer what looks like an easy first-day drive, ie Vancouver International Airport to Whistler, north of Vancouver. It's a two-hour jaunt that can stretch to half a day in weekend or holiday traffic. Better to spend the first night in an airport-area hotel and hit the road refreshed in the morning – especially if you're not accustomed to urban traffic or driving on the right side of the road.

The reverse is equally true. Don't plan a tight schedule that gets you into Vancouver or Calgary and on to the airport the requisite two hours before an international departure. Unexpected traffic can leave you stranded on a freeway as your plane takes off overhead. Allow a safety margin by spending your last night in Canada near the departure airport, or at least in the same city.

Try to arrive with a few dollars in Canadian currency and coins. Luggage trolleys are free in the international arrivals area but must be paid for in some domestic airports. Some trolley stands accept credit cards, usually Visa or Access/MasterCard, but other stands require cash – and currency exchange facilities are located outside the arrivals area.

ATMs, automated teller machines, offer the best currency exchange rates and never close. Star and Cirrus are the most common international ATM networks, but check with your card issuer before leaving home to ensure that you have the proper four-digit PIN (personal identification number) for Canadian outlets. International airports have currency exchange facilities in the international terminal that are open long hours. Domestic terminals and smaller airports have no exchange facilities at all. US dollar and pound sterling travellers' cheques from Thomas Cook and other major issuers are accepted almost everywhere, but travellers' cheques in other currencies must generally be cashed at a bank. Eurocheques and personal cheques drawn on banks outside Canada are generally not accepted.

Canadian airports don't have duty-free shopping for incoming travellers, but it's no great loss. Prices for alcohol and other duty-free items are almost always lower in Liquor Stores, supermarkets and discount stores than in duty-free shops.

Some car-hire companies have cars at Vancouver Airport itself (in a car park just outside International Arrivals), others require that you take a coach to an off-airport facility to pick up your hire car – be sure to ask when making your car reservation.

If hiring an RV, ask the hire company about airport pick-up and drop-off when making your booking. Most hire companies provide free transport to and from their offices, which are usually located some distance from the airport.

Setting the scene

The land
British Columbia. It was named in the 19th century for a river, the Columbia, itself named for an 18th-century American ship that took its name from a 15th-century Italian, Christopher Columbus, who never came anywhere near his 20th-century namesake.

Like its name, BC is a hodge-podge of geography: massive glaciers and bone-dry deserts; rich alluvial plains and sheer granite canyons. Home to one of the greatest cities in North America, BC also lay claim to some of the least developed and least populated land on the continent. It's also a latecomer to the travel scene.

Above
Whistler Mountain

Early explorers
A Chinese manuscript tells of a storm-whipped voyage eastward to a land of enormous trees and red-skinned people around 220 BC, but landfall could have been among the towering redwood forests of Northern California and Oregon as easily as the red cedar and Sitka spruce stands of British Columbia. Chinese and Japanese shipwrecks along the North American coast have been dated as early as the 5th century AD, matching Asian ceramics found up and down the length of the Columbia River. Sir Francis Drake *may* have visited Vancouver Island in 1579 on his voyage to plunder Spanish possessions around the world, but any sure evidence was lost when Drake's logbook burned in an Admiralty fire.

That leaves Juan de Fuca, a Greek sailing for Spain in 1592, as the first outsider to visit BC officially. De Fuca gave his name to the strait between Vancouver Island and Washington State, due south, but neither the First Nations who lived there nor the Europeans who read of them much noticed or cared – possibly because stormy weather prevented de Fuca from landing and seeing BC first hand. It wasn't until Danish captain Vitus Bering sailed east from Russia in the early 1700s that Europe began to pay serious attention to the northwest edge of North America.

What Bering found were enormous populations of sea otters, much prized by merchants in China for their rich, silky fur. Russian hunters and merchants flocked to Alaska to trade with local Native groups for otter pelts. This sparked a race for commerce that brought Spanish, English and American traders to the coast.

Spain got there first. Juan Perez arrived from Mexico in 1774, claiming the Queen Charlotte Islands and Nootka Sound, on the western coast of Vancouver Island. Bruno de Heceta and Juan Francisco de la Bodega y Quadra sailed north in 1775, a trip most notable for what didn't happen. Heceta noted, but didn't bother to explore, 'the mouth of some great river'. It was the Columbia, the easiest way to reach the interior of British Columbia until the transcontinental railway arrived a century later.

Search for the Northwest Passage

The British had their own commercial and strategic agenda. The Admiralty as well as commercial explorers had been searching for a direct route westward across the Atlantic to Asia for nearly two centuries. Parliament had a standing offer of £20,000 to the person who discovered a northern sea route to China and Asian lands south. Innumerable navigators had failed to find the Northwest Passage from the Atlantic side, so Captain James Cook went looking for the Pacific Ocean end of the fabled passage.

The fur trade

Cook never found the passage east, but he did find safe anchorage at Nootka Sound, then controlled by Spain. His officers and men traded with the Mowachat First Nation to obtain sea otter pelts for clothing and bedding against the coming winter.

Cook eventually sailed south for Hawaii, where he was killed in 1779. Charles Clark, the expedition's second-in-command, headed for home by way of Macao. When Macanese merchants discovered the well-worn otter skins, they paid such astronomical prices that the crew threatened to mutiny if they didn't return to Nootka Sound. Clark put down the rebellion and sailed for home, where news of the voyage set off a fur rush. Ships from Boston and New York joined the fray once America's war for independence from Britain ended in 1783. The crush of traders nearly led to war between Britain and Spain, but cooler, more commercial minds prevailed. Both countries mounted expeditions to map the Northwest coast in preparation for diplomatic talks.

Spain sent Bodega y Quadra; Britain sent George Vancouver, who had sailed to Vancouver Island as midshipman under Cook. America wasn't part of the talks, but legal technicalities weren't enough to keep trader Robert Gray away. It was Gray who found and charted the mouth of the Columbia River in 1792, establishing US claims to the region. Later the same year, British and Spanish authorities signed the Nootka Accord, agreeing that the Northwest Coast should be open to traders of all nations.

The Nootka Accord was the high point of European exploration of BC by sea as war engulfed Europe and over-hunting destroyed the otter trade. Spain eventually traded its claims to the Pacific Northwest to America in return for Washington's recognition of Spanish title to California.

As far as Britain was concerned, all the important activity in Western Canada took place on land. British traders had been trading for furs across Eastern Canada for 200 years. In 1670, the Hudson's Bay Company (HBC) had wrangled rights to everything west from

Hudson Bay, a vast, unknown territory called Rupert's Land. Anthony Henday paddled up the North Saskatchewan River from Hudson Bay in 1754 and became the first known White to glimpse Canada's Rocky Mountains. He returned the next spring, canoes nearly swamped under the weight of furs, and set off an overland rush. Competitors followed, including a French-Canadian consortium, the North West Company (NWC) and numerous American companies. The race to find a way through BC to the Pacific Ocean was on.

North West Company partners Alexander Mackenzie, Simon Fraser and David Thompson grabbed an early lead. Mackenzie made his way west to the mouth of the Bella Coola River in 1793, the first White to cross the continent north of Mexico. He returned with tales of a land so filled with wild animals that it looked like a 'stall-yard'.

Americans Meriwether Lewis and William Clark explored west from American territory, reaching the mouth of the Columbia River before returning home in 1806. Fraser battled through treacherous rapids along the Fraser River to the Pacific in 1808. Thompson paddled the entire length of the Columbia in 1811, but reached the Pacific Ocean four months late. He arrived to find American traders who had sailed around Cape Horn building a fort at modern day Astoria.

American presence

That initial American presence seemed of no great import. The NWC peacefully took over Astoria when war broke out between the US and Britain in 1812. When the war ended, the 49th Parallel divided the United States and British America east of the Rockies, and the two countries jointly occupied the unmapped West. When the HBC took control of the NWC in 1821, Britain emerged triumphant with the only economic force that spanned the continent. But British power existed only on paper. On the ground, the West was beyond control.

The Americans, however, were getting restless. In 1825, Britain and the US both recognised Russian authority south to 54°40', the current boundary between Southern Alaska and Northern BC. Americans began talking of 'Manifest Destiny', the idea that they were empowered by divine right to occupy the continent from ocean to ocean. Missionaries who were moving westward to 'civilise the savages' began sending back enticing reports of rich farmland beyond the Rocky Mountains.

The HBC was just as busy, building and strengthening forts at Spokane, Okanagan, Nisqually, Langley and elsewhere to block American expansion. Company farms along the Columbia River and Puget Sound in what is now Oregon and Washington fed both inland forts and a growing export trade to Alaska, Hawaii and Asia. HBC's chief factor, Dr John McLoughlin, systematically directed American immigrants south into present-day Oregon, hoping to retain the Columbia River, the only practical route into British Columbia, the company's most profitable territory.

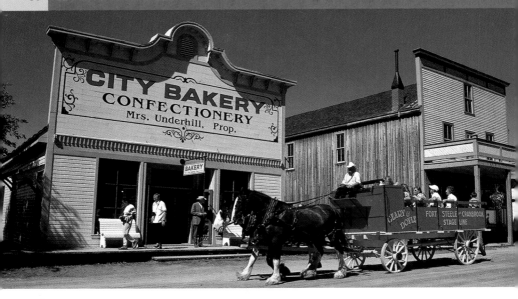

Above
Fort Steele Heritage Town

But the HBC also hedged their position. In 1841, company governor George Simpson and head trader James Douglass moved to Fort Victoria, on the southern tip of Vancouver Island. It was a foresightful move.

US Army surveyors were already mapping a wagon route westward over the Rocky Mountains by way of passes far lower and easier than any in British America. The US Navy paid a 'goodwill' visit to the Pacific Northwest, updating its charts from the Columbia River region north to Vancouver Island and noting the HBC's lack of coastal defences. In 1843, America moved.

The US Senate officially declared Oregon Territory, an enormous tract west of the Rockies, north of California and south of Alaska, to be American. Americans were told it was their patriotic duty and God-given destiny to move west. More importantly, they were given an irresistible lure: 260 hectares for every White US male and 130 hectares for his wife, free for the taking.

Fortunately for Britain, the initial settlers headed south into the Willamette River Valley, south of the Columbia River. But US–British tensions heightened in 1844 when James Polk won the presidential election on the slogan of '54°40' or Fight!', challenging Britain for control north in the West. Since neither country was anxious for a third war, diplomats simply extended the existing boundary, the 49th Parallel, to the Pacific Ocean, then west down the middle of the Strait of Juan de Fuca between Vancouver Island and Washington State.

The HBC lost the Columbia River, the only viable route from interior BC to the coast. Furs from the interior began moving eastward over the Yellowhead Pass, through the Northern Rockies and downriver through Alberta. In coastal areas, the company turned to commerce and farming.

Britain leased all of Vancouver Island to the HBC in 1849 in order to create a colony. Just months later, the Gold Rush in California sent demand for grain, timber, coal and every sort of manufactured product through the roof. Successive gold strikes in Oregon and Washington kept farming and lumbering busy even as a new Royal Navy station at Esquimalt, next to Victoria, boosted coal mining at Nanaimo. Demand for salmon kept salteries, and later canneries, busy.

Settlers, however, were in short supply. Would-be immigrants headed for Oregon and Washington in the western US, where land was less expensive and easier to get to. Until the Canadian Pacific Railway arrived in 1886, the only practicable route to BC was a brutal five-month voyage around the tip of South America. Victoria remained a prosperous but tiny town surrounded by vast forests. Gold changed history, just as it had done in California, Oregon and Washington.

The Gold Rush

HBC traders had been accepting occasional amounts of the precious metal from their First Nation trading partners for years, but the company had never revealed its discoveries, fearing further encroachment by American interests. Faced with growing piles of the stuff in Victoria vaults and rumours of gold finds on the Fraser River starting to circulate, the HBC decided to act. After enacting strict mining licence laws and laying in supplies, the company sent 20kg of raw gold to the nearest mint, San Francisco, early in 1858. The next summer, more than 30,000 miners flooded north from America.

HBC made a fortune supplying the Gold Rush. The company was also terrified that America would take control as easily as it had seized California from Mexico in 1846. Although British on the map, both Vancouver Island and New Caledonia, as the mainland was called, were effectively outside all political control.

The fears were warranted. American miners demanded immediate changes to mining regulations and government practices. A special US Commissioner sent to the Fraser River gold fields to look after American interests reported that it was only a matter of time until both Vancouver Island and the mainland became American by force of population alone. Unless, of course, Washington wanted to act sooner.

While the Americans debated, the British acted. In June 1858, the House of Commons declared the mainland a Crown Colony. Queen Victoria chose the name British Columbia and assigned key officials. A provisional government was declared at Fort Langley in November, then moved to New Westminster (now part of Greater Vancouver), a site Royal Engineers judged more defensible against an expected American invasion. Gold Commissioners and magistrates imposed strict order in the mining camps, a startling contrast to the lawlessness and self-rule that predominated in US mining communities of the time.

The new provincial government also adapted a US-style land distribution system, allowing White settlers to buy up to 65 hectares at

bargain rates – the entire Lower Fraser River Valley was settled, cleare
and planted within nine years. Cattle ranches sprang up across th
province as drovers brought herds north from Washington ar
discovered fine meadows ready for the taking.

Merchants prospered, but every economic downturn prompted ne
calls for union with America, the land most BC residents had
recently left. Talk of a State of British Columbia increased whe
America purchased Alaska from Russia in 1867, bolstered by ha
hearted attempts by Washington to claim BC as compensation f
British support of the (defeated) Confederacy during the US Civil Wa

It was an uneasy time, even as continuing gold discoveries open
the Cariboo, the Kootenays and almost every corner in between. BC
political leaders were firmly British, but business lived or died I
commercial decisions made in San Francisco, not London marke
Ordinary citizens were either recent American immigrants
Canadian-born with little loyalty to any government beyond th
strictly local. Talk of union with America faded after BC voted to jo
the new Dominion of Canada in 1870, a vote bought by promises
an all-Canadian transcontinental railway and strengthened econom
ties east across the Rockies. When the rails finally arrived in 1886, a
obscure lumber town called Vancouver was suddenly catapulted
fame and fortune as Western Canada's richest, most successful ar
most cosmopolitan city.

First Nations

The biggest losers were BC's original First Nations inhabitan
Smallpox and other European disease brought to Mexico by Spani
explorers and conquerors had been steadily moving north and we
following long-established trade routes. Epidemics had begun to swe
through mainland tribes about the time Spanish and English trade
first appeared off Vancouver Island. With little natural resistance
illnesses from measles and the common cold to smallpox, enti
villages were wiped out. Survivors had little chance again
government policies and agents intent on clearing land for Wh
settlement. HBC agents commonly purchased tribal lands, but pri
were pitiful, a few shirts in return for the entire Nanaimo waterfro
and promises to protect traditional hunting and fishing areas we
routinely violated.

Colonial and Dominion officials treated tribes as well as individu
as incompetent imbeciles by policy, regularly confiscating land a
resources 'for their own good'. In 1874, a BC/Canadian Indian Reser
Commission began setting aside lands for First Nations groups. T
region's original inhabitants ended up with 0.34 per cent of t
province. The railways alone were given 8 per cent of BC's mo
commercially profitable and agriculturally useful land, more th
75,600sq km.

Along the coast, First Nations' potlatches and other traditior
practices were outlawed in an effort to destroy traditional culture a

make plague survivors still more dependent upon government. Generations of children were forcibly removed from their families to be raised in church- and government-run residential schools, where the use of Native languages was strictly forbidden and mercilessly punished. Claims for monetary compensation, return of traditional lands and enforcement of long-ignored treaty terms are meeting with a fair degree of success in modern courts.

The railway and the 20th century

The development boom came to an abrupt end with the Panic of 1893. Stock market failures around the world were echoed in bank and railway failures, which brought down businesses and farms dependent upon capital and transportation – which included most of BC. Recovery had to wait for the Yukon Gold Rush of 1898, which brought yet another river of miners north from America. World War I put a damper on growth, but the economy boomed again into the 1920s, as irrigation spread into the Okanagan and other areas thought too dry for successful agriculture. World War II saw the development of the chain saw and other mechanised equipment that allowed the timber industry to leap into a post-war housing boom.

But growth has come neither easily nor quietly. The last patch of virgin forest near Victoria was turned into a wasteland of splintered stumps in the 1970s, sparking furious protests. Plans to expand logging in the Queen Charlotte Islands led to the most massive campaign of civil disobedience in Canadian history – and to the formation of a new national park, Gwaii Haanas, in 1987. Similar efforts in the 1990s to log virgin forests in Clayquot Sound, off the west coast of Vancouver Island, sparked more protests.

Salmon runs, once the mainstay of BC life, have all but disappeared. Overfishing by fleets from the United States, Canada and other Pacific nations is partly to blame, but the despoliation of spawning beds by logging and other human activity is even more destructive.

The not-so-slow decline of resource industries is producing a new economic ethic by reluctant fits and starts. Although clothed in references to Mother Earth and First Nations beliefs, the new model is based in harsh economic choices: resources can be used up, as the sea otter trade, the fur trade, most fisheries, mining and a growing number of timber companies have shown. When the resource is exhausted, the industry dies. Or the resources can be preserved for some less intensive but longer-term use.

Sport fishing, for example, brings more dollars into the local economy than commercial fishing. Recreational use of forests is more profitable in the long run than clearcutting. Mountain climbers, skiers and sightseers spend more money to enjoy an undamaged mountain than mining companies pay to turn it into ore and toxic waste. The outcome of the ongoing battle between resource extraction and resource renewal will shape the face and the psyche of BC in the 21st century.

ove
nderbird Totem

Highlights and touring itineraries

Top ten sights

Not the top ten places visitors to BC actually *go* to, but the top ten not to miss.

• **Barkerville Historic Town** (*page 188*)
The *real* Cariboo Gold Rush that refused to die.
• **Fort Steele Heritage Town** (*page 253*)
A frontier town that has brought the 1890s vividly back to life.
• **Fraser River Canyon & Hells Gate** (*page 193*)
The toughest terrain you're ever likely to drive.
• **Gwaii Haanas National Park, Queen Charlotte Islands** (*pages 117–8*)
Leave the car behind to see nature on the edge.
• **The Hazeltons – (Old) Hazelton, 'Ksan and Kispiox** (*pages 216–7*)
Where the heart of the First Nations beats most powerfully.
• **The Paint Pots, Kootenay National Park** (*page 261*)
The colours and the setting are magical.
• **Nelson** (*page 246–7*)
It looks as good in person as it did on the silver screen.
• **Meadows in the Sky, Mount Revelstoke National Park** (*page 235*)
Wildflower carpets that disappear into empty summer skies.
• **Inner Harbour & Thunderbird Park, Victoria** (*pages 69–70*)
Everyone's vision of what BC *should* look like.
• **Takakkaw Falls, Yoho National Park** (*pages 265–6*)
First Nations visitors were as awe-struck as modern travellers.

The best of BC

These three circular tours start and end in Vancouver, but there's no reason not to pick up either of the last two routes from Calgary. Suggested overnight stops are shown in **bold type**.

Two weeks

The Great Western BC Marathon. You'll ne
time at home to recover from this holiday.
Day 1 Arrive in **Vancouver** (*see page 42*).
Day 2 **Vancouver.**
Day 3 BC Ferries to **Victoria** (*see page 62*).
Day 4 The Island Highway to **Campbell Riv** (*see page 98*).
Day 5 The Island Highway to **Port Hardy** (*s page 101*).
Day 6 BC Ferries' **Discovery Coast** (*see pa 106*) route to Bella Coola.
Day 7 Bella Coola over The Hill to **Anahi Lake/Nimpo Lake** (*see pages 198–201*).
Day 8 Hwy 20 to **Riske Creek** (*see page 201*).
Day 9 Hwy 97 to Barkerville, overnight **Wells** or **Quesnel** (*see page 192*).
Day 10 Hwy 97 to **100 Mile House** (*see pa 191*).
Day 11 Hwy 97 to **Cache Creek** (*see page 18.*
Day 12 Hwy 1 through the Fraser Riv Canyon to Hells Gate and **Hope** (*see pa 127*).
Day 13 Hwy 1 to **Vancouver.**
Day 14 Home.

The Great Interior BC Marathon. You'll ne a few days to rest up from this one, too.
Day 1 Arrive in **Vancouver** (*see page 42*).
Day 2 Hwy 1 to **Hope** (*see page 127*).
Day 3 Hwy 1 through the Fraser River Cany and Hells Gate to **Kamloops** (*see page 138*).
Day 4 Hwy 1 through the Shuswap Lakes **Revelstoke** (*see page 236*).
Day 5 Hwy 1 over Rodgers Pass and Glac National Park to **Golden** (*see page 232*).
Day 6 Hwy 1 through Yoho National Park **Lake Louise/Banff/Canmore** (*see page 273*)
Day 7 Hwy 93 through Kootenay Natior Park to **Radium Hot Springs** (*see page 261*).
Day 8 Hwy 95 to Fort Steele Heritage Tow

and **Cranbrook** (*see page 250*).
Day 9 Hwy 3/3A to Creston, the Kootenay Lake Ferry and **Nelson** (*see page 246*).
Day 10 Hwy 3A/3 to Castlegar and **Grand Forks** (*see page 243*).
Day 11 Hwy 3/97 to **Penticton** (*see page 153*).
Day 12 Hwy 97/3A/3 to Keremeos, Princeton and **Manning Provincial Park** (*see page 132*).
Day 13 Hwy 3 to Hope and **Vancouver**.
Day 14 Home.

Four weeks
See most of BC in a busy month.
Day 1 Arrive in **Vancouver** (*see page 42*).
Day 2 **Vancouver**.
Day 3 BC Ferries to **Victoria** (*see page 62*).
Day 4 Island Highway to Nanaimo and **Campbell River** (*see page 98*).
Day 5 Island Highway to **Port Hardy** (*see page 101*).
Day 6 BC Ferries to **Prince Rupert** (*see page 206*).
Day 7 BC Ferries/fly to **Skidegate**, Queen Charlotte Islands (*see page 120*).
Day 8 **Gwaii Haanas National Park** (*see page 117*).
Day 9 **Gwaii Haanas National Park** (*see page 117*).
Day 10 BC Ferries/fly to **Prince Rupert** (*see page 206*).
Day 11 Yellowhead Highway (Hwy 16) to the Hazeltons and **Smithers** (*see page 218*).
Day 12 Yellowhead Highway (Hwy 16) to Fort St James and **Prince George** (*see page 222*).
Day 13 Hwy 97 to **Barkerville** and **Wells/Quesnel** (*see page 192*).
Day 14 Hwy 97/1 to **Kamloops** (*see page 138*).
Day 15 Hwy 1 through the Shuswap Lakes to **Revelstoke** (*see page 236*).
Day 16 Hwy 1 over Rodgers Pass and Glacier National Park to **Golden** (*see page 232*).
Day 17 Hwy 1 through Yoho National park to **Lake Louise/Banff/Canmore** (*see page 273*).
Day 18 Hwy 93 through Kootenay National Park to **Radium Hot Springs** (*see page 261*).
Day 19 Hwy 95 to Fort Steele and **Cranbrook** (*see page 250*).
Day 20 Hwy 3 to **Creston** (*see page 243*).
Day 21 Hwy 3A to the Kootenay Lake Ferry and **Nelson** (*see page 246*).
Day 22 Hwy 3A/3 to Castlegar and **Grand Forks** (*see page 243*).
Day 23 Hwy 3/97 to **Penticton** (*see page 153*).
Day 24 Hwy 97/97C to Kelowna, Meritt, Kamloops and **Cache Creek** (*see page 187*).
Day 25 Hwy 1/99 to Hat Creek and **Lillooet** (*see page 191*).
Day 26 Hwy 12/1 to Lytton, down the Fraser River Canyon to **Hope** (*see page 127*).
Day 27 Hwy 1 to **Vancouver**.
Day 28 Home.

Vancouver

Ratings

Beaches	●●●●●
Food	●●●●●
Outdoor activities	●●●●●
Scenery	●●●●●
Children	●●●●
History	●●●●
Museums	●●●●
First Nations	●●●

Canada's third-largest city is a small town at heart. Decades of immigration have given Vancouver more foreign-born citizens than any other North American city, yet it remains an essentially Canadian place. Yes, black is the uniform of the day, and hard-eyed attitude the public posture *du jour*, but Vancouver remains a polite, tidy town where everyone seems to know everyone else and quite prefers it that way. Harbour vistas vie with Sydney, Hong Kong and San Francisco for the world's best, while urban views stand in for big-city streetscapes from Los Angeles to London, Moscow and Shanghai. Cosmopolitan Vancouver works hard to remain an overgrown village on the edge of a vast rain forest. Serious mountains rise within sight of City Hall, while *laissez-faire* beaches are just a quick bus ride away and a young, bustling population is ready to enjoy both at the slightest excuse.

Arriving and departing

ⓘ **Tourism Vancouver** *Plaza Level, 200 Burrard St; tel: 604-683-2000; web: www.tourismvancouver.com Open May–Sep, daily 0800 –1800; Sep–May, Mon–Fri 0830–1700, Sat 0900–1700.*

Visitor Centre *Vancouver International Airport international arrivals level. Open daily.*

Most air services use Vancouver International Airport (YVR). Expect to pay an Airport Improvement Fee (AIF) on departure: $5 when travelling within BC and the Yukon; $10 for flights within North America; $15 for flights outside North America. Regional carriers offer a seaplane service from the harbour.

• **VIA Rail** *1150 Station St; tel: 604-640-3741; web: www.viarail.ca*, provides national rail service.

• **BC Rail** *1311 W 1st St, North Vancouver; tel: 604-984-5503; web: www.bcrail.com/bcrpass*, provides most services within the province.

• **Rocky Mountaineer Railtours** *1150 Station St; tel: 604-606-72000; web: www.rkymtnrail.com*, offer rail tours to the Rocky Mountains.

Lion's Gate Bridge

...se Mountain

Capilano Suspension Bridge

First Narrows

99

1A

Stanley Park Drive

Stanley Park

Beaver Lake

Lion's Gate Bridge Road

Burrard Inlet

Aquarium

Lost Lagoon

Lagoon Drive

Coal Harbour

Seabus

Gilford Street

Denman Street

Georgia Street

Pender Street

Canada Place

Waterfront Station

The Lookout

Beach Avenue

English Bay

Barclay Street

Robson Street

Nelson Street

Comox Street

Broughton Street

Pendrell Street

Jervis Street

Barclay Heritage Square

Vancouver Art Gallery

Gastown

Davie Street

Bute Street

Hastings Street

Chinatown

English Bay

Burnaby Street

Bute Street

Thurlow Street

Pender Street

Harwood Street

Burrard Street

Hornby Street

Howe Street

Granville Street Mall

Dunsmuir Street

...ver
...ne
...m

Vancouver Museum

Vanier Park

Pacific Street

Granville Street

Seymour Street

Nelson Street

Smithe Street

Robson Street

Georgia Street

BC Place Stadium

...em of
...opology

Beach Avenue

Burrard Street Bridge

Yaletown

Science World

Cambie Street Bridge

Granville Street Bridge

Granville Island

Steveston

False Creek

University of British Columbia Botanical Garden

Nitobe Memorial Garden

Bloedel Floral Conservatory

Van Dusen Botanical Garden

Main St.

0   500 metres
0   500 yards

ⓘ **The Georgia Straight**
1770 Burrard St; tel:
604-730-7000, a free
weekly newspaper, has the
best listing of local events,
cultural attractions,
performances, cinemas and
other happenings.

• **Highway access** is Hwy 1 (the Transcanada Hwy) from the east and Hwy 99 from the south and north.
• **BC Ferries** *tel: 250-386-3431 or 888-223-3779; web: www.bcferries.bc.ca*, provide a ferry service from Tsawwassen (south of the city) to Victoria and Horseshoe Bay (north of the city) to Nanaimo, both on Vancouver Island.

Getting around

Public transport
BC Transit, *tel: 604-521-0400*, is Canada's largest public transport system, a combination of buses, light rail (SkyTrain) and ferries (SeaBus). All major tourist sites in the lower Mainland area are accessible by public transit, though schedules may not be convenient.
Aquabus Ferries *tel: 604-689-5858*, and **False Creek Ferries** *tel: 604-684-7781*, provide a ferry service around False Creek from Science World west to the Maritime Museum.
   Driving is practical throughout Vancouver, although traffic slows during rush hours (*0730–0930 and 1600–1800*). Left turn lanes are rare and roadways can be narrow, especially in residential areas with kerbside parking. Metered parking is generally available; most car parks accept either coins or credit cards. Watch for cyclists.

Below
Vancouver cityscape

Sights

Barclay Heritage Square $ *Barclay, Nicola, Haro and Broughton Sts. Open daily.*

Roedde House Museum $ *1415 Barclay St; tel: 604-684-7040 for hours.*

Bloedel Floral Conservatory & Queen Elizabeth Park $ *33rd Ave and Cambie St; tel: 604-257-8570. Open daily.*

Canada Place $ *Harbourside at the foot of Howe St. Open daily.*

Capilano Suspension Bridge $$ *3735 Capilano Rd, North Vancouver; tel: 604-985-7474. Open 0800–dusk in summer, 0900–1700 in winter.*

Chinatown $ *Gore, Keefer, Carrall and E Hastings Sts.*

Chinese Cultural Centre $ *50 E Pender St; tel: 604-687-0729, conducts daily walking tours by advance booking.*

Dr Sun Yat-Sen Classical Chinese Garden $ *578 Carrall St; tel: 604-662-3207; web: www.discovervancouver.com/un. Open daily.*

English Bay $ *West of False Creek, between Stanley Park and Point Grey.*

Barclay Heritage Square*

Vancouver's most elegant heritage area preserves nine of the city's few remaining Victorian-era homes. Most are closed to the public, but the **Roedde House****, built in 1893, has become a period museum. All nine homes are surrounded by spectacular period gardens.

Bloedel Floral Conservatory*

Perched atop Vancouver's highest hill in **Queen Elizabeth Park****, the silvery tridetic dome of Bloedel houses the city's largest tropical plant collection. A courtyard behind Bloedel is popular for *tai chi* and similar exercise activities morning and evening. Queen Elizabeth Park, 53 landscaped and wooded hectares, including a quarry next to Bloedel, has become a stunning sunken garden. Walking trails offer broad vistas of Vancouver, the harbour and the mountains beyond.

Canada Place***

The sail-like, white roofline of Canada Place marks Vancouver's cruise ship terminal, convention centre and IMAX cinema. Look for two or three cruise ships at dock during the May–September Alaska cruise season, and vast vistas across Burrard Inlet all year.

Capilano Suspension Bridge***

This 140-m footbridge sways 70m above the Capilano River canyon to a shady forest park on the far side. The original bridge opened in 1889, creating the first tourist attraction on what was then the deserted North Shore of Burrard Inlet. Today's bridge is laced with steel cables that can carry the weight of several fully loaded Boeing 747 passenger planes, but the swaying, bouncing span feels more like a thrill ride when the spring melt turns the river below into a thundering torrent.

Chinatown**

Vancouver's Chinatown is the third-largest Chinese community in North America after San Francisco and New York. What began as a refuge against periodic persecution has become a wealthy community infused by massive immigration from across Asia. Vegetables, fruits, fish and other goods spill from shops on to pavements that are jammed with shoppers all day. **Dr Sun Yat-Sen Classical Chinese Garden*****, the first classical Chinese garden built outside China, is an island of tranquillity.

English Bay***

The protected waters of English Bay, Captain James Vancouver's anchorage in 1792, are popular for kayaking and sailing. The shoreline, especially **Vanier*****, **Hadden***** and **Kitsilano beach parks***** on the south and the **Seawall Promenade***** into **Stanley Park***** on the east, is popular for walking, cycling and rollerblading.

False Creek $ *East beneath the Burrard Bridge, past Granville Island to Science World.*

Gastown $–$$$ *Water St, between Columbia and E Cordova Sts.*

Granville Island $–$$$ *South side of False Creek, beneath the Granville Bridge. Open daily.*

Grouse Mountain $$$ *6400 Nancy Greene Way, North Vancouver; tel: 604-984-0661; web: www.grousemtn.com Trams depart every 15 minutes, 0900–2200.*

Museum of Anthropology $$ *6393 Northwest Marine Dr (University of British Columbia); tel: 604-822-5087; web: www.moa.ubc.ca After Memorial Day weekend–Labour Day weekend open daily 1000–1700, Tue until 2100; after Labour Day weekend–Memorial Day weekend open Tue–Sun 1000–1700, Tue until 2100.*

Nitobe Memorial Garden & UBC Botanical Garden $ *6804 Southwest Marine Dr; tel: 604-822-9666; web: www.hedgerows.com. Open daily.*

False Creek✦✦✦
This shallow inlet stretching east from English Bay along the south side of the inner city has become one of Vancouver's premier recreation areas. The one-time industrial slum has been reborn as a series of marinas, parks and low-rise housing developments with stunning water views, all linked by a walking and cycling trail stretching from Kitsilano Beach to Vanier Park, around False Creek to the Seawall Promenade and circling Stanley Park.

Gastown✦✦✦
Once Vancouver's red-light district, Gastown has become a less risqué but no-less-popular, entertainment district. Many of Gastown's original brick buildings have been renovated as bars, restaurants and offices. Don't miss the **steam clock✦✦** at the corner of Water and Cambie streets, signalling the quarter hour with steam-powered chimes.

Granville Island✦✦✦
One million cubic metres of mud dredged from False Creek nearly a century ago created a metal-bashing haven called Industrial Island. Island factories produced decades-worth of rivets, chain, nails, cement and industrial pollutants. Industry was eased out in the 1960s, the site cleaned up and renamed. As Granville Island, it has become a popular refuge for boaters, artists, shoppers and entertainers. The **Public Market✦✦✦** is Vancouver's best.

Grouse Mountain✦✦✦
Skim the slopes of 1242-m Grouse Mountain by aerial tramway, or hike the Grouse Grind, a rugged walk that gains 850m in 2.9km. Either way, clear-weather views offer the best panorama of Vancouver ground-side of a helicopter. Peak facilities include restaurants, a cinematic exploration of lower BC from the air, kilometres of walking paths, helicopter rides, tandem paragliding, mountain biking down the mountain, and **híwus✦✦✦**, a First Nations dance, song and story-telling show with traditional foods. Grouse is open for skiing in winter.

Museum of Anthropology (MOA)✦✦✦
Canada's top anthropology museum has one of the world's finest collections of First Nations artefacts and art, with modern and antique totems, feast dishes and carvings in wood, stone, gold and other media. Don't miss the outdoor totem poles, directly behind the museum.

Nitobe Memorial Garden✦✦ and University of British Columbia Botanical Garden✦✦
Nitobe is a calm Japanese tea and stroll garden 200m from MOA. The Botanical Garden has more than 400 species of rhododendrons, a 16th-century Physick Garden and thousands of other plants from around the world.

Opposite
Granville Island Bridge

Science World $$
*1455 Quebec St; tel:
604-443-7440; web:
www.scienceworld.bc.ca
Open Mon–Fri 1000–1700,
Sat–Sun 1000–1800.*

Stanley Park $ *North end
of Georgia St; tel: 604-299-
9000 ext 4100. Open daily.*

**Vancouver Aquarium
$$** *tel: 604-685-3364; web:
www.vancouver-aquarium.org
Open daily.*

Steveston $ *West end of
Steveston Hwy, Richmond.*

**Gulf of Georgia
Cannery National
Historic Site $** *12138
4th Ave, Richmond; tel: 604-
664-7908. Open daily.*

**Van Dusen Botanical
Garden $$** *5251 Oak St at
37th Ave; tel: 604-878-9274;
web: www.hedgerows.com
Open daily.*

Science World✦✦
BC's largest science museum uses hands-on displays to explain the natural world for kids, who usually have to push their way through crowds of fascinated adults to reach the exhibits.

Stanley Park✦✦✦
Vancouver has one of the world's finest urban parks, 400 hectares of forest laced with 80km of walking and cycling paths. The most popular path is a 10-km shoreline loop. Highlights include totem poles, sweeping vistas across Vancouver and the North Shore, restaurants, picnic grounds, a rose garden, beaches and horse-drawn wagon tours. **Vancouver Aquarium✦✦✦**, one of the best aquaria in the region, specialises in the Pacific Northwest. Don't miss the whales.

Steveston✦
This former salmon cannery town at the mouth of the Fraser River is still Canada's largest commercial fishing port and a popular local getaway. The **Gulf of Georgia Cannery National Historic Site✦✦✦** is a restored fish-processing plant, all that remains of what was once the world's largest concentration of salmon canneries.

Van Dusen Botanical Garden✦✦
This former golf course has become one of Canada's most comprehensive collections of ornamental plants. Plantings are rotated to provide maximum colour in all seasons.

Vancouver Art Gallery $$ 750
*Hornby St; tel: 604-662-719; web:
www.vanartgallery.bc.ca
Open Fri–Wed 1000–1730,
o 2100 Thur.*

**Vancouver International Airport
art** $ *First Nations artwork
scattered throughout the
international and domestic
terminals.*

**Vancouver Maritime
Museum** $$ *1905 Ogden
Ave; tel: (604) 257-8300;
web: www.vmm.bc.ca Open
daily Victoria Day–Labour
Day 1000–1700; rest of
year, Tue–Sat 1000–1700,
un 1000–1700.*

Vancouver Museum $$
*Vanier Park, 1100 Chestnut
St; tel: 604-736-4431; web:
vanmuseum.bc.ca Open
Jul–Aug, daily 1000–1700;
Sep–Jun, Tue–Sun
1000–1700.*

Vanier Park $ *Chestnut
St, at English Bay; tel: 604-
257-8400. Open daily.*

Vancouver Art Gallery*

This one-time courthouse showcases West Coast artists, as well as travelling exhibitions. The neo-classical exterior is often a shooting location for television and cinema productions.

Vancouver International Airport art***

Vancouver Airport (YVR) has BC's best free collection of First Nations art. Most of the monumental eye-catchers are in the International Terminal, including a trio of totems between the terminal and the car park, and *The Spirit of Haida Gwaii, The Jade Canoe*, a 6m bronze by Bill Reid, with traditional Haida themes on the departure level.

Vancouver Maritime Museum**

Canada's finest Pacific museum is filled with uniforms and memorabilia, including a weavily ship's biscuit nearly 150 years old. Highlight is the *St Roch* National Historic Site, a 1928 ship built for arctic patrol by the Royal Canadian Mounted Police and docked inside the museum. The *St Roch* was the first vessel to sail the Northwest Passage from the Pacific Ocean to the Atlantic Ocean, the first to make the return voyage and the first to circumnavigate North America.

Vancouver Museum**

Canada's largest civic museum includes vast collections of local artefacts as well as a laserium and planetarium. The Orientation Gallery presents two timelines for reference: adults peruse a Timeline Wall; children have a Toy Timeline Wall.

Vanier Park***

Vanier occupies much of the headland on the south side of False Creek inlet. Lawns, marinas, a walking and cycling path and broad views across English Bay make it a popular city escape all year round. The Vancouver Maritime Museum and the Vancouver Museum are both located in the park.

First Nations art

After decades of suppression by Christian missionaries and government policy, BC's aboriginal arts, crafts and cultures have returned to the mainstream. Academic interest at the University of British Columbia and Victoria's Royal BC Museum sparked a revival of totem-pole carving in the 1940s and 1950s. The new totems helped fuel a renaissance of cultural and artistic forms that had all but disappeared outside museum collections. Fifty years later, modern interpretations of traditionally bold, stylised First Nations motifs are everywhere.

Vancouver International Airport has a fine collection of modern First Nations art; UBC's Museum of Anthropology has an even larger collection. MOA's gift shop is filled with affordable reproductions of display pieces. Commercial gallery prices are higher.

Accommodation and food

Hotel space can be tight and expensive in summer but prices drop once the cruise ships head south from September to October.

Hotel Vancouver $$$ *900 W Georgia St; tel: 604-684-3131*, is the *grande dame* of Vancouver hotels and worth every penny.

Listel Vancouver $$ *1300 Robson St; tel: 604-684-8461; web: www.listel-vancouver.com*, is a delightful hotel with art gallery décor.

The Palisades $$$ *202-1288 Alberni St* and **The Residences on Georgia $$$** *101-1288 W Georgia St; tel: 604-891-6100; web. www.palisades-vancouver.com*, are popular with the cinema and TV set in Vancouver for longer stays.

Pan Pacific Vancouver $$$ *999 Canada Place; tel: 604-662-8111; web. www.panpac.com/canada/vancouver/hotels/hotel.html*, rises above Canada Place with the best harbour views in town.

Sutton Place $$$ *845 Burrard St; tel: 604-682-5511; web. www.travelweb.com/sutton.html*, is a highly successful version of traditional luxury.

Vancouverites eat out more often and drink more wine than any other city in North America. The city's young, well-travelled population, vibrant immigrant communities, fresh seafood and healthy economy have transformed food from fuel to celebration. West Coast or Northwest Cuisine is the code for fresh local ingredients (most often seafood) with a light touch on the sauces.

Bali Restaurant $ *1016 W Broadway (near Oak), tel: 604-731-8281*, serves authentic Indonesian Malaysian and Singaporean dishes.

Bridges Restaurant $$–$$$ *Granville Island; tel 604-961-4981*, has reliable seafood and Vancouver's most popular patio.

CinCin $$$ *1154 Robson St (near Bute); tel: 604 688-7338*, keeps winning awards as the city's top (and most expensive) Italian restaurant

Delhi Darbar Restaurant $$ *2120 Main St (near 5th); tel: 604-877-7733*, has the best *dhosas* this side of Delhi and enormous portions of South Indian delights. Don't miss the Sunday brunch with Bombay chat, dozens of small, street vendor-style dishes.

Kalamata $$ *478 W Broadway (at Cambie); tel 604-872-7050*, has the sparkle, bustle and sunny flavours of Greece.

Liliget Feast House $$ *1724 Davie St (near Denman); tel: 604-681-7044,* is Vancouver's original First Nations restaurant.

Phnom Penh $$ *955 W Broadway (near Oak); tel: 604-734-8898,* serves delightfully authentic Cambodian and Vietnamese dishes to fanatically faithful crowds.

Pink Pearl $ *1132 E Hastings (near Clark Dr); tel: 604-253-4316,* has the best Cantonese-style seafood in Vancouver.

Raincity Grill $$$ *1193 Denman (at Morton); tel: 604-685-7337,* pushes the edge with West Coast dishes and Canada's best selection of BC wines by the glass.

Star Anise $$$ *1485 W 12th St (near Granville); tel: 604-737-1485,* serves the city's most successful fusion of Asian and West Coast flavours.

Shopping

Vancouver is gaining a reputation for good-value shopping. **Robson Street** is Canada's answer to Beverly Hills, with blocks of brand name and trendy shops from Burrard to Cardero streets. **Chinatown** has bargains on Asian imports. **A&B Sound** and **Virgin Megastore** are locked in perpetual competition over music CDs and tapes. The edge usually goes to A&B. **Duthie Books** has the city's best selection of Canadiana and travel books. **Mountain Equipment Co-op** *tel: 604-872-6630,* is a good stop for outdoor gear.

On the water

The best way to see Vancouver is from the water. **Vancouver Harbour Tours** *tel: 604-688-7246; web: www.boatcruises.com,* offer daily harbour cruises aboard the city's only authentic paddlewheeler. **Ocean West Expeditions** *tel: 604-898-4979; open daily,* hires kayaks from the English Bay Beach boathouse at Denman and Davie Sts. Kayaks can be taken out on your own or on a guided tour with free lessons.

Suggested tour

Total distance: 80km.

Time: Allow a half-day for driving and 2 days to see the sights. Pick up the circular tour anywhere, but try to avoid commuter traffic *(0730–0930 and 1600–1800).*

Links: The city tour links with ferry routes to Vancouver Island from **Horseshoe Bay** and the lower Fraser River valley on Hwy 1 eastbound toward **Harrison Hot Springs, Hope** and the **Okanagan Valley.**

Route: Start at **Fourth Ave**, on the western edge of Vancouver. This trendy shopping district stretches from Burrard St to Balsam St, where it becomes a residential area headed west toward **Jericho Beach Park**. Watch for cyclists as the road veers to the right and becomes NW Marine Drive towards **Locarno Park**, **Locarno Beach** and **Spanish Banks Beach**, all fronting on English Bay. The parks offer expansive vistas to North Vancouver and east to the inner city and Stanley Park. There is ample parking, particularly near Locarno Park, as well as picnic and recreational facilities.

Pacific Spirit Regional Park begins just west of Spanish Banks. The 770-hectare park surrounds the **University of British Columbia** campus on **Point Grey**. At the first stop sign, turn right on to Chancellor Dr and the car park for the **MUSEUM OF ANTHROPOLOGY (MOA)** ❶, on the right. The outdoor totem exhibition area is over a small rise behind the car park and behind the museum building. Walk the 200m west along Marine Dr to **NITOBE MEMORIAL GARDEN**, on the left.

Marine Dr curves south around Point Grey. Just past the **UBC Botanical Garden**, 2km beyond MOA, move into the left lane. At the first traffic signal, turn left on to 16th Ave. Follow 16th Ave east back into Vancouver and the pleasant, tree-shaded residential neighbourhoods of **Shaughnessy Heights**. The road is a broad parkway, but residential parking frequently blocks the kerb lane.

Follow 16th Ave to Arbutus St and turn north (left). Several blocks north of W 4th Ave are still paved with brick, which becomes slippery in rain. Continue downhill toward **Kitsilano Pool**, Hutton Park and Vanier Park, with English Bay behind.

Follow signs for the **VANCOUVER MARITIME MUSEUM** ❷ and **VANCOUVER MUSEUM**, skirting the edge of **VANIER PARK**. Parking is extremely limited; try the Maritime Museum and the Vancouver Museum.

From the Vancouver Museum, turn south (left) on to Chestnut for one block, then go west (right) on Greer Ave, following signs for the bicycle route on to the **Burrard Bridge**.

After crossing the bridge, continue straight on Burrard St for 10 blocks to Georgia St. Turn east (right) for one block to Hornby St and turn south (right). **The VANCOUVER ART GALLERY** ❸ is on the left. To the right is the **BC Provincial Courts** building, with an urban park and waterfalls rising above street level. Turn south (right) on to Howe St at **Eaton's** department store and west (right) on to Smythe St. Follow Smythe across Burrard to Thurlow and turn south (left) for two blocks to Nelson St. Turn west (right) on to Nelson for four blocks to Nicola St then go north (right) one block to Barclay. Turn east (right) on Barclay to **BARCLAY HERITAGE SQUARE** ❹ and the **Roedde House Museum**.

Take the first left turn after the museum. Continue north to Robson St and turn west (left) to Denman St. Turn north (right) on Denman, following signs for ferries to **Nanaimo** and the **Sunshine Coast**. At Georgia St, turn north (left) toward **Stanley Park**. Stay in the right-hand lane and veer right into the park.

Parking regulations are enforced all year; buy parking coupons at the yellow dispensers. The first car park on the left is convenient for visits to the **VANCOUVER AQUARIUM** ❺ and **horse-drawn tours** of the park. One kilometre beyond is the main parking area and **Totem Pole Display** ❻. Just ahead and on the right are broad views back to the sail-like roofline of **CANADA PLACE**. Expect to see cruise ships docked at Canada place from May to October. Ships returning from Alaska dock around 0800 and depart 1600–1800 the same day. The **Nine O'clock Gun**, on the waterfront just past a bronze statue of a runner, is fired at 2100 each evening. The cannon originally signalled the close of commercial fishing each day.

A lay-by 1km ahead has good views across to North Vancouver. Th bright yellow piles are sulphur waiting to be loaded aboard ships; th tan-coloured piles are wood pulp. The suspension bridge to the left **Lion's Gate Bridge ❼**, leading to the north shore. Just beyon **Brockton Point** is Vancouver's answer to Copenhagen's *Littl Mermaid*, **Girl in a Wetsuit**, a bronze statue of a woman diver in a we suit. A left-hand exit 1km ahead leaves the park back to Georgia S The entrance to **Lion's Gate Bridge**, 1km ahead, is closed 1530–183 to minimise park traffic.

Cross the bridge and turn east (right) on to Marine Dr, following sigr for **North Vancouver, Capilano Canyon** and Grouse Mountain. Tur north (left) at the first traffic signal, Capilano Road. **CAPILAN SUSPENSION BRIDGE** is 3km uphill, on the left. The swayir pedestrian bridge, built a century ago for fishing and logging acces was Vancouver's first tourist attraction. Continue 4km north o Capilano Rd, which becomes Nancy Greene Way, to **GROUS MOUNTAIN** and the peak tram.

Return downhill to Hwy 1. Take the highway eastbound to th **Second Narrows Bridge** and cross **Burrard Inlet**. Take the first ex following signs for the bicycle route on to McGill St. Follow McGi past **Exposition Park** and along the waterfront for 3km. Turn nort (right) on to Wall St and continue through residential areas above th docks for another 2km, then go north (right) on to Dundas St Heatley St.

Turn south (left) on to Heatley to E Pender St. Turn west (righ through the heart of **CHINATOWN ❽**, past the Chinese Cultur Centre behind the large gate on the south (left) side of the street wit the Dr Sun Yat-Sen Chinese Gardens behind.

Turn north (right) on to Abbott St to E Cordova St and turn ea (right) along the edge of **GASTOWN ❾** for two blocks to Columbia S Go two blocks north (left) on Columbia and turn west (left) on Alexander St. At the first stop sign, where the brick pavement begin turn north (right) on to Water St. A flamboyant statue of **Gassy Jac** who built the first bar in Gastown, is on the left. The Steam Clock on the north (right) at Cambie St.

At the end of Water St, turn south (left) into Richards St, immediate west (right) on to W Hastings St, then south (left) on to Howe St. Th **Four Seasons Hotel** is on the east (left) and the **Hotel Georgia** on th west (right) at Georgia St. Cross Georgia. West (right) is the Vancouv Art Gallery, on the east (left) is **Eaton's**. Continue south on Howe and cross the **Granville Bridge**.

Stay in the right-hand lane and follow signs for 4th Ave W, turning c to Pine St, then north (right) following signs for **GRANVILLE ISLAN ❿**. When leaving Granville Island, follow signs for 4th Ave W. Follc 4th Ave one block back to Burrard St.

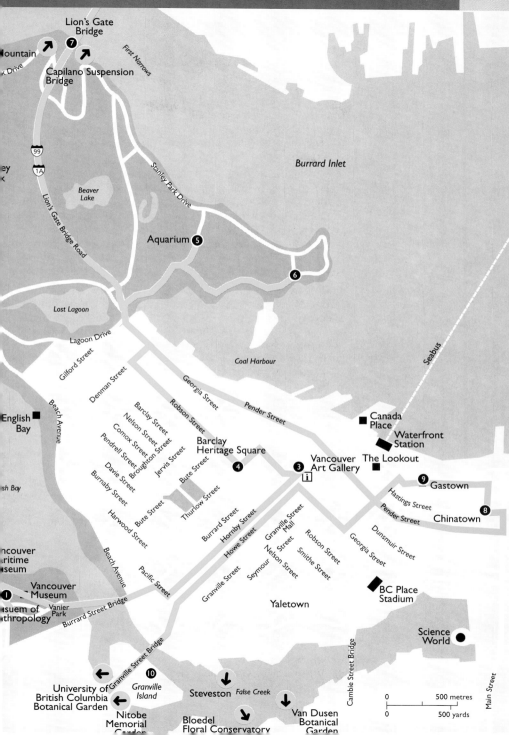

Lion's Gate Bridge 7

Mountain

Capilano Suspension Bridge

First Narrows

Park Drive

99

1A

ley Park

Lion's Gate Bridge Road

Beaver Lake

Stanley Park Drive

Burrard Inlet

Aquarium 5

6

Lost Lagoon

Lagoon Drive

Coal Harbour

Seabus

Gilford Street

Denman Street

Georgia Street

Pender Street

English Bay

Beach Avenue

Barclay Street

Nelson Street

Comox Street

Robson Street

Canada Place

Waterfront Station

The Lookout

Pendrell Street

Broughton Street

Jervis Street

Barclay Heritage Square

Vancouver Art Gallery

4

3

Gastown 9

sh Bay

Davie Street

Burnaby Street

Bute Street

Thurlow Street

Burrard Street

Hornby Street

Hastings Street

Pender Street

Chinatown 8

Dunsmuir Street

Harwood Street

Howe Street

Granville Street Mall

Nelson Street

Robson Street

Smithe Street

Georgia Street

ncouver aritime seum

Beach Avenue

Granville Street

Seymour Street

BC Place Stadium

Vancouver Museum

1

Pacific Street

Yaletown

Vanier Park

useum of nthropology

Burrard Street Bridge

Science World

University of British Columbia Botanical Garden

Granville Street Bridge

Granville Island

10

Steveston

False Creek

Van Dusen Botanical Garden

Cambie Street Bridge

Main Street

Nitobe Memorial Garden

Bloedel Floral Conservatory

0   500 metres

0   500 yards

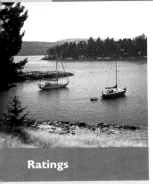

The Gulf Islands

Ratings

Art and craft	●●●●●
Nature	●●●●●
Outdoor activities	●●●●●
Parks	●●●●●
Scenery	●●●●●
Wildlife	●●●●●
Coastal villages	●●●●
Beaches	●●●

An island archipelago spans the Strait of Georgia misnamed the Gulf of Georgia by Captain George Vancouver in 1792. Of the 200 or so Gulf Islands (the San Juans are the same group on the US side of the boundary, five of the major Gulf Islands house 12,000 permanent residents. Within a few hours' reach of Victoria or Vancouver by BC ferry, float plane or water taxi, the dry sunny climate, small retiree and day commuter population, scenery, outdoor activities and arts communities lure visitors to posh inns and bed and breakfasts. Nostalgic vestiges of alternative lifestyles that thrived in relative island isolation in the 1960s can still be found along the rustic side routes and in crafts markets.

Rugged cliffs and smooth beaches lure sailors, kayakers and canoeists on to the water to view pods of orcas and dolphins. Panoramic views from mountaintops entice hikers and cyclists to explore island roads.

GALIANO ISLAND✦✦✦

ℹ **Galiano Chamber of Commerce/Travel Infocentre** *2590 Sturdies Bay Rd; tel: (250) 539-2233; web: www.galianoisland.com* Open to correspond with summer ferry arrivals.

📞 **Go Galiano Island Shuttle $** *tel: (250) 539-0202*, operates from the Sturdies Bay Ferry, with some tours.

How did an island, inhabited for centuries by Coast Salish peoples, get a Spanish name? Answer: Spaniard Dionisio Alcala Galiano sailed a survey ship to the island in 1792.

Spreading 27km long over a narrow, hilly, 57sq km land area, the second-largest and northernmost main Gulf Island concentrates its thousand or so inhabitants in several population centres. Ferries call **Sturdies Bay**. The one main route, Montague Road, goes to Montague Harbour, the other main activity centre, then becomes Porlier Pass Road, stopping short of the island's northern tip.

Many visitors choose to bring or hire bikes, take the **Go Galiano Island Shuttle**, walk, or kayak/canoe between places. Most Galiano's parks provide views of the Strait of Georgia and vistas across to other tiny isles such as the Ballingall Islets, which shelter harbour seals and provide sanctuary for birds.

Dionisio Point Provincial Park $
water access to island's northern tip; web: www.elp.gov.bc.ca/bcparks/explore/parkpgs/dionisio.htm

Montague Harbour Marine Provincial Park
$ 10km northwest of Sturdies Bay at Montague Harbour; web: www.elp.gov.bc.ca/bcparks/explore/parkpgs/montague.htm

Galiano Bluffs Park $
Bluff Rd.

Bodega Ridge $ from Cook Rd on northwest of island; tel: (250) 539-2677.

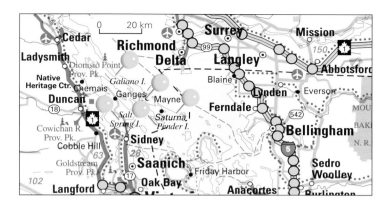

Water-access-only **Dionisio Point Provincial Park❖❖**, backed by forest, has rocky headlands looking out to Porlier Pass. **Montague Harbour Marine Provincial Park❖❖❖** offers a range of activities – walking white-shell beaches or Gray's Peninsula saltmarsh, scuba-diving, spotting shellfish and sea stars at low tide, hiking through a fir, western red cedar and arbutus forest 180m or taking in vistas from a rocky precipice. **Galiano Bluffs Park❖❖** has fine views to Victoria and the San Juan Islands; for another awesome vista, hike up **Bodega Ridge❖❖**.

Mayne Island❖❖

Mayne Island Community Chamber of Commerce; tel: (800) 665-8577. In summer, ask at the **Mayne Island Museum** or get a map-brochure at the Village Bay ferry dock.

Mayne Island Museum $ C4, Miners Bay; tel: (250) 539-2283; web: www.museumsassn.bc.ca/~bcma/museums/mim.html Open Jul–Aug, daily 1000–1700; winter, Sat 1300–1600.

Ferries land at **Village Bay**, a transit depot for the commercial centre at **Miners Bay**, named for prospectors on their way to the Fraser and Cariboo gold rushes between 1858 and the 1860s. Look for fine late-Victorian-era houses. Since then, the 21-km² island has fostered apple and tomato farming and been an island getaway.

Right
Bedwell Harbour

ⓘ **Active Pass
Lighthouse $** *Georgina
Point. Hours vary.*

**Mount Parke Regional
Park $** *off Fernhill Rd. Open
daily.*

Mayne Island Museum✢✢ belies its history as the 1896 Plumper Pass lockup (gaol), exhibiting wreck artefacts. **Georgina Point Heritage Park** is a good picnicking and bird-watching spot, with **Active Pass Lighthouse**✢✢✢, operational since 1885. Cycle Mayne's hills, or hike 270m up **Mount Parke**✢✢✢ for a view east to Vancouver and west to Vancouver Island.

PENDER ISLANDS✢✢

ⓘ **Pender Islands
Infocentre,** *2332
Otter Bay Rd, North Pender;
tel: (250) 681-6541.
Open daily Jun–Sep.*

ⓘ **Mount Norman
Regional Park $**
*South Pender Island, south of
the causeway. Open daily.*

Driftwood Centre
*Bedwell Harbour Rd at Razor
Point Rd has provisions and
hosts the May–Oct
Saturday* **Farmers
Market.**

A narrow causeway joins the 24sq km of Pender's North and South Islands. Ferries put in at **Otter Bay**, North Pender; almost all of the 2000 residents live further south near **Magic Lake**. While all the Gulf Islands have beaches, the Penders' sheltered coves are numerous and easily accessible. Try another panoramic Gulf Island hike up 217-m **Mount Norman**✢✢✢.

For a break from kayaking, horse-riding, swimming and hiking from May to October, visit the (North) Island service area, **Driftwood Centre**, for a Saturday **Farmers Market**✢✢.

SALT SPRING ISLAND✢✢✢

ⓘ **Salt Spring Island
Visitor InfoCentre**
*121 Lower Ganges Rd,
Ganges; tel: (250) 537-5252.
Open daily.*

ⓘ **Gulf Islands
Spinning Mill $** *351
Rainbow Rd, Ganges; tel:
(250) 537-4342. Tours Mon
1200–1330.*

Market in the Park $
*Centennial Park, Ganges.
Open 1st Sat in
Apr–Thanksgiving weekend
0900–1700.*

Salt Spring is a 180-km² island getaway with many of the arts and amenities of a thriving metropolis without the urban angst. Sheep are reared for meat and wool, providing work for some of Salt Spring's 10,000 residents. **Gulf Islands Spinning Mill**✢✢ offer tours of its wool, mohair, llama and alpaca production.

The town of **Ganges**✢✢ is the bustling hub of this island. Local farmers rub elbows with potters and musicians at the **Market in the Park** each Saturday from April to Thanksgiving weekend. In summer, **ArtCraft** pulls together 200-plus island artisans' work for unique souvenir shopping, or visit Salt Spring's 30 or more art galleries.

Ferries call at **Long Harbour**, **Vesuvius Bay** and **Fulford Harbour**. Take time to call ahead to **Bob Akerman's Museum**✢✢, a family collection of Cowichan and First Nations artefacts, historic photographs and Akerman's memories near Fulford Harbour.

The parks introduce what nature offers in the Gulf Islands. The shore **Ruckle Provincial Park**✢✢✢ is rocky, its 486 hectares

ArtCraft $ *Mahon Hall, Ganges. Open daily Jun–early Sep 1000–1700.*

Bob Ackerman's Museum $ *2501 Fulford-Ganges Rd, near Fulford Harbour; tel: (250) 653-4228. Call before arrival.*

Ruckle Provincial Park *$ via Beaver Point Rd; web: www.elp.gov.bc.ca/bcparks/ explore/parkpgs/ruckle.htm Open daily.*

Mount Maxwell Provincial Park $ *Southwest of Ganges, Cranberry Rd to Maxwell Rd. Open daily.*

Mill Farm Regional Park $ *Southwest island section via rough Musgrave Rd. Open daily.*

Right *Salt Spring Island*

Opposite *Otter Bay*

encompassing a sheep farm, several settler homes, fields and forest walks. Hikers enjoy views towards Vancouver Island from **Mount Maxwell Provincial Park❖❖**. Rough roads access the hang-glider heaven atop 698-m **Mount Bruce** in **Mill Farm Regional Park❖❖❖**.

SATURNA ISLAND❖❖

Saturna Island *web: www. saturnatourism.bc.ca*

East Point Regional Park $ *East Point Rd. Open daily.*

Mount Warburton Pike *$ via Staples Rd, west section of the island. Open daily.*

Astronomy aside, the island's 350 residents proudly claim East Point's sandstone formations as the 1791 discovery site of the island by the Spanish schooner *Santa Saturnina*. Saturna's few inhabitants are spread over 31sq km, leaving most businesses close to the **Lyall Harbour** dock, where ferries connect to other Gulf Islands.

Orca-spotting is phenomenal in summer from **East Point Regional Park❖❖❖**, near an 1889 lighthouse. Salmon and raptors, including peregrine falcons, hawks, osprey and eagles, engage in preying upon the small, but numerous, offshore fish. Look for deer and racoons amid forests of fir, spruce and alder, half-hidden in ferny undergrowth.

For vista spotters, 490-m **Mount Warburton Pike❖❖❖** can be climbed or reached via a dirt road, and island arts and crafts run the gamut from tarot readings to goldsmithing, woodworking and *raku* (lead-glazed, Japanese-style pottery).

Above
Waterside restaurant at island
ferry terminus

Accommodation and food in the Gulf Islands

There is no shortage of bed and breakfasts, inns, lodges and country manors to select from, but prices are high. Check with InfoCentres and Provincial Parks for camping; Saturna Island has no public camp pitches. Every ferry landing has a store for provisioning and most have at least one restaurant/pub nearby. Fine dining is often part of a B&B stay.

Hastings House $$$ *160 Upper Ganges Road, Salt Spring Island; tel. (250) 537-2362 or (800) 661-9255; web: www.hastingshouse.com,* may be the poshest collection of lodging buildings in Western Canada, including the original HBC post, secluded on 12 hectares.

Gulf Islands
Online *web:
ww.gulfislands.net*

C Ferries *1112 Fort St,
ctoria, BC V8V 4V2; tel:
50) 386-3431 or (888)
23-3779; web:
ww.bcferries.bc.ca*

C Provincial Parks
outh Vancouver Island
istrict *2930 Trans
anada Hwy, Victoria V9E
<3; tel: (250) 391-2300;
eb:
ww.elp.gov.bc.ca/bcparks*

Hummingbird Pub $$ *47 Sturdies Bay Rd, Galiano Island; tel: (250) 539-5472,* is a good spot to meet local people, with live entertainment in summer. Take the pub's summertime-only red and white shuttle from Montague Bay.

Oceanwood Country Inn $$$ *630 Dinner Bay Rd, Mayne Island; tel: (250) 539-5074,* is a 12-room, Tudor-style waterfront inn with a solarium and fine dining-room, complimented by fresh garden ingredients and one of the best wine cellars in Western Canada. Open Mar–Nov.

Suggested tour

Time: Via BC Ferries, distance depends on route, season and number of islands visited. In summer, June–Labour Day, from Tsawwassen, off BC Hwy 99, 45 minutes south of Vancouver, the run around four islands – but not Saturna Island – could take 5 hours; 6 hours on the direct Tsawwassen–Swartz Bay (Vancouver Island) run, with a return to one of the islands; or as little as 4 hours. Check with BC Ferries before planning a route and verify routing again on the day of travel for exact schedules.

Links: Vancouver (Tsawwassen – see page 42) is the mainland BC link to the Gulf Islands. From Salt Spring Island to Vancouver Island, sail from Vesuvius Bay to Crofton or from Fulford Harbour to **Swartz Bay** (see page 80).

Route: Ferry schedules will shape a tour, especially outside the mid-May–Sept busy season. The best strategy is to start big and work towards wilderness, ie begin with **SALT SPRING ISLAND ❶**, exploring Ganges' art and ambience, hike the trails for **Mount Maxwell Provincial Park** vistas, and work through the other islands as time and routes permit, to **GALIANO's ❷** kayak-loving shoreline and **SATURNA ISLAND's ❸** relative isolation.

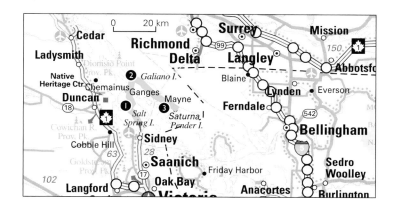

Victoria

Ratings

Architecture	●●●●●
Food and drink	●●●●●
Gardens	●●●●●
Children	●●●●
Historical sights	●●●●
Outdoor activities	●●●●
Scenery	●●●●
Shopping	●●●

ⓘ Tourism Victoria Visitor Info Centre
812 Wharf St; tel: (250) 953-2033; web: www.tourismvictoria.com
Open daily.

Monday Magazine 1069 Blanshard St; tel: (250) 382-6188, free each Friday in shops and newspaper boxes, has Victoria's best listing of current events and reviews.

Victoria doesn't *look* like Western Canada's oldes industrial city. British Columbia's capital has swappe the noise and the grit of old-fashioned metal bashing fo cleaner, more modern technologies without sacrificing on of Canada's greatest concentration of heritage building Older neighbourhoods are filled with lovingly restore storefronts, rambling mansions and social welfar programmes that city founders couldn't have imagined i their worst nightmares.

Victoria wallows in its reputation for espousing th ludicrous and the off-beat. City dwellers from Vancouver t Halifax dismiss Victorians as refugees from the *real* Canad but these self-satisfied refugees have never forgotten th winters they left behind. Canada's mildest climate and quic access to the out-of-doors have attracted a youthful mixtu of urban escapees, artists, ardent environmentalists an would-be entrepreneurs willing to meet establishe politicians and entrenched industrialists in a social fermer that aims to change the political and economic future.

Arriving and departing

Victoria International Airport, *tel: (250) 953-7500*, is 20km and 3 minutes north of downtown Victoria, near Sidney. Taxi **$$$** downtown; **Airporter** *tel: (250) 386-2526*, **$$**; coach service every 3 minutes or **BC Transit $** *tel: (250) 382-6161*.

The **Inner Harbour** has seaplane and helicopter services to Seatt Vancouver, the San Juan Islands, the Gulf Islands, Nanaimo and oth destinations.

By sea
Three million people visit Victoria each year, most of them by wate Advance booking is required on most routes.
• **BC Ferries**, *1112 Fort St; tel: (250) 386-3431* or *(888) 223-3779; we www.bcferries.bc.ca*, serve Swartz Bay, at the north end of the Saani Peninsula; 45 minutes by car from downtown, with vehicle an

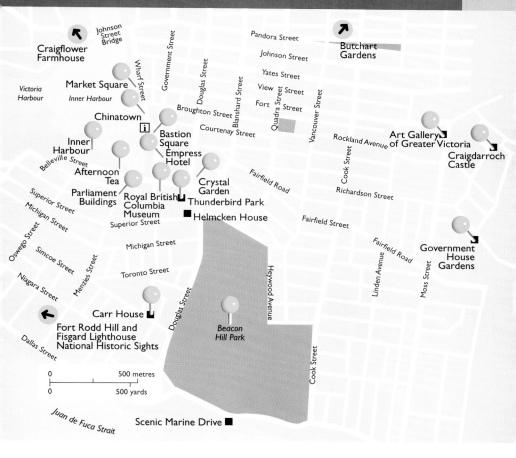

passenger service from Vancouver and the Gulf Islands. Ferry services connect with **BC Transit** in both Victoria and Vancouver.

• **Black Ball Transport** (*MV Coho*), *430 Belleville St; tel: (250) 386-2202*, has a car and passenger service between Victoria's Inner Harbour and Port Angeles, Washington.

• **Victoria San Juan Cruises**; *tel: (800) 443-4552*, has passenger service between Bellingham, Washington and Victoria via Roche Harbor (San Juan Island, Washington) May–Oct.

• **Victoria Clipper**, *254 Belleville, Victoria; tel: (250) 382-8100 or (800) 888-2535; web: www.victoriaclipper.com*, has a daily passenger catamaran service to Seattle with the fastest ships on the route and a car ferry service mid-May–mid-September.

• **Washington State Ferries**, *2499 Ocean Ave, Sidney; tel: (250) 656-1831*, has a vehicle and passenger service to Anacortes, Washington. Credit cards are not accepted, but fares may be paid in either US or Canadian currency.

By land
• All road transport between Victoria and the mainland requires a ferry connection. **Pacific Coach Lines** *210-1150 Station St; tel: (250) 385-4411*, operate between central Victoria and central Vancouver.
• **Esquimalt & Nanaimo (E&N) Railway** *450 Pandora Ave; tel: (250) 383-4324 or (800) 561-8630; web: www.viarail.ca*, has a daily return rail service between Victoria and Courtenay via Nanaimo.

Getting around

Walking is the best way to explore touristic Victoria, a compact area around the Inner Harbour. It's also practicable to explore all but the most distant parts of the city by public transport. **BC Transit** *tel: (250) 382-6161; web: www.transitbc.com*, has a dense network of bus routes throughout Greater Victoria with several discount ticket and pass schemes available at the Tourism Victoria Info Centre.

Driving
Narrow streets, busy traffic and limited street parking make it difficult to explore downtown by car. The best bet is to park and explore on foot, then drive to more distant attractions. There is ample parking on the west side of Wharf Street along the Inner Harbour, as well as parking garages east of Government Street. Parking meter time limits are strictly enforced, especially downtown.

Downtown traffic is usually heavy, but flows smoothly in other areas. Major arteries, particularly Hwy 17 and Hwy 1A, are jammed during rush hours, 0730–0900 and 1600–1800 Mon–Fri. Left turns are extremely difficult anywhere downtown, while scenic country roads on the Saanich Peninsula can be narrow, winding and slow.

Below
Victoria's Inner Harbour

**Art Gallery of
Greater Victoria $$**
040 Moss St; tel: (250)
84-4101. Open Mon–Sat
000–1700, Thu
000–2100, Sun
300–1700.

astion Square $ *Wharf*
t between Yates and Fort
ts. Open daily.

**laritime Museum of
ritish Columbia $$** *28*
astion Sq; tel: (250) 385-
222. Open daily
930–1630.

Afternoon tea

Every hotel, restaurant and café offers its own version of afternoon tea. **Blethering Place Tea Room and Restaurant $$** *206-2250 Oak Bay Ave (Oak Bay); tel: (250) 598-1413*, is favoured by the Tweed Curtain set. **Empress Hotel $$$** *721 Government St; tel: (250) 384-8111*, is overpriced and overtouristed, but it's hard to beat the city's most sumptuous setting. **James Bay Tea Room and Restaurant $$** *332 Menzies St (behind Parliament Buildings); tel: (250) 382-8282*, attracts nearby residents, as well as government and legislative workers. **Tudor Rose Restaurant and Tea Room $$** *253 Cook St (near Beacon Hill Park); tel: (250) 382-4616*, is a neighbourhood favourite.

Sights

Afternoon Tea**

A Victoria tradition, the Empress Hotel serves more than 100,000 of these light meals yearly. Cups of strong tea wash down finger sandwiches, crumpets and scones arrayed on multi-tiered trays amid pots of whipped cream and conserves.

An early 19th-century Duchess of Bedford gets credit for afternoon tea. Desperate to counteract 'that sinking feeling around 5pm', she tried snacking on small sandwiches and tea. The custom caught on, evolving into today's afternoon tea and the more formal version known as 'high tea'.

Art Gallery of Greater Victoria**

Victoria's city art museum concentrates on contemporary Canadian artists, as well as North American and European historical artists and notable Asian artists. The gallery shop is particularly well stocked with affordable reproductions.

Bastion Square*

The Square (actually a long rectangle) is the site of Victoria's first gaol, as well as the original Provincial Court House, used between 1889 and 1962. The Victoria Law Courts Building now houses the **Maritime Museum of British Columbia***, filled with ship models, figure-heads, tools, naval uniforms and the 1860 *Tilikum*, an 11-m dug-out canoe converted to a schooner that sailed from Victoria to England and back between 1901 and 1904.

Beacon Hill Park $
Juan de Fuca Strait between Douglas and Cook Sts; tel: (250) 381-2532. Open daily, most attractions open mid-Mar–mid-Oct.

Butchart Gardens $$$
Brentwood Bay; tel: (250) 652-5256/4422. Open daily 0900; closing varies with the season. Reduced prices in winter.

Carr House $ *207 Government St; tel: (250) 383-5843. Open daily, mid-May–mid-Oct, 1000–1700.*

Chinatown $ *Between Herald, Government, Pandora and Store streets.*

Fan Tan Alley $
Chinatown, between Fisgard St and Pandora Ave. Open daily.

Craigdarroch Castle $$
1050 Joan Cres; tel: (250) 592-5323. Open Jun–Sep, 0900–1930; rest of year, 1000–1700.

Opposite
Bastion Square's Law Courts Building now houses the Maritime Museum

Coloured bricks set into the pavement along View Street west to Bastion Square and south along Government Street to Fort Street then west towards the harbour mark the original stockade where Victoria began.

Beacon Hill Park♦♦♦
This 74-hectare park is named for Beacon Hill, the highest seaside point in Victoria, where signal fires once burned to warn sailors of reefs guarding the harbour entrance. The park is a collection of formal gardens, small lakes and playing fields sloping down to cliff overlooking the Strait of Juan de Fuca. Runners, dog-walkers and sightseers flock to the seaside walkway with its wide vistas across the Strait to the Olympic Mountains in Washington.

Butchart Gardens♦♦♦
Originally a limestone quarry, Butchart has become one of the most popular gardens in Canada. Its 20 manicured hectares are divided into Italian, Japanese, rose and sunken gardens, plus other landscape creations. The gardens are colourful all year and spectacular in summer – as are the crowds. The crush lessens after tour coaches depart at 1530.

Carr House♦
The cream-coloured Victorian building is the birthplace of Emily Carr one of Canada's most famed artists and authors. She took the country by storm in the 1930s with wild, haunting images of forests and totem poles before turning to books that re-created late 19th-century Victoria. A description of Carr's father, 'more English than the English', became an unofficial goal for three generations of Victorians. The house is open for tours daily.

Chinatown♦♦
The oldest Chinese community in Canada began in the 1840s when Victoria was BC's only serious settlement. Don't miss **Fan Tan Alley♦♦♦**, the width of an adult armspan in places. Small shops set into the walls sell everything from haircuts and antique jewellery to New Age crystals and incense in what were once brothels, opium dens and gambling parlours.

Craigdarroch Castle♦♦♦
The castle was the grandest home atop the grandest hill in Victoria a 39-room rough stone castle built by Nanaimo coal baron Robert Dunsmuir. The house was completed in 1889, month after Dunsmuir's death, but his family lived there until 1909. The intricately ornamented mansion is resplendent in carved wood, polished marble and fine paintings, elegantly restored after decades' service as a hospital, music academy, offices and decaying derelict.

Craigflower Farmhouse $ 110
Island Hwy (Hwy 1A and Admiral Rd); tel: (250) 387-4697. Grounds open daily; house open May–Oct, Sun 1000–1700.

Crystal Garden $$ 713
Douglas St; tel: (250) 381-1213. Open daily Jul–Aug, daily 0800–2000; Apr–Jun and Sep–Oct, 0900–1800; Nov–Mar, 1000–1630.

Empress Hotel $ 721
Government St; tel: (250) 384-8111 or (800) 441-1414; web: www.cphotels.ca Open daily.

Above
The Empress Hotel

Craigflower Farmhouse❖❖❖
This 1856 farmhouse was the command centre for one of the Hudson's Bay Company's most successful farms. Most of the furnishings came to BC with Scottish families brought by the HBC to colonise the area. Guides in period costume conduct tours of the interior as well as heritage gardens, orchards and oatfields.

Crystal Garden❖❖
England's Crystal Palace inspired the huge glass house just behind the Empress Hotel. At its debut in 1925, the shining conservatory held the largest indoor swimming-pool to be found in the British Empire. It elegant promenade, ballrooms and tea rooms created one of Canada' most famous landmarks. Today, it is filled with tropical plants, birds butterflies and monkeys.

Empress Hotel❖❖❖
Opened in 1908 by the same architect who built Parliament House the ivy-covered Empress sits surrounded by gardens on what was onc a garbage-filled tidal flat. The posh Edwardian décor in The Empress' original lobby (south end of the building) is worth visiting, if only fo a drink, but beware of Tea Time in summer, when the hotel i swamped with tourists. Corridors in The Empress's first undergroun level are lined with photographs showing the world's upper crust a play around Victoria during the first half of the 20th century.

Fort Rodd Hill and Fisgard Lighthouse National Historic Sites***

The massive seaside fortress protected the naval base and coaling station at Esquimalt, just west of Vancouver, between 1878 and 1956, when missiles replaced coastal defence guns. White Fisgard Lighthouse, atop a rocky islet connected to the mainland by modern walkway, is the oldest lighthouse on the west coast of Canada. The lightkeeper's house has become an excellent lighthouse and shipping museum with broad ocean views.

Government House Gardens***

You can't tour the official residence of BC's Lieutenant Governor, but the 14 hectares of azaleas, blossoming shrubs, formal flower beds, heather, ivy, lawns and rhododendrons are open to the public – unless the British royal family happens to be in residence.

Inner Harbour***

Nearly all of touristic Victoria is packed into a 10-block area along the south and east sides of the Inner Harbour, where the city began about 160 years ago. Ferries from the US dock inside the harbour, as do seaplanes from Vancouver and the rest of Vancouver Island, whale-watching boats, sea kayakers and dozens of pleasure boaters, while tiny ferries dart from shore to shore like water bugs. The best views are from the harbour side of Government Street, across from the Empress Hotel, and from the waterside pedestrian promenade.

Market Square***

The collection of nine red-brick heritage buildings, now an open shopping arcade, were originally shops and storehouses for the docks and industrial areas built to supply successive waves of gold miners, fishing fleets, seal hunters, coal ships and general cargo vessels that sailed into Victoria.

Parliament Buildings***

The imposing buildings at the south end of the Inner Harbour were built by British architect Francis Mawson Rattenbury. Ratz, as he preferred to be called, arrived in Victoria in 1892 and promptly won an Empire-wide competition to build the province's new Parliament House at the age of 25.

He also built the opulent Edwardian Empress Hotel, the Crystal Garden and other ornate edifices in Victoria, before a lurid divorce and lusty remarriage to a woman 30 years younger. Stuffy Victoria ostracised both the *avant-garde* wife, who dared to smoke cigarettes in public, and her new husband. Ratz was murdered by his wife's young lover in 1934, after fleeing to England to escape Victoria's withering disdain.

Royal British Columbia Museum***

Centrepiece of this sprawling museum is a First Nations collection. Enter through the full-sized Kwaktuil chief's house with displays of

Thunderbird Park
$ Belleville and Douglas
Sts; tel: (250) 387-3701.
Open daily.

totems, carvings and chiefly regalia. Even more striking are artefact including story-telling masks, from the apex of First Nations arts an handicrafts in the lucrative decades after first contact with White fu traders and merchants. Many tribes disappeared as smallpox and othe diseases decimated BC's Native population between 1843 and 188. One outbreak of smallpox alone that spread from Victoria in 186 killed 20,000, a third of the Province's non-White population.

Museum curators and collectors also lead excursions from April t October. Local day-trips feature archaeology, sea kayaking, marin biology, bird-watching, snorkelling with salmon, or local history longer trips range as far as the Queen Charlotte Islands (*see page 116*).

Thunderbird Park✦✦✦

Next to the museum is Thunderbird Park, created to display totem poles in the 1940s. As the outdoor poles began to crumble from th effects of weather and time, museum curators sought out carvers t create replacements. Mungo Martin, Chief of the Kwagiulth band nea Fort Rupert, organised a carving group in the 1950s that successfull recreated what had already become a lost art. Many of the pole towering above the park are replicas of Martin's original creation while the originals stand protected inside the museum.

Right
Thunderbird Park

Accommodation and food

Hotel space is tight in summer and less so in winter. Budget–moderate motels line Hwy 1/1A (Douglas Street) north of downtown. Most rooms at all price levels can be booked by credit card through **Tourism Victoria**; *tel: (800) 663-3883.*

Days Inn on the Harbour $$ *427 Belleville St; tel: (250) 386-3451 or (800) 329-7466; web: www.daysinn.com*, is across the street from the Inner Harbour ferry docks, a 10-minute walk from The Empress.

The Empress Hotel $$$ *721 Government St; tel: (250) 384-8111 or (800) 441-1414; web: www.cphotels.ca/cp.htm*, is the most prestigious and most central address in town.

Executive House Hotel $$ *777 Douglas St; tel: (250) 388-5111 or (800) 663-7001*, rises directly behind The Empress with sweeping harbour views from the upper floors.

Laurel Point Inn $$$ *680 Montreal St; tel: (250) 386-8721 or (800) 663-7667*, overlooks the Inner Harbour entrance with modern luxury in contrast to The Empress's Edwardian gloss.

Quality Inn Harbourview $$ *455 Belleville St; tel: (250) 386-2421 or (800) 424-6423; web: www.qualityinn.com*, is an easy stroll along the Inner Harbour from The Empress.

The young, well-travelled Victoria population demands – and gets – the same kind of variety, quality and value you'll find in Vancouver. Advance booking is essential in summer.

Chandlers Seafood Restaurant $$ *1250 Wharf St; tel: (250) 385-3474*, has some of the best seafood in town.

Deep Cove Chalet $$$ *11190 Chalet Rd; tel: (250) 656-3541*, is the best French restaurant on Vancouver Island with one of the largest wine cellars in the province.

Herald Street Café $$ *546 Herald St; tel: (250) 381-1441*, is Victoria's other top seafood choice.

The Sally Café $ *714 Cormorant St; tel: (250) 381-1431*, with its wildly colourful murals, is *de rigueur* for a casual breakfast or lunch with students, artists and local office workers.

Swan's Hotel $$ *506 Pandora Ave; tel: (250) 361-3310*, has one of BC's best breweries, **Buckerfield's Brewery**, on the premises, plus fine Northwest cuisine in a restored heritage building.

Victoria Eaton Centre $ *Government St, Fort–View Sts, top floor; tel: (250) 389-2228* is dependable for a quick lunch or dinner.

Wharfside $$ *1208 Wharf St; tel: (250) 360-1808*, offers great harbour views with tasty fish and pizza, despite the tourist crowds.

Suggested tour

Total distance: 60km, or 110km with all detours.

Time: Allow a half-day for driving and 2 days to see all the sight starting from the southwest corner of Beacon Hill Park, Douglas Stree and Dallas Road. Pick up the circular tour anywhere, but avoid rus hours (*0730–0900 and 1600–1800*), especially downtown.

Links: Victoria connects with the **Gulf Islands** (*see page 56*) and wit routes to **Southern Vancouver Island** (*see page 76*) or **Centra Vancouver Island** (*see page 86*).

Route: Follow Dallas Road east through **BEACON HILL PARK (** along the **Juan de Fuca Strait** separating the US and Canada. Th wooden sign marking Mile 0 of the TransCanada Highway is sceni but the highway now extends west to **Tofino.**

A shoreline walking and cycling path is as popular with runners as it with photographers entranced by the **Olympic Mountains** across th strait.

Detour 1 Dallas Road continues past **Ross Bay Cemetery**, where mo early Victoria citizens can be found. Dallas Road changes names t Hollywood Crescent just beyond the cemetery, then become Hollywood Road as it curves around **Gonzales Bay**, usually called **Fo Bay** for the leavings of its sea birds.

Take King George Terrace to the right, following green Scenic Driv signs. The **King George Lookout**, part of **Trafalgar Park**, ha Victoria's best sea-level view across the Strait to **Port Angele** Washington, 37km due south.

King George Terrace ends at Beach Drive. Go right (east) on Beac Drive along the shores of **McNeil Bay** to the **Municipality of Oa Bay**. Tudor motifs are so popular that the municipal limit is ha seriously called the 'Tweed Curtain'. Beach Drive swings nort through the **Victoria Golf Club**, favoured by strollers. Visito occasionally meet Doris Gravlin, the resident ghost, usually wearing long white dress. Gravlin's body was found in a sand trap in th 1930s. Her husband was suspected of murder, but he drowned befo the investigation was completed.

Just north are **Haynes Park** and the **Oak Bay Marina**. The **Oak Ba Rose Garden** and more than 500 plants from the private estate tha once occupied the area fill the southeast corner of **Windsor Park**, we on Currie Road opposite the breakwater.

Continue north past **Willows Park** and through the massive ston gates of **Uplands**. The posh 1912 housing estate was designed by th Olmsted brothers, who designed New York's Central Park. The 3(hectare **Uplands Park**, part of the original estate plan, is the large

bove
utchart Gardens

tract of undeveloped Garry oak habitat in Victoria. Known as Oregon white oak in the US and British Columbia's only native oak, immense groves of Garry oaks once flourished in the drier meadows of Victoria. Many of the graceful trees became furniture or house beams. Most of the park is undeveloped. Continue 5km north to **Loon Bay**, the **Royal Victoria Yacht Club** and another massive stone gate marking the northern boundary of Uplands. Beach Drive becomes Cadboro Bay Road at Sinclair Road (end of detour).

Detour 2: Follow Cadboro Bay Road to Arbutus Road. Turn left (north) on to Arbutus and keep to the main roads headed north and west through **Mount Douglas Park** to Royal Oak Drive. Take Royal Oak Drive to Hwy 17 northbound. Go left (west) at Keating Cross Road, following signs to **Butchart Gardens**. Return to Victoria via Hwy 17A, passing the **Dominion Astrophysical Observatory** on the way to Hwy 17.

Above
Fisgard Lighthouse, Fort Rodd Hill

Go right (west) on Sinclair Road through th University of Victoria and across th Saanich Peninsula to Hwy 17. Turn lef (south) on Hwy 17 to Victoria. At the end c the dual carriageway, make a sharp left tur on to Douglas Street at the **Town an Country Centre**. Turn right 1km later on t Cloverdale Road, following signs and lan markings for 'Victoria by way of Douglas St At the second traffic signal, turn left on t Douglas to pass **Mayfair Shopping Centr** one of the largest shopping malls o Vancouver Island, and a strip of motels.

The Bay, the modern department stor successor to the Hudson's Bay Compan occupies the southeast corner of Douglas an Herald streets. The bright pink and grey bric **Victoria City Hall** is on the west side c Douglas at Pandora Street.

Continue five blocks to Broughton Street and turn right (west) at th red brick **St Peter's Presbyterian Church**, right again at Broad Stree and again on to Fort Street, one-way eastbound. Follow Fort Stree 2km past **Antique Row** to Moss Street. Turn right (south), followin green signs for the Art Gallery of Greater Vancouver *(end of detour)*.

Head east to skirt Beacon Hill Park, then north up Cook street, right i Richardson Street and left in Moss Street to reach the **ART GALLER OF GREATER VANCOUVER**. From the Gallery, turn right on to Wi Spencer Place, left on to Moss and right on to Fort Street. Turn righ into Joan Crescent to **CRAIGDARROCH CASTLE ❸**.

Exit right into Joan Crescent. Continue to Rockland Avenue, tur right and then immediately left into **GOVERNMENT HOUS GARDENS ❹**. Leave Government House to the left (west) o Rockland. Continue across Moss Street, Cook and Vancouver street where Rockland becomes Courtney Street, to Quadra Street and **Chris Church Anglican Cathedral**, built in 13th-century Gothic style. Tur left (south) on to Quadra, which becomes Arbutus Way in **BEACO HILL PARK**. Continue on to Circular Drive, or follow Park Way to th top of Beacon Hill for views across Victoria and Juan de Fuca Strait an return to Circular Drive. Follow the circle left to Douglas Street and g left. Go right (west) on to Niagara Street two blocks to Governmer Street and turn right (north). **CARR HOUSE ❺** is ahead on the righ (east).

Continue north past the **James Bay Inn** toward Belleville Street, wit the **PARLIAMENT BUILDINGS ❻** on the left and the **ROYAL BRITIS COLUMBIA MUSEUM ❼** on the right. Across Belleville, the **INNE**

HARBOUR **❽** is on the left and **THE EMPRESS HOTEL ❾** on the right. Move to the right lane following Government Street north, passing the **Tourism Victoria Visitor Info Centre** on the left.

Continue past Fort Street with **Eaton Centre** on the right and **Munro's Books** on the left. At View Street, **BASTION SQUARE ❿** and the **Maritime Museum** are to the left.

Detour: Turn left (west) on to Yates Street, then right (north) on to Wharf Street one block later, and move into the left or middle lane. Turn left (west) and cross the sky-blue **Johnson St Bridge** over **Victoria Harbour** to **Esquimalt**. Follow Esquimalt Road west to Admirals Road and turn right (north) to Hwy 1A at **CRAIGFLOWER HOUSE**. Turn left (west) on to Hwy 1A. Go straight to Ocean Boulevard, the first traffic signal beyond the **Juan de Fuca Recreation Centre** (on the south side), following signs for **FORT RODD HILL** and **FISGARD LIGHTHOUSE**. Return via Hwy 1A, which becomes Douglas Street.

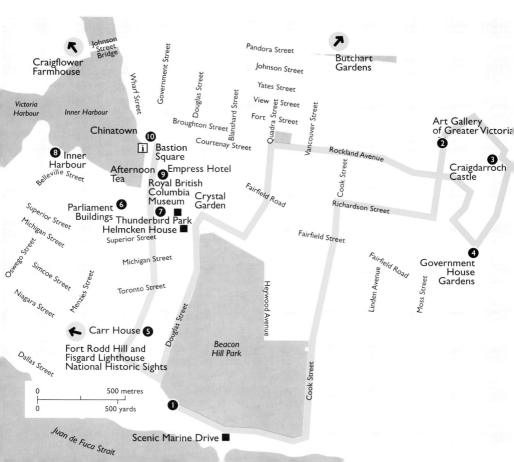

South Vancouver Island

Ratings

Beaches	●●●●
Nature	●●●●
Parks	●●●●
Scenery	●●●●
Walking	●●●●
Children	●●●
Food	●●●
History	●●●

Don't expect to visit Victoria without exploring South Vancouver Island. Routes from Victoria's airport and major ferry terminals include a scenic drive through peaceful farming country east of the city. To the west lie increasingly wild stretches of forest and storm-wracked beach as the Strait of Juan de Fuca opens into the Pacific Ocean. Much of the oceanfront is protected in a series of parks linked by a rugged walking trail.

Inland forests have long since been logged, regrown and logged again in a seemingly endless cycle that despoils land and streams. It isn't until Port Renfrew and the roadless areas north that timber companies relinquish their hold. The variety of outdoor leisure activities, from boating and birding to strolling the lush glades of Butchart Gardens, mountain biking former railway lines and wilderness hiking, have made South Vancouver Island a playground for Victorians of all persuasions.

BOTANICAL BEACH PROVINCIAL PARK✿✿✿

ⓘ Botanical Beach Provincial Park $
3.5km south from Port Renfrew on gravel road. Open daily.

Botanical Beach, at the mouth of the Juan de Fuca Strait, is one of BC's best known, if seldom seen, beaches. Sandstone cliffs drop to a cobble beach and rich tide-pools that have been studied by generations of marine biologists from around the globe. At low tide, the pools are filled with green sea urchins, purple sea stars, scuttling red crabs, the waving green tentacles of anemones and swarms of silvery fish. The best and safest time to visit is near the end of a falling tide (use tide tables for Tofino) just before slack water. Rising tides sweep in rapidly with massive rogue waves scouring what had been dry land an eyeblink earlier.

Rough tides and massive winter storms have eroded cliffs and headlands into swirling stone sculptures topped with Sitka spruce and shore pine. Several easy trails, including Mill Bay, Botany Bay and Shoreline, offer fine views even at high tide. All three trails converge on the Juan de Fuca Marine Trail, which leads 47km to China Beach.

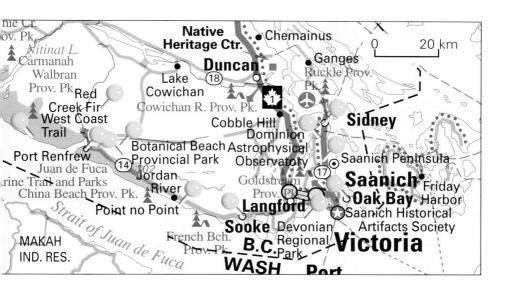

DEVONIAN REGIONAL PARK✦✦✦

Devonian Regional Park $ *William Head Road, 1km west of My-Chosen Café; tel: (250) 478-1344. Open daily dawn–dusk.*

My-Chosen Café $$ *4492 Happy Valley Road; tel: (250) 474-2333, is a local favourite, especially at weekends.*

An easy 1-km nature trail on this former farm leads from the car park past **Sherwood Pond**✦ (once used to water cattle) to the beach at **Perry Bay**✦✦✦, a favourite spot to watch for seals, sea lions and whales. A 5-km trail leads east to **Witty's Lagoon**✦✦✦, but the trail is walkable only at low tide.

Right
Devonian Regional Park

DOMINION ASTROPHYSICAL OBSERVATORY✧✧

The 1.82-m reflecting telescope inside the white dome atop **Observatory Hill** *507 W Saanich Rd; tel: (250) 363-0012; open May–Aug, Sat 0900–2300, Sun and holidays 0900–2000; Sep–Apr, Mon–Fri 0915–1630,* was the world's largest when it opened in 1918 and is still in active use. A scenic access road spirals around the hill to a car park just outside the observatory dome.

EAST SOOKE REGIONAL PARK✧✧✧

East Sooke Regional Park $ *Off Rocky Point Rd; tel: (250) 478-3344. Open daily dawn–dusk.*

South Vancouver Island's prime park has 1422 hectares of semi-wild shore and forest laced with walking trails. The foreshore is framed by twisted arbutus and stunted pines, backed by Sitka spruce, red cedar, hemlock and Douglas fir. Look for bald eagles perched at the edge of the forest, river otters and mink scurrying through piles of tangled driftwood and cormorants diving offshore. Sea lions are common from September to May. Walking routes range from pre-picnic walks to an all-day, 10-km trek along the park shoreline. Tiny spits and offshore islands protect dozens of pocket-sized beaches and picnic spots.

GALLOPING GOOSE TRAIL✧✧✧

Galloping Goose Trail $ *Tourism Victoria Visitor Info Centre, 812 Wharf St; tel: (250) 953-2033; web: www.tourismvictoria.com Trail open daily.*

This linear park (70km long by 10m wide) follows the railbed of the *Galloping Goose*, a 1920s passenger railway that once ran from Victoria to Leechtown, an abandoned mining camp north of Sooke. The almost-level trail meanders through a variety of landscapes from urban streets to dense forest. Popular stretches for walking or cycling are Roche Cove Regional Park (off Gillespie Road in Metchosin) to Matheson Lake Regional Park, about 4km, and through Sooke Potholes Provincial Park (*see page 82*).

JUAN DE FUCA MARINE TRAIL✧✧✧

Juan de Fuca Marine Trail $ *Between China Beach, west of Jordan River (near Port Renfrew), BC Parks; tel: (250) 391-2300; web: www.bcparks.gov.bc.ca Open daily.*

Park and trail cover 47km of spectacular beaches, dazzling marine views, lush coastal forest and rich wildlife habitat. Experienced hikers should allow four days to walk the entire trail, but shorter sections make easy day hikes. **China Beach✧**, just west of Jordan River, has crashing surf 20 minutes from the trail head. **Botanical Beach✧✧✧**, the west end of the trail, is famed for its tide pools and easy walks along the **Mill Bay✧✧✧**, **Botany Bay✧✧✧** and **Shoreline✧✧✧** trails. Other trail access points include **Sombrio Beach✧** and **Parkinson Beach✧**.

PENINSULA TRAIL❖❖❖

Peninsula Trail $
Lochside Dr and Beacon Ave to Quadra St in Victoria.

Scrap the railway but keep the right of way. That's the idea behind the Peninsula Trail, also called the **Lochside Trail** for its starting point. By either name, the walking and cycling trail connects with the Galloping Goose trail at Quadra Street near Greenridge Circle in Victoria. Much of the trail is gravel, passing through forest, fields, hobby farms with pig and turkey pens, open-air museums, and even a field for flying model aeroplanes. Allow three hours one way to cycle the 30km to or from Victoria.

POINT NO POINT❖❖❖

Point No Point $$
1505 West Coast Rd 21km west of Sooke); tel: 250) 646-2020. Open daily.

The point of Point No Point (named by early chartmakers who either saw or didn't see the point, depending on their position) is a 400-m rock pile pounded by ferocious waves. The inn of the same name is a traditional stopping point for modern Victorians on the way to or from Port Renfrew. Afternoon tea is a local classic.

PORT RENFREW❖❖

Port Renfrew
Sooke Travel Infocentre (see page 81) and the Parks Canada West Coast Trail InfoCentre, Hwy 14, 16km west of Sombrio Beach; tel: 250) 647-5434. Open daily 900–1700.

This tiny village at the mouth of the San Juan River is the end of the road on South Vancouver Island. It's also the terminus (or the beginning) of the Juan de Fuca Marine Trail south and east to China Beach, the West Coast Trail north to Bamfield and a maze of logging roads that converge on Cowichan Bay and Duncan (*see page 89*). Expect at least a smattering of hikers, paddlers, beachcombers, fishers and hunters all year, though traffic is heaviest from June to mid-September when hundreds of West Coast Trail walkers pour through town.

Right
Port Renfrew's Botanical Beach

Accommodation and food in Port Renfrew

Don't expect big-city cuisine in this frontier town that caters to outdoor recreationists.

Arbutus Beach Lodge $$ 5 Queesto Dr; tel: (250) 647-5458, is the best restaurant in town and has comfortable bed-and-breakfast accommodation.

Lighthouse Pub $$ Tel: (250) 647-5543, is a good alternative restaurant.

Port Renfrew Hotel & Pub $$ Foot of Government Pier; tel: (250) 647 5541, is a rough and rustic hotel/pub for backpackers and the hunting crowd.

RED CREEK FIR*

Red Creek Fir $
12km from Port Renfrew; ask for directions and (especially) road conditions.

Once thought to be the largest Douglas fir in Canada, this 73-m tree was probably closer to 90m tall before the top blew off in a windstorm sometime in the past 900 or so years. It was left when loggers clearcut the area in 1987. The current record holder is a Douglas fir in the upper Coquitlam watershed that was measured at 94m tall in 1996.

SAANICH PENINSULA**

Saanich Peninsula Chamber of Commerce West side Hwy 17, half-way between Swartz Bay Ferry Terminal and Sidney; tel: (250) 656-0525 or (250) 656-3260; open Mar–Nov. 5th Street and Ocean Avenue; tel: (250) 656-3616; open daily.

BC Aviation Museum $ Norseman Rd; tel: (250) 655-3300; open daily.

Pointing north from Victoria like a thumb, the Saanitch Peninsula is largely open, rolling country. Much of the peninsula is protected from future development within regional parks or agricultural preserves, but Victoria's expanding population has led to traffic congestion and pollution problems. Hwy 17, which leads from the BC Ferries landing at Swartz Bay to central Victoria, is the main traffic artery. Hwy 17A, W Saanich Road, is a more scenic alternative, but considerably slower.

At the tip of the peninsula and Hwy 17 are **Swartz Bay*** and the **BC Ferries terminal**. Just south is **Victoria International Airport** and the **BC Aviation Museum***, which showcases the history of flight in Canada. The emotional highlight is a replica of the Gibson Twin built by Victorian William Gibson in 1910 – the craft flew 60m before crashing into a Garry oak tree, beating the American Wright brothers' 1903 flight record of 36m.

Right
Vintage seaplane

SAANICH HISTORICAL ARTIFACTS SOCIETY*

Saanich Historical Artifacts Society $ 321 Lochside Rd; tel: (250) 52-5522. Open all day arly Jun–Sep, mornings in inter.

The 12-hectare site looks like something of a junk yard from the highway, but the antique farming equipment, model railway, sawmill and almost everything else are maintained in perfect working order. Facilities include a small lake, forest hiking trails, a nature pond and picnic facilities.

SIDNEY*

Sidney Marine Mammal and Historical Museum $ 801 Seaport Place; tel: 250) 656-1322. Open daily summer, weekends in inter.

Sidney Spit Provincial Marine Park $ Sidney Island, 3km from Sidney; tel: 250) 391-2300; open daily.

Princess Margaret Provincial Marine Park Portland Island, 8km from Sidney; tel: (250) 391-2300. Open daily.

The town was built in the 1890s at the terminus of the Victoria and Sidney Railway. The railway is long gone, but the high street, Beacon Avenue, is a pleasant place to wander on a sunny afternoon. Look for bookshops along Beacon Avenue and Third Street, as well as a variety of speciality shops. The waterfront includes several restaurants with pleasant outdoor decks, pubs, parks, a marina and a popular fish market.

At the **Sidney Marine Mammal and Historical Museum***, the mammals are whales, sea lions, sea otters and seals, all common species that are on the decline because of human activities. History exhibits include pioneer artefacts from the 1850s onward as well as period photographs.

Just offshore are **Sidney Spit Provincial Marine Park***** and **Princess Margaret Provincial Marine Park*****. Both are accessible by private boat or by ferry from the marina at the end of Beacon Avenue. The parks offer calm, sandy beaches, open lagoons, meadows and forests teeming with birds, deer and other wildlife.

SOOKE**

Sooke Region InfoCentre Sooke egion Museum, see below.

Sooke Region Museum $ 2070 hillips Rd, Sooke; tel: (250) 42-6351. Open daily 900–1700.

Moss Cottage $ 2070 hillips Rd, Sooke; tel: (250) 42-6351. Open Jul–Aug, aily 0900–1700; Sep–Jun, pen Tue–Sun, 0900–1700. Moss Cottage is part of ooke Region Museum (see bove).

Sooke is the southernmost harbour in Western Canada, a bustling fishing, logging and tourist town. The harbour is protected by **Whiffen Spit*****, a narrow strip of sand, gravel and driftwood nearly 5km long. Both Sooke Harbour and Sooke Basin, a large sheltered backwater, are popular with kayakers.

Sooke was the site of Vancouver Island's first successful steam-powered sawmill and one of BC's last commercial fish traps. **Sooke Region Museum***** tells both stories in lavish detail, as well as recounting a short-lived gold rush at Leechtown and the large First Nations villages that once dominated the area. **Moss Cottage***** is the oldest structure in Sooke, built in 1870 with lumber from the original Muir Mill, itself built around a boiler salvaged from a shipwreck in 1849. The cottage, furnished as a working-class home from 1900, is open all year. Costumed guides explain the displays in summer.

Accommodation and food in Sooke

Mom's Café $$ *2036 Shields Rd; tel: (250) 642-3314*, is a busy local eatery.

Sooke Harbour House $$$ *1528 Whiffen Spit Rd; tel: (250) 642-3421*, is one of the most acclaimed restaurant-hotels in Western Canada, specialising in all-local products: scallops, shrimp, geoducks, whelks, salmon, squid, two dozen types of crab, duck, rabbit and vegetables fresh from the kitchen garden.

SOOKE POTHOLES PROVINCIAL PARK✤✤

Sooke Potholes Provincial Park $
Sooke River Rd, 5km north of Sooke; tel: (250) 391-2300. Open daily.

The potholes, natural holes in the Sooke River filled with cool, clear water, have been a popular summer swimming destination since the 1860s. It is also a place where people come to ride bikes and watch spawning salmon. Expect crowds on hot summer days, but winter visitors are rare.

WEST COAST TRAIL✤✤✤

Port Renfrew is the end or the beginning of the rugged 10-day, 77km trek through bogs, beaches, forests, rivers, rain and sun along the western edge of Vancouver Island. Created as a life-saving route for

West Coast Trail
$$$ *Pacific Rim*
ational Park Reserve, Box
30, Ucluelet, BC V0R 3A0,
r Parks Canada West
oast Trail InfoCentre, Hwy
4, 16km west of Sombrio
each; tel: (250) 647-5434.

sailors shipwrecked on the treacherous coast in the 19th century, the Trail has become of the most popular hikes in Canada. Sixty hikers are allowed to start each day, with groups leaving from Port Renfrew or Pachena Bay (3km from Bamfield) and Nitinat, the midway point. Most permits are booked up months in advance, but a handful are available on a first come, first served basis each day. The trail is part of Pacific Rim National Park Reserve.

WITTY'S LAGOON REGIONAL PARK✦✦✦

Witty's Lagoon
Regional Park $
letchosin Rd; tel: (250)
78-3344; open daily.

Witty's perfectly encapsulates the West Coast with luxuriant forests, clear creeks, a waterfall, long sandy beaches backed by wracks of driftwood, bald eagles, blue herons, seals and passing whales. A 5km trail leads to **Devonian Regional Park** (*see page 77*) at low tide.

Suggested tour

Total distance: 260km.

Time: Allow a half-day to drive east from Victoria and a full day to drive west, or 2–4 days to explore.

elow
usk on Vancouver Island

Links: Combine the south end of Vancouver Island with a visit to Victoria or island routes north.

Route: The south island tour has two sections, east up the Saanitch
Peninsula (70km return) and west to Port Renfrew (190km return).
Drive each section as a day trip from Victoria, or allow at least one
overnight in Sooke or Port Renfrew.

From downtown Victoria, follow Hwy 17 north along the SAANITCH
PENINSULA towards the **Victoria Airport** and the BC Ferries landing
at **Swartz Bay**. The rolling countryside becomes increasingly
agricultural beyond Victoria. Follow exit signs to **SIDNEY ❶**, a lively
seaside town and terminus for Washington State Ferries from the US.
Return southbound on Hwy 17 to Keating Cross Road and turn right
(west) to **Butchart Gardens** (*see page 66*).

From Butchart Gardens, return southbound to W Saanich Road and
turn right (south). The country road winds through 6km of scenic
hills, farms and townships to **Observatory Hill** and the **DOMINION
ASTROPHYSICAL OBSERVATORY ❷**.Continue on W Saanich Road
and follow signs for Hwy 17. Take Hwy 17 into central Victoria or
follow Hwy 1A (Gorge Road) westbound (right) to avoid the central
city and continue the south island tour.

For the western tour, continue along Hwy 1A or the Victoria City Tour Detour to Fort Rodd Hill and Fisgard Lighthouse (*see page 69*) to **Craigflower Farmhouse** (*see page 68*) and **Fort Rodd Hill/Fisgard Lighthouse**. From the Ford Rodd Hill car park, continue straight for 2km to Esquimalt Lagoon. Just offshore is **Royal Roads**, a protected anchorage first charted by Spanish sailors in 1790. At the west end of the lagoon, turn right on to Lagoon Road. At the top of the hill, turn left on to Metchosin Road. Pass Albert Head Lagoon Park and **WITTY'S LAGOON REGIONAL PARK ❸**, 3km to My-Chosen Café and veer right on to William Head Road. Turn right up the narrow avenue of **Lombard Poplars** just past DEVONIAN REGIONAL PARK **❹**. Turn left on to Rocky Point Rd and right 3km later on to Matheson Lake Park Road. Pass East Sooke Regional Park to Gillespie Road. Turn right (north) on to Hwy 14 and turn west (left).

Pass Sooke River Road and the **SOOKE POTHOLES ❺**, the **Sooke River Hotel,** the Sooke Region Museum and continue into Sooke, a small fishing and resort town. Hwy 14 continues west into increasingly mountainous country past the **Shearingham Light** and **Shirley, POINT NO POINT ❻**, the lumber town of **Jordan**, and into **PORT RENFREW ❼**.

Take Hwy 14 back to **Victoria.**

Detour: In good weather, you can follow unpaved logging roads from Port Renfrew to **Lake Cowichan** and **Douglas**, then south along the Island Highway to **Victoria**. Allow half a day for the return trip. Ask about logging road closures and driving conditions in Port Renfrew before setting out.

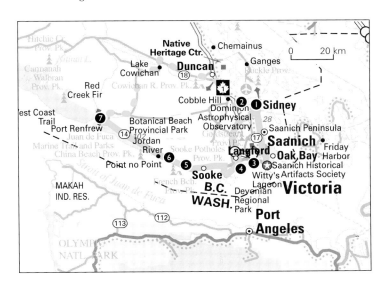

Central Vancouver Island

Ratings

First Nations art	●●●●●
Historical sights	●●●●●
History	●●●●●
National parks	●●●●●
Nature	●●●●●
Beaches	●●●●
Children	●●●●
Outdoor activities	●●●●

Rolling hills, lush valleys, mossy forests, protected harbours, tranquil lakes, art from several First Nations bands and trackless beaches define the central section of Vancouver Island. So do clearcuts, tree plantations, slag heaps and abandoned mining towns. The coal mines that once made Nanaimo one of the richest cities in Canada are long closed, the grimy, sooty waterfronts transformed into sparkling marinas and busy bayside walking paths. Chemainus, Duncan and similar towns once dependent on forest industries have been reborn as tourist centres with museums, murals, totem poles and other artistic productions. Across Vancouver Island, great swaths of beach, island and forest have been preserved within Pacific Rim National Park, much of it unreachable except by foot or by boat. In between lies an irregular chequerboard of natural forest, farmed forest, burgeoning dormitory communities and quiet villages. The area is also becoming BC's second wine region.

CHEMAINUS❖❖

ℹ️ **Chemainus and District Chamber of Commerce** *9796 Willow St (across from Waterwheel Park); tel: (250) 246-4701; web: www.tourism.chemainus. bc.ca Open Mon–Fri.*

Chemainus calls itself 'The Little Town that Did' in memory of its successful transition from timber to tourism. When its mainstay mill closed in the early 1980s, the city paid local artists to paint **murals**❖❖ on the buildings to lure coach tours. The ploy worked, sparking a business boom and three dozen murals.

Centre of the boom is **Waterwheel Park**❖ and the **Chemainus Valley Museum**❖, with local artefacts from the past century. Pick up a Mural Map at the museum or from most local businesses. The 30-plus paintings depict local history from the original First Nations inhabitants of the area to the arrival of Europeans and the development of local timber and agricultural industries. A new sawmill has reopened, but lumber plays second fiddle to a growing arts community.

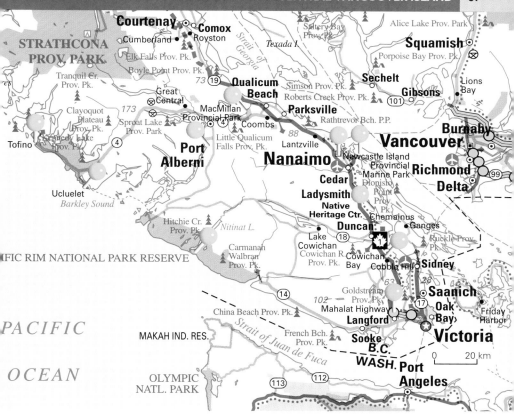

Chemainus Valley Museum $
Waterwheel Park; tel: (250) 246-2445. Open daily.

Waterwheel Park
Willow St. Open daily.

Accommodation and food in Chemainus

Fuller Lake Motel $$ *9033 Trans Canada Hwy; tel: (250) 246-3282*, is the largest motel in the area.

Pacific Shores Inn $$ *Tel: (250) 246-4987* is near ferries and the beach.

Hummingbird Tea House & Restaurant $$ *9893 Maple St; tel: (250) 246-2290*, is a convenient stop.

COWICHAN BAY❖

Cowichan Tourism Association *135 Third Street, Duncan; tel: (250) 715-0709; web: www.cowichan.bc.ca*

This tiny bayside town was once the heart of the entire Cowichan region, stretching from the Malahat Hills north nearly to Nanaimo and west to the Pacific Ocean. Meaning 'warm land' in the Cowichan First Nations language, Cowichan Bay was a major timber and farm port until railway builders opened a station in Duncan in the late 19th century. Most buildings in the one-road town have their front doors on

Bluenose Restaurant $$ *north end of the village; tel: (250) 748-2841*, is a popular local coffee shop and restaurant.

Cow Bay Café $$ *south end of the village; tel: (250) 746-7460*, lures more visitors to its location on Cowichan Bay.

Cowichan Bay Maritime Centre $ *Village centre; tel: (250) 746-4655. Open daily, Apr–Sep.*

Marine Ecology Station *$ Pier 66; tel: (250) 748-4522; web: www.mareco.org Open daily 1200–1700 in summer, weekends autumn–spring.*

Duncan Visitor InfoCentre *381A TransCanada Hwy; tel: (250) 746-4636. Open Apr–Oct, daily; Nov–Mar, Mon–Fri.*

Cowichan Bay Road and their back doors on Cowichan Bay. Th **Cowichan Bay Maritime Centre**✢✢✢ is a combination museum an wooden-boat-building centre. Best views of the town are from th Centre's 100m pier. Pavilions along the pier display histori photographs and boat-related memorabilia.

Marine Ecology Station✢✢ is a combination aquarium and marin research station dedicated to local marine life. Volunteers are usuall

Right
Logging boats

Cowichan Native Heritage Centre $$
200 Cowichan Way; tel: (250) 746-8119. Open daily.

British Columbia Forest Museum $ Hwy 1, just north of Duncan; tel: (250) 746-1251. Open Apr–Oct, daily.

Cowichan Valley Museum $ 120 Canada Ave; tel: (250) 746-6612. Open 1000–1600; Oct–May, 1100–1600 Wed–Fri, Sat 1200–1600.

Freshwater Ecocentre $ 1080 Wharncliffe Rd; tel: (250) 746-6722.

Somenos Marsh Wildlife Refuge $ East side of Hwy 1, north of Duncan; tel: (250) 746-9383.

Englishman River Falls Provincial Park $ Errington Rd; tel: (250) 954-4600.

on hand to explain exhibits in the touch tanks and aquaria, and under the microscopes.

Duncan✦✦✦ became the Cowichan's main town when the railway arrived in the 1880s. A busy commercial and agricultural centre, it is best known for the 40 or so totem poles scattered around town and the **Cowichan Native Heritage Centre**✦✦. Don't miss the multimedia programmes and exhibits on local First Nations history. In summer, a daily **Salmon BBQ**✦✦✦ includes dances and story-telling with an excellent meal.

British Columbia Forest Museum✦ is the forest industry's own vision of BC history. Exhibits include a working lumber mill and steam train, as well as forest machinery and easy-to-understand displays of how trees are cut, sorted and processed.

Cowichan Valley Museum✦✦ offers domestic and industrial artefacts in period settings in a 1912 railway station. The photographic collection is one of BC's best local archives. Park at the museum and follow the yellow footsteps around town to see the entire totem collection.

Freshwater Ecocentre✦ has interactive exhibits on local freshwater habitats and tours of the trout hatchery next door, while **Somenos Marsh Wildlife Refuge**✦✦✦ is good for summer and winter bird-watching.

Englishman River Falls Provincial Park✦✦✦ has a scenic waterfall as well as easy forest walks, picnicking and swimming.

Food in Duncan

Gossips $$ *161 Kenneth St; tel: (250) 746-6466,* uses local ingredients in outstanding Italian-inspired dishes.

Shukla's Curry House $$ *119 Kenneth Street; tel: (250) 746-6460,* is a local favourite for East Indian dishes.

MacMillan Provincial Park✦✦✦

MacMillan Provincial Park $
Cameron Lake. Open daily.

This roadside park includes **Cathedral Grove**✦✦✦, one of BC's only surviving stands of virgin forest accessible by highway. The park is named for Harvey MacMillan, BC's first Chief Forester and later head of what is now MacMillan Bloedel, one of BC's largest timber companies. The virgin grove stands in stark contrast to MacMillan Bloedel clearcuts and plantation projects near by.

Malahat Highway✦✦✦

Malahat Highway winds through the Malahat Hills separating the Saanitch Peninsula from the Cowichan region. Views eastward to the mainland are stunning in clear weather.

NANAIMO*

ℹ Nanaimo Tourist and Convention Bureau *2290 Bowen Rd; tel: (250) 756-0106. Open daily.*

🚢 Nanaimo has BC Ferries terminals, *tel: (888) 223-3779 or (604) 277-0277, at* **Departure Bay** *with a service to Horseshoe Bay and* **Duke Point** *with a service to Tsawwassen.*

🏛 The Bastion $ *Bastion and Front Sts. Open daily, Jul–Sep.*

Nanaimo District Museum $ *100 Cameron Rd; tel: (250) 753-1821. Open May–Sep, Mon–Sun 1000–1800.*

The town developed as a coal centre and remains Vancouver Island's major export centre. The coal docks, foundries and other industries that once lined the harbour have been replaced by marinas, parks and the 4-km **Harbourfront Walkway*****. The shopping malls lining the Island Highway could be anywhere in North America, but the town itself is well worth visiting. Ask for self-guiding walking maps of historic areas and buildings at the Tourist InfoCentre.

The **Bastion***** is the sole surviving Hudson's Bay Company bastion, or fortress, in BC. The white wooden redoubt houses a small museum. Guardsmen in 1850s naval uniforms parade and fire a cannon at noon each day in summer.

Nanaimo District Museum* uses local artefacts to reproduce a coal mine, pioneer town and Chinatown.

Food in Nanaimo

Blackbear Pub $ *6201 Dumont Rd; tel: (250) 390-4800*, is a comfortable local pub.

Scotch Bakery $ *87 Commercial St; tel: (250) 753-3521*, lures locals for breakfast and lunch.

NEWCASTLE ISLAND PROVINCIAL MARINE PARK***

🏛 Newcastle Island Provincial Marine Park $ *Just off Nanaimo; tel: (250) 387-4363.*

This 306-hectare island sheltering Nanaimo Harbour has been home to First Nations villages, coal mines, fish processing plants and resorts. Accessible by ferry from Nanaimo, it has become a favourite getaway for picnicking, walking, swimming and camping.

PACIFIC RIM NATIONAL PARK RESERVE***

ℹ Park Information Centre *Hwy 4, 3km north of Ucluelet–Tofino junction; tel: (250) 726-4212. Open mid-Mar–mid-Oct, daily.*

🏛 Pacific Rim National Park Reserve *west coast of Vancouver Island; tel: (250) 726-7721; web: www.harbour.com/parkscan/pacrim/*

This is three parks in one – the **West Coast Trail*****, stretching north from Port Renfrew, the **Broken Group Islands*****, more than 100 islands in Barkley Sound, and **Long Beach*****, between Ucluelet and Tofino – the only section accessible by road. The 30km of sandy beaches, rocky headlands, forests and bogs are busy in summer and deserted from November to April, except for sea gulls, sea lions and crabs hiding in the tangled driftwood.

Wickaninnish Centre*** *(Long Beach; tel: (250) 726-7333. Open mid-Mar–mid-Oct, daily)* is the main interpretative centre, with a museum, restaurant and elevated walkways with expansive views. The surf-swept sand of Long Beach stretches 10km north.

ght
:ific Rim National Park

ΦORT ALBERNI✧✧

▶ **Alberni Valley Chamber of ommerce** 2533 Redford tel: (250) 724-6535. ɔen daily late spring–early tumn, Mon–Fri in winter.

▶ **Alberni Pacific Railway $$** 4255 'allace St; tel: (250) 723-81. Operates hourly on ɪmmer weekends.

Ꮧberni Valley Museum 4255 Wallace St; tel: 50) 723-2181. Open ɒe–Sat.

Forty kilometres from the Pacific Ocean at the head of a fjord-like inlet, Port Alberni is shifting from mining and timber to tourism, although logging tours remain popular attractions.

Alberni Pacific Railway✧✧ provides a steam train service along the waterfront in summer. The restored 1929 2-8-2 Baldwin Locomotive No 7 spent its entire working life in island logging.

Alberni Valley Museum✧ has a major collection of local First Nations artefacts, as well as an operating steam engine, water wheel and similar practical items.

The ships ***Lady Rose***✧✧✧ and ***Frances Barkley***✧✧✧ provide freight, passenger and sightseeing services to Ucluelet via Bamfield and the Broken Group. Expect to see marine life all year and hikers, kayakers and boaters coming and going to one of BC's most popular marine parks in summer.

Woods Tours✧✧✧ from MacMillan Bloedel are an easy way to see how trees are turned into timber.

Lady Rose and *Frances Barkley* $$ *Harbour Quay; tel: (250) 723-8313.* Operated by the Alberni Transportation Company.

Woods Tours $ *Harbour Quay; tel: (250) 724-7888. Call for tour times.*

Accommodation and food in Port Alberni

The Barclay $$$ *4277 Stamp Ave; tel :(250) 724-7171*, is the large hotel in town.

Coast Hospitality Inn $$$ *3835 Redford St; tel: (250) 723-8111*, ha big-city facilities.

Paradise Café $$ *4505 Gertrude St; tel: (250) 724-5050*, specialises i seafood and steaks.

Steamers $ *Harbour Quay; tel: (250) 723-2211*, is a convenier breakfast or lunch stop on the quay.

Swale Rock Café $$ *5328 Argyle St; tel: (250) 723-0777*, serves seafoo to a largely local crowd.

TOFINO

❶ Tofino-Long Beach Chamber of Commerce *Campbell St; tel: (250) 725-3414. Open daily, Jul–Aug; May–Jun and Sep, weekends.*

⓰ Eagle Aerie Gallery $ *350 Campbell St; tel: (250) 725-3235.*

House of Himwitsa $ *300 Main St; tel: (250) 725-2017.*

West Coast Maritime Museum & Whale Centre $ *411 Campbell Street; tel: (250) 725-2132. Open daily, Mar–Oct.*

This one-time timber town has become a busy tourist centre for Pacifi Rim National Park and **Clayoquot Sound**✦✦✦. Tofino has also become centre for First Nations artists and galleries. **Eagle Aerie Gallery**✦✦ exhibits works by Roy Vickers, one Canada's most commerciall successful First Nations artists.

House of Himwitsa✦✦✦ is a combination First Nations galler restaurant and motel.

The **West Coast Maritime Museum & Whale Centre**✦✦✦ sponsor whale-watching excursions to supplement artefacts from loca shipwrecks and First Nations history.

Accommodation and food in Tofino

Weigh West $$$ *634 Campbell St; tel: (250) 725-3277*, is a water-fror hotel and restaurant popular with visiting fishermen.

Wickaninnish Inn $$$ *Chesterman Beach; tel: (250) 725-3100; wel www.wickinn.com*, gets international attention as one of BC's fines restaurants and most luxurious inns.

Common Loaf Bake Shop $ *180 First St; tel: (250) 725-3915*, is th town's best bakery and café.

UCLUELET✦✦

The logging and fishing village of Ucluelet is trying to switch t tourism, but Tofino gets most of the traffic. Ucluelet is smaller, quiete and more focused on outdoor activities such as kayaking, fishin whale-watching and boating. **Amphitrite Point Lighthouse**✦✦✦ ha

Ucluelet Chamber of Commerce
overnment Wharf (foot of ain St); tel: (250) 726-541. Open daily in summer; on–Fri autumn–spring.

Amphitrite Point Lighthouse $ south downtown. Open daily.

e-Tin-Kis Park $ 1km uth of downtown. Open aily.

overnment Wharf $ ot of Main St.

stunning views of Barkley Sound. Look for migrating grey whales between March and April, raging storms in winter and spectacular sunsets all year.

He-Tin-Kis Park✦✦✦ boardwalk trails wander through old-growth cedar and spruce forests to open shoreline vistas, while **Government Wharf**✦✦✦ is a convenient spot to watch bald eagles, seals and sea lions.

Accommodation and food in Ucluelet

Canadian Princess Resort $$$ *Harbourfront; tel: (250) 598-3366 (reservations from outside North America) and (250) 726-7771 (information and reservations)*, is a historic steamship turned resort, restaurant and mothership for fishing and nature trips into Barkley Sound.

Snug Harbour Inn $$$ *460 Marine Dr; tel: (250) 726-2686; web: www.virtualcities.com/ons/bc/v/bcv5603.htm*, offers plush cliffside suites overlooking a private beach.

Suggested tour

Total Distance: 320km.

Time: Allow a full day to drive from Victoria to Tofino; up to a week for sightseeing.

Links: Continue north to **Port Hardy** and **ferry routes** to the mainland (*see page 108*), take the ferry from **Nanaimo** back to Vancouver (*see page 42*), or return to Victoria.

elow
hemainus mural

Rain forest archipelago

Clayoquot Sound✦✦✦ is the largest surviving temperate rain forest in North America, thanks to Canada's largest-ever civil protest. A provincial decision to allow logging in 1993 sparked hundreds of arrests, road blockades and world-wide boycotts of BC products before most logging permits were rescinded. The 65km-long sound includes 3000sq km of islands, rivers and forests accessible only by air or boat. **Meares**, **Vargas** and **Flores** are the largest and most popular islands. **Hot Springs Cove**, the only natural hot springs on Vancouver Island, is another popular destination. Sea and air operators in Tofino and Ucluelet offer daily trips, weather permitting.

Route: Follow signs for Hwy 1 north from Victoria past **Portage Inl**
and **Thetis Lake Park**. The road swings north at **Goldstream**
Provincial Park to become the **MALAHAT HIGHWAY ❶**. Broa
vistas across the **Saanitch Peninsula** to the mainland and th
Cascade Range are stunning in clear weather, but lay-bys at the 352-r
summit are accessible only from the northbound lanes. The Malaha
Hwy becomes the Island Hwy as it runs north through the rollin
agricultural lands from Duncan to Nanaimo.

Detour: The scenic route follows the direct route 50km north t
Cowichan Bay Road and a rest area 18km north of the **Malaha**
Summit. Turn east (right) through 6km of rolling farmland an
forests dotted with tiny lakes to **COWICHAN BAY ❷** and continu
north. The road becomes Tzouhalem Road at a T-junction just nort
of the roadside historical marker lauding the landing of the fir:
shipload of English settlers in 1862. A second marker is dedicated t
poet Robert W Service, who worked and wrote locally in the earl
1900s.

Continue north, then west, to **Maple Bay**. Take Maple Bay Roa
northeast (right) through 6km of exclusive housing estates to Geno
Bay Road and turn right (east). The narrow road climbs through
range of granite hills to emerge at tiny **Genoa Bay**.

Return to Maple Bay, with **Salt Spring Island** (*see pages 58–9*) ju
offshore. Take Herd Road north and west to Osborne Bay Road an
turn north (right) to Champlain Street. Go east (right) into **Crofto**
Go back up Champlain Street to Crofton Road and turn north (righ
to Chemainus Road, 2km beyond the Fletcher Challenge pulp an
paper mill. Continue north to **CHEMAINUS ❸**.

Chemainus Road runs 10km to the Island Hwy. Turn right (north
towards Nanaimo. At Cedar Point Road, turn right (east) throug

pastoral farmland to Yellowpoint Road and go east (right). Continue past **Roberts Memorial Provincial Park**, a popular summer swimming spot, and back on to Cedar Point Road. At MacMillan Road, turn right to visit the **Harmac Pulp Mill** or continue on to the Island Hwy and **NANAIMO ④**.

Hwy 1 becomes Hwy 19 at Nanaimo, but keeps the Island Hwy name. Continue north along a narrowing strip of flat land along the coast. Just before **Parksville**, take Hwy 4 west towards Port Alberni. The settlement just south of the highway with goats grazing on the roof is **Coombs**, a convenient rest and ice cream stop. The highway climbs past **MACMILLAN PROVINCIAL PARK ⑤**, one of the rare bits of virgin forest left along any highway in BC, then drops down to **PORT ALBERNI ⑥**, the island's most interior Pacific port.

The road continues past **Sproat Lake**, home to the world's largest water bombers (used to fight forest fires), and twists through the increasingly rugged **MacKenzie Range** and **Hydro Hill**, an 18 per cent grade. At the T-junction, go left to **UCLUELET ⑦** or right to **PACIFIC RIM NATIONAL PARK** and the end of the road at **TOFINO ⑧**.

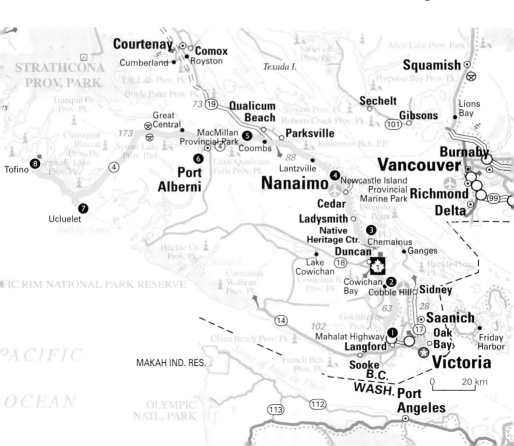

North Vancouver Island

Ratings

Beaches	●●●●●
Children	●●●●●
First Nations art	●●●●●
Mountains	●●●●●
Nature	●●●●●
Outdoor activities	●●●●●
Scenery	●●●●●
Wildlife	●●●●●

The northern portion of Vancouver stretches from warm gentle beaches hundreds of metres wide and kilometre long to treacherous cliffs rising sheer from the turbulen ocean. Logging trucks and heavy equipment share the few northern roads and infrequent hamlets with hunters, fisher RVs and long-distance cyclists, all of them outnumbered b bear, deer and bald eagles.

Just offshore, the Inside Passage between Vancouver Islan and the mainland narrows from a broad marine highway a Parksville to a narrow, twisting channel dotted with jagge rocks and turbulent eddies from Campbell River northward.

Pods of orcas patrol the cold, fish-rich waters, dodgin fleets of cruise ships, humpback whales and sea kayakers. O shore, look for the ornate, richly coloured totem pole created by the First Nations bands which have emerged fror generations of repression and cultural twilight to become major social and economic force once again.

ALERT BAY❖❖❖

ℹ️ **Alert Bay Tourist Information Centre** *118 Fir St; tel: (250) 974-5213. Open daily, Jun–Sep; Oct–May, Mon–Fri.*

⛴️ **BC Ferry**; *tel: (888) 223-3779, from Port McNeill.*

🅷 **'Namgis Burial Ground** $ *Fir St, south of the ferry landing.*

Alert Bay was a hotbed of First Nations resistance to discriminator laws in the 19th and early 20th centuries. The fishing and touri community is an ethnic mix today, but the look and feel are solid Kwakwaka'wakw, or Kwagiulth, as the band is sometimes spelle Don't miss the **Namgis Burial Ground❖❖❖** with its stunning tote poles (the cemetery is closed to the public, but clearly visible from th street), and the **U'mista Cultural Centre❖❖❖**, a longhouse built t display half of a potlatch (*see box, page 101*) collection that w confiscated by government agents in 1922 and returned in 1978 aft decades of wrangling. The rest of the collection is in the **Kwagiult Museum and Cultural Centre** on Quadra Island (*see page 102 U'mista also has an excellent selection of prints, lithographs, mas and other works by First Nations artists. Orcas often swim just off th seawall and bald eagles frequent trees all over the island.

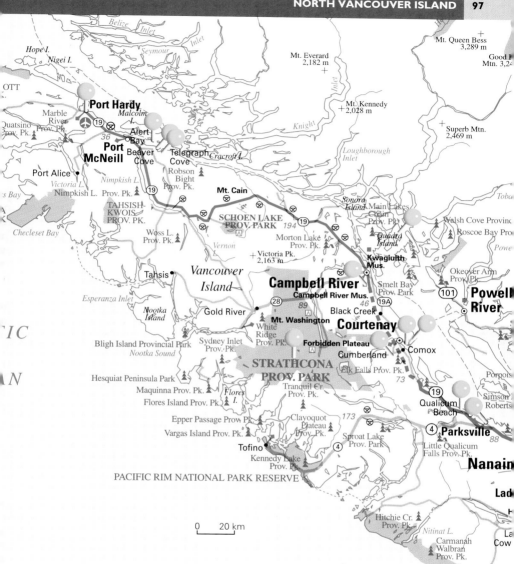

Accommodation and food in Alert Bay

Nimpkish Hotel $$ *Fir St; tel: (250) 974-5716,* is the largest hotel and restaurant on the island.

Orca Inn $$ *Fir St; tel: (250) 974-5322,* has Alert Bay's busiest pub and good water views from most rooms.

BEAVER COVE❖❖❖

ⓘ Beaver Cove $ *12km off Hwy 19 from the North Island Forestry Centre; tel: (250) 928-3023 for summer tours.*

Beaver Cove handles 1.4 million cubic metres of logs annuall Canada's largest dryland sort where logs are separated by specie grade and intended use. The sorted logs are dumped in huge ponds 'booming grounds' in the cove to be chained together, or 'stowed u into rafts 21m wide by 121m long. The rafts are then towed to pu and lumber mills for processing.

CAMPBELL RIVER❖

ⓘ Campbell River and District Chamber of Commerce *Centennial Museum Building, 1235 Shoppers Row, Tyee Plaza; tel: (250) 287-4636; web: www.vquest.com/ crtourism/ Open daily, Jun–Sep; Oct–May, Mon–Sat.*

ⓘ Campbell River & District Public Art Gallery $ *1235 Shoppers Row; tel: (250) 287-2261. Open Jun–Sep, Tue–Sat; Oct–May, Wed–Fri.*

The Museum at Campbell River $ *470 Island Hwy; tel: (250) 287-3103; web: www.island.net/~crm_chin/. Open daily, May–Sep; Oct–Apr, Tue–Sat.*

Island Dive Connection $$ *1621 N Island Hwy; tel: (250) 830-0818.*

Timber is the main industry, but Campbell River is better known fc fishing and scuba diving. The town has become the gateway for Nort Island hiking and trekking, fishing charters, sea kayaking, dive trij and other outdoor activities.

Campbell River & District Public Art Gallery❖ features local artis and representations of the local area by outside artists. **The Museu** **at Campbell River**❖❖❖ looks across Discovery Passage to Cape Mud; on Quadra Island (*see page 98*). Exhibits cover local First Natio history, European exploration and exploitation, and local natur history. Museum field trips to nearby historic sites are particular interesting but must be booked in advance.

Scuba diving❖❖❖ is stunning all year, with protected waters fc beginners, racing tidal currents for thrill seekers and some of Nort America's richest marine environments. Several ships have bee scuttled near by to serve as artificial reefs and scuba dive destination During the spring–autumn salmon runs, look for snorkelling trips th put even non-divers face-to-face with salmon migrating upstream t spawn. Don't even dream about diving the tricky tidal waters withou a local guide; **Island Dive Connection**❖❖❖ is one of the best operators

Accommodation and food in Campbell River

Seafood is always a good choice in a town that has fancied itself th Salmon Capital of BC for most of the past century.

Anchor Inn $$$ *261 Island Hwy; tel: (250) 286-1131*, offers water views

Panache $$$ *1090 Shoppers Row; tel: (250) 830-0025*, is one of the be island restaurants north of Victoria with French-inspired preparatior of local seafood.

Pier Street Café $$ *207-871 Island Hwy; tel: (250) 287-2772*, serve more basic versions of the same fish.

Town Centre Inn $$ *1500 Elm St; tel: (250) 287-8866*, is a basic, goo value choice.

CAPE SCOTT PROVINCIAL PARK✦✦✦

Cape Scott, the northernmost tip of Vancouver Island, is a tough two-day return trek from the trailhead, but an easy 45-minute trail leads to the sandy shores of San Josef Bay. (**Cape Scott Provincial Park $** *63km from Port Hardy by logging road; tel: (250) 954-4600.*)

COURTENAY AND THE COMOX VALLEY✦✦✦

❶ Comox Valley Chamber of Commerce *2040 Cliffe ve; tel: (250) 334-3234. pen daily.*

❷ Courtenay and District Museum $ *60 Cliffe Ave; tel: (250) 34-3611. Open May–Sep, aily; Oct–Apr, Tue–Sat.*

orbidden Plateau Ski rea $$ *Strathcona rovincial Park; tel: (250) 34-4428. Open year-round.*

t Washington Ski rea $$ *Strathcona arkway; tel: (250) 338-386. Open year-round.*

Courtenay and the Comox Valley are amongst the sunniest parts of Vancouver Island, sheltered behind the highest peaks on the island. **Courtenay and District Museum**✦✦✦ occupies the Native Sons Hall, Canada's largest free-span log structure. Highlight is a 14m, 80-million-year-old elasmosaur fossil, the largest marine dinosaur ever found in Canada west of the Rockies.

Forbidden Plateau Ski Area✦✦✦ has some of the best skiing on Vancouver Island in winter and kilometres of hiking, cycling and picnicking in summer. The chairlift and restaurant are open in summer. **Mt Washington Ski Area**✦✦✦ has the highest vertical ski drop on the island. Views of the surrounding mountains are breathtaking in any season. Resort facilities and chairlift are open all summer.

CUMBERLAND✦✦✦

ⓘ Cumberland Chamber of Commerce 2755 Dunsmuir Ave; tel: (250) 336-8313. Open daily, Jul–Aug; Sep–Jun, Mon–Fri.

ⓝ Cumberland Museum and Archives $ 2680 Dunsmuir Ave; tel: (250) 336-2445. Open daily.

Cumberland was the heart of a massive coal field opened by Nanaim coal baron Robert Dunsmuir, who built Craigdarroch Castle i Victoria (*see page 66*). Dunsmuir encouraged ethnic strife amongs British, Chinese, Italian, Japanese, Mexican and other workers t minimise union activities. The last mines closed in the 1960s, but sla heaps, derelict buildings, abandoned mine sites and a downtow: mural showing a once-active Chinese community remair **Cumberland Museum and Archives✦✦✦** explores the dramatic histor of the region, including fatal mine accidents, bitter strikes, martial la and an awe-inspiring collection of period photographs.

PARKSVILLE✦✦ AND QUALICUM BEACH✦✦

ⓘ Parksville and District Chamber of Commerce Hwy 19, south end of town; tel: (250) 248-3613; web: www.chamber.parksville.bc. ca. Open Jun–Sep, daily; Oct–May, Mon–Fri.

Qualicum Beach Chamber of Commerce 2711 Island Hwy (look for the totem pole); tel: (250) 752-9532; web: www.qualicum.bc.ca Open daily.

ⓝ Craig Heritage Park Museum $ 1245 E Island Hwy (at the InfoCentre); tel: (250) 248-6966. Open daily, mid-May–Labour Day.

Qualicum Beach Historical Museum & Power House Museum $ 587 Beach Rd; tel: (250) 752-5533. Open daily in summer.

Parksville and Qualicum Beach are a burgeoning holiday destinatio: backed by kilometres of broad, sandy beach. Each receding tide leave hundreds of shallow pools that warm to tropical temperatures in th summer sun. Anonymous strip malls line much of Hwy 19A, but th twinned towns are worth a visit.

Craig Heritage Park Museum✦✦✦ offers local history and artefacts i heritage buildings moved to the site.

Qualicum Beach adjoins Parksville but has more open beachfron **Qualicum Beach Historical Museum & Power House Museum✦✦** explores local history and the history of electrical power in BC in th town's original brick powerhouse.

Right
Port Hardy thunderbird

Potlatch

The potlatch ceremony was a central feature of First Nations life among coastal bands. Usually held in the quiet winter months, potlatch reinforced traditional authority through performances of sacred rituals and cemented political power by redistributing prodigious quantities of food, trade goods, clothing and household items. The more wealth a leader could give away, the greater his power and influence.

The practice was banned in 1884 as sinful, wasteful and supportive of what Christian missionaries termed a 'decrepit' culture. A few First Nations communities complied, others continued to hold potlatches in secret. In more remote areas, the ban was simply ignored. In 1918, a government agent complained that 'During these gatherings, they lose months of time, waste their substance, contract all kinds of diseases and generally unfit themselves for being British subjects in the proper sense of the word'.

In 1922, federal officials raided potlatch ceremonies and confiscated an enormous collection of ceremonial and sacred objects. The potlatch ban was quietly dropped in the 1950s, along with prohibitions against other traditional First Nations practices, but the 1922 hoard of masks, head-dresses, blankets, baskets, boxes and other regalia wasn't returned until the 1970s. The collection was divided between museums at Alert Bay and Quadra Island. Potlatch ceremonies are again being held publicly, especially in the Queen Charlotte Islands (see page 116).

PORT HARDY✦

❶ Port Hardy and District Chamber of Commerce 7250 Market St; tel: (250) 949-7622. Open daily, Jun–Sep; Oct–May, Mon–Fri.

❷ Port Hardy Museum and Archives $ 7110 Market St; tel: (250) 949-8143. Open daily in summer.

Port Hardy is the end of the road on North Vancouver Island and a centre for North Island outdoor adventures. The walkway along **Hardy Bay**✦✦✦ is a favourite gathering spot for bald eagles and other birds. BC Ferries' terminal is just south at **Bear Cove.**

Port Hardy Museum and Archives✦✦ concentrates on local Kwakwaka'wakw First Nations history and later White arrivals.

Accommodation and food in Port Hardy

Ferry traffic is extremely heavy in summer. Book accommodation well in advance or expect to sleep in the back seat.

Pioneer Inn $$ *Quatse River; tel: (250) 949-7271,* is a quiet choice outside of town.

Port Hardy Inn $$ *Granville St; tel: (250) 949-8525,* is a central, if busy, hotel and restaurant.

Sportman's Steak & Seafood House $$ *Market Street; tel: (250) 949-7811,* offers Greek dishes plus steaks and seafood.

QUADRA ISLAND✦✦✦

ⓘ **Quadra Island Campbell River and District Chamber of Commerce** *Centennial Museum, 1235 Shoppers Row, Tyee Plaza; tel: (250) 287-4636; web: www.vquest.com/crtourism/ Open daily, Jun–Sep; Oct–May, Mon–Sat.*

Quadra Island forms one side of Discovery Passage, off Campbel River. It has numerous sheltered harbours, islets, forests, beaches an streams, but is known mostly for the **Kwagiulth Museum an Cultural Centre**✦✦✦ (**$** *Cape Mudge Village; tel: (250) 285-3733. Ope Jun–Sep, daily; Oct–May, Mon–Sat*), built in the shape of a sea snail. Th museum houses part of the 1922 potlatch collection confiscated b government authorities. The rest of the collection is in the **U'mist Cultural Centre** in Alert Bay (*see pages 96–7*). An active carving an arts centre supplies the museum shop.

STRATHCONA PROVINCIAL PARK✦✦✦

Strathcona Park Lodge $ *Strathcona Provincial Park; tel: (250) 286-3122.*

Strathcona Provincial Park stretches nearly across Vancouver Island to include the tallest mountain on the island (Mt Golden Hinde, 2200m) and the tallest waterfall in Canada (Della Falls, 440m). The **Strathcona Park Lodge✦✦✦** is the best-developed accommodation and activity centre in the largely wilderness park.

TELEGRAPH COVE✦✦✦

Telegraph Cove Resort $$$ *Telegraph Cove; tel: (250) 928-3131; web: www. telegraphcoveresort.com/*

Telegraph Cove was named for a telegraph line at the turn of the 20th century. Surviving buildings, most on stilts above the water, are either museum pieces or part of a busy resort and eco-travel centre with whale-watching trips by boat or kayak.

Suggested tour

Total distance: 360km.

Time: Allow 6 hours to drive from Parksville to Port Hardy; 2–3 days to enjoy the sights.

Links: From Port Hardy, ferry routes lead north to Bella Coola and Prince Rupert (*see page 206*) or retrace Vancouver Island routes south.

Route: Follow Hwy 19 to the adjoining beach towns of **PARKSVILLE** ❶ and **QUALICUM BEACH** ❷. Hwy 19 continues inland, bypassing the beach and cutting at least an hour off the drive to Campbell River, but Hwy 19A along the **Strait of Georgia** is far more interesting.

Detour: From Hwy 19 in **COURTENAY** ❸, go east (right) on to 17th Ave towards **COMOX** ❹, and right again on Comox Road, passing a wildlife viewing area on the Comox River. To visit **Comox Spit** and expansive good-weather views back along the coast, turn right into Balmoral Avenue and right again on to Croteau Road.

Return to Comox Road and turn right on to Lazo Road to **Lazo**, following the blue and white 'scenic drive' signs – watch out for deer grazing along the verges. The road curves around the Canadian Forces Base Comox, with a golf course (open to the public) and the Comox Valley Regional Air Terminal. Ryan Road leads directly back to Hwy 19, or follow back roads to **Little River** and BC Ferries routes to the mainland at **Powell River**, then back to Hwy 19 by way of the **Seal Bay Nature Park**.

Take Hwy 19 north from **CAMPBELL RIVER** ❺ past the turn for **STRATHCONA PROVINCIAL PARK** ❻ to the **Fletcher Challenge Elk Falls Pulp and Paper Mill**, *tel: (250) 287-5594*, with free tours in summer. Signs in the large lay-by overlooking a mill, barge terminal

Left Telegraph Cove

Above
Port Hardy totem pole

and **QUADRA ISLAND**, explain plant operation. Continue north 7km to **Seymour Narrows,** one of the most perilous passages between Vancouver and Prince Rupert. Swift currents churn the Narrows into a boiling mass of white water at flood tide. There's a convenient overlook on the north side of Hwy 19.

Detour: Turn north (right) 29km north of **McNair Lake,** following signs for **Sayward,** one of the few remaining company-owned towns in BC. The road passes clearcuts, tree farms and isolated towns on the way to Sayward, then continues to **Kelsey Bay.** The bay, protected by the rusting hulks of sunken barges, was once the terminus for the BC Ferries route to Prince Rupert that now departs from Port Hardy. Return to Hwy 19 and turn north (right).

Hwy 19 continues north past **Schoen Lake Provincial Park,** a wilderness park best visited by high-clearance vehicles. **Hooma Lake,** 4km north, is a more convenient rest break. A few hectares of old growth forest have been left around the lake shore as habitat for elk and other animals that don't take well to tree farms. One of the few gas stations and restaurants between Campbell River and Port McNeill is in the town of **Woss,** 7km north of the lake and 2km west. The highway skirts **Nimpkish Lake** for 20-plus km beyond the Woss turn-off.

Detour: Turn south (right) off Hwy 19 at the **North Island Forestry Centre;** *tel: (250) 956-3844.* Book summer forest and mill tours by phone in advance. Continue past the centre to a T-junction at the end of the paved road. Turn left, following signs for the Telegraph Cove Resort. Just beyond is **BEAVER COVE** ❽ and a massive dryland sort. Watch the action from a lay-by near the top of the hill just beyond the dryland sort entrance.

Continue another kilometre to a second T-junction. Turn left for **TELEGRAPH COVE** ❾. Return to Hwy 19 and turn north (right).

The highway passes the **Nimpkish Fish Hatchery**, *tel: (250) 974-9556*, with excellent explanations of how poor logging practices and overfishing have blighted salmon runs in recent decades.

An imposing totem pole just across the Nimpkish River was carved in 1966 to commemorate the 1866 political union of Vancouver Island and mainland BC. Six kilometres north is the turn for **Port McNeill** and the ferry to **ALERT BAY** ⑩. Continue north past the turn-off for **Bear Cove** and the BC Ferries terminal, and into **PORT HARDY** ⑪.

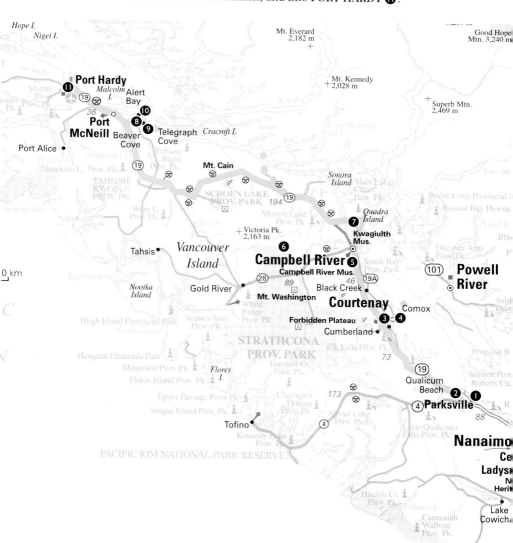

Ferry voyages

Ratings

Children	●●●●●
History	●●●●●
Mountains	●●●●●
Nature	●●●●●
Scenery	●●●●●
Villages	●●●●●
Wildlife	●●●●●
Food and drink	●●●

BC Ferries are the most popular cruise company i Canada. Strictly speaking, the provincially owned ferrie are simply transportation for vehicles and foot passenger but even the most prosaic ferry run from Vancouver t Vancouver Island can take on the air of a cruise when th summer sun shines bright and temperatures climb.

On the north coast, a ferry trip is more adventure tha transportation. Plying the waters of the Inside Passag between Port Hardy and Bella Coola or Port Hardy an Prince Rupert, a ferry voyage is the best way, and most ofte the only way, to enjoy some of North America's mos dramatic coastal vistas in a region where roads are all bu unknown. Expect to see snow-capped peaks dropping steepl into icy blue fjords lined with dark green forests – and don be surprised to see nothing at all if a storm blows through.

DISCOVERY COAST: PORT HARDY TO BELLA COOLA❖❖❖

Below
Bella Coola harbour

Unlike most BC Ferries runs that cater to commuters, commerci traffic and local residents, the Discovery Coast route was created fc tourists. This summer-only service aboard the *Queen of Chilliwack* wa named 'Discovery' for Alexander Mackenzie, who, in 1793, wa the first European to cross North America north of Mexicc Mackenzie emerged from the mountains at Bella Coola t discover that he had finally found the Pacific Ocean.

There are more ghost towns – reminders of the days whe timber and fishing ruled the BC Coast – than moder settlements along the route, but the often-narrow, always-scen channels are seldom empty. Cruise ships and fishing boats mak regular runs between Alaska, to the north, and Canadian por to the south. Pleasure craft throng the protected inlets an passages of the **Hakai Recreation Area❖❖❖**, one of the mo popular areas in BC for sea kayaking.

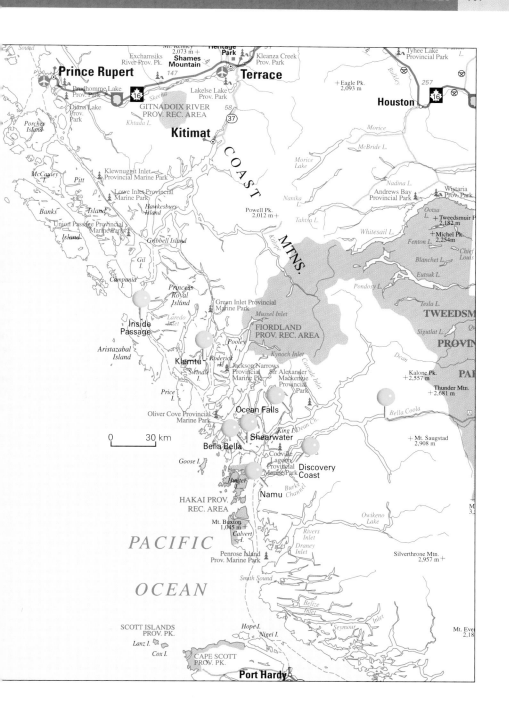

Mt. Remey 2,073 m +

Heritage Park

Exchamsiks River Prov. Pk.

Shames Mountain

Kleanza Creek Prov. Park

Tyhee Lake Provincial Park

Prince Rupert 147

Terrace

Eagle Pk. 2,093 m

257

Houston

Prudhomme Lake Prov. Park 16 Skeena

Lakelse Lake Prov. Park

Diana Lake Prov. Park

GITNADOIX RIVER PROV. REC. AREA 58 37

Khtada L.

Kitimat

Morice

Porcher Island

Sound

Morice Lake

McBride L.

COAST

Nadina L.

Andrews Bay Provincial Park

Wistaria Prov. Park

McCauley I.

Pitt

Klewnuggit Inlet Provincial Marine Park

Lowe Inlet Provincial Marine Park

Nanika L.

Powell Pk. 2,012 m +

Tahtsa L.

Ootsa L.

Tweedsmuir P 2,182 m

Banks Island

Hawkesbury Island

Union Passage Provincial Marine Park

Island

Gribbell Island

MTNS.

Whitesail L.

Michel Pk. 2,254m

Fenton L.

Chief Loui

Gil I.

Kitimat

Blanchet L.

Campania I.

Princess Royal Island

Pondosy L.

Eutsuk L.

TWEEDSM

Inside Passage

Laredo Inlet

Green Inlet Provincial Marine Park

Mussel Inlet

Tesla L.

Sigutlat L.

PROVIN

Aristazabal Island

Pooley I.

FIORDLAND PROV. REC. AREA

Kynoch Inlet

Dean

Kalone Pk. +2,557 m

PAR

Klemtu

Roderick I.

Swindle I.

Price I.

Jackson Narrows Provincial Marine Pk.

Sir Alexander Mackenzie Provincial Park

Thunder Mtn. +2,681 m

Oliver Cove Provincial Marine Park

Ocean Falls

Bella Coola

A

Mt. Saugstad 2,908 m

0   30 km

Shearwater

King I. Dean Ch.

Bella Bella

Goose I.

Codville Lagoon Provincial Marine Park

Discovery Coast

Hunter I.

Namu

Burke Channel

Owikeno Lake

M 3,

HAKAI PROV. REC. AREA

Mt. Buxton 1,045 m +

Calvert I.

Rivers Inlet

Draney Inlet

Silverthrone Mtn. 2,957 m +

PACIFIC

Penrose Island Prov. Marine Park

Smith Sound

Belize Inlet

OCEAN

Seymour Inlet

Mt. Eve 2,18

SCOTT ISLANDS PROV. PK.

Hope I.

Nigei I.

Lanz I.

Cox I.

CAPE SCOTT PROV. PK.

Port Hardy

**Discovery Coast,
Port Hardy–Bella
Coola $$$** *web:
www.discoverycoast.bcferries.
bc.ca. The summer-only route
operates late May–early Jun
and late Sep.*

BC Ferries *1112 Fort
Street, Victoria BC V8V
4V2; tel: (250) 386-3431 or
(888) 223-3779; web:
www.bcferries.bc.ca*

**Hakai Recreation
Area** *tel: (250) 398-
4414.*

The entire voyage takes between 15 and 33 hours, depending on how many of five potential port calls the *Queen* makes. Allow about 5 hours for a return voyage from either Port Hardy or Bella Coola. The ship stays reasonably close to schedule, but don't expect slavish devotion to the timetable. The 100m car ferry also carries kayaks and other small craft that can be dropped off and picked up at irregular stops along the trip. There may be detours when the captain spots a pod of orcas or a humpback whale nearby.

For the best sightseeing, sail the Discovery Coast southbound, Bella Coola–Port Hardy, to enjoy the panorama of mountains surrounding North Bentinck Arm (near Bella Coola) in daylight. For easier driving take a northbound sailing, Port Hardy–Bella Coola. The trip *up* The Hill, a steep gravel section of Hwy 20 just east of Bella Coola, is considerably less thrilling than twisting down the unpaved hairpin curves.

In Port Hardy (*see page 101*), passengers and vehicles board at the Bear Cove ferry dock. In Bella Coola, foot passengers board at the ferry dock, but vehicles must check in at a staging area near the Cedar Inn about 2km from the dock, to pick up a boarding pass before driving to the dock. Check current procedures with BC Ferries when making your booking.

Boarding starts 60 minutes before sailing at both ports, but it's better to board early than late – early arrivals get the coveted seats next to the *Queen's* oversized view windows. Seating is first-come, first-served, so passengers in the know race aboard to drop a jacket or backpack on their preferred window seat, usually in the forward lounge. Hotels, motels and bed and breakfasts at either end of the route can arrange transport to and from the dock for foot passengers.

Reservations are required for vehicles and are *highly* recommended for foot passengers – space is limited and the season short. There may be space on the first few and last few sailings at the last moment, but book four to six months in advance for June to August trips. Reservations can be changed (if space is available on the new date), but each change costs $50 per segment. You can check availability, make reservations and buy tickets by credit card on-line or by telephone.

Summer weather is usually good, but the coastal climate is fickle. Rain, fog and wind are at least as common as sunshine, which comes and goes almost without warning. Stick to comfortable, layered clothing and flat shoes for walking about on deck, up and down outside stairways and on shore. Long trousers, long sleeves, closed shoes and a warm jacket with a hood are likely to be as useful as sunglasses and sun block, even if the weather forecast predicts nothing but sunshine.

Seas will likely be calm no matter what the weather. Except for a short stretch of open water in the Queen Charlotte Sound just north of Port Hardy, a maze of islands protects the entire route from ocean swells and large wind waves.

The Discovery Coast is a tourist cruise, but the *Queen* is no cruise ship: no disco, no casino, no swimming-pool, no sauna, no beauty parlour, no dressy dinners. There is a gym, a couple of stationary bicycles on the solarium deck, as well as a full-service cafeteria, bar, lounge, laundry, showers, video arcade and gift shop. There is also plenty of outside deck space to enjoy the passing scenery while looking for orcas, humpback whales, eagles, seals, dolphins and passing vessels of all sizes. Binoculars and telephoto camera lenses are a must.

The *Queen* has no passenger cabins, but the reclining seats are extremely comfortable for night-long napping. Blankets, sheets and pillows can be hired on board, or bring your own. You can also hire tents on board, or pitch your own on the outer decks (or perhaps indoors, depending on the weather). A popular option is to overnight in Klemtu, Ocean Falls or Shearwater and pick up the ship on a later sailing, but rooms on shore are extremely limited. Book shoreside accommodation first (and explain that you're arriving aboard the *Queen*), then book passage to match your dates ashore.

Port calls stretch from 30 minutes to half a day, depending on the port and day of the week. Arrival and departure times are posted near the Purser's Office, forward of the cafeteria. There are shore excursions in most ports, usually walking tours, traditional dancing, salmon feasts or paddle trips. Buy shore tours as soon as possible after boarding. The better the weather, the earlier excursions sell out.

You can also explore ashore on your own, but watch the time. The *Queen* doesn't wait for late returners. The only departure warning is a long whistle blast 15 minutes before pulling away from the dock.

Below
Bella Coola sunset

BELLA BELLA/MCLOUGHLIN BAY❖

**Bella
Bella/McLoughlin
Bay** *Heiltsuk Band
Administration; tel: (250)
957-2381 and See Quest
Adventures, tel: (250) 957-
2774; web:
www.seequest.com*

The Heiltsuk Band, based at Bella Bella, is opening the door to tourism slowly and cautiously. For now, tourists are generally restricted to McLoughlin Bay, 3km south of the village. The Purser may say that Bella Bella is too far to walk during the short port call, but it's not too far for several local artists to set up shop at the dock when the *Queen* calls, including famed silversmith Peter Gladstone. McLoughlin Bay is also a popular stop for kayakers setting off for or returning from camping trips through the Hakai Recreation Area (*see page 106*).

If the weather is reasonable, that is, blowing anything less than a full gale, walk a few hundred metres down the crushed shell beach to the traditional-style longhouse. Built by Heiltsuk carvers Frank and Kathy Brown, the longhouse is a combination local history museum, First Nations art gallery and simple restaurant specialising in salmon roasted on cedar planks over an open fire.

Brown also takes passengers on a one-hour paddle in the *Glwa*, a traditional Heiltsuk canoe carved from a single cedar log. The trip passes old totem poles, deserted fish canneries, ravens, eagles, orcas, herons, dolphins and often bear and deer before rejoining the *Queen* in the next port, Shearwater.

On ferry trips that stop at Shearwater but not McLoughlin Bay, Brown brings his authentically carved canoe out to meet the ship and take on paddlers. Seats on the canoe are limited and extremely popular with repeat passengers, so sign up immediately after boarding the *Queen*.

KLEMTU✧✧✧

Klemtu *Kitasoo Band Council; tel: (250) 839-1255.*

This is one of the most popular overnight stops on the Discovery Coast, thanks to a bed and breakfast operated by the Kitasoo Band – book accommodation first, then the Discovery Coast sailing that matches your stay.

Most of Klemtu's 300 or so residents turn out to welcome the *Queen*. Main Street is among the longest boardwalks in Canada, skirting two sides of a bay that is alive with bald eagles, dolphins and orcas on the hunt for salmon and other fish. The most popular activity is a three-hour walking tour of town with stops at a busy carving shed and a traditional First Nations feast guaranteed to finish before the ship sails. BYOK – bring your own kayak – or charter boats from band operators for fishing, sightseeing, hiking and camping on nearby islands.

NAMU✧✧✧

BC Ferries *tel: (250) 386-3431 or (888) 223-3779; web: www.bcferries.bc.ca*

Namu is a rarity along the BC coast, a former fish cannery that still has a permanent population. The faded white cannery buildings look like a cinema set against the dense green shoreline forest after the plant closed down in 1970, but a handful of hardy residents find Namu an inviting spot none the less. They aren't alone. Archaeological digs have found 10,000 years' worth of human habitation around the tranquil cove, making Namu the oldest continuously occupied site along the western coast of North America.

OCEAN FALLS✧✧✧

Named for Link Falls, a waterfall that thunders directly into the sea, Ocean Falls was once a thriving pulp mill town at the head of Cousins Inlet. Three thousand people lived here in the mid-20th century, enough to fill a hospital, high school, hotel and Olympic-sized swimming-pool. When the mill closed in 1980 and jobs evaporated, so did most of the people. A few families remain at the original town site, which spreads uphill from the ferry dock, a few more in nearby Martin Valley, but the population more than doubles when *Queen* passengers hit the streets on walking tours. Fishing and sightseeing boat charters are also available, as are a few bed-and-breakfast rooms – book onshore accommodation first, then matching sailing dates.

There's home-made soup, ice-cream and espresso at the one café in town, a fire hall, a modern school and the mouldering remains of a long-closed hotel, but most of Ocean Falls is vanishing beneath a creeping carpet of blackberry bushes, alders and seedling pines. It's hard to miss the occasional splash of colour, usually a bright blue hydrangea in what was once a carefully tended front garden.

Ocean Falls BC
Ferries; tel: (250) 386-3431 or (888) 223-3779; web: www.bcferries.bc.ca

Today's residents wouldn't change much about their town. A hydroelectric dam built for the mill still churns out power, but with no logging and no toxic pulp waste pouring into the ocean, salmon, halibut, eagles, dolphins and other wildlife have returned.

SHEARWATER/DENNY ISLAND❖❖

Shearwater/Denny Island Shearwater Marine Resort, tel: (604) 270-6204 or (800) 663-2370; web: www.shearwater.ca

Flying boats based at Denny Island, opposite Bella Bella, once patrolled the Queen Charlotte Channel for World War II submarine invaders. The base is long gone (so is an early 20th-century fish packing plant), but with the newer name of Shearwater, the sheltered bay has become a base for tourism, sport fishing and maritime traffic. The Shearwater Resort includes a small hotel, fishing charters, restaurant, pub, marina and bed-and-breakfast accommodation.

Look for commercial fishing boats, sailboats and luxury motor yachts tied up to the dock. Crew and passengers are most likely tied up to the bar inside, the only full-service stop between Port Hardy and Bella Coola. The *Queen* ties up long enough for a meal or a drink at the resort. The alternative is to spend several days cycling and hiking the island or boating nearby waters.

INSIDE PASSAGE: PORT HARDY TO PRINCE RUPERT❖❖❖

Inside Passage, Port Hardy–Prince Rupert $$$ 1112 Fort Street, Victoria BC V8V 4V2; tel: (250) 386-3431 or (888) 223-3779; web: www.bcferries.bc.ca

Eagles, whales and mouth-dropping scenery on all sides make this all year car-ferry route the most popular 15-hour cruise in Canada. Look for sheer mountains cloaked with red cedar and Sitka spruce rising from glacier-carved channels, low islands swept clean by winter storms and lighthouses marking channels less than 250m wide.

The entire trip takes place during daylight hours from mid-May to September, when most sailings leave at 0730 and arrive at 2230 the same day. There are twice-weekly departures in early May and one return trip weekly from October to April; check with BC Ferries for off season schedules.

Vehicle spaces *must* be reserved in advance. Foot passengers should also book space, especially June to August when tour groups flock to north-coast ferry trips. Last-minute vehicle space *may* be available mid-September to mid-May, but make reservations four to six months in advance for summer travel.

In Port Hardy, board at Bear Cove, just south of town. In Prince Rupert, follow Second Avenue (Hwy 16) to the ferry dock. Boarding starts one hour before sailing. There's no rush to be first on board in winter, when there are few passengers. In summer, be prepared to scramble for window seats in the forward cabins with the best views or opt for an outdoor seat.

Weather is usually warm and clear (but not always sunny) in summer, while storms are common in winter. The Inside Passage route

is calm and well protected by dozens of islands off the BC coast, but rain, wind, fog and snow blast down from the Arctic in winter.

In any season, most passengers opt to spend the trip in comfortable reclining chairs or in the many lounge areas set with tables and chairs. Private cabins are available at an additional charge. There's also a fine dining-room, complete with silver and white linen tablecloths. Most passengers go for the less expensive cafeteria that serves everything from snacks to full meals. Ferries also have a licensed lounge, video arcade, games, free videos in public rooms and a well-stocked gift shop.

The Inside Passage

Fewer than 5000 people live on BC's central and northern coast, half of them in Bella Coola (see page 200) and another quarter in Queen Charlotte City, in the Queen Charlotte Islands (see page 116). Two hundred years ago, the waters and islands between Port Hardy and Prince Rupert were the realm of First Nations bands who lived well from the bounty of temperate coastal forests and the rich sea. A century ago, the same waters teemed with floating logging camps, pulp mills and fish canneries. Changing economic conditions closed most of those outside industries, leaving the Inside Passage once again a largely First Nations area where humans are vastly outnumbered by the wildlife and the scenery draws visitors from around the globe.

Suggested tours

Time: Allow up to 33 hours to travel the **Discovery Coast** betwee: **Port Hardy ❶** and **Bella Coola ❷** or 15 hours along the **Insid Passage** between **Port Hardy** and **Prince Rupert ❸**.

Links: Both ferry routes meet at **Port Hardy** (*see page 101*), at th north end of Vancouver Island, for the drive south toward **Victori** (*see page 62*). From **Bella Coola** (*see page 200*), it's possible to drive th **Cariboo-Chilcotin** to **Williams Lake** (*see page 202*) and either nort to **Prince Rupert** (*see page 206*) or south towards **Vancouver** (*see pag 206*). **Prince Rupert** is the mainland terminus of the **Yellowhea Highway** (*see page 214*), which continues westwards in the **Quee: Charlotte Islands** (*see page 116*) or eastwards to the **Rocky Mountain** and **Jasper National Park** (*see page 275*).

Route: Both ferry trips fit into a circular driving tour from **Vancouve** to **Victoria** by ferry, up **Vancouver Island** to **Port Hardy** by highway ferry to the mainland at **Bella Coola** or **Prince Rupert**, then south b road to **Vancouver**. Allow 7–10 days for the entire route. It's als possible to combine both ferry voyages by driving to either Port Hard or Bella Coola, taking one ferry route into **Port Hardy** and then takin the second route back to the mainland. Allow 10–14 days for the tw ferry trips, plus long-distance driving on the mainland and an excursions on Vancouver Island.

Both routes are served by car ferries, but don't take *car* too literally. it's street-legal in BC, BC Ferries will carry it: cars, vans, RVs, motc coaches, motorcycles, bicycles, trucks and foot passengers. Both tou can be taken in either direction and both can be made with combination of train, coach and air connections to avoid drivin altogether.

Below
McLoughlin Bay (Bella Bella)

Prince Rupert

Porcher
Island

McCauley
I.   Pitt

Banks   Island

Island

Mountain
147

Terrace

+ Eagle Pk.
2,093 m

Houston

257

Prudhomme Lake
Prov. Park

Diana Lake
Prov.
Park

Lakelse Lake
Prov. Park

GITNADOIX RIVER
PROV. REC. AREA

58

37

Kitimat

Klewnuggit Inlet
Provincial Marine Park

Lowe Inlet Provincial
Marine Park

Hawkesbury
Island

Powell Pk.
2,012 m +

Union Passage Provincial
Marine Park

Gribbell Island

+ Tweeds
2,182 r

+ Michel F
2,254m

Gil
I.

Campania
I.

Princess
Royal
Island

Green Inlet Provincial
Marine Park

TWEE

**Inside
Passage**

Aristazabal
Island

Pooley
I.

Klemtu • Roderick
I.

Swindle
I.

FIORDLAND
PROV. REC. AREA

Jackson Narrows
Provincial
Marine Pk.

Alexander
Mackenzie
Provincial
Park

Kalone Pk.
+ 2,557 m

Thunder
+ 2,681 m

0   30 km

Price
I.

Ocean Falls •

King I.
Shearwater

Bella Bella •

2

+ Mt. Saugstad
2,908 m

Oliver Cove Provincial
Marine Park

Goose I.

Hunter
I.

Cockville
Lagoon
Provincial
Marine Park

Discovery
Coast

•
Namu

HAKAI PROV.
REC. AREA

Mt. Buxton
1,045 m +

Calvert
I.

PACIFIC

Penrose Island
Prov. Marine Park

Silverthrone Mtn.
2,957 m +

OCEAN

SCOTT ISLANDS
PROV. PK.

Lanz I.

Cox I.

Hope I.
Nigei I.

CAPE SCOTT
PROV. PK.

Raft Cove
Prov. Pk.

Quatsino
Prov. Pk.

Port Hardy **1**

19

Queen Charlotte Islands

Ratings

First Nations	●●●●●
History	●●●●●
Nature	●●●●●
Outdoor activities	●●●●●
Parks	●●●●●
Beaches	●●●●
Children	●●●●
Walking	●●●●

Also known as *Haida Gwaii*, Home of the People, the Queen Charlottes are BC's most remote islands. By any name, this isolated, storm-swept, rain-forested archipelago 100km west of Prince Rupert is the best-known corner of Canada that almost nobody has ever seen. There are fewer than 150km of paved roads, more black bears and eagle than humans and barely enough vehicles to fill a small car park in downtown Vancouver.

Home to the Haida, proud, artistic warriors who once ruled the Pacific Northwest coast from cedar canoes, the Charlottes are an ecological wonder snatched from the jaws of timber cutters. Nearly overwhelmed by epidemics, discrimination and logging, the Haida rebounded as a vibrant traditional culture and artistic tradition. Gwaii Haanas National Park preserves links to 10,000 years of Haida history in a wilderness of moss-covered forests and village sites dotted with totem poles slowly crumbling back to earth.

Getting there

Queen Charlotte City Visitor Information Centre
3220 Wharf St; tel: (250) 559-8316. Open daily mid-May–mid-Sep 1000–1900.

Sandspit Airport
open daily mid-May–mid-Sep 0900–1700.

Principal access is by air from Vancouver to Sandspit or **BC Ferries**, *tel: 888-223-3779; web: www.bcferries. bc.ca/* from Prince Rupert to Skidegate Landing.

Getting around

There is no public transport. Hire a car from the Sandspit Airport or Queen Charlotte City, or bring your own vehicle by ferry. Weather is highly variable – rain, fog and sun alternating with blustery winds and dead calm, even in summer.

GWAII HAANAS NATIONAL PARK RESERVE/HAIDA HERITAGE SITE***

One of North America's most spectacular natural areas became a park in 1987 following a stand-off between the Haida and logging companies on Lyell Island. The 1500-sq km park protects rich marine environments, as well as trackless areas of old growth cedar and spruce forest carpeted with moss and orchids, deep fjords, sandy scimitars of beach, enormous colonies of puffins and sea lions, some of the world's largest nesting populations of falcons and bald eagles, and over 500 Haida sites.

Credit isolation for the park's splendour. The only access is by water or air, and only when weather, currents and 7m tides allow. Parks Canada approves operators for day-trips as well as multi-day boat trips and guided or self-guided kayak trips.

On the water, expect to see orcas, humpbacks and other whales, dolphins, porpoises and clouds of seabirds. Black bears roam the intertidal areas, black-tailed deer the meadows and open forests. Bald eagles are common.

ⓘ Gwaii Haanas National Park Preserve/Haida Heritage Site $$ *Tel: (250) 559-8818; web: www.harbour.com/parkscan/ gwaii/ Open daily, entry by commercial tour or individual permit. For permit reservations tel: (250) 387-1642 or (800) 663-6000.*

ⓒ Rose Harbour Guest House $$ *Rose Harbour, Gwaii Haanas National Park; web: www.island.net/~rosehgh/, has bed-and-breakfast accommodation with hot water, but no electricity.*

Gwaii Haanas Guest House $$ *Rose Harbour, Gwaii Haanas National Park; tel: (250) 559-8638; web: www.gwaiihaanas.com/, has similar bed-and-breakfast accommodation.*

Most Haida village sites have been reclaimed by the forest, but a few remain visible. All were once marked by forests of totem poles, most removed to museums as smallpox and other epidemics swept Haida Gwaii in the 19th century and villages were abandoned. A few poles remain, decaying, weather-beaten and returning to the earth in keeping with Haida tradition. Haida Gwaii watchmen (guardians) live at major village sites to discourage vandals and over-eager collectors.

Burnaby Narrows✦✦✦ This twisting passage is navigable by small boats at high tide and dry at low tide. Walking is banned to protect the profusion of sea stars, urchins, mussels and other species.

Hotspring Island✦✦ The only natural hot spring in the Charlottes was a traditional Haida healing place. Several soaking pools overlook the waters of Ramsay Passage.

Rose Harbour✦✦✦ The tiny community of Rose Harbour is a convenient stop-over for quick trips: fly in from Queen Charlotte City, visit SGaang Gwaii by speedboat and fly out. Rose is also a convenient base for kayak trips.

SGaang Gwaii (Ninstints, Anthony Island)✦✦✦ This abandoned village at the south end of Haida Gwaii was named a Unesco World Heritage Site in 1981. The world's largest collection of totem poles in their original location still stands along the beach.

Skedans✦✦✦ Skedans is the most accessible village site for day-trips.

T'anuu✦✦✦ There are no standing totem poles, but many visible house sites draped with moss. The ashes of famed Haida artist Bill Reid are buried in his ancestral village.

Windy Bay✦✦✦ A modern longhouse here was the focus of Haida battles with logging companies in the 1980s.

Gwaii Haanas under sail

Expert kayakers rate Gwaii Haanas National Park amongst the best water on earth – as famous for swirling currents, racing tides and blasting storms as for protected shores, stunning scenery and rich wildlife. For the rest of us, there's the *Duen*.

Michael Hobbis has been sailing his 22-m, eight-passenger ketch around the Charlottes for more than a decade, exploring remote inlets that larger boats will never see. Inflatable zodiacs take passengers ashore for daily forest hikes with kayaks available for calm waters. The *Duen* visits several Haida sites during her week-long trips, but the route depends on wind, tides and passenger preferences. **Duen Sailing Adventures $$$**, *Box 398, Brentwood Bay, BC, Canada V8M 1R3; tel: (250) 652-8227; web: www.duenadventures.com*

MASSET✧✧✧

ℹ **Masset Travel InfoCentre** *400m ʳom the 'Welcome to Masset' sign, east side of Hwy 6; tel: (250) 626-3982. Open daily, Jun–late Aug.*

ℹ **Old Masset Council** *Eagle Rd; tel: (250) 626-337.*

ℹ **Naikoon Provincial Park $** *Tel: (250) 557-390; web: www.elp.gov.bc.ca/bcparks/explore/parkpgs/naikoon.htm*

🍴 **Haidabucks $** *Main St; tel: (250) 626-5548, is Masset's best café.*

🍴 **Sandpiper $$$** *Collison Ave; tel: (250) 626-3672, specialises in seafood.*

🍴 **Villager Cafe $$** *Orr St; tel: (250) 626-3694, has Chinese dishes.*

🏠 **Copper Beech House $$** *1590 Delkatla; tel: (250) 626-441, is Masset's most comfortable bed and breakfast.*

Masset is a fishing and tourist town at the north end of Graham Island. **Old Masset**✧✧✧, 2km west, is Canada's largest Haida community with modern totem poles, artist workshops and galleries. To the east is **Naikoon Provincial Park**✧✧✧, stretching to **Rose Spit**✧✧✧, where Haida legend says humans appeared, and south to Tlell. Don't miss **Tow Hill**✧✧✧, a 100-m outcrop of basalt columns with active tidal blowholes at the base. Sandy beaches backed by mossy forest and bog stretch nearly 100km from Tow Hill to Rose Spit and south.

*Right
Masset welcome sign*

PORT CLEMENTS✧

ℹ **Port Clements Museum $** *45 Bayview Dr; tel: (250) 557-576. Open Jun–Sep, Tue–Sun; irregular winter hours.*

Port Clements is a tiny logging supply centre. The top attraction is the **Port Clements Museum**✧, an eclectic collection of early logging paraphernalia and household items. The pleasant **Golden Spruce Trail**✧✧✧, 5km south on the gravel logging road, leads in 10 minutes to the site of a unique golden spruce tree destroyed by a vandal in 1997. Eight kilometres south is the **Haida Canoe**✧✧✧, a partially carved wooden canoe abandoned in the forest over a century ago.

QUEEN CHARLOTTE CITY❖❖

 Queen Charlotte City Visitor Information Centre
3220 Wharf St; tel: (250) 559-8316. Open daily, mid-May–mid-Sep 1000–1900.

The administrative centre for the Charlottes is also the archipelago' largest town. Serious people live here, trying to pursue the area' traditional fishing and lumbering, while Haida arts and crafts are fo sale in local galleries.

Accommodation and food in Queen Charlotte

Hecate Inn $$ *321 Third Ave; tel: (250) 559-4543* or *800-665-3350*, i the most modern motel in the islands.

Under the Covers $$ *tel: (250) 559-8384*, is a central bed and breakfast.

Howler's Pub & Bistro $$ *tel: (250) 559-8600*, has Charlotte's bes beer selection and restaurant views.

Hummingbird Café $$ *Sea Raven Motel; tel: (250) 559-8583*, has the town's best seafood selection.

SKIDEGATE❖❖

Haida Gwaii Museum $
Qay'llnagaay, east off Hwy 16, 1km north of Skidegate Landing; tel: (250) 559-4643. Open Jun–Sep, Mon–Fri 1000–1700, and weekend afternoons all year.

Pronounced 'skid-e-git', this one-time mission settlement is a Haid village. The **Band Longhouse❖❖** has a fine **totem pole❖❖❖** overlookin the water. Just south of town is the **Haida Gwaii Museum❖❖❖**, with collection of local totem poles and the world's largest collection o carvings in argillite, a type of slate. Just off Hwy 16 is the **Spirit Lak Trail❖❖❖**, a moderate 3km, 90-minute hike through second-growth and old-growth forest around two small lakes.

TLELL❖

Cacillia's Bed & Breakfast $$ *tel: (250) 557-4664*, is a rustic log home behind beach dunes.

Naikoon Provincial Park *tel: (250) 557-4390; web: www.elp.gov.bc.ca/ bcparks/explore/parkpgs/ naikoon.htm Open daily.*

Tlell River House $$ *tel: (250) 557-4211*, is Tlell's most dependable restaurant and only hotel.

This one-time ranching town has become an artistic centre, where roadside signs announce galleries. Tlell is also the southern entry fo **Naikoon Provincial Park❖❖❖** with camping, hiking, and the 192 wreck of the timber ship *Pesuta*.

Suggested tour

Total distance: 300km.

Time: 2–4 days by road; 7–10 days by water.

Links: BC Ferries to Prince Rupert (*see page 206*) or air to Vancouve (*see page 42*).

Sandspit*

This scattered village has the Charlottes' major airport.

Accommodation in Sandspit

Sandspit Inn $$$ *tel: (250) 637-5334 or 800-666-1107; web: www.sandspitinn.com,* is next to the airport.

Route: From the airport at **Sandspit ❶**, drive east along **Shingle Bay** to the ferry at **Alliford Bay**. If time allows, take an hour to walk the **Dover Trail**, just west of **Haans Creek**, through dense thickets of alders, red cedar and Sitka spruce. The Haida peeled strips of bark from cedars to make rope, baskets, clothing and other items, leaving long, triangular scars on the trees. The ferry to **Skidegate Landing** is free, the return ferry is $$.

From the landing, follow traffic uphill and around to Hwy 16, the Yellowhead Hwy. Queen Charlotte City is 4km to the right (west); Skidegate, Tlell, Port Clements and Masset to the left (east).

North of **SKIDEGATE ❷**, the highway passes **Balanced Rock**, beyond a small sign east of the highway. Continue north along **Jungle Beach**, a tangle of driftwood stretching nearly 10km. The road follows the shoreline to **TLELL ❸**, near **Naikoon Provincial Park**.

From Tlell, Hwy 16 turns inland to **PORT CLEMENTS ❹**, a tiny logging supply centre. The Golden Spruce Trail and the Haida Canoe are off the logging road just south of town. Return to Port Clements and continue 38km to **MASSET ❺**, at the north end of Graham Island.

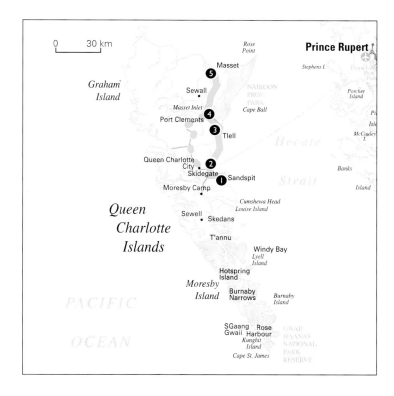

Lower Fraser Valley

Ratings

Children	●●●●●
Gardens	●●●●●
History	●●●●●
Scenery	●●●●●
Museums	●●●●
Outdoor activities	●●●●
Parks	●●●●
Beaches	●●●

The lower section of the Fraser River Valley is the heart o BC, and not just for the flat, rich farmlands that keep Vancouver well supplied with milk and vegetables. BC began along the Fraser with the creation of the Hudson's Bay Company post at Fort Langley in 1827. The Fraser River gold rush in the 1850s opened the interior to the outside world and transformed BC into a Crown Colony in 1858 to thwart American expansion from the south.

The Lower Fraser is a microcosm of BC. It was the first section of the mainland to be explored by Whites, the first to be settled and the first to feel the impact of over development. Half of BC's population lives, works and play in the Lower Fraser River Valley, yet despite population an pollution, the Fraser remains the most productive salmon stream in the world.

FORT LANGLEY✦✦✦

ℹ Fort Langley & District Chamber of Commerce *23245 Mavis St (in the heritage train depot); tel: (604) 513-8787/888-1477. Open daily May–Sep; Oct–Apr Mon–Fri.*

This small rural town began as a Hudson's Bay Company trading for in 1827. The original site was about 4km downstream, but the fort wa moved a decade later to be closer to HBC's rich grain fields an pastures. When word of gold deposits on the Fraser finally leaked o in the 1850s (HBC had tried to downplay earlier reports in order t retain control), Fort Langley was promptly overrun by 30,00 goldseekers, most of them Americans. With only a handful of HB men on the scene, the company worried that their mainland holding would be annexed by the US. On a rainy November day in 1858, B was declared a Crown Colony at the fort's 'Big House' and the Britis government took control.

The gold rushes eventually declined and HBC closed its fort, but th town thrived as an agricultural and residential centre. Today, a rebui Fort Langley National Historic Park is the centrepiece of a thrivi tourism trade.

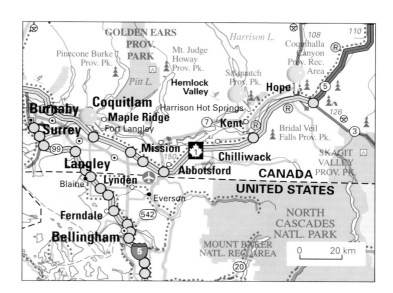

BC Farm
Machinery and
gricultural Museum $
31 Kings St; tel: (604)
8-2273. Open daily
r–mid-Oct.

>maine de
namberton Estates $
64 216 St, Langley; tel:
>4) 530-1736. Open daily
ar–Dec; Jan–Feb,
>n–Sat.

rt Langley National
istoric Park $ 23433
avis St; tel: (604) 513-
77; web:
vw.parkscanada.pch.gc.ca
en daily.

ungley Centennial
useum $ Mavis and King
; tel: (604) 888-3922.
en May–Sep, daily;
t–Apr, Tue–Sat.

The collection at the **BC Farm Machinery and Agricultural Museum**✧ emphasises 20th-century farm machinery, most of it used locally and much of it displayed outdoors. Inside displays concentrate on household items and logging equipment.

Domaine de Chamberton Estates✧✧✧, the only estate winery in the Fraser Valley, concentrates on French and some German varietals.

Fort Langley National Historic Park✧✧✧ was established by the Hudson's Bay Company as a fur-trading centre, but the local fur supply was quickly trapped out and the fort was moved to its present location in a lush agricultural region adjacent to a traditional First Nations trading site. With help from local Sto:lo bands, HBC created the salmon-packing industry, shipping 300-kg barrels of salted salmon to markets across the Pacific and creating BC's first major export trade. HBC farmers fed customers from Hawaii and Alaska to California and the Company's own inland settlements.

News of gold deposits along the Fraser changed BC forever. American miners flooded north from California, some of them stopping in Victoria to obtain the required mining permits, others simply sailing up the Fraser River to the head of navigation at Fort Langley. The HBC found itself in a quandary: as the only source of food, supplies and transport, the Company was profiting hugely. But the influx of Americans threatened annexation by the US.

The HBC's solution was to turn its mainland holdings into a Crown Colony and let London deal with the American problem. British Columbia was declared in November 1858, at a ceremony in the Chief Trader's house, the 'Big House', at Fort Langley.

Colonial status was the death of Fort Langley. Competitors moved into fishing, farming and commerce. Navigation was extended to Hope, then to Yale, destroying the fort's role in shipping. BC's capital moved to New Westminster, then Victoria, eclipsing the fort's political power. The fort finally went out of business in 1886 and fell into ruin.

The site became a National Historic Park in 1955 and was reconstructed for BC's centenary in 1958. Most of the storehouse is original (the building was used as a barn for decades), but the rest of today's Fort Langley, from the log palisade to the imposing white Big House and Blacksmith's shop, is modern reconstruction. Living history volunteers conduct tours year-round, with regular demonstrations of barrel-making, blacksmithing, cooking, clerking and trading. A small Visitor Centre museum just outside the palisade covers the history of the fort.

Langley Centennial Museum** offers more, complete explanation of Sto:lo First Nations settlements in the lower Fraser Valley and later agricultural expansion than the Fort Langley visitor centre, as well as a look at local agricultural history. Don't skip the recreated general store, Victorian parlour and homesteader's kitchen.

Below
Trading beaver pelts at Fort
Langley

Accommodation and food in Fort Langley

Cedaridge Country Estates $$$ *9260 222 St; tel: (604) 882-8570,* has an indoor swimming-pool and the usual luxury accommodation extras.

The Marr House $$$ *tel: (604) 888-6455,* is Fort Langley's most elegant restaurant.

Spill the Beans $ *9124 Glover Rd; tel: (604) 888-3434,* is a good stop for coffee or light meals.

Wendel's Bookstore & Café $ *9233 Glover Rd; tel: (604) 513-2238,* has Fort Langley's best selection of local-interest books as well as a popular all-day café.

HARRISON HOT SPRINGS✦✦

Harrison Hot Springs Chamber of Commerce *499 Hot Springs Rd; tel: (604) 796-25. Open daily May–Oct; Nov–Apr, Mon–Fri.*

Sasquatch Provincial Park $ *Rockwell Dr; tel: (604) 824-2300; reservations, tel: (604) 689-9025. Open daily.*

Harrison Public Hot Pool $ *Hot Springs Rd and Esplanade Ave. Open daily.*

There's been a hotel and mineral baths at Harrison Lake since the 1880s, but the hot springs themselves are out of sight along the western lakeside, a 10-minute walk from the Harrison Hot Springs Hotel. The lake has a broad sandy beach, boating and fishing, with camping and hiking along the water and up nearby mountainsides. A small tourist town sits on the south shore.

Surrounding forests are the haunt of Sasquatch, a legendary hairy forest giant that has been reported as far south as the Trinity Alps in Northern California. Hikers are more likely to spot deer, squirrels, Canada geese and the occasional beaver.

Although named for the shy, oversized creature of the northern forests, **Sasquatch Provincial Park✦✦✦** is actually one of the more popular spots for camping, hiking and boating on the lower mainland. Attractions include four lakes surrounded by rugged mountains. Look for mountain goats on the **Slollicum Bluffs✦✦✦** just north of **Deer Lake✦✦✦**.

Harrison Lake✦✦ is 60km long and favoured by windsurfers and sailors for the heavy winds blowing southward most afternoons. Lake tour boats depart daily from the dock in front of the Harrison Hot Springs Hotel in summer. There's a wide swimming beach directly in front of the town as well as marina facilities.

The actual hot springs supplying **Harrison Public Hot Pool✦✦✦** are about 2km away, but insulated pipes keep the sulphur- and potassium-rich water too hot to touch. The indoor soaking and swimming-pool is cooled to 38°C.

Accommodation and food in Harrison Hot Springs

Harrison Hot Springs Hotel $$$ *Hot Springs Rd; tel:(604) 796-2244,* is a full-service resort and spa on the shores of Harrison Lake.

Above
Harrison Hot Springs

Jorg's Cafe $ *105-196 Esplanade; tel: (604) 796-2824,* lures locals fc simple but filling meals.

Kitami Restaurant $$ *318 Hot Springs Rd; tel: (604) 796-2728,* serv great Japanese food, and gets plenty of visiting Vancouverites wh want a taste of home.

La Cote d'Azur $$ *310 Hot Springs Rd; tel: (604) 796-8422; web: www.lacotedazur.com*, serves excellent French dishes with a better-than-small-town wine list.

Quality Hotel $$ *190 Lillooet Ave; tel: (604) 796-5555; web: www.harrisonhotsprings.com*, is the best value in town, across the street from the lake.

HOPE✦✦

Hope & District Chamber of Commerce *919 Water e; tel: (604) 869-2021. ben daily Jun–Sep; ct–May, Mon–Fri.*

Hope Museum $ *919 Water St; tel: 04) 869-7322. Open daily ay–Sep.*

Japanese Gardens $ *emorial Park, Third and rk streets.*

inter Gardens $ *52892 nker Rd, Rosedale (exit 5 off Hwy 1); tel: (604) 4-7191. Open daily.*

oquihalla Canyon ecreation Area and thello Tunnels $ *10km st from Kawkawa Lake; : (604) 824-2300. Open ily; tunnels closed in winter e to ice.*

Sitting at the head of the lower Fraser River Valley, Hope was long the head of navigation upriver and an important transfer point for goods and gold moving between the interior and the coast. Navigation eventually moved upstream to Yale, but railway traffic revitalised the town, which has developed into a booming centre for hiking, river rafting, cycling, fishing, soaring, mountain biking and other outdoor activities. Camera crews from Vancouver and Hollywood regularly use Hope for film shoots.

Highlight of **Hope Museum**✦✦ is a restored ball mill from a nearby mine. Other displays cover Sto:lo life in the area, early White settlers and Canada's treatment of its Japanese citizens during World War II. The calm meditation garden in the **Japanese Gardens**✦✦✦ is dedicated to the 2300 Japanese-Canadians who were interned in barns at Tashme, 24km east, during World War II.

Minter Gardens✦✦✦ doesn't have quite the advertising budget or the formality of Victoria's Butchart Gardens (*see page 66*), but Butchart can't begin to match Minter's setting against the Cascade Range. Eleven themed areas include rose gardens, the largest collection of Penjing rock bonsai outside China, a maze and Canada's largest floral flag.

Coquihalla Canyon Recreation Area & Othello Tunnels✦✦✦ This is the canyon where Rambo blazed his name in *First Blood*. It's also one of the most famous sets of railway tunnels in Canada, carved through solid granite for the Kettle Valley Railway to the Kootenay region between 1910 and 1916. The almost flat 2.8-km return stroll includes four tunnels and pleasant views of the rushing Coquihalla River.

The KVR ran between Hope and Nelson (*see page 246*), but was plagued by snow, washouts and rock slides. A 130m washout just north of the Othello Tunnels closed the railway permanently in 1959. Most of today's Coquihalla Highway (*see page 144*) follows the old KVR railbed, including one section which cost $300,000 per mile to build in 1914.

Accommodation and food in Hope

Quality Inn $ *350 Hope-Princeton Hwy; tel: (604) 869-9951*, is on the outskirts of Hope.

Skagit Motel $$ *655 3rd Ave; tel: (604) 869-5220*, is quiet and central.

Above
Minter Gardens

Dee's Café **$** *875 Water St; tel: (604) 869-5534*, has Hope's be espresso, cookies, soups and quick meals.

New Golden Star Restaurant $ *377 Hope-Princeton Hwy; tel: (604) 86 9588*, is Hope's best Chinese choice.

Suggested tour

Total distance: 130km, or 260km as a long day trip from Vancouver.

Time: Allow 2 hours to drive to Hope, plus at least 2 hours each fo Fort Langley and Minter Gardens and time to soak in Harrison He Springs.

Links: This route links with **Vancouver** (*see page 42*) to the west ar the **Cascade Mountains** (*see page 130*) or the **Gold Rush Trail** (*s page 186*) to the east.

Route: From Central **Vancouver**, take either Broadway or Hwy 7A ea to Hwy 1, the TransCanada Highway, eastbound towards Hope. On across the **Fraser River**, the freeway runs through a mixture of rur farmland and small towns in the **Lower Fraser Valley**.

The flat plain stretching from the river to the base of the Cascades is or of BC's prime agricultural areas. Dairy herds alternate with fields raspberries, blueberries, strawberries and grain, with the occasional hor farm and llama pasture. Try to resist the temptation to speed along th freeway – the RCMP set up frequent radar speed traps in both direction Drivers who keep within 8–10kph of the posted speed limit may get stern warning, but seldom a speeding ticket. Many Vancouver rad stations include speed trap locations in their traffic reports.

Much of the farming land east of **Langley** has gone into agricultural preserve that gives owners tax incentives to continue farming rather than selling out to the suburban sprawl of Greater Vancouver. *Farm Fresh Guide*, available at tourist infocentres, petrol stations and tourist stops throughout the valley and in Vancouver, maps farms in the Langley area selling produce to the public. *The Harvest Guide*, with similar free distribution, covers the valley from **Abbotsford** east towards Hope.

The town of **Langley** is a busy farming and commercial. Follow freeway signs to **FORT LANGLEY** ❶, its older, smaller and more sedate cousin.

Detour: From Fort Langley, drive north to the **Fraser River** and the free ferry to **Albion**, on the north side of the river. Take Hwy 7 to the east (right), following signs to Harrison Hot Springs to rejoin the route.

From Fort Langley, return to Hwy 1 and continue eastward. **Abbotsford** calls itself the Raspberry Capital of the World. It's hard to wax ecstatic about neat rows of raspberry plants, but Minter Gardens draws raves and visitors from around the world – exit north on to Hwy 9 and follow signs to the left (west) just after crossing the Fraser River.

Return to Hwy 9 and turn left (north) through maize fields and dairy pastures toward **Agassiz**, which fancies itself the 'Corn Capital of BC'. Follow signs towards Hwy 7 and **HARRISON HOT SPRINGS** ❷, then return to Hwy 1 and continue east to **HOPE** ❸.

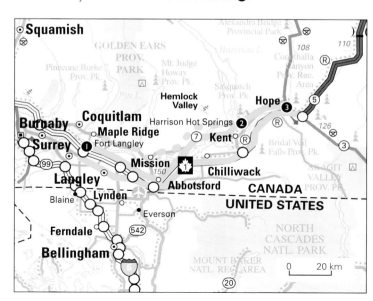

The Cascade Mountains

Ratings

History	●●●●●
Mountains	●●●●●
Scenery	●●●●●
Children	●●●●
Nature	●●●●
Outdoor activities	●●●●
Walking	●●●
Wildlife	●●●

The Cascades aren't the tallest mountains in BC, nor the highest, but they're far and away the most scenic, the most rugged and the most inaccessible by road. Only one highway crosses the range east–west, the Crowsnest, which follows a gold rush trail built for pack mules in the 1860s. The modern roadway is wider, smoother and not nearly as steep as the early track, but the snow-capped peaks, rushing rivers and dense forests that gradually give way to cacti and desert sand are as memorable today as they were to early surveyors.

The Cascades also form one of BC's most obvious political and economic barriers. Nearly the entire population of the province lives west of the mountains. With a few exceptions such as the Okanagan Valley and isolated towns on major highways, the countryside from Hope eastwards become increasingly wild, rugged and invitingly empty.

APEX ALPINE MOUNTAIN RESORT✧✧✧

Apex Alpine Mountain Resort $$$
Green Mountain Rd, Apex Mountain Provincial Recreation Area; tel: (250) 292-8126; web: www.apexresort.com Open all year.

With a reputation as the sunniest of Canada's Cascade ski resorts Apex also has some of the best alpine skiing near the Okanagan Valley. The main lift is open in summer to carry walkers, mountain bikers and sightseers up to alpine meadows. Camping, horse-riding and back-country trail trips are also available in summer.

HEDLEY✧✧

Hedley Heritage Museum; *tel: (250) 292-8422. Open daily.*

This is one of the best preserved of BC's Cascades boom towns. Hedley has dwindled to less than a tenth of its pre-World-War-I population of 5000, but many of its old buildings remain. So does the **Nickel Plate Mine✧✧✧**, perched on a mountain slope 1000m above the town. A 3-km aerial tramway hauled a bonanza in gold, silver and copper down to mills in Hedley, but the good times were cut short by falling commodity prices and World War I labour shortages. Surviving mine building

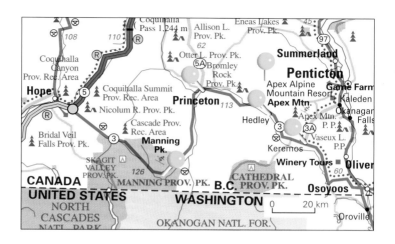

Wild Goat Gift Shop $ *Hedley Heritage Museum*, has snacks and small meals when the museum is open.

looming far above Hedley have been restored and are open for guided tours in summer. Tours depart from the **Hedley Heritage Museum***, which has a fine collection of local mining artefacts and period photographs. Gold panning is still allowed in the Similkameen River just south of town, but trout fishing is likely to be more productive.

KEREMEOS***

Keremeos & District Chamber of Commerce *Memorial Park (in the town centre); tel: (250) 499-5225. Open daily Jun–Sep.*

Crowsnest Vineyards $ *Sunrise Dr, just east of Cawston; tel: (250) 499-5129. Open daily.*

The Grist Mill at Keremeos $ *Upper Bench Rd; tel: (250) 499-2888. Open daily May–Oct.*

Perched on a bench above the Similkameen River, Keremeos still looks and feels like the frontier town it once was. Orchards and pastures stretch nearly to the main street, which is lined with false-front wooden buildings and well-used pick-up trucks. The village began as a First Nations town big enough to convince the Hudson's Bay Company to build a trading post, and slowly grew as settlers started cattle ranches, fruit orchards and, more recently, vineyards. **Crowsnest Vineyards*** offers broad mountain vistas from the tasting room.

The Grist Mill at Keremeos*, an 1877 water-powered mill, is BC's only surviving 19th-century mill with the original machinery intact and working. Built next to Keremeos Creek, the grounds have been turned into a heritage garden surrounded by more modern orchards. The BC Heritage Trust site is open all year, but costumed interpreters operate the mill and demonstrate period farming and household tasks in summer. The tea room is an excellent summer lunch stop.

South Similkameen Museum* fills the former Provincial Police building and gaol with its pioneer artefacts and antique police uniforms.

Cliffs of basalt columns soar 30m in the blazing sun at **Keremeos Columns Provincial Park***. A survey error in the 1930s left the columns on private land outside park boundaries; ask permission to hike the 8-km trail from the house at the end of the paved road.

🄷 South Similkameen Museum $ *6th Ave and 6th St; tel: (250) 499-5445. Open Jun–Aug, Tue–Sat 1000–1600; by appointment the rest of the year.*

Keremeos Columns Provincial Park $ *North on Hwy 3A, east at the cemetery. A 16-km return hike from the end of the pavement.*

The Red Bridge $ *Just west of Keremeos and south of Hwy 3.*

St Lazlo Estate Winery $ *Upper Bench Rd; tel: (250) 499-2856. Open daily.*

The faded **Red Bridge**✦ over the Similkameen River was built as a railway bridge around 1907. When the line was abandoned, the bridge was converted to highway use. Deep pools just below the bridge are popular local swimming holes during the blazing days of summer.

St Lazlo Estate Winery✦ spreads across the upper bench above the Similkameen River providing expansive views of Cascade peaks in every direction. The wines are largely Hungarian- and German-inspired.

Right
Keremeos Mill

MANNING PROVINCIAL PARK✦✦✦

🄸 Manning Provincial Park Visitor Centre *Hwy 3, 1km east from Manning Park Resort.*

🄷 Manning Provincial Park $ *Hwy 3; tel: (250) 840-8836; camping reservations, tel: (604) 689-9025.*

Originally created as a game preserve, Manning displays jagged, snow capped peaks, alpine meadows, deep valleys, teal-blue lakes and dense forests. Vegetation and wildlife are as varied as the terrain, from wild rhododendrons and magnificent stands of red cedar to bears foraging along the highway, deer, beaver, chipmunks, and hoary marmots, the park symbol carved into a gigantic sign at the western entrance.

Hwy 3 bisects the park, with the primary facilities, the **Manning Park Resort**✦✦✦ and the **Visitor Centre**✦✦✦, midway between Hope and Princeton, 68km in either direction. Resort facilities include the only indoor accommodation (chalets, cabins and hotel rooms), restaurant and supply/gift shop in the park. The Visitor Centre has a small natural history museum with free trail guides and other park information.

Manning Park Resort $$ *Manning Provincial Park; tel: (250) 40-8822; web: www.manningparkresort.com*

Beaver Pond $ *South side of the highway, 500m east of the Visitor Centre. Open all year.*

Cascade Lookout $ *Paved road from Manning Park Resort area. Open in summer only.*

Heather Trail $ *Trail head at Blackwall Peak Meadows. Open in summer only.*

Rein Orchid Trail $ *Trail head 100m west of amphitheatre car park off Gibson Pass Rd.*

Rhododendron Flats $ *South side of the highway, just beyond the Summallo Grove.*

Summallo Grove $ *South side of the highway, 1km from the west park entrance.*

Manning is a year-round outdoor recreation centre, with alpine and Nordic skiing in winter and extensive trails for hiking, mountain biking and horse-riding in summer. There are also several short, self-guiding nature trails, many accessible only in summer, as well as multi-day backpacking routes and several campgrounds accessible by car.

Two major rivers rise from the Cascades within Manning. The Skagit River curls westward through the park and the adjoining **Skagit Valley Provincial Recreation Area**✧✧✧, then disappears into a series of hydroelectric reservoirs south of the US border to drain into Puget Sound near Seattle. The Similkameen River runs east through the Cascades and eventually drains into the Okanagan River and then into the Columbia River in Washington State.

Beaver Pond✧✧, created by beavers damming a small stream, offers excellent bird-watching during May and June. The sometimes paved, sometimes gravel trail stretches 500m.

A summer-only paved road leads 9km from the highway at the Lodge to **Cascade Lookout**✧✧✧, with grand views back to the valley surrounding the Manning Park Lodge and Visitor Centre and nearby mountains. A good gravel road climbs another 6km to **Blackwall Peak Alpine Meadows**✧✧✧ and sublime vistas invisible from lower look-outs. The meadows shimmer with wild flowers from late July to mid-August.

Heather Trail✧✧✧ follows a carpet of wild flowers more than 24km long and up to 5km wide stretching from Blackwall Peak to Third Brother Mountain and beyond. Road access is from the Blackwall Peak Alpine Meadows car park.

Rein Orchid Trail✧✧✧ explores bog and riverside terrain filled with native orchids, ferns and other wetland flora. The flat, 15-minute trail is only 500m long.

Rhododendron Flats✧✧✧, a flat 2-km walking trail, goes through one of the few naturally occurring groves of rhododendrons in the Cascades. Red blossoms are at their height early–mid-June most years.

A 700m trail (wheelchair accessible in most seasons) in **Summallo Grove**✧✧✧ circles through a towering riverside grove of red cedar and Douglas fir.

PRINCETON✧✧

The town was originally called Vermilion Forks for the red pigment mined by First Nations bands. The name 'Princeton' dates from an 1860 visit to Eastern Canada by the Prince of Wales. Once a mining and cattle town, Princeton has become the commercial centre of the south Cascades region. Most of the major mines have closed in recent years, prompting residents to turn their colourful history into profitable tourism. Several downtown buildings sport new western-themed murals, while the Chamber of Commerce promotes walking tours and gold panning.

Princeton and District Chamber of Commerce 57 Hwy 3 (east end of town); tel: (250) 295-3103; web: www.town.princeton.bc.ca/ Open daily Jun–Sep; Oct–Apr, Mon–Fri.

Princeton and District Pioneer Museum and Archives $ 167 Vermilion Ave; tel: (250) 295-7588. Open daily Jul–Sep; Oct–Jun, weekends (or by appointment).

Gold panning $ Check with the Chamber of Commerce for location and pans.

Vermilion Bluffs $ Behind Home Hardware, Bridge St and Fenchurch Ave.

Princeton and District Pioneer Museum and Archives*** has an outstanding collection of fossils, including some of the earliest known examples of fossilised citrus trees, apple trees and salmon. There are also exhibitions of local mining equipment and pioneer artefacts.

Gold prospectors followed the Similkameen River northward in the 1850s, panning and dredging as they went, but small flakes of gold continue to wash out of the Cascades with every spring melt. The Chamber of Commerce runs a **panning reserve*** on the river and hires out pans.

The Okanagan First Nations bands who lived at **Vermilion Bluffs*****, when Hudson's Bay Company explorers first appeared in the early 1800s, called the place *Yak Tulameen*, 'place where red earth is sold'. The band mined red ochre, vermilion sulphate, from cliffs along the Tulameen River, just west, and sold it at a well-established market-place where Princeton now stands.

Accommodation and food in Princeton

Princeton Hotel $$ *258 Bridge St; tel: (250) 295-3355*, is the oldest restaurant in Princeton.

Villager Motel $$ *Hwy 3; tel: (250) 295-6996*, is the largest and newest motel in town.

The Dewdney Trail

In the 1860s, it was easier to travel east–west through the United States than through BC, and easier still to travel north–south along the many river valleys that connected the two countries. When gold was discovered at Wild Horse Creek, near **Cranbrook** (see page 250), American miners and merchants flooded north, threatening to undermine already tenuous British authority. The solution: Surveyor Edgar Dewdney blasted a mule trail 1.2m wide through 400km of mountains, desert and forests from Hope to the East Kootenays in just seven months.

The Dewdney Trail opened the southern reaches of BC to the coast for the first time. As mining grew, so did the trail, expanding from mule trail to wagon road and automobile road, Hwy 3. With a boost from the Kettle Valley Railway, road access slowly focused the province's southern communities on Vancouver and Victoria and away from closer, more accessible commercial centres in the United States.

Opposite
Coquihalla Highway

Above
Keremeos Mill

Suggested tour

Total distance: 240km.

Time: Allow half a day to drive from Hope through the Cascades to the Okanagan Valley and 2–4 days to explore Manning Provincial Park.

Links: Go west to the **Lower Fraser River Valley** (*see page 122*) and Vancouver (*see page 42*), north to **Kamloops** (*see page 138*), the **Gold Rush Trail** (*see page 186*) or the **Okanagan Valley** (*see page 148*).

Route: From **HOPE** ❶ (*see page 127*), go east on Hwy 3, the Crowsnest Highway, named for the Crowsnest Pass near the BC–Alberta border. The freeway turns north toward **Kamloops** at Hwy 5, the **Coquihalla Highway** (*see page 144*), while Hwy 3 reverts to two lanes. Hwy 3 largely follows the **Dewdney Trail**, the first rough mule track cut through the wilderness to supply Kootenay gold fields in the 1860s.

Look for the raw scar of the **Hope Slide** looming above the north side of the highway 10km beyond the junction. One side of the mountain, 1983m high by 1km wide, slid into the valley in 1965. The slide raised the valley floor by 70m and blocked the highway for weeks.

Continue east past the wooden carving of a hoary marmot into **MANNING PROVINCIAL PARK** ❷, the most scenic (and the slowest) section of the Crowsnest. The road is winding and occasionally steep, the scenery distracting and the wildlife sometimes close enough to cause traffic jams.

The road turns north after leaving the park, heading for the former mining town of **PRINCETON** ❸. The highway follows the Similkameen River as it cuts through increasingly dry terrain eastward toward **HEDLEY** ❹. By **KEREMEOS** ❺, the mountains have taken on the look of desert, although streambeds and river courses are still lined with green – as are growing tracts of fruit orchards and vineyards. The highway takes a final plunge over **Richter Pass** (682m) before dropping into the true desert of the **Okanagan Valley** (*see page 148*) at **Osoyoos** ❻ (*see page 152*).

Detour: From Keremeos, take Hwy 3A north and east to **Skaha Lake** (*see page 153*) in the central **Okanagan Valley** (*see page 148*).

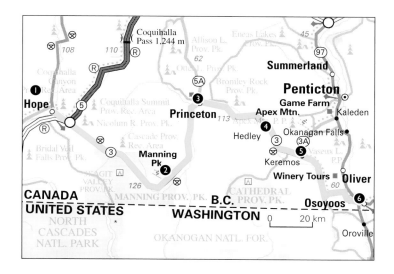

Kamloops

Ratings

Cowboys	●●●●●
First Nations	●●●●●
History	●●●●
Outdoor activities	●●●●
Scenery	●●●●
Beaches	●●●
Parks	●●●
Sport	●●●

B C's largest city, at least in terms of area, takes its name from a Secwepemc First Nations word, *Kamloopa*, the 'meeting of the rivers'. Straddling the junction of the North Thompson and South Thompson rivers, Kamloops spreads across 31sq km of river valley and hillside that have become the centre of BC's ranching industry.

In prior decades, scarlet-clad huntsmen rode to hounds across the rolling hills in noisy pursuit of wild foxes (or coyotes, depending on the luck of the hunt). Those same hills today are sprouting housing estates or provincial parks, depending on the luck of conservationists.

In the old city centre, on the low south bank of the Thompson River, dozens of stately brick buildings rise along shady streets that lead to sandy riverfront beaches. Outlying districts have more ice-rinks, playing fields, gymnasiums and tennis courts than many countries can claim.

Sights

🔘 **City of Kamloops Fire Museum $**
1205 Summit Dr; tel: (250) 372-5131. Open Mon–Fri; tours Tue, Thu.

Farmers Market $
Victoria Street, 4th–5th Ave – Wed; St Paul St, 2nd–3rd Ave – Sat. Open mornings May–Oct.

City of Kamloops Fire Museum✦
The museum is part of the city's main fire hall, with tours occasionally interrupted by genuine emergency calls. Fires excepted, there's almost always a fire-fighter on hand to explain the intricacies of fire suppression equipment and technologies dating back to 1884.

Farmers Market✦✦✦
The weekly farmers market started as a place for local farmers to sell their products, but has become a popular cultural and educational venue. Look for anything from a 4-H Club parade with chickens and rabbits to live music, square dancing and suggestions on how to control garden bugs without pesticides – plus a better selection of fresh fruits, vegetables, breads, cheese and picnic supplies than any store in town.

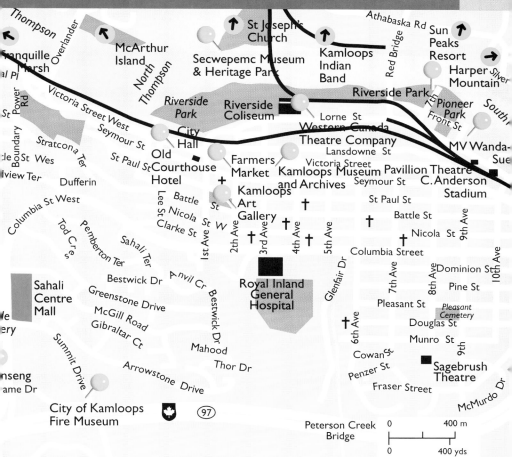

Ginseng✧✧✧

Kamloops has become a major ginseng-growing region – the areas of black sunscreens protecting the shade-loving plants from the fierce summer sun are the world's largest single source of ginseng. Few ginseng growers welcome visitors, but the processors do. The two biggest, **Canadian Imperial Ginseng**✧✧✧ and **Sunmore Ginseng Factory**✧✧✧, offer daily tours and product samples as well as display gardens.

Harper Mountain✧

Kamloops' traditional family ski hill is a short drive from town with alpine and Nordic skiing in winter. There are day-use facilities only, and lifts are less developed than newer competitor Sun Peaks, but prices are also considerably lower.

Canadian Imperial Ginseng $ 1274 McGill Rd; tel: (250) 851-380. Open daily.

Sunmore Ginseng Factory $ 925 McGill Pl; tel (250) 374-3017. Open daily.

Harper Mountain $$ 042 Valleyview Dr; tel: (250) 372-0336. Open year-round.

⓫ Kamloops Art Gallery $ 207 Seymour St; tel: (250) 828-3543. Open Tue–Sat; extended hours in summer.

Kamloops Indian Band $ 315 Yellowhead Hwy; tel: (250) 828-9700.

Kamloops Museum and Archives $ 207 Seymour St; tel: (250) 828-3576. Open Tue–Sat 0930–1630; extended hours in summer.

Kamloops Symphony Orchestra $$ 335 Victoria St; tel: (250) 372-5000. Concerts Nov–Apr.

Kamloops Water Slide $$ Hwy 1, 19km east; tel: (250) 573-3789. Open late May–Labour Day.

McArthur Island $ North Kamloops via McKenzie Ave or 12th St; tel: (250) 828-3580. Open daily.

Below
St Joseph's Church

Kamloops Art Gallery*

The gallery, which claims to be the largest public art exhibit in interior BC, concentrates on local artists and publishes a free walking tour to private downtown galleries.

Kamloops Indian Band***

The Kamloops Band is one of 17 modern Secwepemc (Shuswap) bands and the most economically successful. Much of the Band's land along the North Thompson and South Thompson rivers has been leased out to thriving industrial parks, farming and grazing operations. Profits support a successful Band community as well as the **Kamloops Powwow Days***, held each August, one of the largest First Nations gatherings in North America.

Kamloops Museum and Archives**

Three floors of displays explore local Secwepemc First Nations history, Hudson's Bay Company activities, gold rushes, ranching and cowboy history, local Chinese culture, Victoriana and natural history. The museum's collection of Secwepemc baskets is one of the best in the province. Exhibits include an 1842 log building from the HBC fort on what is now the Kamloops Indian Reserve on the north bank of the South Thompson River, two Victorian-era house interiors, a Victorian medical office and a late 19th-century general store.

Kamloops Symphony Orchestra*

The 50-member orchestra presents a full concert schedule from autumn to spring, plus outdoor summer concerts at Sun Peaks and other area venues.

Kamloops Water Slide*

Kamloops' only water park has slides, hot tubs, wading pools and miniature golf next to the area's largest RV park.

McArthur Island**

Recreation is big business in Kamloops, with 84 baseball diamonds, 73 soccer fields, 5 tennis courses, 5 ice arenas, 40 gymnasia, golf courses … and McArthur Island. The North Shore island is all recreation, with golf course, cycling trails, swimming, tennis, football, soccer, rugby, baseball and more. McArthur is also a wildlife mecca, with a butterfly garden, viewing platform to spot beavers, muskrats, yellow-bellied marmots, squirrels, red foxes and river otters, hides for bird-watching and an extensive native-plant walk.

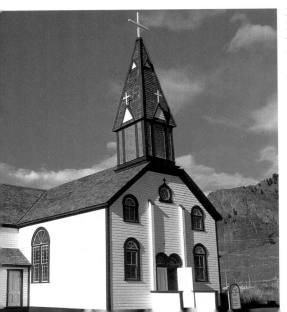

Old Courthouse Hostel✧✧✧

Kamloops' 1909 courthouse has been restored as a youth hostel, retaining the original Gothic-style arched windows and stained glass. The main courtroom, with the judge's bench, jury seats, witness box and prisoner's box intact, has become the dining area and lounge.

Riverside Park✧✧✧

The city's first riverfront park features a rose garden, tennis, swimming, walking trails, water park and a 5000-seat coliseum.

Secwepemc Museum & Heritage Park✧✧✧

The Secwepemc (pronounced she-whep-m,) or Shuswap First Nations controlled a vast territory from Kamloops west to the Fraser River, north to Soda Springs and east to the Rockies for millennia before the Hudson's Bay Company built its first fur-trading fort at Kamloops in 1812.

The Secwepemc traditionally lived a semi-nomadic life, following fish, game and food plants from spring to autumn and returning to permanent villages with the first winter snows. One of the largest and oldest of the villages occupied the northeastern shore of the confluence of the two Thompson Rivers, land that eventually became the Kamloops Indian Reserve.

A 4-hectare Heritage Park covers the ancient village site, which includes remains of dwellings at least 2400 years old. Reconstructed houses and archaeological excavations show changes in house styles and sizes from 5000 years ago to first contact with the HBC in the early 19th century. The Park also has exhibits of heritage and native food plants and a traditional salmon fishery. In summer, band performers offer traditional song, dancing, theatre and story-telling as well as salmon barbecues in a traditional summer lodge.

The museum building was once part of the Kamloops Indian Residential School. Exhibits include most of the artefacts found in the Heritage Park outside, as well as artefacts from digs throughout traditional Secwepemc lands and a fine collection of archival photographs. Museum displays put a distinctly Secwepemc spin on local history, detailing the legal and moral transgressions committed by White settlers that are largely ignored by the Kamloops Museum.

St Joseph's Church✧✧✧

The white steeple of St Joseph's was first raised in 1846, but the current building has been resorted to its early 1900s look, complete with stained-glass windows and bright interior paintings. Don't miss the cemetery, directly across the car park, with grave markers ranging from simple wooden crosses to ornate totemic carvings.

Sun Peaks Resort✧

Calling itself BC's newest year-round mountain resort, Sun Peaks has skiing in winter (882m vertical drop, groomed runs, open glades and

Tranquille Marsh $
10km west of North Kamloops on Tranquille Rd. Open daily.

Two River Junction $$
Columbo Lodge, Lorn St and Mt Paul Way; tel: (250) 314-3939. Shows Tue, Thu, Sun, May–Oct; advance booking required.

MV Wanda-Sue $$
Moored at the foot of 10th Ave; tel: (250) 374-7447. Cruises May–Sep daily.

Western Canada Theatre Company $$
1025 Lorne St; tel: (250) 372-3216. Regular productions Oct–Mar.

snowboarding) and fishing, golf, hiking, horse-riding, mountain biking, music festival, swimming and tennis in summer. Base facilities include hotels, condominiums, lodges, restaurants and shopping.

Tranquille Marsh**

This BC Wildlife Watch viewing site overlooks an extremely active waterfowl habitat. Look for trumpeter swans, Canada and snow geese, herons, ducks and dozens of other species, especially during the spring and autumn migrations. Follow Red Lake Road a few kilometres to spot bighorn sheep.

Two River Junction*

This western-frontier-themed dinner show evokes local history with a lively musical review based very roughly on the gold rush era 1880–1910.

MV Wanda-Sue**

Long-time resident George Slack dreamed of seeing a paddle-wheel boat on the Thompson River, so he built one. The 26-m sternwheeler carries 100 passengers on two-hour narrated river cruises.

Western Canada Theatre Company**

Kamloops has one of the few professional theatre companies in the province outside Vancouver and Victoria. The programme emphasises well-known productions that have already garnered a following in London or New York.

Accommodation and food

Accommodation is usually easy to find, although advance booking is wise during the summer holiday period. Motels are concentrated along Hwy 5 and off Hwy 1 at exits 366–369. For more expensive digs try along Columbia St (exit 369), which curves from the highway down to the old town centre near the river.

South Thompson Inn & Guest Ranch $$$ *North of the South Thompson River, 15 minutes east off Hwy 1; tel: (250) 573-3777,* is an expansive horse-farm-cum-resort set in 26 hectares next to the Rivershore Golf & Country Club – guests get preferred tee times.

A growing population has brought new life to Kamloops' restaurants. Don't expect the kind of cutting edge Northwestern fare common in Vancouver and Victoria, but there's more than steaks, burgers and meatballs on offer.

Apollon $$ *369 Victoria St; tel: (250) 372-5852,* in the old town centre is a good choice for Greek dishes.

Bagel Street Café $ *428 Victoria St; tel: (250) 372-9322,* in the old town centre, is popular for breakfast and light lunches.

Above
Kamloops countryside

Stockmen's Restaurant $$ *540 Victoria St; tel: (250) 372-2281*, has become the hottest steak restaurant in BC's biggest cowboy town.

Taka $$ *270-1210 Summit Dr (Columbia Place Mall); tel: (250) 828-0806*, has Kamloops' best Japanese cuisine.

Kamloops *1290 W TransCanada Highway (exit 368); tel: (250) 374-3377; web: www.city. kamloops.bc.ca Open daily Jul–Aug; Sep–Jun, Mon–Fri.*

Weather The BC interior is given to extremes: +40°C and blazing sun in summer; -40°C and drifting snow in winter. Both extremes are arid.

Suggested tours

Total distance: 3km.

Time: 2 hours' walking, 4 hours' cycling. The Kamloops Museum has self-guiding maps and brochures for both tours.

Route: The North Kamloops cycle tour has seven stops between Riverside Park and the **Tranquille Sanitarium** by way of **MCARTHUR ISLAND ❶**.

The museum's recommended walking tour includes 30 stops in the old city centre, Nicola Street–Riverside Park and Fourth Street–Lee Road. Start at the old **Calvary Temple** (185 Seymour Street, across 2nd Avenue from the **KAMLOOPS MUSEUM AND ARCHIVES ❷**), the oldest public building in town. It opened in 1887 as St Andrew's Presbyterian Church. Just uphill was Kamloops' posh residential district between the 1880s and 1914, with imposing residences along St Paul, Battle and Nicola streets between 1st Avenue and Lee Road.

Walk west along Seymour Street to the English-Gothic-style **OLD COURTHOUSE HOTEL ❸** (7 W Seymour Street), now a youth hostel. Diagonally across 1st Avenue is the **Cigar Factory** (297 1st Avenue), built in 1895 and converted to a bakery in 1913. Continue down 1st Avenue to the **Bank of Commerce** (118 Victoria

Coquihalla Highway

Created for Expo '88, the World's Fair that put Vancouver on the international map, the Coquihalla shaves 90 minutes and uncounted grey hairs off the drive between Hope and Kamloops. Cruise smoothly from four-lane Hwy 1 on to four-lane Hwy 5 at Hope and you can make the run from Vancouver to BC's inland capital in a comfortable 5 hours – without bending a single speed limit!

BC's only toll road is actually a second attempt to conquer the Cascade Range between Hope and Kamloops. The first try, the Kettle Valley Railway (*see page 151*), was plagued by runaway trains, washouts, rockslides, avalanches and massive snowfalls until Canadian Pacific Railways finally gave up and closed the line in 1959. The Coquihalla follows much of the old KVR route through the Cascades, but a panoply of modern engineering marvels keeps the highway open through the same choke-points where the railway failed year after year: massive snow sheds, avalanche diversion channels, snow dams, arcing bridges and howitzer emplacements to blast hanging snowpacks are well worth the $10 toll.

The highway is a microcosm of BC scenery. From the lush forests and rough coastal mountains around Hope, the roadway climbs sharply into the older, more rounded peaks of the Cascades. As the climate becomes drier toward the interior, trees become smaller and moss is displaced by the sparse, semi-arid grasses of the Fraser Plateau.

ght
owbird jet in one of
amloops' parks

Street), which looks almost as it did when built in 1904. Straight ahead is **RIVERSIDE PARK** ❹, originally the site of a sawmill, gristmill and brickyard.

Victoria Street is one of the most scenic sections of Kamloops, lined with well-preserved buildings. One of the most imposing is the **Fuoco Block** (No 219), erected during the boom years between 1910 and 1914. The 1905 **Kamloops Inn** (No 345) was the site of the city's first fire hall. The **Ellis Goodman Block** (No 371) was home to a successful drugstore partnership, with an apothecary shop at street level and professional offices on the floors above. The **Plaza Hotel** (No 405), opened in 1927 in pseudo-Spanish style, was the first hotel in Kamloops built specifically for automobile traffic. Turn uphill along 4th Avenue to Seymour Street. The **Elks Lodge** (409 Seymour Street), also built in 1927, shows similar Spanish design details. Continue west along Seymour Street back to the Calvary Temple.

Also worth visiting

Lac de Bois Grasslands Provincial Park *North of Kamloops; tel: (250) 851-3000.* Open daily, no developed facilities or water.

Above
Lac du Bois

Eastern unit Take exit 374 from Hwy 1 at Kamloops. Follow Hwy north over the South Thompson River to Halston Avenue (second se of traffic lights). Take Halston west (left) over the North Thompso River. At the first traffic signal beyond the river, turn right (uphill) t Westsyde Road. Move to the left-hand lane and drive straight up th hill through the housing estates on Lac du Bois Road. Enter the par when the road turns to gravel at the cattle guard.

Western Unit Take Hwy 1 exit 369 or 374 toward the Kamloop Airport via Tranquille Road. From the airport, continue west towar Tranquille. At the Tranquille Sanatorium, turn right, over the railwa tracks, and up a long hill.

Dewdrop Lake is straight ahead, along the flats; **Tranquille Rive Canyon** is uphill.

To explore the grasslands, head for the eastern unit, accessible fro Hwy 5. For lakes and canyons, drive the western unit, off Tranquil Road beyond the Kamloops Airport. Either way, Lac du Bois is wh. Kamloops looked like before it was Kamloops, complete with sweepir vistas, red lava cliffs, canyons ringing with waterfalls, arid grassland dry forests, hidden lakes and rolling fields of wild flowers stretching t the horizon.

Lac du Bois is also BC's largest publicly owned grassland. Establishe in 1996, it accommodates multiple and not always compatible use from walking and mountain biking to grazing, logging, all-terrain vehicle driving, fishing, hunting and no-entry ecological preserves in three separate grassland communities.

Ecologists go dewy-eyed over the only-in-Kamloops opportunity to see all three types of bunchgrass native to North America west of the Rocky Mountains. Flower lovers rave about the variety: buttercups, biscuit root, mariposa daisies and yellow sagebrush are only the beginning, with flowering seasons that can range from May into July, depending on rainfall, exposure and elevation.

Bird-watchers think they're in heaven: sharp-tailed grouse, sapsuckers, hairy woodpeckers, flammulated owls and dozens of other species use the grasslands in every season. It's nearly impossible not to see cows, or at least evidence of their recent presence; visitors who know where to look can expect to spot California bighorn sheep, coyotes, foxes, moose, mule deer, rattlesnakes and waterfowl.

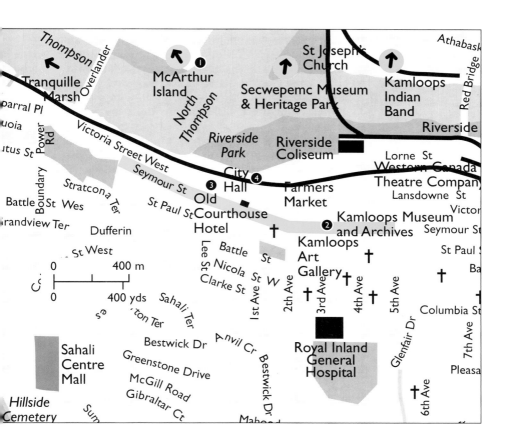

Okanagan Valley

Ratings

Food and drink	●●●●●
Wineries	●●●●●
History	●●●●
Scenery	●●●●
Beaches	●●●
Children	●●●
Outdoor activities	●●●
Wildlife	●●●

The Okanagan Valley is touted as Canada's only true desert, but leave the sand shoes at home – true desert is all but impossible to find anywhere in the valley. Decades of irrigation have pushed cacti and other desert creatures into few isolated ecological reserves, as lush fruit orchards, vegetable fields and vineyards spread from the Okanagan River up every arable hillside, bench and plateau.

The valley itself follows a string of lakes linked together by the Okanagan River, the remnants of an immense glacial river that carved a broad north–south rift through the mountains. The Cascade Range blocks most rain-bearing clouds from the Pacific Ocean; the even higher Monashee Mountains to the east capture what moisture remains. The Okanagan sits in the rain shadow of both ranges, a desert that has blossomed into BC's fruit basket, wine cellar and most popular interior holiday destination.

BRITISH COLUMBIA WINE INFORMATION CENTRE❖❖❖

This is the single most complete source of information about wine in BC, with experimental plantings, a tasting room and the best commercial selection of BC wine in the province. (**British Columbia Wine Information Centre** $ *888 Westminster Ave W, Penticton; tel (250) 490-2006; web: bcwineinfo.com. Open Mon–Fri 0930–1700, Sat–Sun 1100–1700.*)

DOMINION RADIO ASTROPHYSICAL OBSERVATORY❖❖❖

Sitting at the bottom of a shallow valley, DRAO's towering white radio dish, surrounded by an array of smaller antennae, looks more like *Star Wars* than the Okanagan.(**Dominion Radio Astrophysical Observatory** $ *White Lake Rd, 9km from Kaleden Jct; tel: (250) 493-4355. Open daily.*)

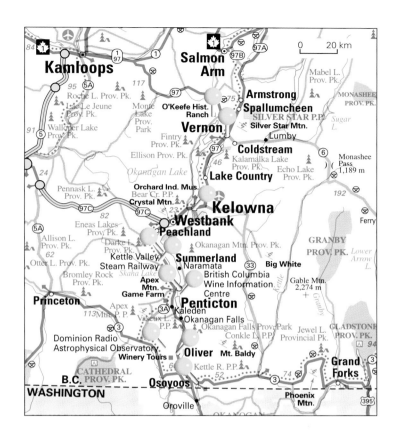

KELOWNA✦✦

Kelowna Visitors and Convention Bureau *544 Harvey Ave (Hwy 97); tel: (250) 861-515; web: www.kelownachamber.org Visitor centre open daily.*

Kelowna began as an 1850s Roman Catholic mission, but soon expanded into lumber and fruit. The 128-km² expanse of Okanagan Lake moderates winter weather while the dry, sunny climate produces dependable crops of apples, peaches and grapes.

Lake and sun have also made Kelowna a popular holiday destination. Vast areas of beaches, parks and mountain forests offer sailing, fishing, hiking, house-boating and skiing. The defunct Kettle Valley Railway creates magnificent easy walking and mountain biking.

The 1917 Laurel Packing House, now the **BC Orchard Industry and Wine Museum**✦✦✦, displays the history of Okanagan fruit growing and packing with period photographs and hands-on equipment displays. The Wine Museum has a few wine-related displays in a retail shop.

Pleasant **City Park**✦✦✦ stretches 1km from the foot of the floating bridge across Lake Okanagan to the white sculpture, *The Sail*, merging into the waterfront and marina.

BC Orchard Industry and Wine Museum $ *1304 Ellis St; tel: (250) 763-0433. Open Tue–Sat.*

City Park $ *Lakeshore, from the floating bridge to the white sculpture 'The Sail'.*

Father Pandosy Mission $ *Venvoulin and Casorso roads, southeast from the city centre; tel: (250) 860-8369. Open daily Apr–Oct.*

Geert Maas Sculpture Gardens, Gallery and Studio $ *250 Reynolds Rd; tel: (250) 860-7012. Open May–Oct, Mon–Sat, or by appointment.*

Kelowna Art Gallery $ *1315 Water St; tel: (250) 762-2226. Open daily.*

Kelowna Centennial Museum $ *470 Queensway; tel: (250) 763-2417. Open daily Jul–Aug; Sep–Jun, Tue–Sat.*

Kelowna Land & Orchard $ *2930 Dunster Rd; tel: (250) 763-1091. Tours daily May–Oct.*

KVR Bike Trails $ *Myra Canyon, June Springs and Chute Lake. Check with the CVB for current conditions and instructions – access roads may or may not be passable by passenger cars.*

Father Pandosy Mission✦✦✦, a rough-hewn Oblate Mission, founded in 1859 by Fr Charles Pandosy, was the first non-Native settlement in the Okanagan. The original log buildings have been heavily but accurately restored.

The **Geert Maas Sculpture Gardens, Gallery and Studio** complements the sculptor's more traditional indoor gallery, while the **Kelowna Art Gallery**✦ has a growing collection of BC art and artists. Exhibits at **Kelowna Centennial Museum**✦✦ include an 1861 trading post, a traditional First Nations pit house and Kelowna's first radio station.

One of the Okanagan's orchard giants, **Kelowna Land & Orchard**✦✦ offers regular tours, fruit and juice samples and a small museum.

KVR Bike Trails✦✦✦, restored railbeds from the abandoned **Kettle Valley Railway**, offer spectacular canyon and mountain views for walkers and mountain bikers with a maximum 2 per cent grade. **Myra Canyon**✦✦✦ offers the best views; the first trestle is an easy 15-minute walk from the car park. The next 12km to **June Springs**✦✦✦ crosses 17 trestles and two tunnels.

Right
Kettle Valley Railway bike trail

**Okanagan Valley
Wine Train $$$**
*creation Ave, Ellis–Richter
; tel: (250) 712-9888.
en May–Oct and Dec,
ekends.*

ay Monk $ *1055 Camp
; tel: (250) 766-3168.
en daily.*

ission Hill Winery $
*30 Mission Hill Rd; tel:
50) 768-7611. Open daily.*

**uail's Gate Vineyard
tate Winery $** *3303
ucheire Rd; tel: (250) 769-
51. Open daily.*

**ammerhill Estate
'inery $** *4870 Chute
ke Rd; tel: (250) 764-
00. Open daily.*

Okanagan Valley Wine Train✧✧ is a tourist-only train which offers wine-country excursions between Kelowna and Vernon.

Wineries✧✧✧ Most of the dozen or so in the area offer free tours and tastings. **Gray Monk**✧✧✧ is one of the oldest wineries in the Okanagan and still among the best. **Mission Hill Winery**✧✧✧ has spectacular views across Okanagan Lake from the winery tasting room. **Quail's Gate Vineyard Estate Winery**✧✧✧ doesn't have a grand building, but some of the Okanagan's grandest ice wines. **Summerhill Estate Winery**✧✧✧, BC's largest producer of sparkling wines also, has stunning views across the valley from a deck just outside.

Accommodation and food in Kelowna

Wicklow Bed & Breakfast $$ *1454 Green Bay Rd, Westbank; tel: (250) 768-1330,* overlooks Okanagan Lake.

Café Soleil $$ *2424 Main St, Westbank; tel: (250) 768-1030,* serves California-tinged continental dishes.

Divinos $$ *594 Bernard Ave; tel: (250) 860-8477,* offers Italian-Continental.

Woodfire Bakery $ *2041 Harvey Ave; tel: (250) 762-2626,* is a local favourite for breakfast and lunch.

ℇETTLE VALLEY STEAM RAILWAY✧✧✧

**Kettle Valley
Steam Railway $$**
*404 Bathville Rd,
mmerland; tel: (250) 494-
22. Operates May–Oct.

This 16-km section of track is all that remains of the Kettle Valley Railway that once linked Nelson with Hope. The train, pulled by a 1924 Shay steam locomotive engine, offers stupendous views across the Okanagan Valley.

)'KEEFE RANCH✧✧✧

O'Keefe Ranch $ *tel:
(250) 542-7868; web:
ww.okeeferanch.bc.ca Open
ay–Oct, daily 0900–1700.*

Started in 1867, the O'Keefe became one of the largest cattle ranches in the region. The ranch headquarters (*Hwy 97, 12km north of Vernon*) grew into a small town with church, general store and post office. Living history interpreters sound as though they just stepped off the range.

)LIVER✧✧

This orchard and vineyard town lived by ranching until a Provincial irrigation project turned jobless World War I veterans into farmers. **The Ditch**, the original irrigation canal, is still used. Most of the

ⓘ Oliver & District Chamber of Commerce *End of 36205 93rd St near Okanagan River; tel: (250) 498-6321. Open daily May–Oct; Nov–Apr, Mon–Fri.*

ⓗ Oliver and District Heritage Society Museum and Archives *$ 9728 356 Ave; tel: (250) 498-4027. Open Tue–Sun in summer, by appointment in winter.*

Wineries: Gehringer Bros *$ Road 8; tel: (250) 498-3537.*

Hester Creek *$ Road 8; tel: (250) 498-2784.*

Inniskillen Okanagan Vineyards *$ Road 11; tel: (250) 498-6663.*

Tinhorn Creek *$ Road 7; tel: (250) 498-3743.*

ⓧ Nikko's Greek Taverna *$ 36041 97 St; tel: (250) 498-6565, has good lamb dishes.*

Okanagan River was canalised in the 1950s for more irrigation an flood control. Exhibits in **Oliver and District Heritage Societ Museum and Archives**◇, the former Provincial Police building, cove natural history, early mining activities and irrigation.

Wineries◇◇◇ Oliver created the **Golden Mile** as a marketing ploy t lure visitors to a string of award-winning wineries located on the we side of Hwy 97 just south of town. **Gehringer Bros**◇◇◇ leans towar traditional German-type wines. **Hester Creek**◇◇◇ produces more moder styles, influenced by California rather than Europe. **Inniskille Okanagan Vineyards**◇◇◇, owned by the Inkaneep First Nation (Osoyoo Indian Band), produces intense, flavourful wines. **Tinhorn Creek**◇◇ shines with reds and has Valley views from the winery deck.

Okanagan wine

Wine has been a familiar Okanagan product for decades, but high-quality wine is a new arrival. The change started in 1988, when Provincial authorities encouraged grape growers to pull out old vineyards that were filled with table grapes and high-yield, low-quality wine grapes. The replacements were Cabernet Sauvignon, Chardonnay, Riesling, Merlot, Sauvignon Blanc, Pinot Noir and similar varieties. The province also revised antiquated licensing laws that favoured high production over high quality and introduced the **VQA**, the Vintners Quality Alliance, BC's answer to appellation and quality control schemes in France, Germany, Italy and California.

OSOYOOS◇

ⓘ Osoyoos Chamber of Commerce *Jct of Hwys 3 and 97; tel: (250) 495-7142. Open daily.*

Just north of the US border, Osoyoos sits in the same Sonoran deser made famous by Sonora, Mexico. The hottest Osoyoos day on recor was 42.8°C. Osoyoos Lake draws visitors eager to bake on sand beaches and water-ski in almost-warm water, but irrigation has turne the desert into a literal fruit basket: apples, peaches, pears, grape plums and cherries from surrounding hillsides appear in roadside frui stands in summer.

Sandy strands are a way of life. **Gyro Beach**◇ and **Communit Beach**◇ are in the centre of town. **Desert Centre**◇◇◇, one of th Okanagan's few surviving pockets of desert, has 3km of boardwalk and interpretive kiosks. Look for greasewood, rabbit brush, sage burrowing owls, spadefoot toads, yellow badgers and rattlesnakes.

Osoyoos Museum◇, an 1891 log schoolhouse, has exhibits o Inkaneep settlement and local irrigation projects.

Beaches $ *Downtown and lakeside parks.*

Desert Centre $ *West on 46 Ave; tel: (250) 495-*[cut]*470; www.desert.org* *Open daily.*

Osoyoos Museum $ *Community Park; tel: (250)* *495-2582. Open daily* *May–Sep.*

Osoyoos Oxbows Fish and Wildlife Management Reserve $ *Road 22 E, 7.5km north* *from Osoyoos. Open daily.*

Osoyoos Oxbows Fish and Wildlife Management Reserve* is all that remains of the natural Okanagan River, with marshes, ponds and open channels providing vital wildlife habitat.

Accommodation and food in Osoyoos

Motels are concentrated along Hwy 3 E (Main St), the spit crossing Osoyoos Lake at the south end of town.

Inkaneep Point Lodge $$$ *10 minutes north from Osoyoos; tel: (250) 495-6353*, is on a small peninsula with private beaches on two sides.

Sunrise Inn $$ *5506 Main Street; tel: (250) 495-4000*, is the newest motel; continental breakfast is included.

Campo Marina $$ *Richter Pass Motor Inn, Hwy 3 E; tel: (250) 495-7650*, has the best Italian food in the South Okanagan.

PENTICTON***

Penticton and Wine Country Chamber of Commerce *888 Westminster Ave W; tel: (250) 493-4055; web: www.penticton.org Open daily May–Oct; Nov–Apr, Mon–Fri.*

Penticton Museum and Archives $ *785 Main St; tel: (250) 490-451. Open Tue–Sat.*

Rafting $ *Okanagan Lake–Skaha Lake. Summer only.*

Skaha Lake $ *South of Penticton.*

Skaha Climbing Bluffs $ *South of town, off S Main St.*

SS Sicamous $ *On the beach off Lakeshore Dr; tel: (250) 492-0403. Open daily Jun–Sep; Oct-May, Mon–Fri.*

Sitting between Okanagan Lake and Skaha Lake, Penticton has beaches on two sides and mountains behind. The traditional lure – peaches and beaches – is being pre-empted by vineyards, wineries and outdoor recreation.

Look for First Nations artefacts and pioneer memorabilia in the **Penticton Museum and Archives***.

The screams of summer delight are coming from tyre tubes and rafts floating 7km down the canalised Okanagan River from Okanagan Lake to Skaha Lake. Operators set up temporary shop on the south shore of Okanagan Lake; prices include transport back to the starting point.

Skaha Lake*** remains popular for sailing, boating, fishing, sightseeing and swimming off beaches at the north end, near Penticton. **Skaha Climbing Bluffs*****, overlooking Skaha Lake, have pleasant hiking trails through the sage and Ponderosa pine as well as granite slabs, chimneys, faces and overhangs for rock monkeys.

The 72-m restored sternwheeler **SS *Sicamous**** sailed Okanagan Lake between 1914 and 1935.

Accommodation and food in Penticton

Clarion Lakeside Resort $$ *21 Lakeside Drive W; tel: (250) 493-8221*, spreads along Okanagan Lake.

God's Mountain Chalet $$ *South of town above Skaha Lake; tel: (250) 490-4800*, is a whimsical, whitewashed, Greek-style villa perched between vineyards and a sheer drop into Skaha Lake.

Granny Bognars' $$ *302 W Eckhardt; tel: (250) 493-2711*, has an excellent local wine list to match its Northwest cuisine.

1912 $$$ *Kaleden; tel: (250) 497-6868*, serves what may be the best Northwest dishes in the valley.

Villa Rosa $$ *795 Westminster Ave W; tel: (250) 490-9595* concentrates on northern Italian dishes.

SUMMERLAND✧✧

ⓘ Summerland Chamber of Commerce *15600 Hwy 97 (north end of town); tel: (250) 494-2686. Open daily May–Oct; Nov–Apr, Mon–Fri.*

Pacific Agri-food Research Centre $ *4200 Hwy 97 S (across from Sunoka Beach); tel: (250) 494-6385. Gardens open daily, interpretative centre open Mon–Fri.*

ⓘ Sumac Ridge $ *307 Hwy 97 (north of town); tel: (250) 494-0451. Open daily.*

Summerland Sweets $ *Canyon View Rd; tel: (250) 494-0377. Open daily Jul–Aug; Sep–Jun, Mon–Sat.*

Summerland Museum $ *9521 Wharton St; tel: (250) 494-9395. Open Jun–Aug, Mon–Sat; Sep–May, Tue–Sat afternoons.*

ⓘ Cellar Door Bistro $$ *Sumac Ridge Winery; tel: (250) 494-3316, offers French-styled Northwest dishes and picnic items.*

The small town is a major fruit-growing centre, sitting at the junction of three fertile valleys. The name was coined by an early developer who made a fortune subdividing the lakeside, adding irrigation and luring winter-weary farmers from Manitoba and Alberta. The Kettle Valley Steam Railway (*see page 151*) still steams over 16km of track.

The **Pacific Agri-food Research Centre**✧✧✧ is a Dominion experimental farm which opened in 1914 to develop fruit varieties better suited to the semi-arid Okanagan climate. English-style ornamentals soon followed, all open to the public.

The hilltop **Sumac Ridge**✧✧✧ winery is worth a visit just for the valley view – the outstanding wines are a bonus.

If it's sweet and based on fruit, you'll find it at **Summerland Sweets**✧: candies, syrups, jams, wines and more, all from local orchards.

The artefacts at the **Summerland Museum**✧✧ are local, but the KVR irrigation and fruit-growing history are valley-wide.

Right
Summerland peaches

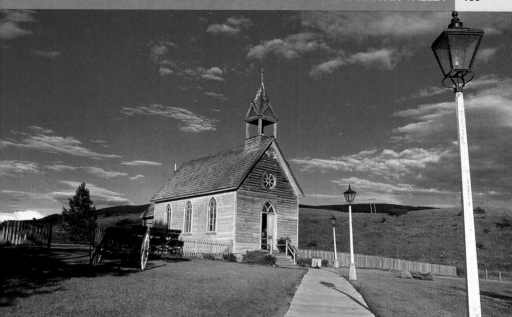

ERNON✧✧

Vernon Tourism
6326 Hwy 97; tel:
(0) 542-1415. Open daily.

**Greater Vernon
Museum and
chives $** 3009 32nd
; tel: (250) 542-3142.
en Jun–Sep, Mon–Sat;
–May, Tue–Sat.

**n Klip Theatre
mpany $$** Tel: (250)
9-2921 for performances.

Outdoor recreation and original red brick buildings at affordable rents have turned Vernon into a thriving and surprisingly trendy town at the north end of the Okanagan Valley. The city sits between three lakes, **Kalamalka**✧✧✧, **Okanagan**✧✧✧ and **Swan**✧✧✧, all lined with sandy beaches. The acclaimed O'Keefe Ranch (see page 151) is northwest.

Greater Vernon Museum and Archives✧✧ is the best place for agricultural history, including the region's first commercial orchards, planted in 1891 by Lord Aberdeen, later to be Governor-General of Canada.

Sen Klip Theatre Company✧✧✧, one of Canada's few First Nations theatre groups, is gaining a reputation worldwide for blending traditional themes and modern arts.

Accommodation and food in Vernon

The Vernon Lodge $$ 3914 32nd St; tel: (250) 545-3385, has a real stream, BX Creek, running through the lobby.

Café Asiago $$ 3202 31st Ave; tel: (250) 542-3970, is Northwestern with Italian touches.

Italian Kitchen Company $$ 2916 30th Ave; tel: (250) 558-7899, offers unalloyed Italian.

ove
Keefe Ranch, near Vernon

Above
Kalamalka Lake looking to Vernon

Suggested tour

Total distance: 160km.

Time: 4 hours to drive; 2–5 days for winery touring.

Links: The Okanagan Valley connects west through the **Cascad Mountains** (*see page 130*) to **Vancouver** (*see page 42*), via Hwy 97C **Kamloops** (*see page 138*) or via Hwy 97/97A to the **Shuswap Lak** (*see page 158*).

Route: From **OSOYOOS ❶**, take Hwy 97 north through a mixture fruit orchards, vegetable fields and vineyards coaxed from the dese by intensive irrigation. Irrigation projects have been so successf that Canada's only desert has been reduced to a few endanger pockets of cacti and burrowing owls. Continue north to Oliver.

Detour: From the Osoyoos Oxbows Fish and Wildlife Manageme

Reserve, continue east a few hundred metres to the main road and turn left. Follow the eastern shore of the river past some of the newest vineyards and wineries in the Okanagan to **OLIVER** ❷ .

From Oliver, the Okanagan Valley narrows toward **Vaseux Lake**, a bird, mountain goat and California bighorn sheep sanctuary. Beyond the lake lies **Okanagan Falls**, now a minor rapid at the south end of Skaha Lake. The road climbs the hillside above the lake before dropping back down to water level at **PENTICTON** ❸ , perched between **Skaha Lake** and **Okanagan Lake**.

Detour: From Penticton, follow secondary roads to the east of Okanagan Lake to **Naramata** for additional winery visits.

Continue north on Hwy 97 past **SUMMERLAND** ❹ and **Peachland** to **KELOWNA** ❺ and **VERNON** ❻ .

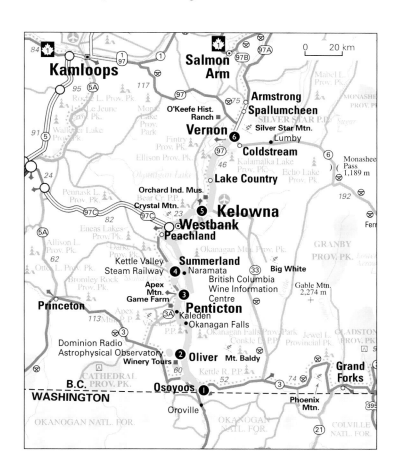

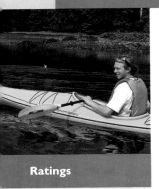

Shuswap Lakes

Ratings

Lakes	●●●●●
Mountain scenery	●●●●●
Children	●●●●
Outdoor activities	●●●●
Parks	●●●●
History	●●●
Nature	●●●
Towns	●●●

There's more than meets the eye – or the main highway in the Shuswap Lakes region: lakes, long and narrow, more like flat, calm rivers than broad lakes, but also soaring mountains, breathtaking runs of salmon, sandy beaches and eye-popping scenery that is easy to reach and forever beyond the touch of even rough logging roads.

The Shuswap is arguably the most scenic section of the entire 8047-km stretch of Highway 1 between St John's, Newfoundland and Victoria, BC. Wild, historic, filled with tiny towns, the Shuswap welcomes bald eagles and grizzly bears with the same equanimity it shows to fleets of luxury house-boats and some of the best ice-cream on either side of the Rocky Mountains. Highways follow rail lines, which traced lakeshores and river canyons past rugged peaks and foaming waterfalls. If you can't find it in the Shuswap, it may not exist.

CHASE✦✦✦

ⓘ **Chase and District Chamber of Commerce** *400 Shuswap Ave; tel: (250) 679-8432. Open daily Jul–Aug; Sep–Jun, Mon, Wed, Fri.*

ⓝ **Niskonlith Lake Provincial Park $**
8km northwest from Chase on Niskonlith Lake; tel: (250) 851-3000; web: www.elp.gov.bc.ca/bcparks/ explore/parkpgs/niskonli.htm Open Apr–Oct.

A carpenter from New York who was lucky enough *not* to strike gold in the Cariboo instead found fortune building a timber and cattle town. Chase is better known today for its outdoor recreation opportunities – canoeing down 58km of calm water to Kamloops, fishing, house-boating, hiking, swimming, golf and winter skiing. The town is surrounded by calm pine forests at the head of Little Shuswap Lake. The municipal beach is particularly scenic and popular.

The **Chase Museum & Archives✦✦**, the former Blessed Sacrament church, is filled to the rafters with the town's first physician's office, the gleaming mahogany bar from an early hotel, an antique barber's chair and everything in between. (**Chase Museum & Archives $** *100 Shuswap Ave; tel: (250) 679-8432. Open Jun–Aug, daily.*)

Niskonlith Lake Provincial Park✦✦✦ has camping, magnificent wild-flower displays from May to June and good rainbow-trout fishing year-round.

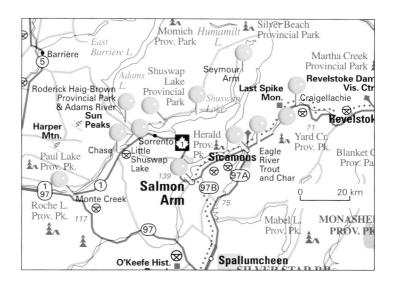

CRAIGELLACHIE❖

A stone cairn and railway-station-type souvenir shop commemorates the driving of the last spike to complete the Canadian Pacific Railway in 1885 (**$** *Hwy 1, east from Sicamous; tel: (250) 837-5345; web: www. revelstokecc.bc.ca/vacation/lspike.htm; gift shop open daily in summer*).

EAGLE RIVER TROUT AND CHAR❖❖❖

This small fish farm sells fresh trout and char, as well as smoked fillets or whole fish, a fine addition to any picnic (**$** *Hwy 1, 1km east from Yard Creek Provincial Park; tel: (250) 836-4245; open daily in summer*).

LITTLE SHUSWAP LAKE❖❖❖

Little Shuswap is the smallest of the Shuswap Lakes, but has the most accessible beaches from Hwy 1 (**$** *North and east from Chase to the Adams River and Little River*).

MONTE CREEK❖

The small town and railway station are best known as the site of an abortive railway robbery by 'Gentleman Bandit' Bill Miner in 1906 that netted around $15. Miner was captured, sentenced to life in

Monte Creek $ *Hwy 1, 31km east from Kamloops.*

prison, escaped, and eventually landed in a US prison for la robberies. A romantic version of his story surfaced in a 198 Hollywood film, *The Grey Fox*, filmed in the area.

RODERICK HAIG-BROWN PROVINCIAL PARK & ADAMS RIVER❖❖❖

Roderick Haig-Brown Provincial Park & Adams River $ *North from Hwy 1 at Squilax; tel: (250) 851-3000; web: www.elp.gov.bc.ca/bcparks/ explore/parkpgs/roderick.htm*

The park surrounds and protects 11km of the Adams River betwe Adams Lake and Little Shuswap Lake. The river has one of the heavi runs of sockeye salmon in the world, well over a million of the brig red fish fighting their way up the Fraser and North Thompson riv to spawn every fourth year. (The next major, or dominant, run occ in 2002.) Off-years merely feature a few hundred thousand salmo plus attendant bears, eagles, ravens, mink, gulls and other wildli Observation decks provide a clear view of spawning with naturali on hand during the height of the late summer–autumn salmon runs

SALMON ARM❖

Salmon Arm & District Chamber of Commerce *751 Marine Park Dr NE; tel: (250) 832-2230. Open daily in summer, Mon–Fri in winter.*

RJ Haney Heritage Park & Museum $ *Hwy 97B, 4km east from Salmon Arm; tel: (250) 832-5243; web: www.museumsassn.bc.ca/ ~bcma/museums/rjhhpm.html Open Jun–Aug, Tue–Sat 1300–1700; or by appointment.*

Rotary Peace Park and Public Wharf $ *Marine Park Dr at the lake.*

The commercial centre of the Shuswap Lakes region, Salmon Arm v born as a fruit and dairy town on the rich flood plain of the Salm River, which enters Shuswap Lake here. The town and the south a of Shuswap Lake were named 'salmon' for the massive runs of salm that made their way from the Pacific Ocean each year. The salm disappeared when faulty railway construction blocked the Fraser Ri at Hells Gate (*see page 190*) in 1912, destroying the fish run. Ev without the salmon, Salmon Arm is a popular port to hire hou boats, floating RVs, to explore the far reaches of Shuswap Lake.

The **RJ Haney Heritage Park & Museum**❖❖❖ includes a histo church, farm buildings and schoolhouse.

Rotary Peace Park and Public Wharf❖❖❖, a 250-m pier and walkw curves out from the park with excellent views of shorebirds a waterfowl. At least 150 different species of birds nest around the mou of the Salmon River each spring. Best breeding displays are Ap to June.

Accommodation and food in Salmon Arm

Motels line Hwy 1 through town, or, to explore Shuswap Lake water, hire a house-boat.

Salmon Arm Bay Houseboat Vacations $$ *tel: (250) 832-2745; w www.twinanchors.com/sabay.htm*, is one of several local operators.

Shuswap Lake Houseboat Association *tel: (250) 836-2450*, li house-boat operators around the lake.

SEYMOUR ARM✧✧✧

A few old buildings still line the streets, but the restaurant, pub, general store and a small hotel are all at the wharf on Bughouse Bay. The town is accessible by road in summer and by ferry from Sicamous all year. (**Seymour Arm** *North end of Seymour Arm, the northernmost arm of Shuswap Lake, 47km north from Anglemont by logging road.*)

SHUSWAP LAKE✧✧✧

The narrow, H-shaped lake is the most popular house-boating destination in BC, perhaps in Canada. The 1000km of shoreline tends to be steep, with no shoals or reefs, or soft and sandy. Warm summer weather means few storms and no heavy waves. Nineteen species of fish keep anglers busy all year. (**Shuswap Lake $** *The lake stretches from Sorento, south to Salmon Arm, east to Sicamous and north to Seymour Arm; web: www.shuswap.com*)

SHUSWAP LAKE PROVINCIAL MARINE PARK✧✧✧

ⓘ Shuswap Lake Provincial Marine Park $ *26 sites around Shuswap Lake; tel: (250) 851- 8000; web: www.elp.gov.bc.ca/bcparks/ explore/parkpgs/shmarine.htm*

The park has less than 1000 hectares, but is scattered around 26 sites on the shores of Shuswap Lake. Most of the units are accessible only by water and are extremely popular with summer house-boaters.

Right
Shuswap Lake

David Thompson

The Thompson River is named for David Thompson, Canada's most important and least acknowledged White explorer. In two decades of travel, this North West Company trader logged 90,000km by canoe, foot and horse, mapping four million square kilometres of Western Canada plus major sections of Washington, Idaho, Oregon and Montana in the US.

Along the way, Thompson found the source of the Columbia River at Columbia Lake (1807), pioneered Athabasca Pass through the Rockies (1811) and mapped the entire length of the Columbia River.

Thompson's greatest achievement, travelling the Columbia River to the Pacific Ocean, was also his greatest disappointment. He arrived just in time to find American fur traders, who had sailed from Boston, feverishly building Fort Astoria. Their 1811 post eclipsed British claims to what would become Oregon and Washington and led to the division of Western America along the 49th parallel. Thompson's precise maps were used well into the 20th century, but the explorer, having retired to Montreal, died in poverty.

SICAMOUS✣✣

ⓘ Sicamous and District Chamber of Commerce *110 Finlayson St (near Government Dock); tel: (250) 836-3313; web: www.sicamous.com Open daily in summer, Mon–Fri in winter.*

ⓘ D Dutchman Dairy *$ Hwy 1, 1km east from Sicamous; tel: (250) 836-4304. Open daily.*

ⓘ Shuswap Lake Ferry Service $$ *tel: (250) 836-2200. Service to Seymour Arm all year.*

The name comes from a Secwepemc word that means 'narrow' o 'squeezed in the middle', a good name for the tiny narrows betwee Mara and Shuswap lakes. The one-time railway camp has become resort town that is especially popular with house-boaters – loca operators have more than 300 vessels for rent, no experience required **D Dutchman Dairy**✣✣✣, a local dairy, has 50 flavours of wha aficionados call BC's best commercial ice-cream. Even coach tours sto for a cone – highly recommended is the banana and black walnut.

Right
The SS *Sicamous*

For those who don't want to drive their own boats, **Shuswap Lake Ferry Service**✧✧✧ offers regular vehicle and passenger ferry (all year) and sightseeing (summer only) services between Sicamous and Seymour Arm.

Accommodation and food in Sicamous

Motels and restaurants line Hwy 1 and Hwy 97A from Vernon.

Sicamous Inn $$ *tel: (250) 836-4117*, is the largest in town, with the best facilities.

YARD CREEK PROVINCIAL PARK✧✧✧

Yard Creek Provincial Park $
Hwy 1, 15km east from Sicamous; tel: (250) 851-3000; web: www.elp.gov.bc.ca/bcparks/explore/parkpgs/yard.htm Open May–Sep.

This wet, upland forest has excellent bird-watching and pleasant hiking trails beneath hemlock and cedars along a sparkling creek, and is a popular camping and picnic spot.

Suggested tour

Total distance: 160km.

Time: 3 hours to drive; 2–5 days to explore.

Links: Kamloops (*see page 138*) is just west on Hwy 1; **Revelstoke** (*see page 236*) and the **Columbia River** (*see page 230*) just west.

Route: Hwy 1 follows the **South Thompson River** west past **MONTE CREEK ❶**. The high cliffs on the north side of the river have been eroded into an irregular series of columns and buttresses that can take on fantastic shapes in the late afternoon light. The earliest known human remains in BC, a man trapped in a mudflow about 8000 years ago, were found along **Gore Creek**, near the north end of the bridge at **Pritchard**.

Road and river climb slowly to **CHASE ❷**, a ranching and lumber town on the south shore of Little Shuswap Lake, the west end of a vast lake system that extends north (Adams Lake) and west (Shuswap Lake).

Just east of Chase is a lay-by for **Chase Falls**, an easy and popular short hike. Just beyond is **Squilax Mountain**, home to a herd of Rocky Mountain bighorn sheep which often descend the bluffs on the south side of Hwy 1. The **Jade Mountain Lookout**, 2km east, offers broad views of Little Shuswap Lake. Just beyond is the **North Shuswap (Squilax) Bridge** over the **Little River**. The 4-km river between the two Shuswap lakes was once a thriving trade centre for Secwepemc (Shuswap) First Nations. The river is better known today for trout fishing in February, March and October.

Above
Black bear

Detour: Little Shuswap Lake Road runs west around the north side of Little Shuswap Lake to **Quaaout Lodge**, a resort and outdoor recreation centre owned by the Squilax/Little Shuswap Lake First Nation. The popular resort is jammed mid-July when the Nation hosts the annual **Squilax Powwow**, drawing attendees from across North America.

Squilax-Anglemont Road runs northeast from the bridge to a turn for the **RODERICK HAIG-BROWN PROVINCIAL PARK ❸** and the Adams River, or continue along the north shore of **SHUSWAP LAKE ❹**.

A 40-km paved road links the hamlets of **Lee Creek, Scotch Creek, Magna Bay** and **Anglemont**, all with campgrounds, bed and breakfasts and cabins for rent. **SEYMOUR ARM ❺** is another 45km north on a good gravel road. Return to Hwy 1 at the Squilax Bridge or take the Shuswap Lake Ferry to Hwy 1 at Sicamous.

Hwy 1 continues east from the bridge to **Squilax**, little more than a general store and hostel, and on to **Sorrento**. The tiny community swells to more than 4000 in summer when motels, resorts, RV parks and campgrounds fill up. Hwy 1 climbs south from Sorrento.

Also worth visiting

Turn downhill at **Canoe Point Road** to Shuswap Lake at **Sunnybrae Provincial Park, Herald Provincial Park** and **Paradise Point**, one of the few sites in **SHUSWAP LAKE PROVINCIAL MARINE PARK ❻** that can be reached by land. Return to Hwy 1.

The main highway emerges on a hillside high above Shuswap Lake and sweeps down into the rich agricultural valley leading to **SALMON ARM ❼**. Continue along the lakeshore past the junction with Hwy 97B, which leads south to **Vernon** and the **Okanagan Valley** (*see page 148*). If the valley seems hazy, blame the lumber mill at Canoe, which still burns sawdust and other waste. The best place to admire Shuswap Lake is the **Shuswap Rest Area**, a picnic area 15km east from Canoe on the north side of Hwy 1.

SICAMOUS ❽ is just beyond, straddling the narrow junction of Shuswap Lake and **Mara Lake**, stretching southward. Hwy 97A leads south into the Okanagan Valley. Hwy 9 continues eastward past the Dutchman Dairy, a must-taste ice-cream stop, following the **Eagle River** past **YARD CREEK PROVINCIAL PARK ❾**. Just beyond is **EAGLE RIVER TROUT AND CHAR ❿**, a good stop for smoked trout and char just 11km before **CRAIGELLACHIE ⓫**, where the transcontinental Canadian Pacific Railway was completed in 1885.

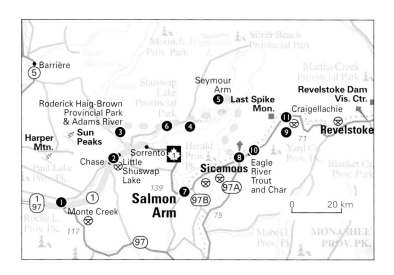

Railway journeys

Ratings

Children	●●●●●
Heritage	●●●●●
Railways	●●●●●
Scenery	●●●●●
Mountains	●●●●
Desert	●●●
Food and drink	●●●
Forests	●●

No industry was more influential in the development of Southwestern Canada, especially British Columbia, than the railways. Settlers, miners, gold rush prospectors and immigrants raced west to claim land or resources; many took the trains. Returning to developed Eastern Canada were the raw materials from the land, forests, ocean and rivers, along with cultivated crops and cattle. The *quid pro quo* for BC's entry into the Canadian Confederation as a province in 1871 was the assurance from the Canadian Pacific Railway and the Federal government in Ottawa that a transcontinental railway would be built. Fifteen years later, Vancouver was quickly transformed from a backwater to a full-fledged city when the promise was fulfilled and it became the terminus railway hub controlling the overland flow of passengers and freight.

Present-day routes, demarcated by Mile Markers, wind through craggy mountain massifs, crawl through river canyons, traverse deserts and ranchlands, and skirt shimmering lakes.

CARIBOO PROSPECTOR❖❖❖

ⓘ Cariboo Prospector $$$ BC Rail Ltd, 1311 W 1st St, North Vancouver; tel: (800) 663-8238, (800) 339-8752 or (604) 984-5246; web: www.bcrail.com/bcrpass/bcrpsca.htm Runs three times weekly.

Route: North Vancouver–Whistler–Lillooet–Exeter/100 Mile House–Williams Lake–Quesnel–Prince George

It's a 13.5-hour trip from North Vancouver to Prince George at Mile Marker 462.4, though many opt for a return summer day trip to Whistler, which includes breakfast and dinner at your seat on the train and a Whistler gondola ride. It's a train remarkable for its engineering: lightweight, self-propelled passenger cars called Budd Cars.

For those who venture north of Howe Sound, Squamish and the mountains around Whistler, the train travels inland along the Fraser River most of the distance to Prince George from its junction with Cayoosh Creek at Lillooet. Near Clinton, enter Cariboo Gold Rush and ranching country – rolling pastures, barns and cowboys. Ranching heartland is at Williams Lake. If pausing at Quesnel, don't miss the well-restored historic Gold Rush town of Barkerville (*see page 188*).

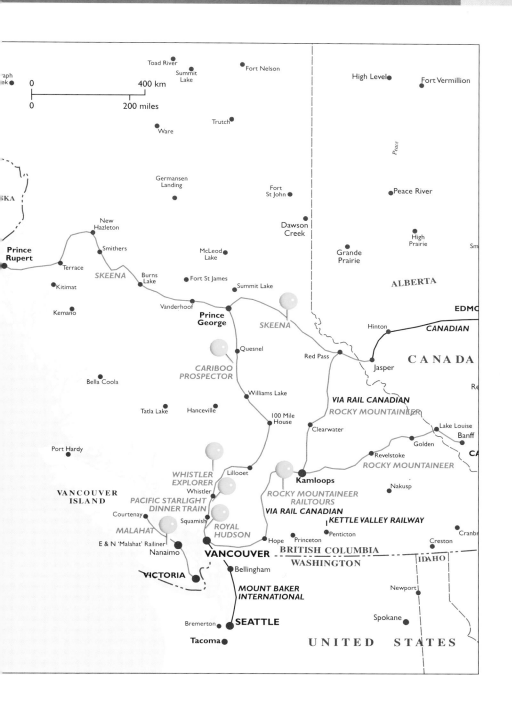

0 | 400 km

0 | 200 miles

Toad River
Summit Lake
Fort Nelson
High Level
Fort Vermillion
raph ek
Trutch
Ware
Peace
SKA
Germansen Landing
Fort St John
Peace River
New Hazleton
Dawson Creek
High Prairie
Sm
Prince Rupert
Smithers
McLeod Lake
Grande Prairie
ALBERTA
Terrace
SKEENA
Burns Lake
Fort St James
Kitimat
Kemano
Vanderhoof
Summit Lake
EDMO
Prince George
SKEENA
Hinton
CANADIAN
Quesnel
Red Pass
Jasper
CANADA
CARIBOO PROSPECTOR
Williams Lake
Bella Coola
Tatla Lake
Hanceville
100 Mile House
Clearwater
VIA RAIL CANADIAN
ROCKY MOUNTAINEER
Lake Louise
Banff
Golden
Re
Port Hardy
Revelstoke
ROCKY MOUNTAINEER
C
WHISTLER EXPLORER
Lilloeet
Kamloops
Nakusp
VANCOUVER ISLAND
Whistler
ROCKY MOUNTAINEER RAILTOURS
PACIFIC STARLIGHT DINNER TRAIN
VIA RAIL CANADIAN
MALAHAT
Courtenay
Squamish
ROYAL HUDSON
KETTLE VALLEY RAILWAY
Cranb
E & N 'Malahat' Railiner
Nanaimo
Hope
Princeton
Penticton
Creston
VANCOUVER
BRITISH COLUMBIA
WASHINGTON
IDAHO
VICTORIA
Bellingham
Newport
MOUNT BAKER INTERNATIONAL
Spokane
Bremerton
SEATTLE
Tacoma
UNITED STATES

E & N 'Malahat' Railiner✧✧

ⓘ **E & N 'Malahat' Railiner $$** *VIA Rail Canada, 450 Pandora Ave, Victoria; tel: (800) 561-8630 or (250) 383-4324; web: www.viarail.ca/en.trai.nord. html#01 Runs daily.*

Route: Victoria–Duncan–Nanaimo–Parksville–Courtenay

The *Malahat* makes scheduled stops but will also stop on request, fine way to venture beyond Duncan's totem poles, Nanaimo's Bastion near the marina and Parksville's swimming beach. The 33 Chemainus murals are worth a stop, a wallside composite history of First Nation first settlers, Chinese merchants, lumberjacks, fishers and the rail Unlimited stopovers are permitted with standard ticketing, but there is no provision for left luggage, so travel light.

Pacific Starlight Dinner Train✧✧✧

ⓘ **Pacific Starlight Dinner Train $$$** *BC Rail Ltd, 1311 W 1st St, North Vancouver; tel: (800) 363-3373, (800) 339-8752 or (604) 984-5246; web: www.bcrail.com/starlight/*

Route: North Vancouver–Porteau Cove–North Vancouver

It is light when you board the nine-car train at 1815 in North Vancouver, dressed up for a fine dining experience. The train, which also offers Sunday brunch and Murder Mystery evenings, serves supper with entrées such as guinea fowl, beef tenderloin or Coho salmon in either Salon or Dome Car seating. Each car has a 1930s or 1940s name and pedigree.

Runs May–early Oct,
Wed–Sun; early
Oct–Thanksgiving, Fri–Sat.

Porteau Cove was served by steamships until 1955 when a railway link between Vancouver and Whistler gutted the waterborne traffic. The route leaves North Vancouver for West Vancouver's waterside vistas and posh residences, Horseshoe Bay and Howe Sound's craggy shoreline to the watersports paradise at Porteau Cove.

ROCKY MOUNTAINEER RAILTOURS***

ⓘ Rocky Mountaineer Railtours $$$ 1150
Station St, Vancouver; tel:
(604) 606-7200 or (800)
665-7245; web:
www.rockymountaineer.com
Runs May–early Oct, with
Dec winter trips.

Route: Vancouver–Kamloops–Banff or Vancouver–Kamloops–Jasper

The *Rocky Mountaineer* trains, always photographed against stunning Banff National Park scenery in brochures, live up to their billing as the 'Most Spectacular Train Trip in the World'. Self-adulation aside, the *RM* took a route abandoned by VIA Rail in 1989 and in a decade built a heavily booked tourist train which offers good steward service, food and, above all, stunning scenery. Stewards, Onboard Service Attendants, also provide a narrated history of points of interest *en route*, interpret natural history, provide books and talk about their personal research of the region.

Expect occasional stops or slow-downs for wildlife spotting. The *Rocky Mountaineer* waits for commercial traffic, so schedules are not precise, enhancing the feeling of travelling back in time when nature

Below
The *Rocky Mountaineer* train
passes through Banff National
Park

(rockslide, avalanche or flood) or business (a railway with more priority) could affect railway operations.

GoldLeaf Service, with roomy seats, has much-coveted dome car views, whose windows are kept clean despite often misty or rainy weather. White linen and flower-vase dining is below the dome car level. Signature Service passengers benefit from access to landings between cars, a spot favoured by photographers. Meals served at your seat are box lunches of excellent quality. Snacks are non-stop.

The *RM* provides a tabloid newspaper upon boarding, a Mile Marker by Mile Marker key to the routes, scenery, historic men, engineering feats, commercial development and ethnology the train passes through. With the tabloid guide, it's impossible to be lost even though the *RM* traverses about 1000km and seven (roughly) 200-km divisions over track controlled by two railway companies – the Canadian National and the Canadian Pacific.

The *RM* trains to Jasper or to Banff follow the same route from Vancouver as far as Kamloops. Leaving Vancouver, the train also leaves urban density behind for the green grass suburbs and lakes east. At Hope, the *RM* travels up the Fraser River Canyon, gathering a collective gasp at gondolas moving across the river almost into the train at Hells Gate. As the train criss-crosses the Fraser and Thompson river canyons, who can resist the sight of an occasional raft upriver near Suicide Rapids or the evocatively named Jaws of Death Gorge?

The route turns east to Kamloops where passengers disembark and spend the night.

Below
Kamloops VIA train crossing
the North Thompson River

Kamloops–Jasper Along the Jasper Route on the second day, the *RM* follows the North Thompson River past Blue River and halts briefly at the lovely Pyramid Falls for photographers. Mountains begin to fill the view, with the Premier and Cariboo Ranges to the west and the Monashees east. Eastwards, the *RM* approaches the Rockies and enters Mount Robson Provincial Park, with 3954m Mount Robson ahead. Yellowhead Pass, used by the Grand Trunk Pacific and Canadian Northern Pacific Railways in prior days is the crossing rejected by the CPR as not southerly enough to protect Canadian interests against American railways. Mount Edith Cavell is on the right as the train approaches Jasper.

Kamloops–Banff The route to Banff from Kamloops skirts the edge of the Shuswap Lakes and Sicamous houseboat population. Eighteen kilometres east at Craigellachie, a cairn commemorates the driving of the final spike to inaugurate the transcontinental railway by the CPR in 1885. A graceful bridge crosses the Columbia River to Revelstoke, gateway to Mount Revelstoke and Glacier National Parks. Lights dimmed, the *RM* moves in through the arrow-straight 8-km-long Connaught Tunnel through Mount MacDonald, built in 1913 to avoid the avalanche disasters constantly plaguing Rogers Pass. There is another pause to admire the 149m-long Stoney Creek Bridge arching 100m over the creek. Having crossed the Columbia Mountains, the route briefly follows the Columbia River south to Golden.

The *RM* moves east up into Yoho National Park to Field along the Kicking Horse River. A short stop at Field, surrounded by dramatic golden mountains with hanging glaciers where fossils are rife, aid appreciation of the flat town area beneath the massive peaks which the CPR used as a stopping point for transcontinental trains and passengers. There is no RM passenger disembarkation, merely a short wait for clearance on the track for the final haul over the Rockies.

Just east of Field are the Lower and Upper Spiral Tunnels, the double figure-8 solution to a too-steep grade up a mountain called the Big Hill. The Lower Spiral through Mount Ogden turns 230 degrees over its 900m, and the 1001m-long Upper Spiral Tunnel through Cathedral Mountain swivels 250 degrees – before both emerge 15m higher than when the train entered either tunnel. The *RM* crosses into Alberta and Banff National Park at the Continental Divide, passing close to Lake Louise before heading down the Bow River Valley to Banff Townsite.

Passengers not returning by train to Vancouver can continue to Calgary on the *Rocky Mountaineer*.

Below
Royal Hudson steam train

An exhausting but rewarding all-day motorcoach tour taking in the Icefields Parkway and the TransCanada Hwy to Banff can be booked for either direction, with stops at Athabasca and Sunwapta Falls, Peyto Lake and Lake Louise.

ROYAL HUDSON***

Royal Hudson $$ *BC Rail Ltd, 1311 W 1st St, North Vancouver; tel: (800) 663-8238 or (604) 984-5246; web: www.bcrail.com/bcrpass/bcrhudsn.html/ and www. mountain-inter.net/~chadwick/hudson/hudson. htm Runs mid-May–Sep, Wed–Sun. Can be combined with MV Britannia in one direction, and booked through BC Rail.*

Route: North Vancouver–Squamish

One of BC's most famous and beloved rail excursions takes just two hours and operates only half the week in summer. The CPR steam locomotive engine No 2860, built in 1940, carries the royal British coat of arms in tribute to its engine class (H14-6-4). King George VI and Queen Elizabeth had this class of engine to pull their train on a 1939 Canadian visit, and the king designated its type 'Royal Hudson'. Only five Royal Hudsons survive, No 2860 being the only one in operation.

The views of Howe Sound along the 'Sea to Sky route' are spectacular. Bunker C Bear, the train mascot, entertains children as parents watch the views. In Parlour Class, enjoy brunch on the way up to Squamish or afternoon high tea while returning to North Vancouver. Rail buffs won't miss a Squamish stopover for **West Coast Railway Heritage Park***** vintage rolling stock.

THE SKEENA***

The Skeena $$$ *tel: (800) 561-8630 or (604) 640-3741; web: viarail.ca/en.trai.nord. html#01 Runs three times weekly.*

Route: Jasper–Prince Rupert

A stop in Prince George is a welcome pause along the 1160km route which follows the track of the early 20th-century Grand Trunk Pacific Railway. *The Skeena* leaves Jasper National Park heading west over the Yellowhead Pass, passing by the landmark Mount Robson, generally following the Fraser River to Prince George. West is the land of First Nations and the Gitxsan, preserving the world's largest collection of standing totem poles in the Hazeltons. For the last 225km to Prince Rupert, *The Skeena* threads through its namesake canyon, often giving credence to the Skeena's name (it means 'river of mists').

WHISTLER EXPLORER***

Whistler Explorer $$$ *BC Rail Ltd, 1311 W 1st St, North Vancouver; tel: (800) 663-8238 or (604) 984-5246; web: www.bcrail.com/bcrpass/bcrwhis.htm Runs late May–Sep.*

Route: Whistler–Kelly Lake

This railway journey provides a four-hour out/nine-hour back tourist excursion following the Gold Rush Trail from the magnificent mountains around Whistler Resort through the Pemberton Valley to remote Kelly Lake. A 1000-m rise in elevation takes the railway through flower meadows and changing forest. Walk a quick circuit around the lake during the 45-minute stop before reboarding. Lunch is served on the return leg.

BC Railway Museums: **Canadian Museum of Rail Travel**◆ *Cranbrook* (see **The Crowsnest** *page 250);* **Kwinitsa Station Railway Museum**◆◆ *Prince Rupert (see* **Prince Rupert** *page 209);* **Prince George Railway and Forestry Museum**◆◆◆ *Prince George (see* **Prince George** *page 226);* **Revelstoke Railway Museum**◆ *Revelstoke (see* **Columbia River** *page 236);* **West Coast Railway Heritage Park**◆◆◆ *Squamish (see* **Howe Sound & Whistler** *page 180).*

BC Ferries *tel: (888) 223-3779 or (250) 386-3431; web: www.bcferries.ca. Provides connections with* The Skeena *at Prince Rupert, and Vancouver Island's E & N 'Malahat' to Vancouver.*

Suggested tours

Time: 4–7 days depending on connections and season.

Links: For major stations, see **Vancouver** *(see page 42)*, **Victoria** *(see page 62)*, **Kamloops** *(see page 138)*, **Jasper** and **Banff** *(see* ***Alberta Rockies*** *page 270)*, **Prince George** *(see page 222)* and **Prince Rupert** *(see page 206)*. **Central Vancouver Island** *(see page 86)* covers stops on the E & N 'Malahat'. At Prince Rupert, disembarking *Skeena* passengers can take an Inside Passage **Ferry Voyage** *(see page 113)* to Port Hardy. The *Royal Hudson* takes the **Howe Sound & Whistler** route *(see page 176)*.

Route: All three railway companies offer combination packages with each other, as well as motorcoach and ferry connections where appropriate. Most tourist rail excursions run from approximately May to September, depending on route and snowfall. There are also regular routes such as VIA Rail's transcontinental 'Canadian' train from Vancouver to Toronto with *en-route* stops in Kamloops, Jasper, Edmonton, Saskatoon, Winnepeg, Sioux Lookout and Sudbury Junction.

A cross-province railway excursion provides an excellent introduction to geography before hiring a car and taking to the road. Rail buffs will want to take the train to see the two western provinces with varied scenery and rolling stock.

Coast to Rockies Triangle: Eastern Loop

Take the **CARIBOO PROSPECTOR ❶** from **Vancouver** to **Prince George**. The next morning, board **THE SKEENA ❷**, continuing its run to **Jasper**. The following day, board the **ROCKY MOUNTAINEER ❸** on its northern route from **Jasper** to **Kamloops**. Overnight and re-board the Rocky Mountaineer to **Vancouver.**

Interior to Coast: Western Loop

Take the **CARIBOO PROSPECTOR** from **Vancouver** to **Prince George** Board **THE SKEENA** going west. At **The Hazeltons**, the route begins to follow the curls and curves of the broad, high-walled super-scenic **Skeena River Valley** to **Prince Rupert**. Catch a BC Ferry to **Port Hardy** at the north end of **Vancouver Island**. Take a motor coach to **Courtenay** and board the E & N 'MALAHAT' ❹ to **Victoria**. BC Ferries connect **Victoria** and **Vancouver**.

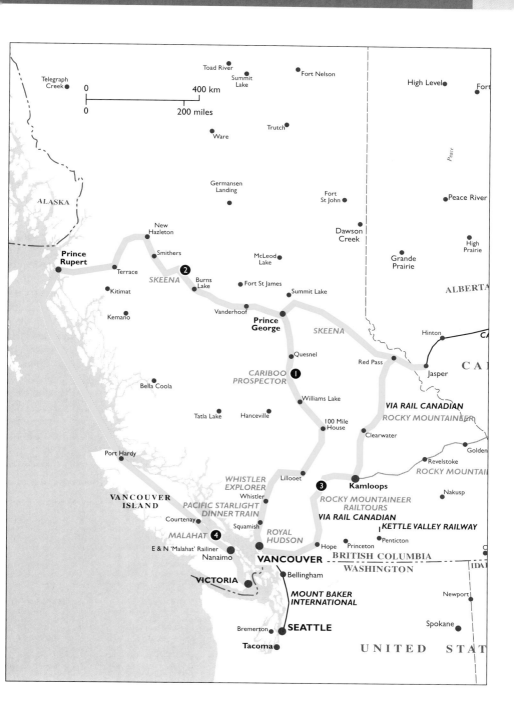

Telegraph
Creek

Toad River

Summit
Lake

Fort Nelson

High Level

Fort

0

400 km

0

200 miles

Trutch

Ware

ALASKA

Germansen
Landing

Fort
St John

Peace River

New
Hazleton

Dawson
Creek

High
Prairie

**Prince
Rupert**

Smithers

McLeod
Lake

Grande
Prairie

ALBERTA

Terrace

SKEENA

Burns
Lake

Fort St James

Summit Lake

Kitimat

Vanderhoof

**Prince
George**

SKEENA

Hinton

CA

Kemano

Quesnel

Red Pass

CA

Bella Coola

*CARIBOO
PROSPECTOR*

Williams Lake

Jasper

VIA RAIL CANADIAN
ROCKY MOUNTAINEER

Tatla Lake

Hanceville

100 Mile
House

Clearwater

ROCKY MOUNTAI

Port Hardy

*WHISTLER
EXPLORER*

Lillooet

Golden

Revelstoke

ROCKY MOUNTAIN

**VANCOUVER
ISLAND**

Whistler

*PACIFIC STARLIGHT
DINNER TRAIN*

Kamloops

Nakusp

*ROCKY MOUNTAINEER
RAILTOURS*

VIA RAIL CANADIAN

Courtenay

Squamish

MALAHAT

*ROYAL
HUDSON*

KETTLE VALLEY RAILWAY

E & N 'Malahat' Railiner
Nanaimo

Hope

Princeton

Penticton

VANCOUVER

BRITISH COLUMBIA

IDA

VICTORIA

Bellingham

WASHINGTON

*MOUNT BAKER
INTERNATIONAL*

Newport

Bremerton

SEATTLE

Spokane

Tacoma

UNITED   STAT

Peace

Howe Sound and Whistler

Ratings

Coastal scenery	●●●●●
Outdoor activities	●●●●●
Skiing	●●●●●
Children	●●●●
Nature	●●●●
Entertainment	●●●
Food and drink	●●●
Villages	●●●

They call it the Sea to Sky Highway, Hwy 99 on most maps. By either name, it curls and twists along the glacier-carved shores of Howe Sound, north of Vancouver, to the base of Whistler Mountain, one of North America's most acclaimed, most visited and most challenging mountain resorts. It is also one of the most scenic drives in southern BC, if not the easiest.

Much of the roadway is carved into the sheer cliffs hugging Howe Sound. The frequent 'No Stopping' signs warn of rockfalls and avalanche hazard, not lack of lay-bys. The few legal stopping spots provide picture-postcard views of BC Ferries plying the protected waters of the sound with trackless mountains rising barely beyond reach. More mountains rise just behind the highway, some pocked with the remains of enormous mining operations, some never touched and all cut by streams rushing from the sky back to the sea.

BRACKENDALE EAGLE RESERVE❖❖❖

ⓘ Brackendale Eagle Reserve $
Brackendale, Government Rd. Park at the dike and walk to the viewpoint on the river. Best eagle viewing Dec–Feb.

The Eagle Reserve lies along both banks of the Squamish River north of Squamish, providing winter habitat and food for between 2000 and 3000 bald eagles in mid-winter. Eagles flock to the river to feed on spawning fish, a feeding frenzy that usually peaks around Christmas and tapers into mid-February, when the eagles disperse. Eagles can be observed from a riverside walk and observation point on the east bank or from the water with rafting and kayaking operators out of Squamish.

BRANDYWINE FALLS PROVINCIAL PARK❖❖❖

Centrepiece of the park is Brandywine Falls, a 66-m cataract erupting from atop an ancient lava bed. The falls viewpoint is an easy 10-minute walk through the forest. The name dates from an early brandy versus wine bet over the height of the falls by two early railway surveyors – neither had cash, so one bet brandy and the other wine. (**Brandywine Falls Provincial Park $** *Hwy 99, 37km north of Squamish; tel: (604) 898-3678; web: www.elp.gov.bc.ca/bcparks/explore/parkpgs/ brandywi.htm. Open daily.*)

BRITANNIA BEACH❖

This wide spot in the beach along Howe Sound was once a busy support and supply town for the Britannia Mine, the largest producer of copper in the British Empire between 1930 and 1935. Today, it's a centre for arts and crafts shops, small galleries, a general store and an

Britannia Beach *Hwy 99, 33km north of Horseshoe Bay.*

BC Museum of Mining National Historic Site *$$ Tel: (604) 896-2233. Open daily May–Oct; year-round for pre-booked tours.*

ever-changing list of restaurants and bistros. The car park just east Hwy 99 is also a popular spot for RCMP radar speed traps.

During some 70 years of operation, the massive Britannia Bea Mine produced more than 600 million kg of copper. The facili closed in 1974 but has re-emerged as the **BC Museum of Mini National Historic Site**✦✦✦, with nearly the entire plant battered b intact. Facilities include mining museum displays in the herita support buildings just off the highway to the east. Outdoor displa include a 355-tonne 'Super Mine' truck and other massive equipme Guided tours take visitors inside the mine and tunnels to see slushe muckers, drills and one of the last surviving gravity-fed o concentrators in the world. If the site looks familiar, it probably The spooky, rust-stained shop that seems to spill down t mountainside has starred in nearly 100 cinema and TV productions recent years.

BROHM LAKE INTERPRETATIVE FOREST✦

Brohm Lake Interpretative Forest *$ Hwy 99, 13km north of Squamish; tel: (604) 898-2100.*

There's fishing in the shallow lake and swimming in clear water th seldom warms to more than frigid. Eleven kilometres of trails le through 400 hectares of forest with spreading views of the **Tanta Mountain Range**✦✦✦ and one of the largest ice fields in North Americ

GARIBALDI PROVINCIAL PARK✦✦✦

Garibaldi Provincial Park *$ East of Hwy 99, Squamish–Whistler; tel: (604) 898-3678; web: www.elp.gov.bc.ca/bcparks/ explore/parkpgs/garibald.htm Highway signs indicate trail access. Open daily but weather may make access difficult.*

There is no road access into the wilderness park, but well-develop trail systems lead to five of the most popular camping and hiki areas – **Black Tusk/Garibaldi Lake**✦✦✦, **Cheakamus Lake**✦✦✦, **Diamo Head**✦✦✦, **Singing Pass**✦✦✦ and **Wedgemount Lake**✦✦✦. In summer, lo for azure-blue lakes, vast meadows of wild flowers, untouched stan of Douglas fir, yellow and red cedar, mountain hemlock and lodgepc

Right
Timber bridge

pine, depending on altitude. The entire park gets heavy snow in winter, but Diamond Head is particularly popular with experienced Nordic skiers and snow campers. The park is also accessible via trails from Whistler.

HORSESHOE BAY✤✤

North Vancouver InfoCentre 131 East nd Street, Horseshoe Bay, orth Vancouver; tel: (604) 87-4488. Open daily in summer, Mon–Fri autumn–spring.

Named for its shape, this protected bay opens on to the head of Howe Sound, a convenient terminal for service to **Nanaimo** (see page 90) on Vancouver Island, as well as more local services from **BC Ferries**. The small town just above the ferry docks offers restaurants, pubs, shopping and a pleasant park with views across the harbour from beneath spreading shade trees. (**BC Ferries** End of Hwy 1; tel: (250) 386-3431 or (888) 223-3779; web: www.bcferries.bc.ca)

MURRIN PROVINCIAL PARK✤

Murrin Provincial Park $ Hwy 99, 3km orth of Britannia Beach; tel: 04) 898-3678. Open daily.

The park was named for a former general superintendent of the Britannia Beach Mine, who shared his summer cottage, tiny Brown Lake and surrounding trails with mine employees. It is popular for walking, picnicking, swimming, fishing, sunbathing and novice to intermediate rock climbing. More experienced climbers head for **Stawmus Chief**, just up the road.

PORTEAU COVE PROVINCIAL PARK✤✤✤

Porteau Cove Provincial Park $ Hwy 99, 25km north of orseshoe Bay; tel: (604) 89-3678. Camping reservations; tel: (604) 89-9025; web: www.elp.gov.bc.ca/bcparks/ explore/parkpgs/porteau.htm Open daily.

The cove was once an important ferry landing on Howe Sound, but is better known today for beachcombing, fishing and scuba diving. Several ships have been scuttled just off the beach to the north of the pier for divers to explore. The cove is also a good point to watch for the Royal Hudson steam train en route between North Vancouver and Squamish in summer (see page 173) and is the turn-around point for the Pacific Starlight dinner train from North Vancouver (see page 168). The actual cove is at the more protected south end of the park, beyond the camping area.

SHANNON FALLS PROVINCIAL PARK✤✤✤

Shannon Falls Provincial Park $ Hwy 99, 7km north of Britannia Beach; tel: (604) 89-3678. Open daily.

You can hear Shannon Falls, the third highest in BC, from the car park. The 335-m cataract is a five-minute walk along a pleasant but well-worn forest trail. Best time to visit is shortly after noon, when the sun highlights the falls dropping from the cliff high above. Expect crowds in summer, including motor coach tours en route to Whistler.

SQUAMISH✧✧

ⓘ Chamber of Commerce Serving Squamish, Britannia Beach & Furry Creek
37950 Cleveland Ave (the main street); tel: (604) 892-9244. Open daily.

ⓝ Soo Coalition for Sustainable Forests
$ 1498 Pemberton Ave; tel: (604) 892-9766. Open Mon–Fri.

West Coast Railway Heritage Park $$ *3km north on Hwy 99 to Centennial Way, then 1km west; tel: (604) 898-9336. Open daily May–Oct.*

Squamish Estuary $
West from Third Ave beyond Vancouver St, just southwest of town.

The word *squamish* means 'Mother of the Winds' in the language of the Coast Salish, the local First Nations group – it's an accurate description of local weather. Daytime sun heats the sheer rock face surrounding Squamish, creating afternoon updrafts that build into world championship windsurfing gusts.

Squamish is also a timber town of two minds. Forestry jobs and incomes are slowly declining while hiking, kayaking, cycling, fishing, rock climbing and other outdoor activities are growing in economic importance – and luring a growing number of outsiders who hate nothing so much as the sight of logging trucks, pulp mills and clear cuts. Outdoor recreation is winning, but timber interests are stringing out their measured withdrawal as long and as gracefully as possible.

Soo Coalition for Sustainable Forests✧✧✧, the timber industry advocacy group, arranges mill and forest tours.

The **West Coast Railway Heritage Park✧✧✧** is a must-see for rail buffs with more than four dozen vintage railway carriages and locomotive engines. Highlights include a gleaming 1890 Executive Business Carriage panelled in hand-rubbed teak, a restored Colonist Car that once carried migrants across the prairies on hard benches, the only surviving steam locomotive engine from the Pacific Great Eastern Railway that once served Howe Sound and a gargantuan orange snowplough.

Squamish Estuary✦✦✦ has excellent bird-watching, especially during the spring and autumn migrations.

Accommodation and food in Squamish

Howe Sound Inn & Brewing Company $$ *37801 Cleveland Ave; tel: (604) 892-2603*, the only brewpub on the Sound, concentrates on local fish and seasonal vegetables with hotel rooms upstairs.

Sunflower Bakery $ *38086 Cleveland Ave; tel: (604) 892-2231*, is a good source for light lunches or picnic supplies.

TAWMUS CHIEF PROVINCIAL PARK✦

The 652-m Chief lures thousands of climbers and hikers every year. There are at least 180 different ascent routes, including a rugged walking trail that gains 550m in just 2.5km. The rocky plug is the second largest granite monolith in the world after Gibraltar. Best spot to watch rock climbers is from a lay-by on the eastern side of the highway, about 1km north of the park entrance. (**Stawmus Chief Provincial Park $** *Just north of Shannon Falls; tel: (604) 989-3678; web: www.elp.gov.bc.ca/bcparks/explore/parkpgs/stawamus.htm Open daily.*)

elow
we Sound

WHISTLER✧✧✧

ⓘ **Whistler Resort Association** *4010 Whistler Way, Whistler, BC V0N 1B4; tel: (604) 932-2394; web: www.whistler-resort.com*

Created in the hope of luring the Olympic Winter Games to Canada in the 1960s, Whistler developers haven't let decades of lukewarm interest from the International Olympic Committee slow things down. North America's most successful mountain development may have started as a ski resort, but it has become just as successful – and just as busy – in summer.

Two mountains, Whistler and Blackcomb, have been trimmed and groomed for just about every mountain activity known to man or estate developer: skiing, golf, hiking, mountain biking, fishing, kayaking, rafting, canoeing, shopping, eating, drinking, climbing and snowboarding are only the beginning. The ski season extends well into summer, thanks to lifts that access high-altitude glaciers. A few hundred metres below, families with hiking boots and backpacks can watch for deer, marmots, bears and other wildlife amid alpine meadows and open forest.

At the base is Whistler Village, an entirely artificial and hugely successful European-style pedestrian village packed with hotels, restaurants, shops, cafés, clubs, plazas, bridges, creeks, gazebos, musicians and magicians, none of them more than a 10-minute stroll away. Relaxing? No, but Whistler was designed for excitement, glamour and glitz and has very largely succeeded.

Right
Whistler Mountain

Whistler InfoCentre Hwy 99 d Lake Placid Rd; tel: 04) 932-5528.

Whistler Museum and Archives $ 4329 Main St; : (604) 932-2019. Open ly.

The original activity centre was Whistler Village, at the foot of Whistler Mountain. The Village still has more restaurants, more shops and more variety than the rest of the resort. A short walk across the valley is Upper Village, a more expensive, more exclusive and less frenetic enclave surrounding Chateau Whistler. Smaller valleys to the south are filled with condominium developments that rely largely on the Village for services and entertainment.

For activity information in any season, contact the **Whistler Resort Association** and the **Whistler Activity and Information Centre** in the **Whistler Village Conference Center**. Shops near the gondola base in Whistler Village hire out bikes, skates and other equipment in summer and skis or snowboards in winter.

Summer is Whistler's value season, as well as its most active. At the base, five lakes are strung like turquoise and green beads on a necklace, woven together with 20km of mostly paved trails for easy walking, cycling and rollerblading. Six lakeside parks offer broad lawns, sandy beaches and full picnicking facilities with sailing, windsurfing, boating and fishing.

Both Whistler and Blackcomb lifts remain open (except for short maintenance periods in autumn), with summer skiing on Blackcomb and hiking or mountain biking on both mountains. Other possibilities include golf, climbing, backpacking, hang-gliding, heli(copter)-hiking, jet boating, flightseeing and hayrides.

Winter is Whistler's *raison d'être*, with 200-plus named runs and three dozen lifts. Blackcomb has the longest lift-serviced vertical in North America, 1609m, as well as the longest uninterrupted fall-line skiing on the continent. Whistler comes a close second, with 1530m of vertical served by lifts. Then there's Nordic skiing on valley golf courses and trails, ice-skating, snow shoeing and sleigh rides.

Even if you're only spending the day at Whistler, check out **Chateau Whistler**✦✦✦ in the mountains. Canadian Pacific didn't break the bank building Canada's grandest 20th-century resort hotel, but it looks like they did. It's an enormous castle-like building beneath a copper-green roof that still manages to feel comfortable, thanks to touches such as Mennonite hooked rugs and quilts and First-Nations-inspired twig furniture. The Great Hall and the Mallard Bar are best for gawking.

Whistler is short on history, but the **Whistler Museum and Archives**✦ makes the best of skiing gear from the 1960s, fishing souvenirs from the 1920s and local logging paraphernalia.

Accommodation and food in Whistler

Most Whistler hotels, inns, condos and other accommodation have their own booking number, but it's easier to book through the **Whistler Resort Association**; *tel: (604) 664-5625* or *(800) 944-7853*. Expect two- to three-night minimum stays in high season (Jan–Mar), the lowest rates Nov–Dec and Apr, and mid-range rates the rest of the year.

Chateau Whistler $$$ *Upper Village; tel: (604) 938-8000*, is undisput Queen of the Mountain.

Fireplace Inns $$ *Whistler Village; tel: (604) 932-3200*, is one of tl better mid-range hotels with kitchens and plenty of room for familie

Pan Pacific Lodge Whistler $$$ *Whistler Village; tel: (604) 905-299* has full-kitchen suites a few steps from both Whistler and Blackcon gondolas.

Residence Inn $$ *Upper Village; tel: (604) 905-3400*, has a prime ski-i ski-out location midway up the base of Blackcomb Mountain.

Araxi Ristorante $$ *Whistler Village; tel: (604) 932-4540*, gets raves f its pasta and wine list.

Caramba $$ *Town Plaza; tel: (604) 938-1879*, is the liveliest Itali restaurant at Whistler.

Ingrid's Village Café $ *Whistler Village; tel: (604) 932-7000*, is wor the out-the-door queues for vegetarian dishes.

Thai One On $$ *Upper Village; tel: (604) 932-4822*, is a calm refu with Thai dishes as good as any in Vancouver.

Zeuski's Taverna $ *Town Plaza; tel: (604) 932-6009*, is cheerful, che and always busy.

WHISTLER INTERPRETATIVE FOREST✦✦

🛈 Whistler Interpretative Forest $ *Hwy 99, 9km north of Brandywine Falls Provincial Park; tel: (604) 932-5535. Open daily.*

There's an extensive and well-marked network of hiking ar mountain biking trails throughout a working forest between Hwy and Garibaldi Provincial Park. Watch for logging trucks and be sure park entirely off the roadway. Almost directly across Hwy 99 **Function Junction**, a catchy name for a perfectly ordinary service ar for Whistler Resort. There are bakeries, hardware stores, a brewer plumbers, electrical supplies and all the other mechanical and servi functions that resorts like to keep out of sight and out of mind.

Suggested tour

Total distance: 120km.

Time: 2–4 hours, depending on traffic.

Links: The Sea to Sky Highway connects to **Vancouver** (*see page 42*) the south, or continue north on Hwy 99 to the **Gold Rush Trail** (*s page 186*) near **Hat Creek Ranch** (*see page 190*).

Route: From Vancouver, take the **Lion's Gate Bridge** north over tl First Narrows to **West Vancouver**. Take Hwy 1, the TransCana

Highway, westbound, following signs for the BC Ferries terminal at **HORSESHOE BAY** ❶, Squamish and **WHISTLER**.

Hwy 1 runs to the ferry line-up at Horseshoe Bay. Hwy 99, the **Sea to Sky Highway**, continues north, hugging the cliffs above **Howe Sound**. The twisting highway is narrow and verges are almost non-existent, especially in winter when snowbanks crowd the road. There are a number of scenic lay-bys, none of them accessible from the northbound lanes. If time permits and the weather is clear, continue to **PORTEAU COVE**, north of Horseshoe Bay, and turn back for the views.

The roadway opens up just south of Porteau Cove, a one-time ferry landing for Howe Sound ferry service that has become a popular park for beachcombing, fishing, boating and scuba diving. Eight kilometres north is **BRITANNIA BEACH** and the Britannia Mine, a museum that was once the largest copper producer in the British Empire. Just north is **SHANNON FALLS PROVINCIAL PARK**, with one of the highest waterfalls in BC, a five-minute walk from the car-park, and **STAWMUS CHIEF**, a massive peak that is a favourite with rock climbers.

Continue north to **SQUAMISH** ❷, a timber town that is turning towards outdoor recreation. The highway turns inland past **BROHM LAKE** and **BRANDYWINE FALLS PROVINCIAL PARK** before passing Function Junction, a small service community for **WHISTLER** ❸ and its resort.

The Gold Rush Trail

Ratings

Historical sights	●●●●●
History	●●●●●
Outdoor activities	●●●●●
Scenery	●●●●●
Children	●●●●
Museums	●●●●
Parks	●●●●
Nature	●●●

The Fraser River and Cariboo Gold Rush transformed BC from a distant source of furs into a major presence on the world stage. Nearly every product, every place, every attitude that is a part of BC today has its roots in Gold Rush. Most of the province's major highways began as Gold Rush trails, many interior towns exist because they once filled Gold Rush needs. Even timber, largest of BC's traditional industries, owes much to the insatiable Gold Rush demand for wooden buildings, railway sleepers and fuel.

Who made the first gold discovery and where may never be known. First Nations traders brought small amounts of gold to the Hudson's Bay Company for years, but the fur trading giant hid its shining secret, rightly fearing that an influx of gold miners would disrupt its profitable monopoly. The Gold Rush that created the province broke the company.

ALEXANDRA BRIDGE PROVINCIAL PARK❖❖❖

Alexandra Bridge Provincial Park $
Hwy 1, 22km north from Yale. Open daily.

The small park surrounds the 1926 **Alexandra Suspension Bridge❖❖** that still spans the Fraser Canyon. An easy walking path follows the original roadbed down to the old bridge and across the foaming river on an open grating. The suspension bridge replaces an 1863 bridge at the same spot, which itself replaced a ferry just downstream at Spuzzum. The new Alexandra Bridge is north of Spuzzum.

ASHCROFT MANOR❖❖

Ashcroft Manor $
10km south of Cache Creek; tel: (250) 453-9983. Open daily.

Built in 1862 as a roadhouse for the Cariboo Wagon Road, Ashcroft grew into a prosperous farm, ranch, mill and social centre in the sagebrush and cactus desert south of Kamloops. The manor also served as one of BC's earliest courthouses. Most of the complex burned down in 194. but a church and the roadhouse, now a tearoom and museum, survived

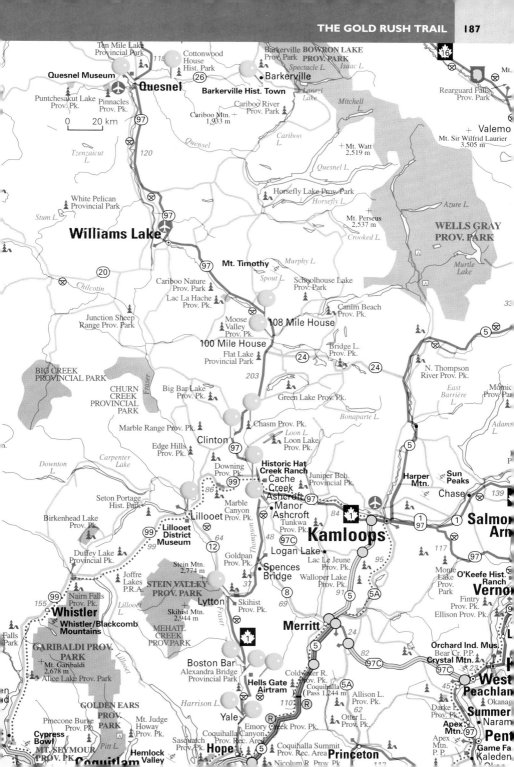

Ten Mile Lake
Provincial Park
118
Cottonwood
House
Hist. Park
Quesnel Museum
Pinnacles
Prov. Pk.
26
Quesnel
Puntchesakut Lake
Prov. Pk.
97
Barkerville Hist. Town

Barkerville
Prov. Park
**BOWRON LAKE
PROV. PARK**
Spectacle L.
Isaac L.
Barkerville
Lanezi
Lake
Mitchell
L.

16
Mt.
Rearguard Falls
Prov. Park

+ **Valemo**
Mt. Sir Wilfrid Laurier
3,505 m

Cariboo Mtn.
1,933 m
Cariboo River
Prov. Park
Cariboo
L.
+ Mt. Watt
2,519 m

0   20 km

97

Quesnel

120

White Pelican
Provincial Park

Quesnel L.

Mt. Perseus
2,537 m

Azure L.

**WELLS GRAY
PROV. PARK**

Tzenzaicut
L.

Horsefly Lake Prov. Park
Horsefly L.

Murtle
Lake

Williams Lake

97

Crooked L.

20
Chilcotin

97   **Mt. Timothy**
Murphy L.
Spout L.
Schoolhouse Lake
Prov. Park

5

Cariboo Nature
Prov. Park
Lac La Hache
Prov. Pk.

Moose
Valley
Prov. Pk.

108 Mile House

Canim Beach
Prov. Park

N. Thompson
River Prov. Pk.

Junction Sheep
Range Prov. Park

100 Mile House
Flat Lake
Provincial Park

203

Bridge L.
Prov. Pk.

24

24

East
Barrière

Momic
Prov. Pa

**BIG CREEK
PROVINCIAL PARK**

Downton
L.

**CHURN
CREEK
PROVINCIAL
PARK**

Fraser

Carpenter
Lake

Marble Range Prov. Pk.

Big Bar Lake
Prov. Pk.

Clinton

Chasm Prov. Pk.
Loon L.

Green Lake Prov. Pk.

Bonaparte L.

Adams

5

Edge Hills
Prov. Pk.

97

Loon Lake
Prov. Pk.

Harper
Mtn.

Sun
Peaks

Chase

139

Birkenhead Lake
Prov. Pk.

155

99

Seton Portage
Hist. Park

Downing
Prov. Pk.

86

99

**Historic Hat
Creek Ranch**

Marble
Canyon
Prov. Pk.

Juniper Bch.
Provincial Pk.

**Cache
Creek**
Ashcroft

• **Manor**
Ashcroft

Tunkwa
Prov. Pk.

84

Juniper Bch.
Provincial Pk.

1
97

1

**Salmo
Arm**

Duffey Lake
Prov. Pk.

99

Lillooet

**Lillooet
District
Museum**

64

12

Goldpan
Prov. Pk.

Thompson

48

97C

Kamloops

O'Keefe Hist.
Ranch

117

97

Joffre
Lakes
P.R.A.

Stein Mtn.
2,774 m

**STEIN VALLEY
PROV. PARK**

Lillooet L.

37

**Spences
Bridge**

8

Logan Lake
Lac Le Jeune
Prov. Pk.

Walloper Lake
Prov. Pk.

95

5A

Vernor

Monte
Lake
Prov.
Park

Fintry
Prov. Pk.

Whistler

99

Nairn Falls
Prov. Pk.

**Whistler/Blackcomb
Mountains**

**MEHATL
CREEK
PROV. PARK**

Lytton

Skihist
Prov. Pk.

Skihist Mtn.
2,944 m

1

Fraser

69

91

5A

Ellison Prov. Pk.

**GARIBALDI PROV.
PARK**

+ Mt. Garibaldi
2,678 m
Alice Lake Prov. Pk.

Boston Bar

Alexandra Bridge
Provincial Park

Merritt

24

5

82

97C

Orchard Ind. Mus.
Bear Cr. P.P.
Crystal Mtn.

97C

23

**West
Peachlan**

Falls
Park

d

**GOLDEN EARS
PROV.
PARK**

Mt. Judge
Howay
Prov. Pk.

Harrison L.

**Hells Gate
Airtram**

Yale

Coldwater R.

Coquihalla
(Pass 1,244 m

5A

Allison L.
Prov. Pk.

Otter L.
Prov. Pk.

62

Okanag

Summer

Naram

Apex
Mtn.

97

Pen

**Cypress
Bowl**

Pinecone Burke
Prov. Pk.

**MT. SEYMOUR
PROV. PK.**

Coquitlam

Pitt L.

**Hemlock
Valley**

Sasquatch
Prov. Park

Hope

Emory Creek Prov. Rec. Area

Coquihalla Canyon
Prov. Rec. Area

1103

5

R

Coquihalla Summit
Prov. Rec. Area

Princeton

Nicolum R. Prov. P

Darke L.
Prov. Pk.

45

Apex
Mtn.
P.P.

Game Fa
Kaleden

BARKERVILLE HISTORIC TOWN❖❖❖

⑪ Barkerville Historic Town $ *Hwy 26, 8km east from Wells; tel: (250) 994-3302; web: www.heritage.gov.bc.ca/bark/bark.htm Open daily 0800–2000; costumed interpreters and full services mid-May–mid-Sep.*

For most of the 1860s, Barkerville was the biggest town north of Sa Francisco and west of Chicago. More than 100,000 hopeful miner and hangers-on travelled the Cariboo Wagon Road to Barkervil between 1862 and 1870. They turned what had been a shanty tow into a city so rich and so confident that it very nearly outdid Victori in a bid to become the capital of BC.

The gold along Williams Creek ran out in little more than a decad but the town survived to become a thriving heritage site. More tha 125 buildings remain, most of them original, if heavily restored. Th bordellos and dance halls never reopened, but restaurants, theatre churches, stores, bakeries, photographers and a Chinese grocery al back in business during the summer months. In winter, the onl residents are park wardens and ground squirrels.

For a better sense of just how far Barkerville lies from the rest of BC walk (or ski in winter) the last 1.6km of the old wagon road west 1 Richfield with *A Walk to Richfield*, a self-guiding map keyed to 1 historic sites. The map is available at the Barkerville Visitor Centr Most visitor facilities are in Wells.

Below
Barkerville's main street

OSTON BAR✧

Boston Bar Hwy 1,
11km north from Hells
e.

Local First Nation residents named the settlement for the 'Boston men', or Americans, who swarmed over the gravel bar in search of gold. The town survived as a supply centre for later traffic and is now a lumber town.

HASM PROVINCIAL PARK✧✧✧

**Chasm Provincial
Park $** Hwy 97, 20km
:heast from Clinton; tel:
0) 398-4414.

The Painted Chasm (open Jun–Sep) is an enormous river-carved gash through 120m and 15 million years of lava atop the Fraser Plateau. The 1.5km gorge shows multiple layers of reds and yellows that are especially brilliant in late afternoon sun.

LINTON✧

**Clinton and
District Chamber
Commerce** 1522
iboo Hwy; tel: (250) 459-
:0; web:
v.village.clinton.bc.ca/
:n daily in summer,
¬–Fri in winter.

**South Cariboo
Historical Museum**
419 Cariboo Hwy; tel:
0) 459-2442. Open
–Sun 1100–1600.

Straddling the junction of two wagon roads, Clinton was originally called Junction, a name discarded when Queen Victoria decided her Colonial Secretary needed a town named in his honour. Little has changed in the years since.

Clinton remains a quintessential cowboy town where everyone knows everyone else and if you have to ask directions, you most definitely don't belong. Most of the horseback trail riding, hiking, rafting and other outdoor activities take place at guest ranches scattered in the hills and valleys to the west.

South Cariboo Historical Museum✧✧✧, set in an 1890s schoolhouse, chronicles the transition from Gold Rush to cowboy country. Most of the people featured in displays can be found at the **Pioneer Cemetery**, just north from town.

Accommodation and food in Clinton

Many area ranches have discovered that guests are more profitable (and less laborious) than huge cattle herds. The self-proclaimed Guest Ranch Capital of BC has facilities ranging from rustic to ritzy.

Big Bar Guest Ranch $$ tel: (250) 459-2333; web: www. bigbarranch.com, was one of the first and is still among the best for families – horse-riding, hiking, river rafting, backcountry camping trips, Nordic skiing and similar activities are geared for beginners.

Moondance Guest Ranch $$$ tel: (250) 459-7775; web: www. bcguestranches.com, is a luxury ranch with private cabins, gourmet meals and wood-fired saunas.

COTTONWOOD HOUSE HISTORIC PARK✥✥

Another of the roadhouses *en route* to Barkerville, Cottonwoc was a family residence from 1874 to 1951. Period buildings inclu the main house, root cellar and a double barn, all explained costumed interpreters (*$ Hwy 26, 28km east from Hwy 97; tel: (25 992-3997; web: www.heritage.gov.bc.ca/cott/cott.htm; open May–S 0800–1700).*

EMORY CREEK PROVINCIAL PARK✥

Once the site of Emory City, the park commemorates the thousands Chinese workers who built the Canadian Pacific Railway. When Wh miners abandoned the town, Chinese workers moved in and reportec recovered twice as much gold from tailings, the refuse left from mini operations, as the Whites had found in the first pass (*$ Hwy 1, 18 north from Hope; tel: (604) 924-2200; web: www.elp.gov.bc.ca/bcpar explore/parkpgs/emory.htm; open Apr–Oct).*

HAT CREEK RANCH✥✥✥

Hat Creek Ranch $ Hwys 99 & 97; tel: (250) 457-9722; web: www.heritage.gov.bc.ca/hat/ hat.htm Open daily 1000–1800; services and costumed interpreters May–Sep.

Still a working ranch, Hat Creek is the last intact roadhouse on t Cariboo Wagon Road. The 20 heritage buildings include one of t largest barns in BC. Stagecoaches and wagon trains used ran facilities until automobiles began using the road in 1916. Facilit include trail rides, ranching demonstrations, museum displays anc summer First Nations village.

HELLS GATE✥✥✥

Hells Gate $$ Hwy 1, 10.5km north from Alexandra Bridge Provincial Park; tel: (604) 867-9277; web: www.hellsgate.bc.ca/ Open Apr–Oct.

An average of 850,000 cubic metres of water blasts through a spa about the width of a city street every second. River rafters run t rapids daily in summer, but only one steamboat, the *Skuzzy*, ev made it upstream, winching through the raging narrows with bo driven into the rock.

The rapids are more fearsome now. In 1913, a careless Canadi National Railway construction crew touched off a landslide tl choked the river and blocked the salmon run for years. Fish ladd built between 1945 and 1946 helped, but modern salmon runs are l than one-third the pre-1913 volume, even in the best of years.

For the best view of the rapids, ride the **Airtram**✥✥✥ 152m down a across the canyon to a museum, restaurant, gift shop and viewi platform. A suspension bridge crosses the river just downstream a railway trains pass every half-hour.

00 Mile House❖

South Cariboo Visitor Info Centre
2 Cariboo Hwy 97 S; tel:
0) 395-5353; web:
w2.bcinternet.net/
00mile/sccofc

This small town is the service centre for the Central Cariboo and a major Nordic skiing area in winter. It began as a Cariboo Road stage stop in the 1860s. Seventy years later, Lord Martin Cecil, Marquis of Exeter, began and headquartered his Emissaries of Divine Light sect here.

08 Mile House❖❖❖

The one-time roadhouse has become a museum with a collection of heritage buildings moved to the site, including one of the largest log barns in Canada (*$ Hwy 97, 13km north from 100 Mile House; tel: (250) 971-5288; open May–Sept, daily 1000–1800*).

ILLOOET❖❖

Lillooet and District Chamber Commerce 790 Main
tel: (250) 256-4308.
en May–Oct, daily.

Lillooet Museum $
790 Main St; tel: (250)
5-4308. Open May–Oct,
y.

Mile-0-Motel $$
616 Main St; tel: (250)
5-7511, is central and
nfortable.

The main streets of Lillooet are extraordinarily wide to allow the 20-team ox wagons that worked the Cariboo Wagon Road to turn around. The **Mile Zero Cairn**❖❖❖ opposite the Visitor InfoCentre is Mile 0 for the roadhouses and supply points north.

Lillooet Museum❖❖❖ shares a former Anglican church with the Visitor InfoCentre and a trove of mining and pioneer artefacts. A self-guiding museum map lists 15 historical sites on Main Street alone.

ht
s Gate mural

LYTTON✦

ⓘ Lytton and District Chamber of Commerce *400 Fraser St; tel: (250) 455-2523. Open daily Jun–Sep; Oct–May, Mon–Fri.*

Lytton lives by logging and **river rafting✦✦✦**. Companies based here in up and down the Fraser and North Thompson rivers for trips th last a few hours to a few days. Five kilometres of riverfront have a been set aside as a **Gold Panning Recreational Reserve✦✦✦** with han panning only. Ask for information and pans at the **Lytton Museum** which is devoted to the Cariboo Wagon Road and mining history *Next to the InfoCentre; open daily in summer).*

QUESNEL✦✦✦

ⓘ Quesnel and District Visitor Information Center *Le Bourdais Park, 705 Carson Ave; tel: (250) 992-8716. Open daily May–Sep; Oct–Apr, Mon–Fri.*

ⓗ Heritage Corner *Carson and Front Sts.*

Quesnel and District Museum and Archives *$ 705 Carson Ave; tel: (250) 992-9580; web: www.city.quesnel.bc.ca Open daily May–Sep; Oct–Apr, Mon–Fri.*

Sitting at the confluence of the Quesnel and Fraser rivers, Quesnel the last river town before the final overland trek to the gold fields Barkerville. There's still enough gold in the rivers to keep prospect busy. Much of the river has been staked, or claimed, but there's pub panning at the river junction.

Heritage Corner✦✦✦ is the centre of town, marked by mass steamboat and mining machinery in the riverfront park and a sce 1929 bridge across the Fraser River.

Highlight of the **Quesnel and District Museum and Archives✦✦** an extraordinary collection of area photographs from 1865 onwards

Accommodation and food in Quesnel

Cariboo Hotel $$ *254 Front St; tel: (250) 992-2333,* is central.

Cascade Inn $$ *383 St Laurent St; tel: (250) 992-5575,* is quiet and n the river.

Heritage House $$ *102 Carson J St; tel: (250) 992-2700,* is in original Hudson's Bay Company trading post.

YALE✦✦✦

Historic Yale Museum $ 31179 ■ouglas St; tel: (604) 863-324; web: ~ww.heritage.gov.bc.ca/yale/ ■le.htm Open daily Jun–Sep; ⊃ring and autumn, ✓ed–Sun.

St John the Divine Church $ Next to the ■useum.

A handful of people still live in this Gold Rush boom town, though most of the town centre is a pleasant historic district. The interior of the 1859 Anglican **St John the Divine Church**✦✦✦ remains almost unchanged since its consecration. It's the oldest church in BC still on its original foundations. **Yale Museum**✦✦✦, in an 1868 house, is filled with period photographs and exhibits concentrating on the two Sto:lo villages that were once here and Gold Rush memorabilia. Ask about gold panning at **Foreshore Park**✦✦✦, on the riverfront. Costumed interpreters give guided tours in summer, including lantern tours of the pioneer cemetery.

Suggested tour

Total distance: 600km.

Time: Allow 2 days to drive from Hope to Barkerville and a week to explore along the way.

Links: From Hope, Hwy 3 runs east through the **Lower Fraser River Valley** (see page 122) to **Vancouver** (see page 42) and west to the **Cascades** (see page 130) and the **Okanagan Valley** (see page 148). From Cache Creek, Hwy 1 leads east to **Kamloops** (see page 138) and the **Shuswap Lakes** (see page 158). At Quesnel, Hwy 97 continues north to **Prince George** (see page 222).

Route: From **Hope** ❶ (see page 127), Hwy 1 follows the **Fraser River** north into the **Fraser River Canyon** past EMORY CREEK PROVINCIAL PARK to YALE ❷, as far upriver as First Nations canoes and later steamboats ever travelled. Simon Fraser walked down the Fraser Canyon in 1806, complaining that 'We had to pass where no human being should venture. Yet in those places there is a regular footpath impressed, or rather indented, by frequent travelling upon the very rocks.' Gold discoveries along the Fraser River and further north brought calls for a road through the canyon.

By 1864, Royal Engineers had blasted the **Cariboo Wagon Road** through to Lytton, opening the interior to miners, loggers and settlers. Hwy 1 follows the same route, and usually the same roadbed.

Hwy 1 continues north past ALEXANDRA BRIDGE PROVINCIAL PARK ❸ to HELLS GATE ❹, the narrowest spot along an already narrow canyon. The Sto:lo First Nation pegged logs to the canyon wall to create a trail along the sheer rock face. Today, a tram crosses the narrow rapids, which has become a popular destination for kayakers and river rafters.

BOSTON BAR ❺ is one of the few Gold Rush towns along the Fraser River to survive into the modern era. Hwy 1 snakes high above the river toward **Siska**, one of 11 Nlaka'pamux Nation communities along the Fraser Canyon. Several tribal artists are building worldwide reputations carving soapstone from traditional quarries near by. **Siska Art Gallery and Band Museum** (*tel: (250) 455-2539*) displays and sells local art as well as CDs by the Siska Halaw Singers and Drummers.

The highway continues along the canyon to **LYTTON** ❻, at the confluence of the coffee-coloured Fraser and the icy-blue Thompson rivers. The Gold Rush wagon road crosses the river to Hwy 12 climbing through increasingly arid country along the Fraser to **LILLOOET** ❼ and **HAT CREEK**.

Alternative route to Hat Creek: Continue north on Hwy 1 along the canyon of the **North Thompson River**. **Skihist Provincial Park**, 8km north, has fine views of the semi-desert canyon, rafters floating downstream and trains passing on the opposite bank. Lay-bys 5km north

BC gold rushes

Hollywood epics have cast trappers, farmers and Mounties as the romantic heroes of Western Canada, but gold miners deserve the credit for transforming a frontier into a Province.

The story begins with the Hudson's Bay Company, which occasionally accepted bits of gold from its First Nations trading partners but decided not to publicise its steady trickle of mineral wealth. HBC governors feared the kind of rush that had spelt disaster for established businesses in California, which had been wrecked by the tens of thousands of Argonauts who flooded west in 1849.

In early 1858, the HBC relented and shipped about 20kg of raw gold to the nearest mint, San Francisco. The shipment ignited a frenzy. Every craft that could float sailed north, jammed with miners headed for the Fraser River to Hope and beyond.

More than 30,000 miners flooded through Victoria between May and July 1858, nearly all of them Americans. Business prospered, but Government trembled. British authority was little more than a thin line of HBC trading posts. There was nothing to prevent the unruly American mobs from seizing BC as easily as they had taken California from Mexico a decade before.

Britain replaced HBC commercial control with direct rule in November 1858, throwing the company into a decline from which it never recovered. James Douglas, former chief agent for HBC, then governor of Vancouver Island, became governor of the newly created Crown Colony of British Columbia. He promptly requested British road builders, British troops and British magistrates to enforce British law.

The gambit succeeded. Bewigged justices backed by a handful of soldiers, and eventually the Royal Canadian Mounted Police, kept BC British through waves of miners rushing north to mineral strikes on the Boundary, Similkameen and Thompson rivers, the Okanagan Valley, Cariboo Mountains, the Yukon and the Kootenay Mountains. By the time the dust had settled around the turn of the 20th century, Gold Rush trails had grown into a network of roads, railways and ferry routes that is still recognisable today.

overlook **Little Hells Gate**, a popular spot to watch salmon leaping upstream in autumn and rafters shooting the same rapids in summer. Most rafts launch just upstream from **Goldpan Provincial Park**.

Eleven kilometres north are **Spences Bridge** and **Murray Falls**, tumbling over red cliffs directly into the river. Watch for ospreys nesting in tall trees along the river (the nests look like untidy piles of sticks) and bighorn sheep on nearby cliffs. In winter, sheep often descend to lick salt from the highway. There are several seasonal ice-cream and fruit stands north of town.

ASHCROFT MANOR ❽, 13km north, is a welcome splash of shady green against the desert hills on the way to Cache Creek and the junction with Hwy 97. Hwy 1 turns east toward **Kamloops** (*see page 138*). Continue north on Hwy 97 to Hat Creek.

At Lillooet, turn on to Hwy 99, which corkscrews up rolling benchlands along the original wagon road track. Some of the natural terraces are irrigated, others are covered by low black sheets of plastic that shade crops of ginseng. Near the top of the grade is the hamlet of **Pavilion** and the **Pavilion General Store**, one of the oldest buildings in BC still on its original site. The mountain vistas are stunning and the store is the only ice-cream and cold-drink stop in the dusty summer heat.

The Cariboo Wagon Road continues north to **Kelly Lake** and Clinton as Pavilion Mountain Road, a steep gravel road that is passable in good weather. The highway loops east and south into **Marble Canyon**, named for 1000m cliffs of red and yellow marble, before emerging at **HAT CREEK RANCH ❾** and Hwy 97.

The hills turn green as the road climbs and conifers replace sagebrus on the way to **CLINTON** ❿, a centre for cattle and guest ranches. Ju: north is **CHASM PROVINCIAL PARK** ⓫, a vast gorge cut through 1 million years of lava eruptions. Increasing rainfall brings denser fores on the way north to **100 MILE HOUSE** ⓬ and **108 MILE HOUSE** ⓭ one-time roadhouses named for the distance from Lillooet on th Cariboo Wagon Road.

Further north through the forests is **150 Mile House**, the last sto before **Williams Lake** (*see page 202*) and Hwy 20 west across th Chilcotin to **Bella Coola** (*see page 200*).

Hwy 97 continues north to **Soda Creek**, the terminus of the Caribo Wagon Road and the head of navigation along 650km of the Uppe Fraser River to Quesnel and **Prince George** (*see page 222*). Rai replaced steamboats in the 1920s, but carbon dioxide still bubbles int the creek from calcium carbonate in the streambed.

There are few signs of settlement to the north until **Marguerite Ferry** an unpowered ferry across the Fraser and the **Fort Alexandri Monument**. The monument marks the end of Alexander Mackenzie 1793 journey down the Fraser and the site of an 1821 North Wes Company trading post. Mackenzie turned back on the advice c Dalkeh traders, and returned upstream to **QUESNEL** ⓮ and struck ou overland to reach the Pacific Ocean at Bella Coola.

From Quesnel, turn east on Hwy 26 through the mountains t **COTTONWOOD HOUSE HISTORIC PARK** ⓯, another Gold Rus: roadhouse. Eleven kilometres east is **Blessing's Grave Historic Par** surrounding the isolated grave of one of the handful of miner murdered during the hectic years of the Cariboo Gold Rush. Just eas is **Wells**, born in a second Cariboo Gold Rush during the 1930s, an **BARKERVILLE** ⓰, the gold mining centre so many thousands c miners laboured so long to reach.

Publican creates backwater

Williams Lake (*see page 202*) missed the Cariboo Gold Rush when a pub owner declined a short-term loan to Cariboo Wagon Road builders. Instead, the contractors built through 150 Mile House, where a more obliging publican made the loan and a quick fortune on the new road traffic. Williams Lake languished until the 1920s when the railway, now BC Rail's **Cariboo Prospector** (*see page 166*), arrived from Lillooet.

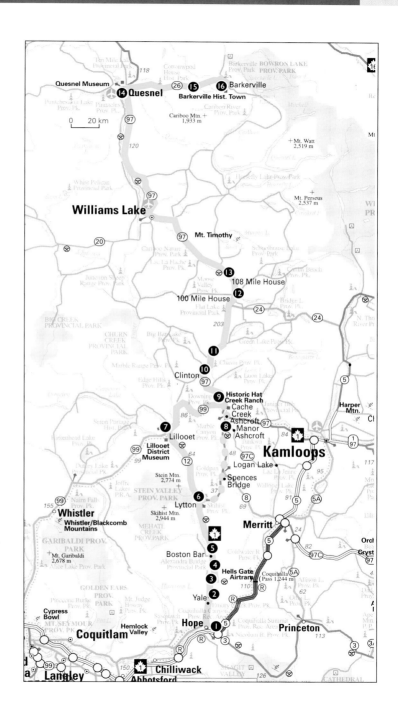

Cariboo–Chilcotin

Ratings

Mountains	●●●●●
Nature	●●●●●
Outdoor activities	●●●●●
Parks	●●●●●
Scenery	●●●●●
Children	●●●●○
History	●●●●○
Wildlife	●●●●○

This is Canada's answer to the Wild West, a semi wilderness of forests, mountains, lakes and prairies, land where towns are small, few and *very* far between. It's land where ghosts of gold seekers haunt decaying ghos towns that once eclipsed Vancouver, a land where cattl outnumber people and dreams grow as big as the sky is wide

The Cariboo lies east, dense forests that stretch from th Cariboo Mountains, in eastern BC, to the Fraser River. Th Chilcotin is west, a great grassy plain rising from the Frase and running to the feet of the Coast Range, home to some c the largest cattle ranches on earth and vast tracts that hav yet to be properly mapped.

West again is the glacial crest of the Coast Range, droppin precipitously into the Pacific Ocean. It's hard to get here and once arrived, even harder to forget.

ALEXIS CREEK✧

Alexis Creek *112km west of Williams Lake.*

With nearly 250 people, this Chilcotin metropolis has petrol, a RCMP station, post office, grocery store and a BC Forest Service office

Accommodation in Alexis Creek

Chilcotin Hotel $$ *tel: (250) 394-4214,* is the only hotel and restaurant in town.

ANAHIM LAKE✧✧✧

This largely First Nations village is the largest in the West Chilcotin and a centre for fishing the Dean and other

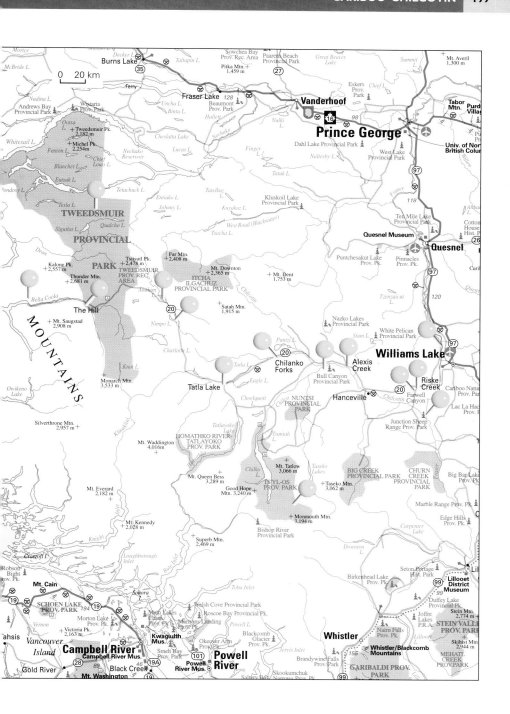

0   20 km

Morice L.
McBride L.

Decker L.
Burns Lake

Taltapin L.

Sowchea Bay
Prov. Rec. Area

Paarens Beach
Provincial Park

Great Beaver
Lake

Summit

Mt. Averil
1,300 m

Pitka Mtn.
1,459 m

Ferry

Eskers
Prov.
Park

Chief L.

Tabor
Mtn.

Purd
Villa

Fraser Lake 128

Uncha L.

Beaumont
Prov. Park

Binta L.

Hallett

Nulki
L.

Vanderhoof

98

Prince George

Univ. of Nor
British Colu

Nadina L.
Andrews Bay
Provincial Park

Wistaria
Prov. L.

Nechako
Reservoir

Outsa
L.

Tweedsmuir Pk.
2,182 m

Michel Pk.
2,254 m

Whitesail L.

Fenton L.

Chief
Louis L.

Blanchet L.

Eutsuk L.

Pondosy L.

Tetachuck L.

Tesla L.

TWEEDSMUIR

Sigutlat L.

Qualcho L.

Dean

PROVINCIAL

Kalone Pk.
2,557 m

Tsitsutl Pk.
2,478 m

PARK

Thunder Mtn.
2,681 m

TWEEDSMUIR
PROV. REC.
AREA

Bella Coola

The Hill

Mt. Saugstad
2,908 m

Cheslatta Lake

Lucas L.

Finger

Dahl Lake Provincial Park

West Lake
Provincial Park

97

118

Kluskoil Lake
Provincial Park

West Road (Blackwater)

Tsacha L.

Entiako L.

Johnny L.

Kuyakuz L.

Far Mtn.
2,408 m

Mt. Downton
2,365 m

ITCHA
ILGACHUZ
PROVINCIAL PARK

Mt. Dent
1,753 m

Ten Mile Lake
Provincial Park

Cotton
House
Hist. P

Quesnel Museum

Quesnel

26

Puntchesakut Lake
Prov. Pk.

Pinnacles
Provincial Pk.

Cari

97

Quesn

MOUNTAINS

Monarch Mtn.
3,533 m

Silverthrone Mtn.
2,957 m

Knot L.

Owikeno
Lake

Klinaklini

Mt. Waddington
4,016m

Anahim

Nimpo L.

Charlotte L.

Satah Mtn.
1,915 m

20

Nazko Lakes
Provincial Park

Puntzi L.

Tatla L.

Stum L.

White Pelican
Provincial Park

20

**Chilanko
Forks**

**Alexis
Creek**

Williams Lake

97

Bull Canyon
Provincial Park

20

**Riske
Creek**

Cariboo Natu
Prov. Par

Tatla Lake

Eagle L.

Choelquoit

Chilco
L.

NUNTSI
PROVINCIAL
PARK

Hanceville

Farwell
Canyon

Chilcotin

Lac La Hac
Prov. P

120

Tenzaicut L.

Tatlayoko
Lake

HOMATHKO RIVER-
TATLAYOKO
PROV. PARK

Tsuniah L.

Junction Sheep
Range Prov. Park

Mt. Queen Bess
3,289 m

Chilko L.

Mt. Tatlow
3,066 m

Taseko
Lakes

BIG CREEK
PROVINCIAL PARK

CHURN
CREEK
PROVINCIAL
PARK

Big Bar Lake
Prov. Pk.

Mt. Everard
2,182 m

Good Hope
Mtn. 3,240 m

TSYL-OS
PROV. PARK

Taseko Mtn.
3,062 m

Marble Range Prov. Pk.

Mt. Kennedy
2,028 m

Knight

Monmouth Mtn.
3,194 m

Edge Hills
Prov. Pk.

Superb Mtn.
2,469 m

Bishop River
Provincial Park

Carpenter
Lake

Downton

Cracroft I.

Loughborough
Inlet

Boat Inlet

Toba Inlet

Seton Portage
Hist. P.

Lil

**Lillooet
District
Museum**

Birkenhead Lake
Prov. Pk.

99

99

Robson
Bight
ov. Pk.

Mt. Cain

Sonora

Duffey Lake
Provincial Park

Joffre
Lakes
P.R.A.

Stein Mtn.
2,774 m

**STEIN VALLE
PROV. PARK**

19

**SCHOEN LAKE
PROV. PARK** 194

19

Vernon

Morton Lake
Prov. Pk.

Victoria L.
2,163 m

Kwagiulth
Mus.

Nymph Lakes
Prov. Pk.

Walsh Cove Provincial Park

Roscoe Bay Provincial Pk.

Matsons Landing

Powell L.

Blackcomb
Glacier
Prov. Pk.

Whistler

Nairn Falls
Prov. Pk.

155

Skihist Mtn
2,944 m

MEHATL
CREEK
PROV. PARK

**Vancouver
Island**

Campbell River
Campbell River Mus.

28

89

Black Creek

Okeover Arm
Prov. Pk.

Smelt Bay
Prov. Pk.

101

**Powell
River Mus.**

**Powell
River**

Jervis Inlet

Brandywine Falls
Prov. Pk.

**Whistler/Blackcomb
Mountains**

Skookumchuck

**GARIBALDI PROV.
PARK**

ahsis

Gold River

Mt. Washington

19A

Mt. Washington

Saltery Bay

Narrows Prov.

99

AC Christensen General Store tel: (250) 742-3266, is the best source of area information and supplies.

nearby rivers. **Anahim Lake Resort** offers fishing, air taxi service, hiking, riding and general relaxation. The locally renowned August Stampede is authentic here, much less commercial than early July's Calgary Stampede. (**Anahim Lake Resort $$** *Hwy 20; tel: (250) 742-3200.*)

BELLA COOLA❖❖

Tourism Bella Coola *10 Cliff St; tel: (250) 799-5268 or (888) 863-1181. Contact the TIC for information about the Bella Coola Valley Museum, Mackenzie Highway, open Jun–Sep.*

Acwsalcta Nuxalk Nation School $ *4km east off Hwy 20.*

Hagensborg *Hwy 20, 18km east of Bella Coola.*

Sir Alexander Mackenzie Provincial Park and Mackenzie Rock $ *60km west on Dean Channel, no land access. Ask about transport at the museum.*

Thorsen Creek Petroglyphs $ *Off Hwy 20, east of Bella Coola. Ask for directions at the museum.*

Captain George Vancouver sailed up fjord-like North Bentinck Arm to Bella Coola in 1793, just weeks before Alexander Mackenzie walked down the narrow valley to the sea. Norwegian farmers arrived in 1894 to share the valley with Nuxalk (Bella Coola) First Nations. Town and fjord are ringed by sheer mountains, providing endless opportunities for fishing, hiking and outdoor adventure.

The **Acwsalcta Nuxalk Nation School**❖❖❖ has some of the finest First Nations artwork on public display along the coast.

Bella Coola Valley Museum❖, in a 19th-century schoolhouse and surveyor's cabin, has Hudson's Bay Company relics and Norwegian goods.

Norwegian farmers at **Hagensborg**❖ were Bella Coola's first non-Native residents in modern times. Many of the century-old homes and barns show adze marks produced by the original builders.

Mackenzie Rock in **Sir Alexander Mackenzie Provincial Park**❖❖ was the final stop of Mackenzie's 1793 trek across Canada. He painted a message in vermilion and bear grease, *Alexander Mackenzie, from Canada, by land, the twenty-second of July, one thousand, seven hundred and ninety-three*, which was later chiselled into the rock.

The **Thorsen Creek Petroglyphs**❖❖❖ are dozens of carvings lining rocks along the creek.

Accommodation and food in Bella Coola

Bella Coola Valley Inn $$ *Mackenzie St; tel: (250) 799-5316*, is the best motel in town and the closest to the BC Ferries dock.

Tallheo Cannery $$ *Across the harbour from Bella Coola; tel: (250) 982-2344; web: www.centralcoastbc.com/tallheo*

BULL CANYON PROVINCIAL RECREATIONAL AREA❖❖❖

This pleasant picnic and camping stop along the grey-green Chilcotin River was a cattle round-up point and the site of a decisive battle between Tsilhqot'in and Secwepemc bands. (**Bull Canyon Provincial Recreation Area $** *Hwy 20, 6km west of Alexis Creek; tel: (250) 398-4414; web: www.elp.gov.bc.ca/bcparks/explore/parkpgs/bullcan.htm*)

CHILANKO FORKS✧✧✧

Chilanko Forks *62km west of Alexis ʀeek.*

Chilanko Forks is a traditional Chilcotin town with a general store and petrol station. A marsh by the airport access road is good for beaver and muskrat-spotting.

ᶠARWELL CANYON✧✧✧

Farwell Canyon *19km south of Hwy 20 ₒm Riske Creek.*

ᵢght
.ᵣwell Canyon

The Chilcotin River has cut a deep canyon through soft golden cliffs, creating flat-topped hoodoos (columns of rock formed by erosion) capped by sand dunes that shift with the wind.

ᵀHE HILL✧✧✧

The Hill *Hwy 20, east of Bella Coola.*

The final barrier to land travel between Bella Coola and the rest of BC was finally breached in 1953 – by local bulldozer operators who were tired of government highway engineers saying a road down the sheer western face of the Coast Range was impossible. Views from the single-track gravel road are stupendous, but there are no verges or lay-bys.

ᵁNCTION SHEEP RANGE PROVINCIAL PARK✧✧✧

This isolated park protects the world's largest herd of California bighorn sheep, as well as some 40 or so butterfly species and countless birds (**$** *15km south of Hwy 20; tel: (250) 398-4414; web: www.elp.gov. bc.ca/bcparks/explore/parkpgs/ junction.htm).*

ᴺIMPO LAKE✧✧✧

Dean River Resort *$$ tel: (250) 742-₃1.*

This 12-km lake claims to be BC's floatplane capital for the many daily charter flights to remote rivers and lakes. **Dean River Resort** is the most comfortable of several lake-front fishing resorts.

ᴿISKE CREEK✧

Riske Creek *46km west of Williams Lake.*

The tiny farming town of Riske Creek is named after a 19th-century Polish farmer, an early settler in the area.

Accommodation and food in Riske Creek

Chilcotin Lodge $$ *Riske Creek; tel: (250) 659-5646,* is a former hunting lodge turned bed and breakfast, restaurant and campground.

TATLA LAKE✦✦✦

 **Tatla Lake $** *109km from Alexis Creek.*

Lake and town provide the half-way point between Williams Lake and Bella Coola. Nordic skiing is a popular winter activity, rivalling lake diving in the summer for appeal.

TS'YL-OS PROVINCIAL PARK✦✦✦

Lakes and streams in this undeveloped wilderness produce one-quarter of the entire Fraser River salmon run. Apart from two gravel roads off Hwy 20, the only access is by air, boat, horse or foot (**$** *100km south of Hwy 20 from Lees Corner; tel: (250) 398-4414; web: www.elp.gov.bc.ca bcparks/explore/parkpgs/ts.htm*

TWEEDSMUIR PROVINCIAL PARK✦✦✦

Tweedsmuir is 980,000 hectares of wilderness outside a narrow corridor along Hwy 20. The best easy walks are on the Bella Coola side along the **Atnarko River Spawning Channels✦✦✦**, where grizzly and black bears *always* have the right of way (**$** *Headquarters on Hwy 20 east of Bella Coola; tel: (250) 398-4414; web: www.elp.gov.bc.ca/bcpark explore/parkpgs/tweed.htm).*

WILLIAMS LAKE✦

❶ Williams Lake and District Chamber of Commerce *1148 S Broadway (Hwy 97, south end of town); tel: (250) 392-5025; web: www.lake.com Open daily Jul–Aug; Sep–Jun, Mon–Fri.*

This is the only real town between Hope and Quesnel, a cowboy city that has expanded into forestry, mining, agriculture and tourism.

Williams Lake's public gallery, the **Stationhouse Gallery✦✦** concentrates on BC artists, while **Williams Lake Museum✦✦✦** focuses on the ranching, rodeo and cowboy history of the Cariboo–Chilcotin region.

Scout Island Nature Centre✦✦✦, a small marsh, has lakeside walking paths, wildlife watching and a summer nature centre.

Suggested tour

Total distance: 465km.

Time: Allow 10–12 hours to drive; 2–5 days to explore.

Fraser Inn $$ 285 Donald Rd; tel: (250) 98-7055; web: www.fraserinn.com, is the largest hotel in town.

Mowat's Waterside $$ 397 Borland; tel: (250) 392-7395, is a bed and breakfast a short walk from Scout Island.

Great Cariboo Steak Company $$ Fraser Inn, 285 Donald Road; tel: (250) 398-7395, known for oversized steaks.

Hearth Restaurant $$ 99 3rd Ave; tel: (250) 398-8831, in the Cariboo Friendship Society, has open-beam First Nations décor.

Stationhouse Gallery $ / N Mackenzie Ave (old BC Rail station); tel: (250) 392-1113. Open daily.

Williams Lake Museum 113 N 4th Ave; tel: (250) 392-7404. Open Jun–Sep, Mon–Sat; Oct–May, Tue–Sat.

Scout Island Nature Centre $ West end of town, off Hwy 97 east of city centre; tel: (250) 398-8532. Open daily.

Links: From Bella Coola, BC Ferries **Discovery Coast** route (*see page 106*) leads south to **Port Hardy** and **North Vancouver Island** (*see page 96*). From Williams Lake, the **Gold Rush Trail** (*see page 186*) leads north toward **Prince George** (*see page 222*) or south toward **Hope** (*see page 127*).

Route: From **WILLIAMS LAKE** ❶, take Hwy 20 west to the **Fraser River**. The river marks the edge of the **Chilcotin Plateau**, which stretches west toward the **Coast Range**. **Becher's Prairie** forms the eastern section of the plateau, rolling grasslands dotted with boulders deposited by retreating glaciers. Nest boxes on fence posts help attract birds which feast on the clouds of mosquitoes hovering above the thousands of tiny lakes and ponds scattered across the Chilcotin.

The enormous antennae rising from the prairie form part of the Loran-C navigation system. A good gravel road 9.5km west leads 16km east to the fairy-tale hoodoos of Farwell Canyon and **JUNCTION SHEEP RANGE PROVINCIAL PARK** ❷.

Detour: Follow the gravel road along the rolling curves of the almost treeless plain to **FARWELL CANYON** ❸ and a wooden bridge over the **Chilcotin River**. There are early First Nations rock paintings on the overhang at the south end of the bridge. Local Tsilhqot'in fishers net salmon from the river in summer and autumn, drying their catch on racks near by. The road loops 50km loop back to Hwy 20 at **Lees Corner**.

The bright yellow log buildings 1.5km west of the turn-off are the town of **Riske Creek** ❹. Continue west, following traditional wooden fences snaking along the road. One of the best views across the Chilcotin is from a hilltop rest area 35km west of Chilcotin Lodge and Riske Creek. Another gravel road leads south to **Hanceville**, named for Tom Hance, the first rancher in the area, and **TS'YL-OS PROVINCIAL PARK** ❺.

Hwy 20 continues westwards to **ALEXIS CREEK** ❻, the largest town in eastern Chilcotin, 10km west. **BULL CANYON PROVINCIAL RECREATION AREA** ❼ is another 9km west. Views westward are stunning as the road gradually rises toward **CHILANKO FORKS** ❽ and a section of gravel highway.

Continue west toward Tatla Lake. There's a wonderful view across the lake and valley from a hilltop viewpoint 15km west of Chilanko Forks. **Pollywog Marsh**, 12km west of the lay-by, is a pleasant lakeside rest stop. **TATLA LAKE** ❾, another 10km west, is the western edge of the Chilcotin Plateau and halfway to Bella Coola. It's a pleasant drive in summer, but don't be taken in by the weather. Winter temperatures regularly hit -50°C with 50kph winds driving blinding blizzards.

Kleena Kleene is well into the slowly rising foothills of the Coast Range. The road continues up toward **NIMPO LAKE** ❿, where pavement begins again for the benefit of several lakeside fishing lodges.

Just west is the **Dean River**, famed for fine steelhead and trout fishing. A highway marker commemorates the 1864 **Chilcotin War**, when Tsilhqo'tin warriors killed 18 roadbuilders, packers and settlers who were attempting to cut a route from Bute Inlet (opposite Campbell River on Vancouver Island) across the Chilcotin to the Cariboo gold fields. Five of the warriors, including the war chief, were executed by Colonial troops, but the road was abandoned, sparing the Chilcotin from smallpox and land-hungry settlers for a few more years. A provincial enquiry in 1993 granted five posthumous pardons and a memorial was erected.

The pavement disappears again at **ANAHIM LAKE** ⓫, the closest the Chilcotin has to a modern town. Gravel roads lead north along the Dean River, but check locally for conditions before setting out. Beyond the last tyre tracks lies the Nuxalk-Carrier Grease Trail east to the Fraser and west to Bella Coola.

From Anahim Lake, the gravel road climbs into the Coast Range and **TWEEDSMUIR PROVINCIAL PARK** ⓬, which begins at 1524-m **Heckman Pass**. There are good views of the multicoloured **Rainbow Mountains** from the **Tsulko River**, east of the pass. Local First Nation bands mined obsidian from the Rainbows, a string of ancient volcanoes stained red, yellow and purple by mineral deposits.

Just west of Heckman Pass is a brake check stop at the top of **THE HILL** ⓭. There are no verges, no guard-rails and no lay-bys in a 19-km

Alexander Mackenzie and the Grease Trail

North West Company explorer Alexander Mackenzie has gone down in Canadian history as 'The First Man West' for his 1793 overland crossing to the Pacific Ocean at Bella Coola. Mackenzie was the first non-Native to cross North America beyond Mexico and return to tell the tale, but it was hardly a trail-breaking wilderness expedition. Mackenzie and company were shepherded every step of the way along an ancient network of trails and trade routes that spanned the continent. In the Chilcotin, he followed the Great Road, the Nuxalk-Carrier Grease Trail linking coastal Heiltsuk, Kwakwaka'wakw and Nuxalk First Nations with the interior. The trail was named for the Dakelh (or Carrier) peoples who traded oolichan oil for furs, obsidian and other goods from the Coast Range to the Rockies. Part of the rugged route has been reborn as the **Alexander Mackenzie Heritage Trail/Nuxalk-Carrier Grease Trail**, 420km from Quesnel (see page 192), on the Fraser River, to Bella Coola. The foot and horse track parallels Hwy 20 from Tweedsmuir Provincial Park at **Burnt Bridge**, 49km east of Bella Coola, to the sea.

stack of single track, hairpin turns that drops 1300m to the head of the Bella Coola Valley. Use low gear to creep down (or up) the 18 per cent grade to prevent brakes from overheating and failing.

A hard road surface begins again at the bottom of The Hill, running through dense forest along the Atnarko and Bella Coola rivers. The valley opens and broadens toward the sea. **Hagensborg** still has many of the square-cut, hand-hewn buildings left by early Norwegian settlers a century ago. The town of **BELLA COOLA** ⑭ sits at the mouth of the Bella Coola River, at the head of **North Bentinck Arm**.

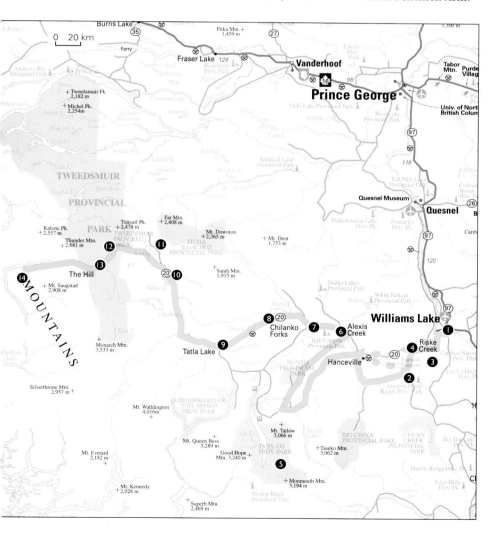

Ratings

Children	●●●●●
Nature	●●●●●
Scenery	●●●●●
Art	●●●●
History	●●●●
Museums	●●●●
Outdoor activities	●●●
Parks	●●●

ⓘ Visitor InfoCentre
100 First Avenue (at McBride Street, Hwy 16); tel: (250) 624-5637; web: www.pgonline. com/tourism/princerupert/ index.html Open daily.

Weather Bring rain gear. Prince Rupert gets more than twice as much rain as Vancouver, an average of 2552mm annually.

Prince Rupert

Prince Rupert is BC's most famous transit hub, the city that everyone goes through but almost no one comes to. Convoys of RVers and independent travellers drive through the city on the way to and from Vancouver Island or the Queen Charlotte Islands via BC Ferries. Schools of sport fishers fly through on the way to isolated lodges up and down the BC coast and along interior mountain rivers. Even the train passengers who roll through the centre of town are on the way to somewhere else, usually a circular tour that combines rail, motor coach and ferry from Vancouver to Vancouver by way of Vancouver Island and Prince Rupert.

What they're missing is a pleasant, albeit damp, city that is big enough to offer good food, good coffee and good Internet connections but small enough to be walkable and friendly. It's a hub worth exploring.

Getting there

Air The Prince Rupert airport is on Digby Island, west of downtown with ferry and bus connections to the city centre terminal in Ruper Square Mall. If leaving by air, be sure to check bus schedules as well a airline schedules – miss the bus and you miss the flight.

Floatplane flights use the **Seal Cove Seaplane Base** east from downtown.

BC Ferries *Ferry Terminal at the end of Hwy 16, 2km west of downtown tel: (250) 386-3431 or (888) 223-3779; web: www.bcferries.bc.ca.* BC Ferries connect with **Port Hardy** *(see page 101)* on Vancouver Islan and **Skidegate** *(see page 120)* in the Queen Charlotte Islands.

Road *Hwy 16*, the *Yellowhead Highway*, is the only road link with th rest of BC.

VIA Rail *1st Avenue, on the waterfront; tel: (250) 627-7589 or (800) 561 8630; web: www.viarail.ca*

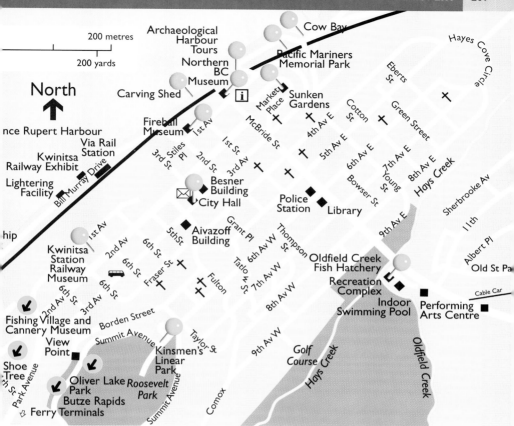

North

↑

200 metres

200 yards

Archaeological Harbour Tours

Northern BC Museum

Carving Shed

nce Rupert Harbour

Kwinitsa Via Rail Station
Railway Exhibit

Lightering Facility

Bill Murray Drive

hip

Kwinitsa Station Railway Museum

Fishing Village and Cannery Museum
View Point

Shoe Tree

Park Avenue

Ferry Terminals

Oliver Lake Park
Butze Rapids

Roosevelt Park

Borden Street

Summit Avenue

Kinsmen's Linear Park

Taylor St

Comox

Summit Avenue

Cow Bay

Pacific Mariners Memorial Park

Sunken Gardens

Market Place

McBride St

Fireball Museum

1st Av

3rd Stiles Pl
2nd St
3rd St
3rd Av

1st St

Besner Building
City Hall

Aivazoff Building

5th St
6th St
6th St
Fraser St

2nd Av
1st Av

Grant Pl

Fulton

8th Av W

9th Av W

Golf Course

4th Av E

5th Av E

6th Av E

7th Av E

8th Av E

Bowser St
Young St

Police Station   Library

Cotton St

Green Street

Eberts St

Hayes Cove Circle

Hays Creek

Sherbrooke Av

11th

Albert Pl

Old St Pa

Thompson St

7th Av W

Tatlow St

Oldfield Creek Fish Hatchery

Recreation Complex

Indoor Swimming Pool

Performing Arts Centre

Cable Car

Oldfield Creek

Hays Creek

Dreams delayed

Prince Rupert is a speculator's dream become reality, albeit several decades delayed. In the early years of the 20th century, railway baron Charles Hays envisioned a great port and gleaming city amid the rain forests of Northern BC. The commercial lure was location, days closer to Asian markets than Vancouver.

Hays sailed to England to raise capital for his grand project, then capped a successful trip by sailing home aboard the maiden voyage of the grandest ship afloat, the *Titanic*. When the *Titanic* sank, so did Hays' dreams. Planned hotels were never built. Trains rolled into Prince Rupert just in time to hit World War I. The Grand Trunk Pacific railroad came to Prince Rupert, but then disappeared in 1919, absorbed by the Canadian National Railway. Prince Rupert stagnated as an out-of-the-way fishing port. It took another World War and 50 years for transpacific shipping to catch up with Hays' vision. Cargo ships can dock at the railway terminal in Prince Rupert and have their cargoes halfway across the continent by the time competitors dock in Vancouver.

Sights

Archaeological Harbour Tours $
Museum of Northern BC; tel: (250) 624-3207 and Metlakatla Development Corp; tel: (250) 628-3201. Tours daily Jun–Sep.

Butze Rapids $ Off Hwy 16 south of town.

Carving Shed $ One block east from the Museum of Northern BC; tel: (250) 624-3207. Open irregular hours.

City Hall $ 3rd Ave W and 3rd St.

Cow Bay $ East from downtown.

Firehall Museum $ 200 1st Avenue W; tel: (250) 624-4475. Open daily in summer; by appointment in winter.

Kinsmen's Linear Park $ A long greenbelt around Prince Rupert. The InfoCentre has self-guiding map brochures.

Archaeological Harbour Tours✦✦✦

In the late 1700s, ten Tsimshian First Nations bands, around 800 people, lived in some 60 villages around present-day Prince Rupert harbour, one of the largest population centres on the entire continent. The village sites are still there, complete with petroglyphs, midden and spectacular island scenery. The Museum of Northern BC (see page 209) and the Metlakatla Development Corporation offer daily boat tours with experienced guides. Three-hour trips stop at Metlakatla, former utopian community founded in 1862 on the site of an ancient village, plus other sites along the Venn Passage. A day-long tour visit Pike Island, which has had at least three Tsimshian villages over the past 2000 or so years.

Butze Rapids✦✦

The narrow rapids reverse flow with the tide, with the boiling foaming water at its most scenic as the tide falls. The Tsimshian calle the white foam floating from the rapids *kaien*, which became the name of the island Prince Rupert occupies.

Carving Shed✦✦✦

Part of the Museum of Northern BC, the carving shed houses totem poles and other works in wood in the making. Carvers are usually happ to explain the significance of the traditional designs and images.

City Hall✦✦✦

Inside are ordinary municipal offices, but the outside is art deco. To the side is a small plaza with a fine totem pole and statue of city founder Charles Hays.

Cow Bay✦✦✦

Named for cattle that were made to swim ashore to a dairy in 1901, Cow Bay is a combination fishing harbour and trendy haven. Look for coffee shops, bistros, restaurants and boats. Mailboxes, garbage cans and other surfaces are decorated with Jersey spots and similar bovine motifs.

Firehall Museum✦

Fire buffs make a pilgrimage just to see Prince Rupert's beautifull restored 1925 REO Speedwagon fire engine. The museum display dozens of badges, patches and pins donated by visiting firemen from around the world and firefighting equipment dating back to the town's beginnings in 1906.

Kinsmen's Linear Park✦✦

Less a park and more a system of interconnected walking paths an greenbelts, Kinsmen's offers a circular tour of Prince Rupert, from the

Kwinitsa Station Railway Museum $
*acific Place, 1st Ave and Bill Murray Way; tel: (250) 627-1915. Open May–Sep, daily; Oct–Apr, by appointment.

Museum of Northern BC $ 1st Ave W and McBride St; tel: (250) 624-3207. Open Mon–Sat 0900–2000, Sun 0900–1700 in summer; Mon–Sat 0900–1700 in winter.

ferry terminal at the waterfront to Cow Bay and around to the seaplane base at Seal Cove, along a creek to McClymont Park and back to the centre of town through a strip of cedar forest along Hays Creek. Sections of the park may be closed for maintenance; check routes at the InfoCentre.

Kwinitsa Station Railway Museum**
The 1911 building was one of 400 identical stations built on the Grand Trunk Pacific line between Prince Rupert and Winnipeg, Manitoba. Only four stations survive; this one was barged 75km down the Skeena River in 1985 and restored as a railway museum.

Museum of Northern BC***
The airy, longhouse-style building is one of the finest museums in BC, as well as offices for the Tsimshian Tribal Council. The focus is 10,000 years of local Tsimshian history (the name means 'people going into the river of mists'), stretching from islands off Prince Rupert and up the Skeena River as far as Kitselas Canyon above Terrace (*see page 219*). The Tribal Council is heavily involved in museum research and displays, documenting village sites, artefacts and oral histories, creating databases and publishing a variety of scientific and popular books. Museum and Council also co-operate on archaeological tour programmes to take visitors to village sites on outlying islands and explain artefacts in their original setting.

North Pacific Historic Fishing Village & Cannery Museum***
BC's oldest surviving salmon cannery (and a National Historic Site) is the last of 19 salmon canneries that once dotted the shores of the lower Skeena River. More than 1200 canneries from Alaska south to

Right
Prince Rupert's shoe tree

North Pacific Historic Fishing Village & Cannery Museum $ *1889 Skeena Dr, Port Edward (11km off Hwy 16 at the south end of Kaien Island); tel: (250) 628-3538. Open daily, programmes May–Sep.*

Sacramento, California, were part of the trade at its height in the earl 20th century before refrigeration and fish farms made fresh salmon fillets an everyday commodity. The cannery is being restored to show the fishing and canning process as well as daily life a century ago. The setting, a long waterfront boardwalk, docks and employee housing overlooking Inverness Pass, is one of the most scenic in the area.

Oldfield Creek Fish Hatchery✵
Started as a classroom project in the late 1970s when local coho

Oldfield Creek Fish Hatchery $ *Off Vantage Rd from Hwy 16; t: (250) 624-6733. Open daily.*

Oliver Lake Park $ *Off Hwy 16, 6km south of Prince Rupert.*

Pacific Mariners Memorial Park $ *North and east from the Museum of Northern BC, overlooking the harbour.*

Shoe Tree $ *Hwy 16 south of Prince Rupert. Ask for directions at the InfoCentre.*

Sunken Gardens $ *East from the Carving Shed.*

Totem Tour $ *Self-guided walking tour.*

salmon runs had dwindled to just nine spawning fish, the hatchery has played a visible role in increasing the salmon population and heightening local concern over the impact that logging and other human activities can have on fish habitat and survival. Local high-school students convinced city authorities and local service organisations to contribute time, labour and money to build a small salmon hatchery and restore spawning beds in Oldfield Creek. Salmon spawned at Oldfield have been used to recreate runs on other local streams that had lost their entire native fish population.

Oliver Lake Park✢✢✢
This small park protects a section of muskeg and wet forest that includes carnivorous plants and naturally stunted trees (visible from boardwalks) that look like carefully tended bonsai specimens.

Pacific Mariners Memorial Park✢
This harbour-front park commemorates a local fishing boat that disappeared in a storm with all hands. Displays include a stature depicting a fisherman at his wheel surrounded by a wall listing local sailors lost at sea and the restored wreckage of a small Japanese fishing boat that drifted from Japan to BC in the 1980s.

Shoe Tree✢✢✢
No one is quite sure how or when the *Tree of Lost Soles* got its start, but decades of mis-matched shoes have ended up nailed to the trunk, draped in the branches and piled around the base of this huge tree.

Sunken Gardens✢✢✢
The gardens were originally dug as the foundation for a 1920s provincial courthouse that was later moved a few hundred metres closer to town. The site was used for storage during World War II and later turned into a public garden.

Totem Tour✢✢✢
Tsimshian carvers have created dozens of totem poles and other wooden carvings that have been erected around Prince Rupert. The InfoCentre and Museum have self-guided tour brochures to totems throughout Kaien Island.

Accommodation and food

Motel Row is along 2nd Avenue W, between the ferry docks and downtown.

Cow Bay B&B $$ *Cow Bay; tel: (250) 627-1804*, is the most popular bed and breakfast in Cow Bay.

The Crest Hotel $$$ *222 W First St; tel: (250) 624-6771; web:*

Above
Prince Rupert harbour

www.cresthotel.bc.ca, has the best water views and the most expensive hotel rooms in town.

Inverness Lodge $$ *North Pacific Cannery Village; tel: (250) 628-3375* is the only accommodation on the National Historic Site.

Breaker's Pub $$ *Cow Bay; tel: (250) 624-5900*, is the liveliest waterfront restaurant in town.

Cow Bay Café $$ *Cow Bay; tel: (250) 627-1212*, uses local fish in Trinidadian-inspired dishes.

Cowpuccino's $ *Cow Bay; tel: (250) 627-1395*, specialises in desserts and coffees.

Smile's Seafood Café $$ *Cow Bay; tel: (250) 624-3072*, is the oldest and best-known fish restaurant in Prince Rupert.

The Waterfront Restaurant $$$ *222 W First St (Crest Hotel); tel: (250) 624-6771*, is the most elegant eatery on the North Coast with the best water views in Prince Rupert. If dinner is too dear, soak up the sunset views for the price of a drink.

Suggested tour

Total distance: 3km.

Time: 2–3 hours on foot.

Route: Prince Rupert's origins as a planned town are still obvious, at least in the downtown area, where streets are wide and boulevards grand. From the **KWINITSA STATION RAILWAY MUSEUM** ❶ at Pacific Place, walk up Bill Murray Drive to 1st Avenue W. Turn right (west) to 3rd Street and right again (south) to **CITY HALL** ❷, at the corner of 3rd Street and 3rd Avenue W, with its totems and statue of Prince Rupert founder Charles Hays.

Follow 3rd Avenue W to the left (east) to McBride Street (Hwy 16). Turn left (north) to the Visitor InfoCentre and another totem. To the right are the **SUNKEN GARDENS, CARVING SHED** and **Prince Rupert Archives**. The **MUSEUM OF NORTHERN BC** is ahead, next to **PACIFIC MARINERS MEMORIAL PARK**, with the **FIREHALL MUSEUM** to the left on 1st Avenue W. The InfoCentre and Museum of Northern BC have an excellent self-guided walking tour brochure with more details and route suggestions. In summer, the museum operates guided walking tours with local tales at historic sites.

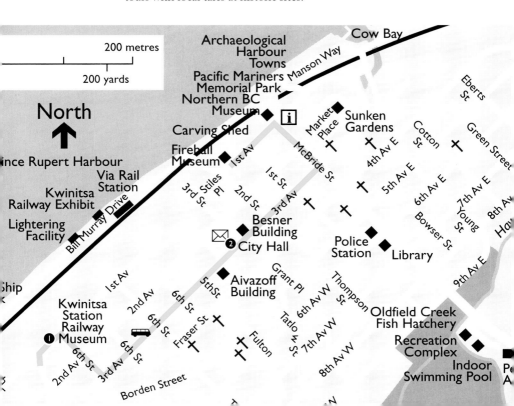

The Yellowhead Highway: Prince Rupert to Prince George

Ratings

First Nations art	●●●●●
History	●●●●●
Mountains	●●●●●
River scenery	●●●●●
Children	●●●●○
Geology	●●●●○
Outdoor activities	●●●●○
Parks	●●●●○

The northern interior is a vast plateau, in parts heavily forested, elsewhere rolling grasslands, all of it ringed by jumbled mountains that remain impassable outside the occasional river valley twisting towards the Pacific Ocean. To the west lies the Skeena, the 'River of Mists', the mystical half-seen heartland of a vibrant First Nations enclave and a traditional route through the Coast Range. Further east lie rolling farm and forest lands dotted with lakes and marshes that eventually drain into the mighty Fraser River.

A century of logging, mining and agriculture has wrought visible changes, but the human population is as scattered today as it was when Simon Fraser paddled through on his way south in 1806. Wilderness is seldom more than a few minutes away from even the largest towns, a region where moose, deer, bears, cougars and wolves still roam a largely empty land at will.

EXCHAMSIKS RIVER PROVINCIAL PARK✦✦✦

An old-growth Sitka spruce forest dominates this small park at the confluence of the Exchamsiks and Sitka rivers. It's crowded during salmon season (thanks to excellent fishing) and nearly deserted the rest of the year. (**Exchamsiks River Provincial Park** $ *Hwy 16, 30km east from Telegraph Point Rest Area; tel: (250) 847-7320; web: www.elp. gov.bc.ca/bcparks/explore/ parkpgs/exchamsi.htm*)

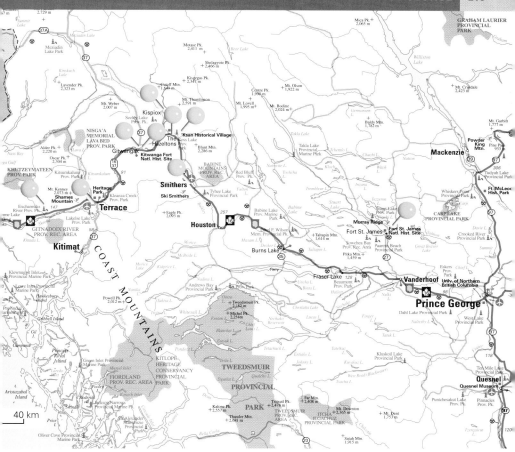

The Yellow Head

Hwy 16, the Yellowhead Highway, is named for an enigmatic French Canadian trapper, Pierre Hatsinaton. Called Tête Jaune, or Yellow Head, for his brilliant blond hair, Hatsinaton popularised a Fur Brigade route along the **Yellowhead Pass** (*see page 263*) through the Rocky Mountains that still serves as BC's main land link to the east. Local legend says Yellow Head hid a rich cache of furs near **Tête Jaune Cache** (*see page 263*), just east of today's **Mount Robson Provincial Park** (*see page 262*), in the early 19th century, but disappeared before he could carry them east. Both man and legend were popularised in the 1939 film classic *Tay John*, directed by Howard O'Haggan.

FORT ST JAMES*

ⓘ Fort St James Chamber of Commerce 115 Douglas Ave; tel: (250) 996-7023. Open daily.

ⓘ Fort St James National Historic Site $ Hwy 27, 68km north from Hwy 16; tel: (250) 996-7191; web: www.harbour. com/parkscan/fsj/ Open May–Sep, 0900–1700.

Originally called Nak'azdli, the town has been a major Dakelh (Carrier) settlement for millennia. Today, it lives on timber and tourism.

Simon Fraser paddled down Stuart Lake to Nak'azdli in 1806. He liked the 300-km string of rivers and lakes so much he dubbed it 'New Caledonia' and established the first White trading post in the territory of the Dakelh, the widest-ranging traders in interior BC. When the Hudson's Bay Company absorbed Fraser's North West Company in 1821, Fort St James became the chief post for the entire mainland area. Despite its importance, the harsh winters, gruelling isolation and monotonous diet of fresh salmon, smoked salmon and dried salmon made Fort St James the Siberia of the North American fur trade.

The HBC post, now **Fort St James National Historic Site***, survived until the 1930s and was later restored to its 1890 appearance. The major buildings are original, including the fur warehouse, fish cache, men's house, officers' quarters and dairy, all staffed by living-history interpreters in period costume. The Visitor Centre museum has excellent displays on the Dakelh people.

GITWANGAK**

The town name means 'place of rabbits', but you're more likely to see **totem poles*** dating back to the 1870s across the street from St Paul's Anglican Church*, with stained-glass windows 400 years old and a Norse-style bell tower.

THE HAZELTONS***

ⓘ Hazeltons and District Chamber of Commerce Hwys 16 and 62; tel: (250) 842-6071. Open Apr–Sep, daily.

ⓒ Bulkley Valley Motel $$ New Hazelton; tel: (250) 842-6817, is in the town centre.

28 Motel $$ New Hazelton; tel: (250) 842-6006, is the largest motel in the area.

There's a trio of towns: **South Hazelton***, a modern highway settlement; **New Hazelton***, an early railway town; and **Hazelton*** the original riverside settlement on the banks of the upper Skeena. All three are dominated by **Mt Rocher Débroulé**, the mountain of rolling stones, named by early miners who dodged frequent rockfalls. The Gitxsan call it **Stii Kyo Kin**, 'Stands Alone', the centrepiece of an ancient city-state and still the Gitxsan cultural capital, heart and soul. There are more standing totem poles in the Hazeltons than anywhere else in BC, as well as a 'Hands of History' 113km driving loop to **Kitwanga** – follow the information signs showing a stylised hand with an all-seeing eye in the palm.

Hazelton, a busy river port from the 1860s until the Grand Trunk arrived in 1912, could be a film set today. The slow-paced town is filled with false-front wooden buildings from the more prosperous Victorian era. The Chamber of Commerce has maps of self-guiding driving and walking tours that begin at the main Tourist InfoCentre on Hwy 16.

Opposite
Fort St James

KISPIOX✧✧✧

Kispiox *Hwy 62, 13km north of Hazelton.*

This ancient (and now tiny) Gitxsan village has a magnificent stand of 15 totem poles, including a rare carving of a crying woman, inside a grassy enclosure. The **Bent Box Gallery** and **Hidden Place Gallery**, both open most days in summer, feature fine local carving and other artworks. Anglers may recognise the name for the world-class salmon and steelhead fishing along the Kispiox River.

KITWANGA FORT NATIONAL HISTORIC SITE✧✧✧

This sculpted hill held one of the largest Tsimshian fortifications in the Skeena River region. The cedar plank redoubts and wood palisade protected a Grease Trail leading 100km north to the Nass River. A flaming battle in the early 1800s destroyed the complex. (**Kitwanga Fort National Historic Site $** *Hwy 37, 5km north of Hwy 16; tel: (250) 559-8818; web: www.harbour.com/parkscan/kf/*)

KSAN HISTORICAL VILLAGE✧✧✧

'Ksan Historical Village $ *Hwy 62, km north of New Hazelton; el: (250) 842-5544; web: ww.ksan.org/ Open daily r–Sep; shorter hours in inter.*

'Ksan is the visible heart of Gitxsan culture. The model village and museum occupy the site of Gitanmaax, a cluster of villages at the junction of the Skeena and Bulkley rivers that has been settled for at least 7000 years. A short, shady forest walk from the car-park leads to seven brightly decorated cedar plank longhouses and a growing collection of totem poles. The buildings house a museum, gift and art shop, carving shed and band meeting rooms.

SMITHERS❖❖

ⓘ Smithers Chamber of Commerce *1411 Court St; tel: (250) 847-5072; web: www.bulkley.net/~smicham*

ⓜ Bulkley Valley Museum *$ Hwy 16 and Main St; tel: (250) 847-5322. Open Mon–Sat.*

Smithers Art Gallery *$ Hwy 16 and Main St; tel: (250) 847-3898. Open Mon–Sat.*

Babine Mountains Recreation Area *$ Old Babine Lake Rd; tel: (250) 847-7320.*

Driftwood Canyon Provincial Park *$ Old Babine Lake Road, 11km northeast of Smithers; tel: (250) 847-7320.*

Tyhee Lake Provincial Park *$ On Tyhee Lake, 16km southeast of Smithers; tel: (250) 847-7320; web: www.elp.gov.bc.ca/bcparks/ explore/parkpgs/tyhee.htm Camping reservations, tel: (604) 689-9025.*

ⓒ Chez Josette B&B *$$ McCabe Road; tel: (250) 847-8743, is a quiet bed and breakfast that opens on to hiking and skiing trails.*

Hudson's Bay Lodge *$$ 3251 Hwy 16 E; tel: (250) 847-4581; web: www.hudsonsbaylodge.com, is the largest hotel in the region.*

The economic centre of the Bulkley River Valley, Smithers dominated by the classic alpine form of **Hudson Bay Mountai** 2621m. The faux-Alpine décor along the main street, complete wi red brick sidewalks and a statue of a man playing an alpenhorn, adds kitschy touch. Like most interior towns, Smithers grew up on timbe but has diversified into agriculture, sport fishing and outdo recreation in recent years.

Bulkley Valley Museum❖ highlights development in the Bulkle Valley. Look for local artists and local themes at the **Smithers A Gallery**❖.

The 32,000-hectare **Babine Mountains Recreation Area**❖❖❖ offe some of central BC's finest hiking through sub-Alpine meadow glacial-fed lakes and rugged peaks.

Created to protect slate cliffs filled with plant, animal and inse fossils 50 million years old, **Driftwood Canyon Provincial Park**❖ also offers picnicking and pleasant forest walks. The good gravel roa continues 35km west to Hwy 16 at Moricetown. Watch for moose ar deer, especially early and late in the day.

Tyhee Lake Provincial Park❖❖❖, a small bit of Bulkley River Vall along Tyhee Lake, provides a habitat for a variety of birds, squirrel beaver, black bears and moose. Beach and campground are popul local getaways.

`ERRACE

Terrace and District Chamber Commerce *4511 Keith e; tel: (250) 635-2063. en Mon–Fri.*

Heritage Park $ *Kerby Rd; tel: (250) 5-3000. Open Apr–Sep, ys vary.*

ouse of Sim-Oi-Ghets *W Kalum Rd; tel: (250) 8-1629.*

orthern Lights Studio Gardens $$ *4820 lliwell Ave; tel: (250) 638-03.*

Once a major steamboat stop, Terrace is better known now for salmon and bears. World-record salmon have been caught in the Skeena River within walking distance of the town centre. The municipal emblem, the white Kermode bear, tends to keep to the woods, but is occasionally spotted along quiet side roads.

Nine original log buildings have been collected into an excellent regional museum, **Heritage Park****, filled with period photographs and artefacts. Costumed guides lead tours in summer.

House of Sim-Oi-Ghets**, a gallery run by the Kitsumkalum Band, offers the best selection of First Nations arts and crafts in the area.

The calm Japanese-style gardens at the **Northern Lights Studio & Gardens*** attract as many visitors as the studio and gallery.

Accommodation and food in Terrace

Alpine House Motel $$ *4326 Lakelse Ave; tel: (250) 635-7216*, is a quiet motel within walking distance of downtown.

Dante's Restaurante $$ *4606 Lazelle Ave; tel: (250) 635-7229*, offers good Northern Italian dishes.

Suggested tour

Total distance: 740km.

Time: One very long day driving, 3–4 days to explore.

Links: The Yellowhead Highway links with **Prince Rupert** (*see page 206*) and the **Queen Charlotte Islands** (*see page 116*) to the east and the **Gold Rush Trail** (*see page 186*) to the south via Hwy 97.

Route: From **Prince Rupert**, take Hwy 16 south. The highway passes several scenic parks with fishing, hiking and grand vistas before reaching the **Skeena River**. The name means 'river of mists' in the language of the Tsimshian and Gitxsan First Nations who have lived in the region since the end of the last Ice Age and perhaps longer. Swirling mists and low-hanging clouds often hide surrounding mountain peaks and the opposite shore.

The Skeena Canyon has been a highway for thousands of years, first for First Nations canoes, then paddlewheel steamboats, the Grand Trunk Pacific Railway and now Hwy 16. Harbour seals have been spotted 100km inland feasting on salmon and oolichan migrating upriver to spawn. Bald eagles, bears, ravens and other predator/scavengers are common sights. The best river viewpoints (mist permitting) are **Basalt Creek**, about 20km east from the first sight of the river, and **Telegraph Point**, 33km beyond.

Above
Terrace Heritage Park

The highway passes **TERRACE ❶**, named for the natural terrac
along the Skeena River, a major steamboat stop until the GTP arriv
in 1912. The small timber and sport fishing town is a good place to s
Kermode (ker-mode-ee) bears, a subspecies of black bear that is hone
blond-white in colour. The Kermode is a spirit bear in local Fir
Nations lore, given to punishing evil-doers and rescuing the deservir
in distress. These days, it's the Kermode that needs help as logging ar
other human activities cut into wild habitat.

From Terrace, the road swings north past **Usk**, a steamboat town th
has all but disappeared, to **GITWANGAK ❷**, with a turn t
KITWANGA FORT NATIONAL HISTORIC SITE ❸, and continues c
to the three **HAZELTONS ❹**.

Detour to Kispiox: From the Visitor InfoCentre at New Hazelton, tak
Hwy 62 left (north) to cross over the single-track **Hagwilget Bridg**
hanging 76m above the boiling Bulkley River. The Gitxsan ar
Wet'suwet'en First Nations built a bridge of wooden poles lashe
together with cedar bark rope over the gorge at the same site.

The highway crosses gently rolling pastures to **'KSAN HISTORICA**
VILLAGE ❺ and on to Hazelton, the head of navigation on tr
Skeena River. The road narrows and follows the Kispiox River north t
the Gitxsan village of **KISPIOX ❻**. Return to Hwy 16.

The highway leaves the Skeena just west of the Hazeltons to follow tr
Bulkley River eastward. The river is squeezed to just 15m .
Moricetown, which has been a traditional Wet'suwert'en fishing sp
for at least the last 4000 years. The small town is named for an ear
missionary priest.

SMITHERS ❼ is the largest town in the Bulkley Valley, laced by several small rivers and streams. The Yellowhead climbs out of the valley to **Houston**, a sport fishing town that proudly proclaims its number-one money spinner with an 18m fly-fishing rod cocked above the **Houston and District Chamber of Commerce**; *tel: (250) 845-7640*. The highest point on the entire Yellowhead Hwy is 40km east at **Six Mile Summit**, 1423m. Downhill lies the **Lake Country**, filled with lakes, meadows and second-growth forests.

Detour: From a turn-off just west of **Vanderhoof**, take Hwy 27 north for 68km to **Stuart Lake** and Fort St James, the former HBC post. Return to Hwy 16.

The highway rolls east through **Vanderhoof**, a logging town that has turned to ranching. The geographic centre of BC is 10km east, marked by a roadside cairn. The highway continues east through rolling forests to **Prince George** (*see page 222*).

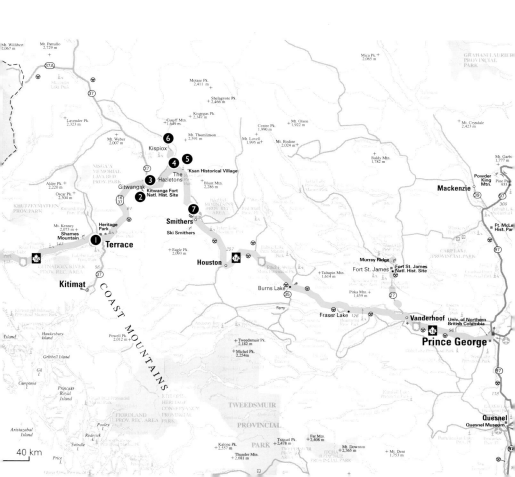

40 km

Prince George

Ratings

Children	●●●●
Geology	●●●●
History	●●●●
Parks	●●●●
Mountains	●●●
Outdoor activities	●●●
Scenery	●●●
Wildlife	●●

Alexander Mackenzie paddled past the junction of th Fraser and Nechako rivers in 1793 without even noticin the massive confluence in a heavy morning mist. Simo Fraser had better visibility in 1807; he stopped long enoug to build a small trading post on the flat bowl below loomir cliffs cut by the two rivers. And that was the last most of th outside world heard of the place until the Grand Trun Pacific Railway arrived on the way west to Prince Rupert.

Almost a century later, Prince George remains an isolate if vital, crossroads. Roads, railways and air routes hav replaced river conduits for people, goods and informatioı but road and rail seldom stray far from river routes in BC rugged interior. A smoothly undulating carpet of fore cloaks a rolling plateau dotted with lakes and laced k sparkling rivers tumbling toward the Pacific.

Getting there

Prince George is the primary transportation hub for northern BC. A rail and road routes headed north–south and east–west all cross at th junction of the Fraser and Nechako rivers.

Air
Prince George Airport *Sintich Road, 10km south of downtown, off H\ 97 S.* Prince George is one of the busiest inland airports in BC, wi frequent service from Vancouver and other major cities around t\ western side of North America. A shuttle bus and taxis serve dow town, or hire a car at the airport.

Rail
BC Rail *tel: (250) 561-4033; web: www.bcrail.com/bcr*, provides servi south to Vancouver via the **Cariboo Prospector** (*see page 166*), whi follows the Cariboo Gold Rush route via Lillooet, Whistler and Ho\ Sound. **VIA Rail** *tel: 800-561-8630; web: www.viarail.ca*, runs west

ⓘ Tourism Prince George and Area
1198 Victoria St; tel: (250) 562-3700; web: www.tourismpg.bc.ca Open daily.

Visitor InfoCentre
Junction of Hwys 16 and 97; tel: (250) 563-5493. Open May–Sep.

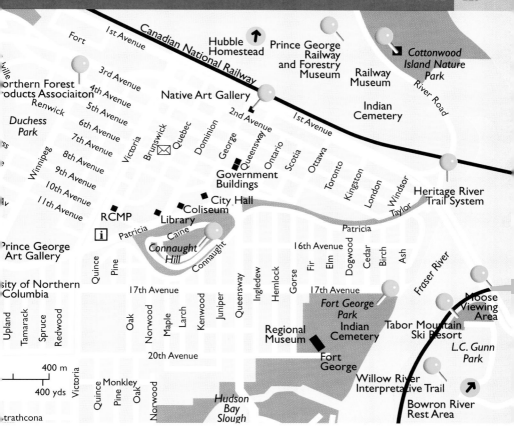

Prince Rupert and east to Jasper, Alberta, via the **Skeena**, which runs through the Skeena River Valley and the Yellowhead Pass.

Road

Prince George sits at the junction of Hwys 97/16, two of Western Canada's most important highway corridors. Hwy 97 runs south to Hwy 1 and Vancouver and north to Dawson Creek, Fort Nelson and into Alaska. Hwy 16, the Yellowhead Highway, runs west to Prince Rupert (and, via ferry, to the Queen Charlotte Islands) and east through the Yellowhead Pass to Jasper, Alberta, and on to Eastern Canada.

Sights

Bowron River Rest Area $ Hwy 16, 55km from Prince George.

Bowron River Rest Area*

The Upper Bowron River Valley has become the world's largest tree farm, with 53,000 hectares, following an infestation of spruce bark beetles that devastated the existing forest.

Connaught Hill Park $ *Centre of town, off Queensway.*

Cottonwood Island Nature Park $ *Off River Road, 2km northeast from downtown.*

Fort George Park $ *Off the end of 20th Ave.*

Fort George Railway $ *Fort George Park; tel: (250) 562-6877. Operates weekends and holidays May–Sep.*

Above
Fort George Railway

Connaught Hill Park✦✦✦

This volcanic plug overlooking downtown has become one of the m popular parks in Prince George for its easy walking trails and 360-deg views. The park is most crowded at noontime in good weather wh workers from city offices flock to the summit for an outdoor lunch.

Cottonwood Island Nature Park✦✦✦

Look for a variety of migratory birds in this 32-hectare wildlife rese skirting the Nechako River just west of its confluence with the Fraser

Fort George Park✦✦

Fort George was the name Simon Fraser gave to the small post he b over the winter of 1807–8, located on today's riverside park site. T park also holds the traditional burial grounds for the Lheidle T'enn First Nations. Nearby South Fort George was the head of navigation the upper Fraser River where paddlewheel steamboats unloaded ca and passengers well into the 20th century.

The park has become a well-loved family playground, in large p thanks to the **Fort George Railway**✦✦✦. The narrow-gauge railw opened in 1978, but the 1912 six-tonne Davenport 0-4-0 Locomot engine, a dinky in railway terminology, was used to build the Gra Trunk Pacific Railway Line. The station is modelled on one of GT standard designs that was used for more than 200 stations across and Alberta. Most of the original stations were built on the north si of the tracks in order to maximise sun and warmth on the sou facing platforms and block frigid winds from the north and west.

Fraser-Fort George Regional Museum $ *Fort George ...rk; tel: (250) 562-1612. ...en daily May–Sep ...00–1700; Oct–Apr, ...e–Sun.*

...eritage River Trail ...stem $ *Along the ...chako and Fraser rivers.*

...bble Homestead $ *...tchell Road, 40km north ... Hwy 97; tel: (250) 960- ...00. Open daily May–Oct.*

...oose Viewing Area $ *...y 16, 29km east from ...nce George. Car park is on ... north side of the ...hway.*

...tive Art Gallery $ *...00 3rd Ave; tel: (250) ...4-7726. Open daily.*

...orthern Forest ...oducts Association $ *...0 1488 Fourth Ave; tel: ...0) 564-5136.*

...ince George Art ...llery $ *2820 15th Ave; ... (250) 563-6447. Open ...ly May–Sep; Oct–Apr, ...e–Sun.*

...ince George Railway ...d Forestry Museum $ *...0 River Rd (next to ...tonwood Park); tel: (250) ...3-7357. Open May–Sep, ...—Mon.*

Also in the park, the **Fraser-Fort George Regional Museum**⁺ has a hands-on science centre for children as well as exhibits concentrating on local transportation from dugout canoes to modern railways.

Heritage River Trail System⁺⁺⁺
An 11-km loop of broad gravel trails follows the Nechako River from the Cameron Street Bridge east around Cottonwood Island Park, past the confluence of the Fraser River and south to Fort George Park. The trail turns inland along Hudson Bay Slough, then cuts through town to Carrie Jane Gray Park. Follow Camey Street N back to the Cameron Street overpass.

Hubble Homestead⁺⁺⁺
A vital roadhouse in the early years of the 20th century, the Homestead stood at the south end of the Giscome Portage, which connects the Arctic and Pacific watersheds over the Continental Divide. The homestead declined in importance after a 1919 road cut the portage out of commercial transportation routes. Costumed interpreters provide guided tours of the homestead and trading post.

Moose Viewing Area⁺⁺⁺
A forest fire in 1961 turned Grover Forest into rolling meadows filled with the kind of tender new growth that moose love to browse. The best views are from a raised platform an easy five-minute walk from the car park.

Native Art Gallery⁺⁺
This is the best (but not the only) selection of both Interior and Coastal First Nations art products in the area.

Northern Forest Products Association⁺
Timber is the biggest industry in north-central BC as well as the industry with the biggest image problem. Most mills and forest operations offer tours to show off their best side. A few tours are self-guided, most require advance booking and all are free. The NFPA has contact information and telephone numbers for mills, forests, tree nurseries and other facilities from Prince Rupert east to Valemont and north to Fort Nelson.

Prince George Art Gallery⁺
The city's biggest gallery space shows touring exhibitions as well as local and regional artists.

Prince George Railway and Forestry Museum⁺⁺⁺
Heaven for steam buffs, the museum celebrates the history of the GTP (now part of the Canadian National Railway) and the Pacific Great Eastern (now part of BC Rail). The site shows a restored section house, GTP's 1914 Penny Station, a railway worker's bunkhouse, an early BC

Tabor Mountain Ski Resort $$ *Off Hwy 16, 20km east from Prince George; tel: (250) 963-7542.*

University of Northern British Columbia $ *3333 University Way; tel: (250) 960-5678.*

Willow River Interpretative Trail $ *Hwy 16, 34km east from Prince George.*

Telephone building and a heritage fire hall. Rolling stock includes 1903 Russell snow plough and a 1913 CPR steam crane, both working order.

Tabor Mountain Ski Resort◆◆◆

Tabor Mountain is Prince George's own ski hill, a 244m vertical dr with lifts and a busy day lodge.

University of Northern British Columbia◆◆

Canada's newest autonomous university has planted its futuris campus atop Cranbrook Hill, overlooking Prince Rupert from t south. Choose from a self-guided indoor tour that weaves through t main buildings all year or an outdoor walk better taken in summ than in winter.

Willow River Interpretative Trail◆◆◆

The Canadian Institute of Forestry has created an excellent series forest and streamside walking trails that explore several differe hardwood, softwood and stream habitats. Allow between 45 minu and 2 hours for the signed trails.

Accommodation and food

The University and a booming economy have given Prince George a better selection of accommodation and restaurants than might be expected in the middle of the northern forests.

Bon Voyage Motor Inn $$ *4222 Hwy 16 W; tel: (250) 964-2333*, 6km west of Hwy 97, is the newest motel in town.

Coast Inn of the North $$$ *770 Brunswick St; tel: (250) 563-0121*, is the best hotel in town.

Credo Manor $$ *6872 O'Grady Road; tel: (250) 964-8142*, is a quiet, comfortable bed and breakfast near the University campus.

Downtown Motel $$ *650 Dominion St; tel: (250) 563-9241*, is just a block from the civic centre.

Bagel Street Café $ *1493 3rd Ave; tel: (250) 563-0071*, is a good breakfast stop, or pick up sandwiches for a picnic.

Earls Place Restaurant $$ *1440 E Central; tel: (250) 562-1527*, specialises in Northwestern dishes, especially salmon and game.

Galitas $$ *1148 7th Ave; tel: (250) 564-5951*, is one of the few Spanish restaurants north of Vancouver.

Oodles Pasta House $$ *1310 5th Ave; tel: (250) 563-5400*, is a popular Italian pasta place.

Suggested tour

Total distance: 260km.

Time: Allow 1 long day or 2 days for easier sightseeing.

Links: From Prince George, the **Yellowhead Hwy** (*see page 214*) links with **Prince Rupert** (*see page 206*) to the west and the **BC Rockies** (*see page 258*) to the east. To the south, Hwy 16 links to the **Gold Rush Trail** (*see page 186*) at Quesnel.

Route: This circular tour runs north to one of the only waterfalls in north-central BC, through forest and muskeg (bog) to Fort St James and back to Prince Rupert along the Yellowhead Highway.

Take Hwy 97 north through pastoral farmlands to the **Salmon River**. About 36km north of Prince George is a marked side-road to the **HUBBLE HOMESTEAD** ❶ and **Giscome Portage Trail**. The homestead was established in 1904 as a waystation for travellers crossing the Arctic–Pacific Continental Divide. Waterways north of the divide, which runs between **Teapot Mountain** and **SUMMIT LAKE** ❷, 15km north, flow into the Arctic Ocean; waterways south of the divide flow into the Pacific.

At **Bear Lake,** head west on the Davie Bear Forest Service Road, excellent gravel road that leads to the **CROOKED RIVER ❸** ar beyond. The meandering river was a major transport route for t Sekanni and other First Nations, as well as Alexander Mackenz Simon Fraser and other explorer/traders. The many lakes, rivers ar streams support a wide variety of wildlife, from Canada geese, loor blue-winged teal, ospreys, bald eagles and hawks to bears, beaver muskrats, moose and deer. **Fisher Lake** and **Merton Lake** ha particularly scenic picnic and camping sites.

Logging roads offer clear views of logging practices, includir clearcuts, in which broad swaths of forest are stripped of all trees. T logged areas may be replanted or left to regenerate naturally, b either way end up looking like a disaster zone for decades. The on useful effect is to reveal the landforms hidden by dense forest. Jr past the Weedon Forest Service Road (Road 300) is an area of lo: narrow ridges formed during the last Ice Age, around 10,000 years a; when glaciers a kilometre thick covered this northern plateau.

The road forks just west of the **Muskeg River.** Take the south fo (1500 Road) to continue the tour. The north fork, Davie Muskeg For Service Road, leads 7km to **Muskeg Falls.** A short, easy trail leads fro the car park to the 20-m falls, one of the few waterfalls that h developed in the area since the glaciers retreated.

The tour continues to the south end of **GREAT BEAVER LAKE ❹,** o of the most scenic lakes in the area accessible by road. Continue we past the **MURRAY RIDGE SKI HILL ❺** to a logging truck weighi station. Take the sharp turn south to **FORT ST JAMES ❻** *(see page 2)* and Hwy 27. Follow Hwy 27 south to Hwy 16, the Yellowhead Hwy, ju west of **VANDERHOOF ❼,** and turn left (east) back to Prince George.

Gravel road precautions

Some public highways are part-paved, part-gravel, while other major roads, including Forest Service roads and logging roads, are entirely gravel. Gravel roads important enough to be shown on highway and tourist maps are well maintained, but require special driving precautions, particularly in areas with active logging.

Logging trucks and other industrial vehicles *always* have the right of way. Most are equipped with radios.

In an active logging area, try to follow a log truck so the driver can notify oncoming traffic. Don't follow so close as to choke on dust, but don't fall back so far the driver loses sight of you.

Don't pass a logging truck unless the driver signals you to go around.

If a logging truck pulls over beside the road and stops, you should, too – there's almost certainly another truck headed your way along a section of road too narrow for two vehicles to pass safely.

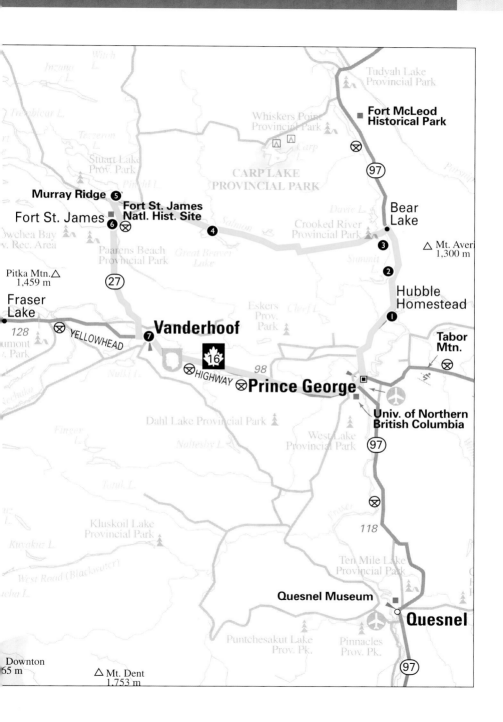

Columbia River

Ratings

Mountains	●●●●●
National parks	●●●●●
Nature	●●●●●
Scenery	●●●●●
Outdoor activities	●●●●
Children	●●●
Geology	●●●
History	●●●

Subtly, the long and mighty Columbia River begins i much-dammed and thwarted route 2044km to tl Pacific Ocean from Columbia Lake, a long but unpr possessing body of water visible from a lay-by along Hw 93/95. Bird migration along the Columbia Valley is awesom in spring and autumn; migration of humans over one of tl world's snowiest mountain areas at Rogers Pass is almost awe-inspiring because of the sheer technical skill it takes keep the pass open against avalanche.

While Parks Canada wages 'snow wars', this is railwa country, from the hub at Golden at the north end of tl Columbia Valley to Revelstoke west of the Selkirk Mountai along the fast-flowing Columbia River, west of Golden ov Rogers Pass. Glaciers, old-growth cedars and wild-flow meadows lie in between the two towns, each claiming tl distinction of Gateway to the Columbia.

CANAL FLATS❖

ⓘ Doug Up Bonz $
Look for skeleton sculptures on the east side of Hwy 95 at Canal Flats. Doug's a skilled bone and fossil finder with a gift for sculpture and humour. The bones of birds and small animals become skeletons of impossible creatures, shown off around the property and in the trailer that is his workshop and sales gallery. His mum is an equally fine painter of natural subjects.

There is a small lumbering community here, but the area's claim fame is twofold: the Kootenay River and source of the Columbia Riv in Columbia Lake, separated only by 2km of land (they actually join at Castlegar, *see page 241*), and an 1889 canal built to divert Kootenay River water away from valley farms. Too narrow locks were the canal's downfall. The *North Star*, only the second vessel to pass through, wrecked the locks and system in 1902. (**Canal Flats** *historic point, Hwy 93/95 at south end of Columbia Lake.*)

WELCOME TO
CANAL FLATS
SOURCE OF THE MIGHTY COLUMBIA

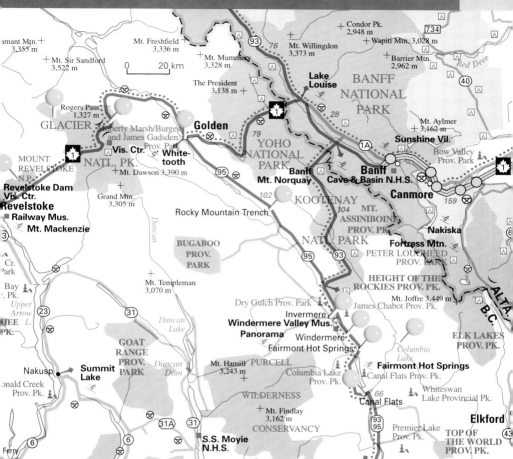

COLUMBIA LAKE*

Columbia Lake
South of Fairmont Hot Springs on the east side of Hwy 93/95.

Look for a lay-by on the east side of Hwy 93/95 and a sign announcing 'Columbia Lake–Source of Columbia River Which Empties into Pacific Ocean at Astoria-Oregon', that is, 2044km southwest of the headwaters! Spiky golden hoodoos (eroded columns of rock) rise sheer above Dutch Creek at the lake's north end.

FAIRMONT HOT SPRINGS*

Here you can soak in the 43°–48°C odourless hot springs, Canada's largest natural hot pools, long used by Ktunaxa (Kootenay) peoples. From several vantage points, including the Mountainside Golf Course, the forest-bound resort looks westward to the craggy line of the Purcell

ⓘ **Fairmont Hot Springs $$** *Fairmont Hot Springs Resort off Hwy 93/95; tel: (250) 345-6311 or (800) 663-4979; web: www.fairmontresort.com* Open year-round with a **Ski Hill $$**.

Hot Pools $ *Open daily 0800–1000.*

⊕ **Mountainside Golf Course $$$** *tel: (250) 345-6314 or (800) 663-4979*, one of two 18-hole courses, offering magnificent views over the Columbia River Valley.

Mountain Range. Hiking, biking, horse-riding and winter skii supplement the pools' attraction for the RVers, lodge guests ar another 750,000 visitors who make an annual pilgrimage to the reson

Where there's a will

Ornery Major A B Rogers, described by Parks Canada as 'short, sharp and rough-tongued', was driven to find a pass over the Rockies suitable for a railway. In 1881, he tried the pass's west side, and 'Many a time I wished myself dead.' In 1882, he approached from the east and 'felt like a piece of liver'. He had found a viable pass through the mountains. The impetus? The CPR had promised to name the pass after him and paid a $5000 bonus. In ornery style he never cashed the cheque.

GOLDEN❖

ⓘ **Golden & District Chamber of Commerce Visitor InfoCentre** *500 N 10th Ave; tel: (250) 344-7125 or (800) 622-4653. web: www.rockies.net/columbia-valley/ Open daily.*

Trains, lorries, rivers, an active sawmill, tourists and outdoo enthusiasts (hang-gliders, rock climbers, whitewater kayakers ar rafters, mountain bikers, hikers and anglers) all use Golden as convenient valley-floor base. Here is the confluence of the Columb and Kicking Horse rivers and access to Yoho National Park (*see pa 264*) or Glacier National Park (*see below*). Mountains rise along bo sides of the valley, causing spectacular sunsets over the Purcells, drama much needed in this rather pedestrian service centre.

Accommodation and food in Golden

Golden Rim Motor Inn $$ *1416 Golden View Rd; tel: (250) 344-221* has views of the Columbia River Valley.

Sportsman Motel $ *1200 12th St N; tel: (250) 344-2915*, is quiet ar away from the highway.

Legendz $ *1405 W TransCanada Hwy; tel: (250) 344-5059*, serv delicious steak and creamy eggs, with other Marilyn Monroe ar James Dean era specialities.

GLACIER NATIONAL PARK❖❖❖

Opposite
Glacier National Park

The northern Selkirk Mountain Range, the birthplace of Nort American technical climbing – mountaineering – in 1888, is a land snow and around 400 active glaciers, including **Illecillewaet Glacie**

Glacier National Park $ *Mount* *elstoke and Glacier* *ional Parks* *dquarters, 3rd St and* *npbell Ave, Revelstoke;* *(250) 837-7500; web:* *v.harbour.com/parkscan/* *ier/*

gers Pass Centre *ers Pass; tel: (250) 814-* *3 or (250) 837-7500.* *n daily May–mid-Jun and* *·Sep–Oct, 0900–1700;* *Jun–mid-Sep,* *0–2030; Nov, Thu–Mon* *0–1700; Dec–Mar,* *.0–1700.*

gers Pass *69km east of* *elstoke, 72km west of* *len, on Hwy 1 in Glacier* *ional Park.*

visible from Hwy 1 on a clear day. Waterfalls and wild flowers are abundant in season. If travelling east, you will see 14.6-km Mount Macdonald Tunnel, North America's longest railway tunnel, built after hundreds died between 1885 and 1911 trying to keep the Rogers Pass open on the surface. A series of snowsheds protects traffic from avalanches as 'Snow Wars' keep Rogers Pass open in winter. The twin keys: constant monitoring and 105mm howitzers deployed to blast snow along avalanche paths.

Rogers Pass✦✦✦ Many peaks poke the sky at 3700m, catching shrouds of snow which avalanche dangerously below. Major A B Rogers, who discovered the 1382m pass, noted, 'Our eyesight caromed from one bold peak to another for miles in all directions. The wind blew fiercely across the ridge and scuddy clouds were whirled in eddies behind the great towering peaks of bare rock. Everything was covered with a shroud of white, giving the whole landscape the appearance of snow-clad desolation.' **Rogers Pass Centre** offers excellent explanations of the Snow Wars waged by the CPR and more currently by Parks Canada and the Royal Canadian Horse Artillery to keep the TransCanada Highway open. **Abandoned Rails Trail** follows Hwy 1 past side-paths and snowsheds 1.3km to the **Rogers Pass Monument**✦, which commemorates completion of the TransCanada Highway in 1962, the first alternative to rail transit over the pass.

Accommodation and food in Glacier National Park

Best Western Glacier Park Lodge $$$ *Rogers Pass; tel: (250) 837-2* or (800) 528-1234. The only non-camping accommodation in the p provides 50 rooms next to the Rogers Pass Centre, with a restaura 24-hour cafeteria and petrol station.

INVERMERE*

ⓘ Invermere Columbia Valley Chamber of Commerce Visitor InfoCentre *651 Hwy 93/95 Crossroads, Windermere; tel: (250) 342-2844 or (250) 342-6316; web: www.adventurevalley. com/chamberofcommerce Open daily 0900–1700.*

ⓝ James Chabot Provincial Park $ *North end of Windermere Lake; web: www.elp.gov.bc. ca/bcparks/explore/parkpgs/ james.htm*

At the northwest corner of Windermere Lake, the area's commerc centre south of Golden boasts September to October kokanee salm spawning in its end of the 15km-long lake, and lakeside **Jam Chabot Provincial Park**** with a swimming beach and watersports.

Opposite
Mount Revelstoke National Park

MOBERLY MARSH/BURGES AND JAMES GADSDEN PROVINCIAL PARK*

ⓝ Moberly Marsh/ Burges and James Gadsden Provincial Park $ *West of Hwy 1 north of Golden.*

Most drivers don't stop in the rush to and from Golden, but migrat waterfowl do along this stretch of marsh between the TransCanada H 1 and the Columbia River. Spot muskrats and ospreys from a 3.5-riverbank **Dyke Trail****.

MOUNT REVELSTOKE NATIONAL PARK ❖❖❖

Mount Revelstoke National Park $
unt Revelstoke and
cier National Parks
adquarters, 3rd St and
mpbell Ave, Revelstoke;
(250) 837-7500 or
0) 837-6867; web: www.
bour.com/parkscan/
rev/ Wardens at
adows in the Sky
kway have park
ormation.

ant Cedars Trail $
n west of east boundary
Mount Revelstoke
tional Park.

**eadows in the Sky
arkway) $** 3km east of
elstoke in Mount
elstoke National Park.
ailers are prohibited
ond the parkway trailer
king area 0.5km from
y 1.

Unlike the Rockies National Parks, which were spurred on by the CPR and the need for an all-weather automobile route (Kootenay), this park was a result of City of Revelstoke citizens' building a trail to the mountain's summit, and lobbying for a road. That road, Meadows in the Sky Parkway, draws thousands of mid-summer visitors to the rich displays of wild flowers.

Giant Cedars Trail ❖❖❖ Rainforest in the interior of BC? Eight-hundred-year-old Western red cedar trees along a 0.5-km boardwalk tell the tale. The damp, mossy streambed is dim, but vibrant with many hues of green. Virgin old-growth forest boasts standing cedars so thick with branches that little water falls through when it rains.

Meadows in the Sky ❖❖❖ Stop at the elaborate archway Welcome Station entrance to the 26-km Meadows in the Sky Parkway for information. Depending on the severity of the past winter, the parkway may be closed part of the way up, even though the route is normally open early July to late September. Enjoy the winding, 16-switchback drive past fine views of Revelstoke and the Columbia River. Waterfalls plummet off rock walls covered with ferns and greenery as the parkway rises through forests of cedar, hemlock, fir and spruce. Park at Balsam Lake and take the Summit Shuttle to the wild-flower meadows or hike the colourful carpet by way of the 1-km Summit Trail to the top.

Revelstoke Viewpoint
The people of Revelstoke worked hard to establish a national park here. In 1908, they cut a trail up the mountain and in 1911 they persuaded the Province of British Columbia

Belvédère Revelstoke
Les résidents de Revelstoke n'ont rien épargné pour préserver la beauté de cet endroit. En 1908, ils ont tracé un chemin sur la montagne et en 1911, ils ont réussi à persuader le gouvernement de la Colombie-Britannique de commencer la route vers le

Elec. 760 m

REVELSTOKE❖

ⓘ Revelstoke InfoCentre *Junction of TransCanada Hwy 1 and Hwy 23 N; open summer.*
Revelstoke Chamber of Commerce *204 Campbell Ave; tel: (250) 837-5345 or (800) 487-1493; web: www.revelstokecc.bc.ca/ Open Mon–Fri 0830–1200, 1300–1630.*

Snow sports *web: www.revelstokecc.bc.ca/ snow/start.htm*

ⓝ Piano Keep Gallery *$ 117 Campbell Ave; tel: (250) 837-6554.*

Revelstoke Dam *$ 4km north of Revelstoke; tel: (250) 837-6515.Open May–mid-Jun, 0900–1700; mid-Jun–mid-Sep, 0800–2000; mid-Sep–Thanksgiving, 0900–1700.*

Revelstoke Railway Museum *$ Victoria Rd, Revelstoke; tel: (250) 837-6060 or (877) 837-6060; web: www.railwaymuseum.com. Open daily Jul–Aug, 0900–2000; May, Jun, Sep, 0900–1700; Apr, Oct, Mon–Sat 0900–1700; Nov, Mon–Fri 0900–1700; Dec–Mar, Mon–Fri 1300–1700.*

No one seems to know why there are bear statues and sig everywhere in this railway hub and recreation centre in the middle the Selkirk and Monashee Mountains. Ask and the answer is there lots of bears around here. Trains constantly roll, click and gri through town. **Grizzly Plaza**❖ *(Mackenzie Ave, Victoria Rd and First St)* the venue for nightly concerts in July and August. Rail and Columl River transportation propelled Revelstoke into existence in the 188(The Chamber of Commerce has *Heritage Walking & Driving* a *Railway Heritage Driving Tour* brochures.

Think of the loveliest piano you've ever seen, then multiply t pleasure of the **Piano Keep Gallery**❖❖❖ dedicated to the instrumer from pre-Mozart harpsichords to modern concert grand pianos, lovingly restored and equally lovingly explained.

BC Hydro operates **Revelstoke Dam**❖ and generating station, a mt for those fascinated by waterway engineering and the intricacies changes to the Columbia River. Get an individual talking wand at t entrance for a self-guiding tour through the powerhouse and circ galleries, tailrace and powerhouse control room. Take a lift 175m up the top crest of the dam and look both up and downstream.

It's not large, but the **Revelstoke Railway Museum**❖❖ is a go introduction to the challenges faced by CPR engineers and offici who encountered avalanches, difficult soil, steep grades, harsh wint and labour strife while constructing and maintaining the railw Prized are Business Car No 4 and Mikado P-2k class locomotive I 5468, on display in a replica of Victoria's E&N Roundhouse.

Right
Revelstoke Railway Museum

Accommodation and food in Revelstoke

Many Revelstoke motels are near the noisy railway track at the west end of town.

Canyon Motor Inn $$ *1911 Fraser Dr, off Hwy 1 at Columbia River Bridge; tel: (250) 837-5221 or (800) 382-7763,* has small, very clean rooms in a quiet spot near the river.

Piano Keep $$ *815 Mackenzie Ave; tel: (250) 837-2120,* offers bed and breakfast in a multi-storey Victorian heritage house a block from downtown, and is a comfortable and cosy base for exploring the area.

Blue Berry Patch $ *212 Mackenzie Ave; tel: (250) 837-5500,* has delicious breakfast blueberry cornmeal and apple rhubarb muffins, and wraps and sandwiches for lunch.

Three Bears' Sweet Shop $$ *114 Mackenzie Ave, Grizzly Plaza; tel: (250) 837-6575,* has great coffee, salads and home-made soup.

Tony's Roma Restaurant $$ *306 Mackenzie Ave; tel: (250) 837-2176,* presents huge, tasty portions of Italian specialities.

Wheat Sheaf Bakery $ *200 1st St W; tel: (250) 837-3461,* has tasty breads without chemicals, sugar, eggs or dairy products.

ROCKY MOUNTAIN TRENCH✣

Rocky Mountain Trench dividing the ocky and Cascade ountain Ranges from aska to the central USA s the Columbia River at bottom in this area.

Astronauts say this depression between mountain ranges which extends from Alaska along the western side of the Rocky Mountains into the central US is one of the most prominent features on Earth. The rift valley separates ancient Columbia Mountains from the craggier, younger Rocky Mountains on the eastern side, with lush wetlands and cultivated farmland in between.

WINDERMERE✣

St Peter's Anglican Church $ *Kootenay* tel: (250) 342-6644.

The town and its namesake lake are a resort getaway for locals and people from colder climes. **St Peter's Anglican Church✣** was stolen in 1897, removed via a railway flatcar from Donald, 210km north, by residents who wanted a ready-made church when most Donald inhabitants moved to Revelstoke along with the CPR operations.

Suggested tour

Total distance: 310km.

Time: 2 days.

Links: South of Canal Flats on Hw 93/95 to **The Crowsnest** (*see pa* 250). At Radium Junction, go east t Kootenay National Park, or Golden go east to Yoho Nation Parks in **BC Rockies Parks** (*see pa* 258). At Revelstoke, continue we on Hwy 1 to the **Shuswap Lakes** (*s page 158*).

Route: From CANAL FLATS ❶ travel north through the ROCK MOUNTAIN TRENCH ❷ on Hw 93/95 along the west side o COLUMBIA LAKE ❸, headwaters o the **Columbia River.** The wetlan that begin here are amongst th most extensive and richest on eart 26,000 hectares of protected spac From Canal Flats to **Donald,** nor of Golden, is the least-develope section along the Columbia Rive Beyond Columbia Lake's north en are the **Dutch Creek Hoodoo** looming mysteriously on the lef and FAIRMONT HOT SPRINGS ❹ for soaking, swimming, golfin hiking and winter skiing with viev of the Purcell Mountains to th west above the valley floor. North **Windermere Lake,** which ha INVERMERE ❺ on the west sid and WINDERMERE ❻ along th highway side.

❶ **Columbia Valley Chamber of Commerce Visitor InfoCentre** *651 Hwy 93/95 Crossroads, Windermere; tel: (250) 342-2844 or (250) 342-6316; web: www.adventurevalley.com/ chamberofcommerce Open daily 0900–1700.*

At **Radium Junction,** Hwy 93 splits off east from Hwy 95 to Radiu Hot Springs in Kootenay National Park. Hwy 95 continues north alon the Columbia River Valley to **GOLDEN** ❼, at the junction of Hwy 9 and TransCanada Hwy 1 from Yoho National Park.

Continue north on Hwy 1 past **BURGES AND JAMES GADSDE** PROVINCIAL PARK ❽ at **MOBERLY MARSH** ❾ and Donald, whe the CPR line first crossed the Columbia River.

Enter **GLACIER NATIONAL PARK** ❿. **Beaver Valley** has a lovel picnic spot, and wild flowers in summer. Tunnels covering th TransCanada Hwy are snowsheds, built to deflect the hideous impa of avalanches. **Rogers Pass Centre** has a roaring fire, excellent exhib and film depictions of avalanche control and snow management, an a well-stocked bookshop. One kilometre south is the **Rogers Pass Monument** arch to the 1962 TransCanada Highway completion. The **Illecillewaet Glacier** campground and trailhead to a series of trails near the glacier are accessible from Hwy 1, not far south of the monument.

There's a 16-km gap between park boundaries. Almost immediately upon entering **MOUNT REVELSTOKE NATIONAL PARK ⓫**, stop and take the short 0.5-km **Giant Cedars Trail** for a view of BC rain forest. In May, walk the 1.2-km **Skunk Cabbage Trail** for views of the odiferous plants flowering yellow along the **Illecillewaet River.** The park's jewel is the **Meadows in the Sky Parkway**, a 42-km drive to **Balsam Lake** parking and a 2-km shuttle ride or walk to Mount Revelstoke's summit, carpeted with wild flowers in mid-summer.

Descending quickly from the park, enter **REVELSTOKE ⓬** to visit the Revelstoke Railway Museum, Revelstoke Dam and the amazing collection at Piano Keep Gallery.

Opposite
Mount Revelstoke Mountain
Meadows Trail

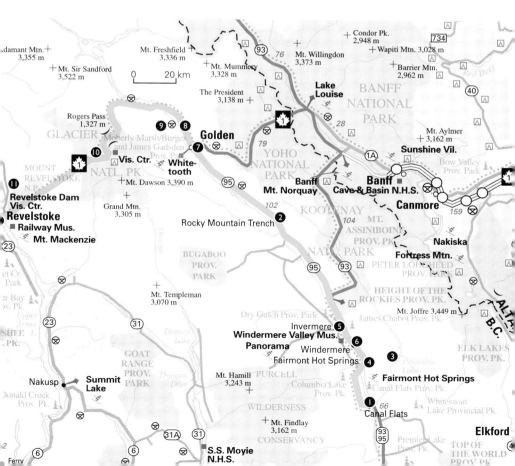

The Kootenays

Ratings

Geology	●●●●●
History	●●●●●
Mountains	●●●●●●
Children	●●●●
Outdoor activities	●●●●
Parks	●●●●
Architecture	●●●
First Nations	●●

This region takes in the West Kootenays through the Purcell, Selkirk and Monashee Ranges, heaven for lovers of rugged mountains and lakes. Linked by just one highway which follows the first track hacked from Hope to Fort Steele during the 1860s, Southern BC is more vertical than horizontal. What little flat space exists between mountain ranges is filled with water more often than not.

Ghost towns abound, no surprise in a region best known for mineral rushes in search of gold, copper, silver and lead as do smelter ruins, decaying mine shafts and long abandoned graveyards slowly disappearing beneath encroaching forests.

The future is as bright as the past. Urban professionals from across Canada have transformed one-time backwaters into modern enclaves surrounded by splendid opportunities for boating, hiking, fishing, skiing and other outdoor recreation.

AINSWORTH HOT SPRINGS❖❖

Ainsworth Hot Springs $$ *Hwy 31, 36km north from Balfour; tel: (250) 229-4212.*

The hot springs flow from a stalactite-filled cave. Spa aficionados swear by the water, which has the highest mineral content of any natural hot springs in Canada. Everyone else swears by the stunning views across Kootenay Lake from the 45°C outdoor baths.

BOUNDARY CREEK PROVINCIAL PARK❖❖

Boundary Creek Provincial Park $ *Hwy 3, just west from Greenwood; tel: (250) 494-6500; web: www.elp.gov.bc.ca/bcparks/explore/parkpgs/boundary.htm Open Apr–Oct.*

A slag heap and crumbling chimney are all that remain of the largest single producer of copper in the world between 1901 and 1918. The park also has pleasant camping and picnicking spots along Boundary Creek.

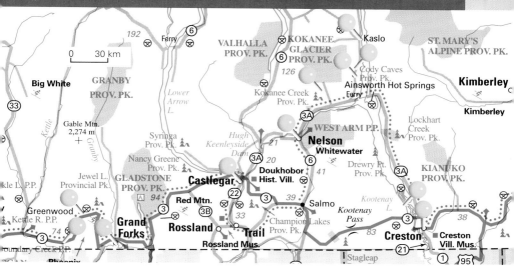

CASTLEGAR✢

Castlegar Chamber of Commerce 1995 6th Ave; tel: (250) 365-6313; web: www.castlegar.com

Hugh Keenlyside Dam $ North of town; tel: (250) 365-5299. Open daily.

Brilliant Suspension Bridge National Heritage Site $ Base of Airport Hill. Park at the south end of the new Kootenay River Bridge and walk 500m down the old highway.

Castlegar Museum $ 400 13th Ave; tel: (250) 365-6440. Open Mon–Sat, 0900–1700.

Doukhobor Historical Village $ Across from the Castlegar Airport; tel: (250) 365-6622. Open daily May–Sep.

Castlegar grew as a railway and mining town at the confluence of the Kootenay and Columbia rivers. Odorous fumes still waft from a pulp mill just below **Hugh Keenlyside Dam✢**, which backs the Columbia into Arrow Lakes, stretching 230km north to Revelstoke (*see page 236*). Doukhobor farms added an important agricultural element to the economy.

When local authorities ignored requests for a bridge across the Kootenay River, the Doukhobors (*see page 242*) designed and built their own span in 1913, which carried Hwy 3 traffic for decades. It forms part of the **Brilliant Suspension Bridge National Heritage Site✢✢✢**.

Castlegar Museum✢, an old CPR station, concentrates on area history from the early days of the 20th century.

Doukhobor Historical Village✢✢✢ is a reproduction of a typical village and includes the communal main house, cottages and workrooms. The furnishings, photographs and artworks are authentic, as are the costumed guides who explain traditional Doukhobor life and beliefs.

The small river island which forms **Zuckerberg Island Heritage Park✢✢✢** was named for a local Russian teacher who built an onion-dome home in the forest. Zuckerberg's home has been restored as a museum and tea room.

Accommodation and food in Castlegar

Fireside Inn $$ 1810 8th Ave; tel: (250) 365-2128, is convenient and central.

Zuckerberg Island Heritage Park $ *9th St and 7th Ave; tel: (250) 365-5511. Open May–Aug.*

Flamingo Motel $$ *1660 Columbia Ave; tel: (250) 365-7978*, has a park-like setting.

Common Grounds $ *692 18th St (Castleaird Pl); tel: (250) 365-3883*, is good for light meals.

The Doukhobors

The name means 'spirit wrestlers' in Russian. It's an apt name for a group of rabid pacifists who lived by the motto 'Toil and a Peaceful Life'. They successfully resisted the Russian Tsars only to be rent by internal divisions and bomb blasts.

Spiritual leader Peter Verigin led the Doukhobors to Canada, eventually settling on flat land across the Columbia River from Castlegar in 1908. Initially ignored by colonial authorities, the Doukhobors built many of the earliest bridges in Boundary Country, including the graceful Brilliant Suspension Bridge over the Kootenay River. About two dozen villages eventually filled *Ootischenia*, the 'Valley of Consolation', most of which is now occupied by Castlegar's airport and golf course.

The new immigrants planted orchards, grain and vegetables while building sawmills, jam factories, pipe works and similar enterprises, but their communal living arrangements, outspoken pacifism and vocal opposition to meat, tobacco and alcohol won few friends locally.

Verigin was killed by a bomb blast in 1924, almost certainly planted by a faction who feared that he was leading the community into mainstream Canadian society. The Doukhobors, along with Hutterites and other communal religious groups, eventually ran foul of laws designed to break up their tightly knit communities. Communal villages have disappeared, but thousands of Doukhobors still live in Boundary Country from Castlegar to Grand Forks. Many of their distinctive farm buildings are still visible along country roads, and Russian restaurants – invariably Doukhobor – are local institutions.

CODY CAVES PROVINCIAL PARK✧

Except for a few ladders, the rugged cave looks much as Henry Cody, an early prospector, first saw it a century ago. Open for guided tours only, paths snake through forests of stalactites, stalagmites and soda straws (**Cody Caves Provincial Park** $ *North of Ainsworth Hot Springs; tel (250) 353-7425. Open June–Oct, guided tours only.*)

CRESTON✦✦

ℹ Creston and District Chamber of Commerce *1711 Canyon St (Hwy 3); tel: (250) 428-4342. Open daily Jul–Aug; Sep–Jun, Mon–Fri.*

ℹ Creston Valley Museum and Archives $ *219 Devon Rd; tel: (250) 428-9262. Open daily May–Oct.*

Creston Valley Wildlife Center $ *Hwy 3, 10km west from Creston; tel: (250) 428-3259; web: www.cwildlife.bc.ca/index.html Open daily.*

A small farming town overlooks a plain where the Kootenay River once sprawled between the Purcell and Selkirk Mountains. The river has been dyked and channelled, creating fertile grain fields. Creston's rural past appears on murals in the town centre.

Highlight of the **Creston Valley Museum and Archives**✦ is a replica of a traditional Kootenay canoe, a 'sturgeon-nosed' craft with ends pointing down into the water.

Creston Valley Wildlife Centre✦✦✦, the interpretation centre for the 6800-hectare Creston Valley Wildlife Management Area, offers guided canoe tours of one of BC's richest wetland areas, also walking trails and educational displays. The area has the largest concentration of nesting ospreys in North America as well as massive bird migrations spring and autumn.

Accommodation and food in Creston

Downtowner Motor Inn $$ *1218 Canyon St; tel: (250) 428-2238,* is central.

Kootenay Rose Coffeehouse $ *129 N 10th Ave; tel: (250) 428-7252,* is the best vegetarian restaurant in the Kootenays.

Rendezvous Restaurant $$ *1230 Canyon St; tel: (250) 428-9554,* has the best steaks.

Uptown Café $ *1417 Canyon St; tel: (250) 428-3565,* lures locals with low prices and huge portions.

GRAND FORKS✦✦✦

An agricultural enclave at the junction of the Kettle Valley and Granby rivers, Grand Forks boomed with the 1900 opening of the Granby Smelter. The smelter closed in 1919, but the glistening mountain of ebony-coloured slag off Granby Road, just north of town, remains.

Right
Creston Valley Wildlife Centre

ⓘ Grand Forks Visitor InfoCentre
7362 5th St; tel: (250) 442-2833; web: www.boundary.bc.ca/

ⓜ Boundary Museum *$ 7370 5th St; tel: (250) 442-3737. Open daily May–Sep; Oct–Apr, Mon–Fri.*

Mountain View Doukhobor Museum $ *Hardy Mountain Rd; tel: (250) 442-8855. Open daily Jun–Oct.*

Phoenix Forest and History Tour $ *Phoenix Rd, 19.5km west from Grand Forks; self-guiding map at museums in Grand Forks or Greenwood; tel: (250) 442-3737. Drivable all year.*

Below
Kootenay Lake

Boundary Museum∗∗ houses artefacts from First Nations to Doukhobors, miners and railways. See the overview, then take a **self-guided tour**∗∗∗ of some of the 300-plus heritage buildings from the mining and railway era with a free museum map.

Mountain View Doukhobor Museum∗∗∗, in a 1912 Doukhobor communal home, overflows with period artefacts and records. Many other Doukhobor buildings are visible along Hardy Mountain Road as it twists back to Hwy 3.

The **Phoenix Forest and History Tour**∗∗∗, a back-road route between Grand Forks and Greenwood, passes many of the former mines, towns and railways that made the Boundary rich in the early 20th century.

Accommodation and food in Grand Forks

Grand Forks Motor Inn $$ *2729 Hwy 3; tel: (250) 442-2127*, is central.

Aromas Espresso Café & Bakery $ *7229 5th St; tel: (250) 442-0119*, is a good stop for breakfast, lunch or picnic supplies.

Chef's Garden Restaurant $$ *4415 Hwy 3 5km south, near Hardy Mountain Rd; tel: (250) 442-0257*, is the best Doukhobor restaurant in BC, serving vegetarian Russian cuisine.

Grand Forks Hotel & Restaurant $$ *7382 2nd St; tel: (250) 442-5944*, runs a close second to Chef's Garden and also has non-vegetarian choices.

GREENWOOD✦✦

Greenwood Museum $ 2 1 4 S Copper St (Hwy 3); tel: (250) 445-6355. Open May–Oct.

Lotzkar Park $ Hwy 3, just south of town.

This booming mining town nearly died after the local mines closed, but was revived as a Japanese-Canadian internment camp during World War II. Some 20 historic buildings have been restored. **Greenwood Museum✦✦✦** packs a major punch in its telling of the mining boom and Japanese internment days.

At **Lotzkar Park✦✦✦**, the best-preserved smelter ruins in North America rise above a barren ridge of black smelter slag that once glowed red hot even at noon. Locals call it a 'corner of hell gone cold'.

KASLO✦✦✦

Kaslo & District Chamber of Commerce 324 Front St; tel: (250) 353-2525. Open May–Oct.

Kaslo was a lumber town before silver and lead strikes brought miners flooding into the Kootenays. Tourism is number one today, thanks to 60 historic buildings and spectacular hiking, mountain biking, fishing, camping and boating.

The beached and meticulously restored *Moie*, at the **SS *Moie* National Historic Site✦✦✦**, sailed Kootenay Lake until 1957, and was the last sternwheeler in regular passenger service in Canada (*$ Front St; tel: (250) 353-2525; open May–Oct for self-guiding tours*).

KOKANEE CREEK PROVINCIAL PARK✦✦✦

Built on the site of a former lakeside estate, the park offers hiking, boating, camping, fishing and **Redfish Creek Spawning Channel✦✦✦**, an artificial spawning channel for Kokanee salmon. Best time to see the bright-red fish is mid-August to mid-September. The park also shelters a major osprey population (*$ Hwy 3A, 20km northeast from Nelson; tel: (250) 825-3500; web: www.elp.gov.bc.ca/bcparks/explore/parkpgs/kokanee.htm; open Apr–Oct*).

KOOTENAY LAKE✦✦✦

This long, narrow lake between the Purcell and Selkirk Mountains was a major navigation route long before it became a prime recreation area. Facilities lie along Hwy 3A, north from Creston to Kootenay Bay. There you can link to Balfour by BC Ferries, with more facilities along Hwy 3A west into Nelson.

Crawford Bay✦ is a collection of artisans producing metalwork, brooms and similar crafts, and a golf course.

Mortician David Brown built the **Glass House✦✦**, a scenic lakeside house, from 500,000 embalming fluid bottles in the 1950s, as he explained, 'to indulge a whim of a peculiar nature'.

Kootenay Lake $ *North from Creston, west to Nelson.*

Crawford Bay *Hwy 3A, 78km north from Creston.*

Glass House $ *Hwy 3A, 25km north from Creston; tel: (250) 223-8372. Open May–Oct.*

Lockhart Beach Provincial Park $ *Hwy 3A, north from Creston; tel: (250) 442-4200; web: www.elp.gov.bc.ca/bcparks/ explore/parkpgs/lockhart.htm*

There's excellent camping and hiking in **Lockhart Beach Provincial Park**❖❖ and the adjacent Lockhart Creek Provincial Park.

Right
Wall mural depicting Steve Martin in *Roxanne*

NELSON❖❖❖

This sparkling Victorian-era mining town was the set for Steve Martin's 1986 film *Roxanne*, a modern version of *Cyrano de Bergerac*. Local painters have enshrined Martin on a mural at the end of Vernon Street. Film publicity helped Nelson re-enforce its current incarnation as a rural refuge for urban professionals who expect high-speed Internet connections and the perfect *latte* after a tough day at the computer.

The imposing **courthouse**❖❖❖ and **city hall**❖❖❖ were designed by Francis Rattenbury, who built the Empress Hotel and Parliament House in Victoria. Costumed guides from the Chamber of Commerce lead walking and driving tours of the town's 350 **heritage buildings**❖❖❖ in summer, or follow self-guiding maps in any season.

Nelson and District Chamber of Commerce *225 Hall St; tel: (250) 352-3433; web: www.city.nelson.bc.ca/ Open daily.*

Chamber of Mines Eastern BC Museum $ *215 Hall St; tel: (250) 352-5242.*

Nelson Museum $ *402 Anderson Street; tel: (250) 352-9813. Open afternoons.*

Lakeside Park $ *Foot of the Nelson Bridge.*

Streetcar No 23 $ *Downtown to Lakeside Park.*

A dozen galleries stage monthly shows by 75 local artists. Maps of Artwalk♦♦♦ are available at the InfoCentre.

The **Chamber of Mines Eastern BC Museum**♦, run by the provincial mining association, has BC's biggest mineral collection. **Nelson Museum**♦, a strictly local collection, emphasises steamboats and mines.

Lakeside Park♦♦♦ is Nelson's most popular recreation area, with sandy beaches, canoe and boat rentals, lawns, playgrounds and greenhouse.

Streetcar No 23♦♦♦ is BC's only operating historic streetcar, making regular runs the length of the city along the lakeshore.

Accommodation and food in Nelson

Heritage Inn $$ *422 Nelson St; tel: (250) 352-5331*, has been Nelson's landmark hotel since the 1890s.

Inn The Garden $$ *408 Victoria St; tel: (250) 352-3226*, is a cheerful bed and breakfast in a historic home.

All Seasons Café $$ *620 Herridge Lane; tel: (250) 352-0101*, offers outstanding Northwest cuisine and the best wine list in Nelson.

Main Street Diner $$ *616 Baker St; tel: (250) 254-4848*, offers solid Greek meals.

Max & Irma's Kitchen $$ *515A Kootenay St; tel: (250) 352-2332*, serves Nelson's best pizza and Italian dishes.

Suggested tour

Total distance: 300km.

Time: It's possible to drive from Creston to Greenwood in one long day, but 2–3 days allows time to enjoy and explore.

Links: The **Okanagan Valley** (*see page 148*) and the **Cascade Mountains** (*see page 130*) lie west from Greenwood on Hwy 3. To the east, Hwy 3 leads to **The Crowsnest** (*see page 250*) and the **BC Rockies** (*see page 258*).

Route: The direct route follows Hwy 3 125km west from Creston past the **Creston Valley Wildlife Centre** and into the **Selkirk Mountains** to 1774m **Kootenay Pass**, the highest paved highway pass in Canada.

The west side of Kootenay Pass twists and turns across five canyons and multiple avalanche chutes. Just west is **Burnt Flat Junction** and Hwy 31, which runs 10km south to the US border at **Nelway** (*open daily 0800–2400*).

Hwy 3 turns north to **Salmo**, then west to **Bombi Summit**, 1214m,

Right
Ferry converted to house on
the shores of Kootenay Lake

with a long descent to the **Columbia River** at Castlegar. The best view of the confluence of the Columbia and Kootenay rivers is from the **Ootischenia Lookout Rest Area**, 8km from the summit on the west side of the highway.

Scenic alternative: The more interesting 150-km route to Castlegar follows Hwy 3A north from Creston along the shores of **KOOTENAY LAKE ❶**, passing **Glass House**, **Lockhart Beach Provincial Park** and **Crawford Bay** on the way to BC Ferries at Kootenay Bay. The 30-minute crossing to **Balfour** is free, but the line-up can take most of the day, especially in summer.

Detour: From Balfour, turn north on Hwy 31 to **AINSWORTH HOT SPRINGS ❷** and **CODY CAVES PROVINCIAL PARK ❸** on the way to **KASLO ❹**. The tiny village has more than 60 heritage buildings, including the SS *Moyie*, a sternwheeler that once carried passengers on the lake. Return to Balfour.

Hwy 3A hugs the north shore of the West Arm of Kootenay Lake. The south shore is all but inaccessible except by boat. The waters between hold record-sized trout and kokanee (land-locked) salmon. What looks like a steamboat cabin perched on the north side of the highway was the upper saloon and wheelhouse of the MV *Nasookin*, once the largest steamboat on Kootenay Lake. The road crosses the bright orange **Nelson Bridge** into **NELSON** ❺, a mining town that has moved into the computer age.

Kootenay Lake empties into the **Kootenay River** just west of Nelson. The highway passes four hydroelectric dams along the river, built to take advantage of the 200m fall from Kootenay Lake at Nelson to the Columbia River at Castlegar. A lay-by 13km west of the junction with Hwy 6 offers a good view of **Lower Bonnington Dam**. A second lay-by 1500m beyond overlooks **Brilliant Dam** and, just downstream toward the Columbia River, the disused Brilliant Suspension Bridge. A modern bridge arcs over the river to **CASTLEGAR** ❻.

Hwy 3 climbs south from Castlegar, then turns west over dramatic canyons toward **Christina Lake**, an important winter range for deer and elk.

Hwy 395 leads south into Washington just beyond the lake, while Hwy 3 continues westbound into **Boundary Country**, a transition zone between the high Kootenay peaks and the drier, more fertile Okanagan Valley to the West.

GRAND FORKS ❼ is the commercial hub of the Boundary Country, an agricultural town that boomed with mineral strikes in nearby hills. Continue along Hwy 3 over **Eholt Summit**, named for an abandoned mining town, to **GREENWOOD** ❽, a one-time mine boom town, which claims modern fame as the smallest city in BC.

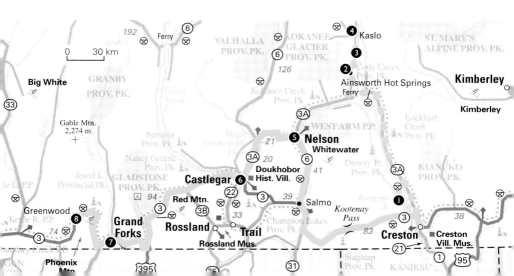

The Crowsnest

Ratings

Heritage	●●●●●
Historical sights	●●●●
Scenery	●●●●
Children	●●●
Museums	●●●
Architecture	●●
Food	●●
Railways	●

Perched east of the Kootenays and south of the Columbia River Valley is a microcosm of BC, with a history of coal and gold mining, lumbering, important freight railway lines and scenic ski alps, complete with a purpose-built Bavarian town. The cheerful-looking crow on Crowsnest Highway signposts belies the massacre of horse-stealing Crow warriors by Blackfoot braves who resented thieves camping in their territory, their nest. Highway 3, called the Crowsnest, spans the Alberta–BC border at Crowsnest Pass and zigzags south and west for several hundred kilometres. A circuit from Cranbrook, the regional hub, links First Nations and Gold Rush town history with scenic recreation lakes, a magnificent falls and an alpine village, famed for accordions and alpenhorns. In winter, this southeast corner of BC is transformed into a winter wonderland of mountains and icy lakes, with major ski resorts at Kimberley and Fernie.

CRANBROOK✣

....

ℹ️ **Cranbrook and District Chamber of Commerce InfoCentre** 2279 Cranbrook St N; tel: (250) 426-5914 or (800) 222-6174; web: www.cranbrook chamber.kootenays.com/ or www.cyberlink.bc.ca/ ~cbkchamber Open daily.

Elizabeth Lake Sanctuary InfoCentre 1101 1st Ave S. Open Jun–Labour Day, 0900–1700.

Aboriginal Ktunaxa lost their camping ground to White settlers in 1870 and to a member of the BC Legislature. Cranbrook became a CPR divisional point and the railway its lifeblood.

Canadian Museum of Rail Travel✣ Train buffs have a field day touring through the self-styled 'Canada's Orient Express', built in 1929 as a nine-car unit for CPR's Trans-Canada Limited for Montréal to Vancouver service. Half the cars are in various states of repair, but the *Argyle* dining-car serves tea and light snacks in a stunning restored carriage.

Canadian Museum of Rail Travel $$ / Van Horne St N at Baker St. (Hwy 3/95); tel: (250) 489-3918; web: www.crowsnest.bc.ca/cmrt Open Jul–Aug, 0800–2000; Easter–Jun, 1000–1800; Thanksgiving–Easter, 1200–1700.

Elizabeth Lake Sanctuary Wildlife Area $ 1101 1st Ave S.

Jimsmith Lake Provincial Park $ 2km west of Cranbrook on Jim Smith Lake Rd; web: www.elp.gov.bc.ca/bcparks/explore/parkpgs/jimsmith. atm Open May–Oct.

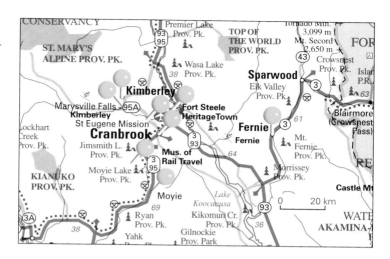

Elizabeth Lake Sanctuary Wildlife Area✺✺ A slice of the Rocky Mountain Trench protects 113 hectares of nature, with a lake-girding trail, a waterfowl viewing hide and a dip-netting pond to peruse fish closely. Coots, killdeer, Canada geese, ruddy ducks, wood ducks, buffleheads and black terns share the lake with muskrats, elk, moose and turtles.

Jimsmith Lake Provincial Park✺ Join the locals swimming, canoeing, picnicking or camping. You can cross-country ski to the lake in winter and lace up some skates to enjoy the ice.

Accommodation and food in Cranbrook

Inn of the South $$ *803 Cranbrook St; tel: (250) 489-4301 or (800) 663-2708.* This motor inn has 101 rooms and a very central location.

Prestige Rocky Mountain Resort $$$ *209 Van Horne St S; tel: (250) 417-0444 or (877) 737-8443.* A modern, posh railway-theme hotel has 108 rooms adjacent to the railway museum.

Super 8 $ *2370 Cranbrook St N; tel: (250) 489-8028 or (800) 800-8000.* Across from the InfoCentre, this chain hotel is clean and comfortable at the quiet north end of town.

Bavarian Chalet $$ *821 Baker St at 9th Ave S; tel: (250) 489-3305.* On Thur–Sat, have the prime rib; otherwise it's a mixture of German specialities and all-Canadian. Closed Sun.

Kootenay Cattle Co $$ *40 Van Horne St N; tel: (250) 489-5811.* One of a chain of regional restaurants, this restaurant's shabby exterior belies the juicy steaks on the menu and its popularity with local people.

FERNIE❖❖

ℹ **Fernie Chamber of Commerce InfoCentre** *Hwy 3 at Dicken Rd (look for the oil derrick); tel: (250) 423-6868; web: www.fernie.net and the delightful humour of www.city.fernie.bc.ca/ Open summer 0900–1900, shorter hours in winter.*

Fernie Alpine Resort $$ *Ski Area Rd; tel: (250) 423-4655; web: www.skifernie.com; Snow Phone: (250) 423-3555. Ski season: open daily late Nov–mid-Apr, 0900–1600.*

Mountains and tourism services are the *raison d'être* for this all-season recreational area, once known for coal-mining and rum-running.

Fernie Alpine Resort ❖❖ An annual 9-m snowfall creates a paradise for alpine and Nordic skiers, snowshoers and snowmobilers. Sleigh rides and dog sledding are other winter options. Mountain bike, ride horse, kayak, raft, hike, fly fish or take a chair-lift ride to scenic views in summer.

Accommodation and food in Fernie

Canadian Spruce Bed and Breakfast $$ *661 4th Ave; tel: (250) 423-6445 or (888) 605-8013; web: www.kci.bc.ca/~cdnsprbb/cdnsprbb.html.* A 1908 multi-storey heritage house with fireplaces, a sitting porch and central location.

Little Witch Log Inn $$ *Hwy 3 at Dicken Rd, next to the InfoCentre; tel: (250) 423-4956; web: www.rockies/~lilwitch/NFMAIN.HTM.* Radiant floor heating completes the cosy feeling of this log-cabin, chalet-style lodge.

Right
Living history at Fort Steele

bove
rt Steele steam train

Wolf's Den Mountain Lodge \$\$ *Ski Area Rd, Fernie Alpine Ski Resort; tel: (250) 423-9202 or (800) 258-7669; web: www.skifernie.com* Open all year, the 42-room lodge offers ski-in, ski-out slope access.

Jamochas Coffee House & Bagel Co \$ *851 7th Ave (Hwy 3); tel: (250) 423-6977.* Cribbage, bread, coffee and atmosphere are welcome after a drive. Open 0800–2200.

ᶠORT STEELE HERITAGE TOWN✦✦✦

**Fort Steele
Heritage Town \$\$**
851 Hwy 93/95 16km
orth of Cranbrook; tel:
50) 417-6000. Open daily
nrise–dusk, with
haracter actors in
ımmer.

The 1864 Kootenay Gold Rush brought settlers to Galbraith's Ferry, later renamed for NWMP Superintendent Sam Steele who brought law and peace to the region. The *de facto* capital of the East Kootenays' rich mining economy lost out and declined when BC Legislator Colonel James Baker got the CPR to build the proposed divisional point in his Cranbrook holdings. The restoration is perfect, with summertime set pieces between neighbours on the street discussing the day's events and politics, all in costume. A bakery, tin-smithy, confectionery, heritage buildings, horse-drawn wagon rides and a steam train provide a well-rounded introduction to Fort Steele's golden years.

KIMBERLEY❖❖

ⓘ Kimberley Visitor InfoCentre *350 Ross St; tel: (250) 427-3666; web: www.cyberlink.bc.ca/~kimbchamber The beerstein waving Happy Hans statue in lederhosen is hard to miss.*

ⓜ Bavarian City Mining Railway $ Cominco Power House Tours $ *Open late Jun–Labour Day, in conjunction with the Railway ride: the Power House tour is a stop en route on the railway.*

At 1113m, Canada's highest city was dedicated to silver, zinc and lead mining production at Sullivan Mine (Cominco), scheduled for closure in 2001. Happy Hans, the world's largest cuckoo clock, Bavarian kitsch and a ski resort have replaced the local mining industry.

Salvaged railway cars at the **Bavarian City Mining Railway** now show off the countryside on the 11-km ride through the scenic countryside.

The mining company wanted to promote fertiliser in 1927. The resultant **Cominco Gardens❖ $** (*306 3rd Ave; tel: (250) 427-2293. Open May–Sept, dawn to dusk. Tea-room open daily in summer 1000–1800*) boast 48,000 blooms annually, with dedicated rose, prairie and Victorian gazebo areas.

In the **Platzl❖ $** (*T-shaped pedestrian street encircled by Wallinger Ave, Howard St, Kimberley Ave and Ross St*), Bavarian architecture, restaurants, shops, wandering accordion players and depictions of the Happy Hans town mascot reflect the transition the town economy has made from mining lead to mining tourists.

Right
Marysville Falls

Accommodation and food in Kimberley

Wild Rose Ranch & Resort $$$ *East of Wasa Lake, north 8km on Wolf Creek Rd; tel: (250) 422-3403 or (800) 324-6188.* A family-owned tourist ranch is purpose-built for horse-riders and fly fishers in a stunning mountain-view setting. Join in as the family drives cattle once a month from May to November.

Chef Bernard's $$ *170 Spokane St, on the Platzl; tel: (250) 427-4820 or (800) 905-8338.* The chef is well known and locally beloved in this Bavarian *schnitzelhaus* which serves excellent pasta dishes. Open daily 0800–2200 (to 2400 in summer*).*

Old Bauernhaus $$$ *280 Norton St, up the ski hill; tel: (250) 427-5133.* Bavaria was never so authentic as in this 350-plus-year-old building dismantled and reassembled here. Open Thur–Mon 1700–2230.

Snowdrift Café $ *on the Platzl; tel: (250) 427-2001.* Big, rich cups of *latte* and home-grown spinach salad with gorgonzola cheese, walnuts, mushrooms, carrots, and wholewheat bread reflect the quality of the menu at this fabulous vegetarian restaurant. Open Mon–Sat 1000–2300, Sun 1200–1800.

MARYSVILLE FALLS✦✦✦

Marysville Falls $
7km south of Kimberley.

An easy 10-minute afternoon walk along rocky Mark Creek to a spectacular crashing 30m cascade is worth a brief stop.

MOYIE✦ AND MOYIE LAKE PROVINCIAL PARK✦✦

Moyie and Moyie Lake Provincial Park $ *31km south of Cranbrook, Hwy 3; web: www.elp.gov.bc.ca/bcparks/explore/parkpgs/moyie.htm Open Apr–Oct.*

Bears roam around the popular windsurfing and swimming lake, which nestles within the Purcell Mountains. Explorer David Thompson's party was almost swept away by Moyie River floods in 1808, but today's 200 residents point with pride to lovely buildings and a well-preserved fire hall which served when the St Eugene Mine silver/lead mine owners became rich before 1898.

ST EUGENE MISSION✦✦

St Eugene Mission $ *515 Mission Rd, Cranbrook; tel: (250) 489-372. Stop by nearby Ktunaxa Tribal office for information and to go inside the church.*

The 1897 white Victorian gingerbread church in the middle of farms on Ktunaxa/Kinbasket St Mary's Reserve is as immaculate inside as out with stained-glass windows and interior supports resembling a barn. Across Old Airport Road is construction on a destination resort centred around the former Kootenay Indian Residential School building.

British Columbia Provincial Parks–Kootenay District *Wasa Lake Dr, Wasa; tel: (250) 422-4200. Information on all Crowsnest area provincial parks.*

Suggested tour

Total distance: 90km for a circuit from Cranbrook. Detours: 97km from Cranbrook to Fernie; 31km south to Moyie.

Time: 2 days.

Links: The **Columbia River** (*see page 230*) lies north of Wasa. Continu south and west of Moyie Lake Provincial Park on Hwy 3, the Crowsnes to Creston and **The Kootenays** (*see page 240*). North of Fernie a Sparwood, Hwy 3 turns east to the Crowsnest Pass and enters Alberta.

Route: CRANBROOK ❶ makes a convenient base with services an facilities, but with this circuit, it's almost as convenient to stay i Kimberley.

Cranbrook's main attraction is the **Canadian Museum of Rail Trav** and the red wooden railway **Water Tower** near by, situated along th Canadian Pacific Railway line where rolling stock provides a realisti background for the historic railway carriages. A graceful reconstructe red-brick **Rotary Clock Tower** (*Baker & Cranbrook Sts*) is the focal poir for a Chamber of Commerce *Heritage Tour* brochure of Cranbrook' Downtown and Baker Hill Residential Area buildings. **Elizabeth Lak Sanctuary Wildlife Area** is an utterly peaceful spot for picnicking an walking the lakeside trail accompanied by birdsong. Follow signs whe crossing Hwy 3 to **Jimsmith Lake Provincial Park**, with non-powere watersports on offer.

Take Hwy 3 to the northeast end of Cranbrook and go left on to Hw 95A. Be prepared to turn right almost immediately on to Old Airpo Road to **ST EUGENE MISSION** ❷ in the bucolic midst of the trib headquarters for the Ktunaxa/Kinbasket First Nation **St Mary's Reserv** The restored historic church is lovely. Ask at the tribal centre to have th church unlocked. Continue along Old Airport Road to rejoin Hwy 95A.

Stop at the bridge in **Marysville** at the south edge of **KIMBERLEY ❸** and hike down Mark Creek for a view of magnificent **MARYSVILL FALLS** ❹. Kimberley's heart is the Platzl, the Bavarian chalet-styl pedestrian plaza, with a cuckoo clock that claims to be the world' largest. It chimes on the hour, revealing the ubiquitous Happy Han yodelling. Catch the Bavarian City Mining Railway excursion train a the Platzl. A short drive up the ski hill offers vistas over the Kootena River Valley. Before leaving town, take in the thousands of blooms a Cominco Gardens.

Continue north on Hwy 95A past **Ta Ta Creek** and turn south at th Hwy 93/95 junction to **Wasa Lake Provincial Park** for swimming i the Kootenay's warmest lake (May–Oct). Follow Hwy 93/95 to **FOR STEELE ❺** for time travel in one of BC's best and most authenti historic site restorations. Return to Cranbrook.

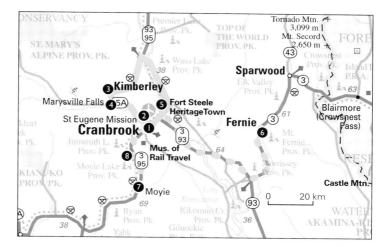

Detour to Fernie: South of Fort Steele, go east on Hwy 3/93. North of **Elko** on Hwy 3 is the **Elk Valley** traversing the Elk River, named for the numerous wapiti spotted by settlers. Coal mining boomed around 1900 from the valley into Alberta, and Fernie and the surrounding area became rich, though plagued by a legendary curse on the mines. **FERNIE ALPINE RESORT** ❻ buzzes with winter activity in a stunning range of mountains.

Detour to Moyie: Take Hwy 3/95 south of Cranbrook to **MOYIE** ❼, a tiny town set on a scenic hillside. **MOYIE LAKE PROVINCIAL PARK** ❽ has watersports and sailing.

Demon King Coal

Fernie became rich on coal deposits, a seam which stretches across the Crowsnest Pass into Alberta at Frank Slide, site of a 1903 disaster when poor coal-mining techniques and water seepage caused 30 million cu m of limestone to slide down Turtle Mountain on to Frank Townsite.

Fernie, too, seemed cursed. Coal Creek Mine developer William Fernie, so the story goes, extracted information about coal deposits from a local Ktunaxa maiden, while pretending to woo her. When the lady was rejected by Fernie, the girl's mother placed a curse on Fernie. Curse or no, the Coal Creek Mine explosion in 1901 killed 128, followed by a 1904 fire which burned the town, and a flood in 1916. A 1964 ritual by local First Nations chiefs was enacted to counteract the curse. Since 1901, though, local people have seen the Ghostrider, said to be the spurned betrothed seated on a horse, and her mother chasing Fernie across the face of Mount Hosmer at the end of each day.

BC Rockies Parks

Ratings

Geology	●●●●●
Mountains	●●●●●
National parks	●●●●●
Nature	●●●●●
Outdoor activities	●●●●●
Scenery	●●●●●
Walking	●●●●●
Wildlife	●●●●●

The Rocky Mountains west of the Continental Divid shelter great rivers, exploding cataracts, emerald-gree lakes, red-rock defiles, thick green forests and slashes colour gushing forth from the earth. Disc-shaped trilobite whose fossils were discovered in Yoho National Par crawled upon this raw, breathtaking landscape half a billio years ago. Kootenay National Park's Radium Hot Spring pools soothed First Nations bathers for centuries. A enduring symbol of the Rockies, Mount Robson, dominat eastward afternoon vistas, a snow-striated massif embrace by forest at its base.

Early explorers looking for fur trade routes west followe streams and whitewater rivers to their headwaters. Th mountains required feats of railway engineering when th imperative to ship goods, settlers, and tourists westwa became financially irresistible. Despite a million visito flowing through each year, there's enough high-count wilderness in the BC Rockies to leave memories untrammelled vastness.

KOOTENAY NATIONAL PARK✤✤✤

ⓘ Kootenay National Park tel: (250) 347-9615; web: parkscanada.pch.gc.ca/ kootenay

West Gate Information Centre Radium Hot Springs Pools; tel: (250) 347-9505. Open late May–late Jun and Labour Day–3rd Fri–Sun of Sep, 0930–1630; late Jun–early Sep, 0900–1900; late Sep–late May, tel: (250) 347-9615 or (403) 522-3833.

Visitors who merely drive through without stopping inadvertently p homage to the park's *raison d'être*. The Banff–Windermere Highw Hwy 93, the route through Kootenay National Park, was built betwe 1912 and 1923 as an all-weather commercial transit road over t Rockies. Motorised touring and holiday-makers never looked back!

The 95-km stretch of Hwy 93 in the park follows the meandering Sinclair and Swede creeks to the Kootenay and Vermilion rivers. T parkway rises east from the Columbia River Valley through a red-r canyon and passes vistas of a ridge of peaks framing the Kooter River before winding up to the Continental Divide at the 1651 Vermilion Pass on the BC–Alberta boundary.

The Kootenay (pronounced 'coo-teh-knee' in Canada), 'people fr beyond the hills', lived and gave character and names to a region fr the peaks of the Rockies to southern interior BC. Descendants c

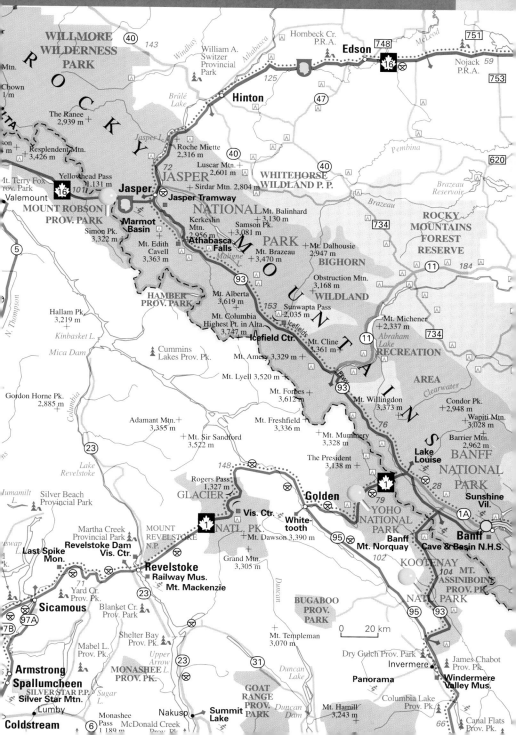

WILLMORE
WILDERNESS
PARK
ROCKY
40 143 Windipay

William A.
Switzer
Provincial
Park

Hornbeck Cr.
P.R.A.

Edson 748
16

Nojack 59
P.R.A.
751
McLeod
753

Mtn.
Chown
1/m

125 Brûlé
Lake
Hinton
47

Pembina

620

The Ranee
2,939 m
Jasper L.
Roche Miette
2,316 m
40

Whitehorse
Wildland P.P.

Brazeau
Reservoir

son
Resplendent Mtn.
3,426 m
72 JASPER
Luscar Mtn.
2,601 m
40

Brazeau
734

ROCKY
MOUNTAINS
FOREST
RESERVE

Mt. Terry Fox
rov. Park
Yellowhead Pass
1,131 m
1011
16
Jasper
Sirdar Mtn. 2,804 m

Valemount
5
MOUNT ROBSON
PROV. PARK
Jasper Tramway
NATIONAL

Mt. Balinhard
3,130 m

11 184

Marmot
Basin
Simon Pk.
3,322 m
Kerkeslin
Mtn.
2,956 m
Samson Pk.
3,081 m
PARK
BIGHORN
Mt. Dalhousie
2,947 m

11

Mt. Edith
Cavell
3,363 m
Athabasca
Falls
Maligne
L.
Mt. Brazeau
3,470 m

WILDLAND

Obstruction Mtn.
3,168 m
Mt. Michener
2,337 m

734

N. Thompson

HAMBER
PROV. PARK
93

MOUNTAIN

Sunwapta Pass
2,035 m
11
Abraham
Lake
RECREATION

Hallam Pk.
3,219 m
Kinbasket L.
Mt. Alberta
3,619 m
153
Icefields

Mt. Cline
3,361 m

AREA

Mica Dam
Mt. Columbia
Highest Pt. in Alta.
3,747 m
Icefield Ctr.

93

Clearwater

Cummins
Lakes Prov. Pk.
Mt. Amery 3,329 m
Mt. Michener

Condor Pk.
2,948 m
Wapiti Mtn.
3,028 m

Gordon Horne Pk.
2,885 m
Columbia
Mt. Lyell 3,520 m
Mt. Forbes
3,612 m
Mt. Willingdon
3,373 m
Barrier Mtn.
2,962 m

Adamant Mtn.
3,355 m
Mt. Sir Sandford
3,522 m
Mt. Freshfield
3,336 m
Mt. Mummery
3,328 m
76
Lake
Louise
28
BANFF
NATIONAL

23
Lake
Revelstoke
148
Rogers Pass
1,327 m
The President
3,138 m
YOHO
NATIONAL
1
79
PARK

Sunshine
Vil.

umamilt
L.
Silver Beach
Provincial Park
GLACIER
Vis. Ctr.
Golden
PARK
1A

Last Spike
Mon.
Martha Creek
Provincial Park
Revelstoke Dam
Vis. Ctr.
MOUNT
REVELSTOKE
N.P.
1
NATL. PK.
White-
tooth
Mt. Dawson 3,390 m
95
Banff
Mt. Norquay
102
Banff
Cave & Basin N.H.S.

swap
7B
Revelstoke
Railway Mus.
Mt. Mackenzie
Grand Mtn.
3,305 m
KOOTENAY
104
MT.
ASSINIBOINE
PROV. PK.

71
Yard Cr.
Prov. Pk.
23
Duncan
BUGABOO
PROV.
PARK

Sicamous
97A
Blanket Cr.
Prov. Park
95
93
NATL. PK.

Shelter Bay
Prov. Park
Upper
Arrow
L.
Mt. Templeman
3,070 m
Dry Gulch Prov. Park
Invermere
James Chabot
Prov. Pk.

Armstrong
Spallumcheen
Mabel L.
Prov. Pk.
MONASHEE
PROV. PK.
23
31
Duncan
Lake
Panorama
Windermere
Valley Mus.

SILVER STAR P.P.
Silver Star Mtn.
Lumby
Sugar
L.
GOAT
RANGE
PROV.
PARK
Duncan
Dam
Columbia Lake
Prov. Pk.

Coldstream
6
Monashee
Pass
1,189 m
McDonald Creek
Nakusp
Summit
Lake
Mt. Hamill
3,243 m
66
Canal Flats
Prov. Pk.

0   20 km

Right
Sinclair Canyon, Kootenay
National Park

**ⓘ Vermilion Crossing
Visitor Centre** *63km
northeast of Radium; no
phone. Open daily Apr–late
May, early Oct Fri–Sun,
holidays 1100–1800; late
May–Sep, 1000–1830.*

linguistically unique and part Plains, part (BC) Plateau group, t
Ktunaxa, Kootenae, Kootenai or Kootenay live in BC and in the U.
in Montana. Foods, hunting traditions, homes, clothing a
ceremonies resemble bits and pieces of neighbouring bands', but we
distinct. Whatever their origins, the Kootenay gathered the brigh
coloured mud running from the mountain streams and soaked wea
bones in the medicinal hot springs.

Kootenay peoples called the coloured earth 'The Place Where t
Red Spirit of the Earth is Taken'. Scientifically, iron oxide stai
water pushing up from three springs beneath the earth red a
yellow, sometimes mixing to brown or orange. The 'vermilion'
which the park's river and pass are named reflect the ochre paint p
reddish colour.

Kootenays gathered the bright mud, formed and baked it into cak
then rubbed off powder as needed and mixed it with rendered anim

Radium/Radium Hot Springs Travel Infocentre *4-7585 Main St W, Radium Hot Springs; tel: (250) 347-9331 or (800) 347-9704; web: www.radiumhotsprings.com,* the southwestern edge of Kootenay National Park, serves the area's population and services centre. There are also hotels in the park above the Radium Hot Springs pools.

Paint Pots *85km northeast of Radium.*

Radium Hot Springs Pools $ *3km east of Radium; tel: (250) 347-9301 (800) 767-1611; web: www.worldweb.com/ParksCanada-Kootenay/rings.html Open mid-May–mid-Oct, 0900–2300; mid-Oct–mid-May, 1100–2100. Enquire about family rates and hire of swimsuits and towels. Massage and reflexology treatments available; tel: (250) 347-9714. There is a summertime poolside restaurant for drinks, sandwiches, burgers, ice-cream and snacks.*

grease for face paint, clothing and tepee decoration and for medicine. When White entrepreneurs started a short-lived ochre mining operation for paint pigments in the early 1900s, they followed Kootenay trading practices by transporting the mud elsewhere, albeit by hand, to Castle Junction (Banff National Park) and on to Calgary by railway.

A 1.6-km return trail traverses varied countryside before reaching the **Paint Pots***, actually three main pools – one red, one yellow and one bright green. Descend from the parking area into a sub-Alpine forest with ferns and wild flowers growing beneath the trees. A swinging suspension bridge bounces and sways across the crashing blue pale waters of the Kootenay River. The land suddenly runs with rivulets of colour as the path ascends by the ruins of mining equipment to the three pots, an oasis of coloured, water-filled pock-marks surrounded by forest. A tiny wetlands offers fine bird-spotting.

The sheer golden-red walls of Sinclair Canyon shelter the site where groundwater sinking 2km down a fault in the earth returns to the surface heated to 44°C. Most of the park's 1.2 million annual visitors make a pilgrimage to the outdoor **Radium Hot Springs Pools**, to soak, swim or absorb the atmosphere of an unpretentious, not-quite-spa experience. The hot, semi-secluded soaking pool is a toasty 40°C; a lap in the swimming-pool afterwards will seem almost bracing at 29°C. Mountain sheep are sometimes spotted clinging to nearby cliffs.

Radium? No, a misnomer, but there is radon, with a minuscule amount of radioactivity. Early 20th-century researchers presumed it was radium, and therapeutic, though a wristwatch emits more radium than the pools! Equally pleasant is the faint-to-odourless atmosphere distinctly lacking in the sulphur experienced in Banff's Cave and Basin National Historic Site (*see page 271*).

Accommodation and food in Kootenay National Park

Alpen Motel $$ *5022 Hwy 93, Radium Hot Springs; tel: (250) 347-9823,* is cheerful with flower-boxes and 14, spotless, no-pet, non-smoking rooms a block from the park portal.

Kootenay Park Lodge $$ *Hwy 93 at Vermilion Crossing; tel: (403) 762-9196 or (403) 283-7482; web: www.kootenayparklodge.com.* To stay in the centre of the park in a log cabin is almost a wilderness experience. Canadian Pacific Railway built the lodge in 1923. There is a licensed restaurant; the gift-shop sandwiches are homemade and scrumptious. Open mid-May–Sep.

Old Salzburg Restaurant $$ *4943 Hwy 93; tel: (250) 347-6553,* matches the style of many nearby alpine-chalet-style motels with Austrian specialities such as schnitzel.

MOUNT ROBSON PROVINCIAL PARK✦✦✦

ℹ Valemount Visitor InfoCentre *99 Gorse Street; tel: (250) 566-4846. Open mid-May–mid-Sept.*

🅝 Mount Robson Provincial Park

TIC *tel: (250)566-4325; web: www.env.gov.bc.ca/bcparks/ explore/parkpgs/mtrobson. htm Visitor Centre at the west end of the park on Hwy 16. Open May–Oct.*

Berg Lake Trail *Car park 2km north of Visitor Centre with trailhead. Advance registration at Visitor Centre required for multiple-day hiking. 23km one-way to end; pre-book for a camp pitch en route. Carry all-weather gear and provisions.*

The Texqakallt/Shuswap aboriginal name, *yuh-hai-has-kun,* says it a] the Mountain of the Spiral Road to Heaven. *If* Mount Robson is ov from behind the often obscuring cloud cover, the sheer rise of i 3954m height is stunningly beautiful. The highest peak in th Canadian Rockies was not scaled until 1913, an assent whic continues to lure only the most experienced climbers today. Wheth driving by on the Yellowhead Hwy, Hwy 16, or stopping for a loo plan on going west in the morning or east in the afternoon for th best-lit views of Mount Robson's face.

The most famous view of Mount Robson and its only slightly le high neighbour, 3426-m Mount Resplendent, is from the Visitc Centre along Hwy 16 at the park's west end. **Berg Lake Trail**✦✦✦ c park is 2km north of the Visitor Centre. From there, it's a several-da advance-registration, 23-km hike to Robson Pass, with limite pitches for self-contained camping along the trail. Short of that Kinney Lake at 7km, famed for still morning reflections of Mour Robson. Beyond is the Valley of the Thousand Falls and no fewer tha 15 glaciers, including the advancing Berg Glacier which 'calves' blu ice into Berg Lake.

East of the Visitor Centre is a short, easy hike through forest 1 the sheer drop of **Overlander Falls**✦✦, named for 1862 prospecto headed for the Cariboo Gold Fields with more determination tha preparation.

Midway through the park, you will spot waterfalls across Moo Lake. Canoe through the rightly named **Moose Marsh**✦✦, a likely plac to find the 450kg beasts browsing. The Fraser River, which has i

headwaters at Fraser Pass in the provincial park, is popular with whitewater rafters where it parallels the Yellowhead Hwy between Red Pass at the west end of Moose Lake and near the Visitor Centre, and below that spot on placid water.

The park's eastern boundary at the 1146m **Yellowhead Pass*** is also the Continental Divide and the provincial border with Alberta at Jasper National Park. The Yellowhead, the lowest pass in this section of the Rockies, was used for centuries by aboriginal peoples, trappers and hunters. Ironically, although it was surveyed in 1872 and known to be the best logistical engineering choice for building a railway line through the Rockies, in 1881 the CPR chose to build the railway over Kicking Horse Pass further to the south, to forestall American railroaders from stealing business from southern Canada.

Tête Jaune Cache*, Yellowhead's purported spot for hiding goods and furs, is at the junction of the eponymous Yellowhead Hwy (16) and Hwy 5. A few buildings and services suffice for the meeting of the roads (pronounced *tay john*) named for trapper Pierre Hatsinaton's golden hair (*see page 263*).

Accommodation and food in Mount Robson Provincial Park

There is a store for provisioning across from the Visitor Centre and two reservation-recommended campgrounds with 144 pitches in the park.

Mount Robson Lodge $$ *log cabins* and **Robson Shadows Campground $** *tel: (888) 566-4821,* are 5km west of the park.

Valemount (*44km southwest of the park*) offers a range of motels.

Yoho National Park❖❖❖

Above
Emerald Lake, Yoho National Park

Few places on earth have both yielded such a rich treasure trove fossils and been the site of almost unimaginable modern engineerir feats. First Nations Cree used the word *yoho* to express av and wonder at a landscape that included rock escarpments, hangir glaciers, waterfalls, emerald lakes, crashing rivers and sheer rang of mountains.

John Palliser's 1857 expedition took three years to scientifical survey Southern Alberta and what would become British Columb. Geologist-naturalist James Hector was assigned to evaluate the riv valley and its steep mountain pass. His skittish horse fell near Wap Falls, knocking him out and frightening Hector's troupe. When recovered, the relieved men named the river Kicking Horse.

Though Hector recommended against transportation across Kicki Horse Pass and in favour of the less precipitous Yellowhead Pa

Yoho National Park tel: (250) 343-83 or (250) 343-6324; b: www.parkscanada.h.gc.ca/yoho.

nerald Lake 11km rth of Field.

further north, nationalist imperative dictated that Kicking Horse be chosen as the Canadian transcontinental railway route, to show encroaching American interests that Canadians could transport their own commodities.

Brilliant, cantankerous Major Albert Bowman Rogers surveyed the passes and recommended that, despite its slope, the Kicking Horse must connect to another pass in the unexplored Selkirk Range to the West (*see Rogers Pass, page 232*) and would be viable. Canadian Pacific Railway general manager, William Cornelius Van Horne, pleasing stockholders and covering up mismanagement scandals, pushed for the Kicking Horse route. The years from 1885 to 1905 saw runaway train crashes on the 4.5 per cent grade, until the spiral tunnels were built.

A CPR engineer taking a break near the railway hub in Field probably thought he was dreaming to see some discs of stone resembling horseshoe crabs in the dirt of Mount Stephen. He had found trilobites.

Smithsonian Institution palaeontologist Charles Walcott, conducting Rockies digs on Burgess Pass within view of Emerald Lake in 1909, recognised the trilobites for what they were: fossils from the Palaeozoic Cambrian period, 500–590 million years old. The Burgess Shale has since yielded 170 fossilised species, more than 65,000 specimens of hard-shelled animals which swam and ate in the sea and underwater reef which extended inland half a billion years ago.

Emerald Lake✦✦✦ Greener than green, green enough to make blue sky pale in comparison, the glassy glacier-formed 28m-deep lake is perfect for canoeing. You can hike, or in winter (usually mid-November to mid-May) snowshoe or Nordic ski the 5-km loop around the lake. Walk clockwise from the wooden car bridge near the parking area for the best views of the President Range northward. The trail's approach to the east and south sides is more lushly forested. Veterans allow a full day to hike a 21-km triangular loop, north from the lake's north end up the Yoho Pass Trail, then south along the flanks of Wapta Mountain on the Burgess Highline Trail to Burgess Pass, then west back to the Lake Loop Trail.

Natural Bridge✦✦✦ Two kilometres up the road to Emerald Lake is one of the most accessible and beautiful attractions in the Rockies parks. A rocky outcropping forms a grey rock tunnel for the green waters of the Kicking Horse River. An afternoon stop is best for drama and photos: walk across the man-made bridge spanning the water to take in alternative viewpoints.

Takakkaw Falls✦✦✦ The winding 15-km road through the Yoho River Valley is filled with waterfalls, a Spiral Tunnel viewpoint, a lay-by for the Meeting of the Waters at the confluence of the Yoho and Kicking Horse Rivers, and a challenging switchback.

Takakkaw (the word means 'wonderful' or 'magnificent' in Cree) Falls consist of sheer, golden cliffs, tufted on the top ridge by a line of

Natural Bridge *3km southwest of Field along the route to Emerald Lake.*

Takakkaw Falls *17km northeast of Field via Yoho Valley Rd.* Because of a switchback section beyond the Meeting of the Waters, trailers are prohibited.

Upper and Lower Spiral Tunnels *Lower Spiral Tunnel Viewpoint is 8km northeast of Field along TransCanada Hwy 1.* Access another viewpoint along Yoho Valley Road by the Kicking Horse River interpretative sign.

Yoho Burgess Shale Foundation $$$ *tel: (800) 343-3006; web: www.burgess-shale.bc.ca,* offers excellent interpretative hikes, including a long, rigorous Burgess Shale/Walcott Quarry hike and a shorter walk up Field's Mount Stephen, with numerous trilobite fossils.

dark green conifers, and water from Daly Glacier above exploding o into space before plunging 254m to the ground. The trail to the fal base from the parking area crosses a bridge before winding up to a ve chilly and thick, misty zone, perfect for rainbows in the afternoon.

Upper and Lower Spiral Tunnels∗∗ If there's a train traversing t tunnels, you're in luck! Most of the time, the vistas of t raw landscape surrounding the 992-m Upper Spiral Tunnel ar 891-m Lower Spiral Tunnel have to suffice to evoke the interpretati sign descriptions.

Imagine the Big Hill west of Kicking Horse Pass, where, because t CPR got a government-granted variance to build track on a grade ov 2.2 per cent, runaway trains were common, a potential death-trap f those on the trains and those maintaining the lines.

For 20 years, death loomed any time a train went west down t Rockies' rise. In 1905, using engineering principles adapted fro Switzerland's St Gotthard Railway Baischina Gorge Tunnels, the C completed a set of $1.5 million tunnels, so perfectly aligned when d that the joining point varied by only 5 cm.

And the innovation? Adding 7km of track in one straight and in rough figure-8 pattern, two spirals within the mountain, reduci speed and eliminating the plunge down the 6.6km Big Hill.

Accommodation and food in Yoho National Park

The small town of **Field** has about a dozen bed and breakfasts. Enqu at the Field Visitor InfoCentre.

Cathedral Mountain Lodge & Chalets $$$ *Yoho Valley Rd; tel: (25 343-6442 or (403) 762-0514; web: www.cathedralmountain.com. L* cabins with fireplaces along the pale blue Kicking Horse River ar stunning views of the mountains near Field make this an alluring m park lodging. A grocery store is good for provisioning before Takakk Falls; the licensed Tea Room Restaurant serves crisp salads, tangy fre tomato soup and delicately prepared fish. Open mid-May–mid-Oct.

Emerald Lake Lodge $$$ *at Emerald Lake; tel: (250) 343-6321 or (8 663-6336; web: www.crmr.com.* Chalets surround the lodge-cum-reso often booked out by executive conferences. The view of canoeists the jewel-coloured lake is without equal. **Cilantro's $$** restaura serves meals and drinks on an umbrella-decked terrace.

Kicking Horse Lodge and Cafe $$ *100 Centre St, Field; tel: 250-3 6303,* has 14 rooms year-round in a chalet-style building, a dinin room and lounge.

Yoho Brothers' Trading Post $$ *Hwy 1, across from the InfoCent* sells sandwiches, First-Nations-style souvenirs and books, and is t meeting place for the Yoho-Burgess Shale Foundation tours.

Opposite
Kicking Horse Pass

Canada's Rocky Mountain National Parks

arks Canada provides a ee tabloid-sized ewspaper with a page of ighlights from each of the x parks: Banff, Glacier, sper, Kootenay, Mount evelstoke and Yoho. The ame summaries can be ound online: ww.worldweb.com/ arksCanada-Banff/Guide/

Suggested tour

Total distance: 550km.

Time: 4 days to drive; can be divided into south (Kootenay and Yoho National Parks) and north (Mount Robson Provincial Park).

Links: The Rocky Mountain Trench along the **Columbia River** (*see page 230*) at Radium is a jumping-off point for Kootenay National Park, and is the gateway to Yoho National Park at Golden. Cross over to the **Alberta Rockies** (*see page 270*) for the transit between parks via the Castle Junction and Icefields Parkway links. From Tête Jaune Cache, continue on the Yellowhead Hwy to **Prince George** (*see page 222*).

Route: From **Radium**, take Hwy 93 east through Sinclair Canyon to the **Radium Hot Springs Pools**, and follow the Banff–Windermere Hwy through KOOTENAY NATIONAL PARK ❶. East of the pools, traverse a red-rock defile. Shallow **Olive Lake** shimmers blue-green with fish-beloved grasses. The highway rises immediately to a superb **Kootenay Valley Viewpoint**, then descends beneath an area favoured by mountain goats to **Vermilion Crossing**. The **Paint Pots** are 22km northwest. Hike a crisscross 0.8-km trail up **Marble Canyon**. At the top of Vermilion Pass is the **Continental Divide** and the **Fireweed Trail** through a 1968 forest-fire area.

Cross into Alberta and **Banff National Park** (*see page 270*) at Castle Junction. Go north on TransCanada Hwy 1 to 3km beyond the Lake Louise exit, and continue on Hwy 1 veering left to the **Great [Continental] Divide** at the BC boundary and west into YOHO NATIONAL PARK ❷ at **Kicking Horse Pass**. The **Lower Spiral**

Geological Rockies

Rockies' peaks and sideways-smashed mountains hint at the siding and crashing which formed them. Inland seas lapped at the area which became the Western Rockies, silt trapping tiny lifeforms as fossils 500,000 years ago. In the Age of Dinosaurs, 160–60 million years ago, volcanoes erupted and faults thrust older rock on top of younger rock. At the bottom was granite; above was sedimentary rock, forming into the striated layers which streak faces of the Rocky Mountain.

Right
Yoho National Park

Tunnel Viewpoint is 8km west. Take the Yoho Valley Road turn-off to Takakkaw Falls, with the Upper Spiral Tunnel Viewpoint and Meeting of the Waters Exhibit *en route*. Return to Hwy 1 and descend the Big Hill to Field Park and Visitor InfoCentre for the Burgess Shale Exhibit. Immediately south is the road to Natural Bridge and Emerald Lake. Rejoin Hwy 1 to Faeder Lake, with pristine mountain reflections, hike a steep 3km trail up the Leanchoil Hoodoos and to Wapta Falls, near where Hector's horse kicked.

To continue through the Rockies, retrace the route up Hwy 1 into Banff National Park, and take Hwy 93, the Icefields Parkway, north to Jasper via Jasper National Park. From Jasper, take Hwy 16, the Yellowhead Hwy, west over Yellowhead Pass through MOUNT ROBSON PROVINCIAL PARK ❸, passing Yellowhead Lake and Moose Marsh. Canoeists paddle Moose Lake; rafters take to the Fraser River. The best views of Mount Robson are from the Visitor Centre near the trail to Overlander Falls. Berg Trail parking is just north. Continue west to Tête Jaune Cache.

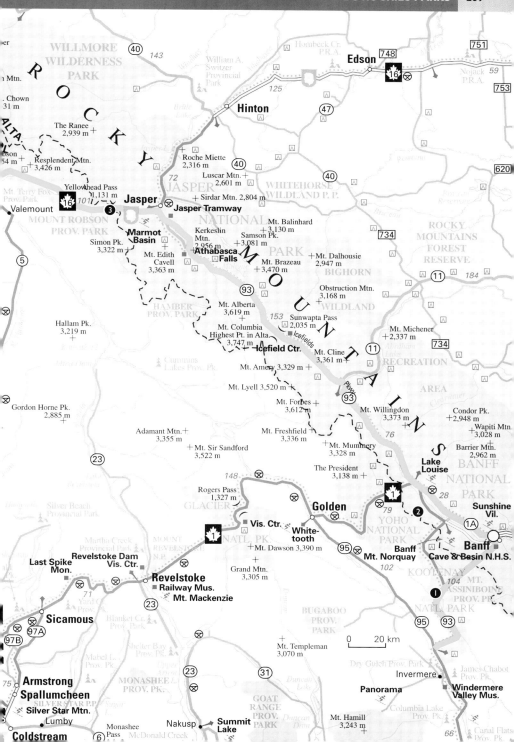

ROCKY
WILLMORE
WILDERNESS
PARK

40 143

751

Edson 748

16 59 Nojack P.R.A.

753

William A.
Switzer
Provincial
Park

125

Hinton

47

620

. Chown
31 m

The Ranee
2,939 m

ALTA.

son
54 m

Resplendent Mtn.
3,426 m

Roche Miette
2,316 m

40

Luscar Mtn.
2,601 m

40

734

Mt. Terry Fox
Prov. Park

Yellowhead Pass
1,131 m

16 101 3

Jasper

72

JASPER

Sirdar Mtn. 2,804 m

WHITEHORSE
WILDLAND P. P.

Valemount

16

Jasper Tramway

ROCKY
MOUNTAINS
FOREST
RESERVE

MOUNT ROBSON
PROV. PARK

Marmot
Basin

NATIONAL

Mt. Balinhard
3,130 m

Kerkeslin
Mtn.
2,956 m

Samson Pk.
3,081 m

Mt. Dalhousie
2,947 m

11 184

5

Simon Pk.
3,322 m

Mt. Edith
Cavell
3,363 m

Athabasca
Falls

PARK

Mt. Brazeau
3,470 m

BIGHORN

Hallam Pk.
3,219 m

HAMBER
PROV. PARK

93

Mt. Alberta
3,619 m

Obstruction Mtn.
3,168 m

WILDLAND

Mt. Michener
2,337 m

734

Mt. Columbia
Highest Pt. in Alta.
3,747 m

153

Icefields

Sunwapta Pass
2,035 m

Gordon Horne Pk.
2,885 m

Cummins
Lakes Prov. Pk.

Icefield Ctr.

Mt. Cline
3,361 m

11

RECREATION

Mt. Amery 3,329 m

Mt. Lyell 3,520 m

93

AREA

Adamant Mtn.
3,355 m

Mt. Forbes
3,612 m

Mt. Willingdon
3,373 m

Condor Pk.
2,948 m

Wapiti Mtn.
3,028 m

23

148

Mt. Freshfield
3,336 m

76

Mt. Sir Sandford
3,522 m

Mt. Mummery
3,328 m

Barrier Mtn.
2,962 m

Rogers Pass
1,327 m

The President
3,138 m

Lake
Louise

BANFF

Silver Beach
Provincial Park

GLACIER

NATL. PK.

1

28

NATIONAL
PARK

Vis. Ctr.

Golden

2

Sunshine
Vil.

Revelstoke Dam
Vis. Ctr.

White-
tooth

79

YOHO
NATIONAL

1A

Last Spike
Mon.

1

Mt. Dawson 3,390 m

95

PARK

Banff

Banff
Mt. Norquay

Cave & Basin N.H.S.

Revelstoke
Railway Mus.
Mt. Mackenzie

Grand Mtn.
3,305 m

102

KOOTENAY

71

23

Sicamous

BUGABOO
PROV.
PARK

NATL. PARK

MT.
ASSINIBOINE
PROV. PK.

97A

95 93

97B

Mt. Templeman
3,070 m

0   20 km

Armstrong
Spallumcheen

23

31

Invermere

James Chabot
Prov. Park

75

MONASHEE
PROV. PK.

Panorama

Windermere
Valley Mus.

Silver Star Mtn.

Lumby

GOAT
RANGE
PROV.
PARK

Mt. Hamill
3,243 m

Columbia Lake
Prov. Pk.

66

Coldstream

6

Monashee
Pass

Nakusp

Summit
Lake

Mt. Chown 3,131 m

Alberta Rockies Parks

Ratings

Children	●●●●●
Mountains	●●●●●
National parks	●●●●●
Nature	●●●●●
Outdoor activities	●●●●●
Scenery	●●●●●
Walking	●●●●●
Wildlife	●●●●●

Canada's best-known natural icons don't disappoint. anything, the peaks are higher and more pristine, th lakes a deeper aquamarine, the rivers an icier blue, the glacie vaster and the animals more evident than seems possible.

The Alberta Rockies, primarily found in Banff and Jaspe National Parks, are heaven for hikers and cyclists, canoeist rafters, skiers and snowshoers, best when explored beyon the confines of a vehicle, motor coach or train window.

The icons also pack the parks with five million annu visitors, most driving through in July and August. They sto barely long enough to shop in Banff Townsite, stroll aroun the Banff Springs Hotel, walk around Lake Louise, dash t the Peyto Lake Viewpoint and haul along the Icefield Parkway. Traverse any trail to add a unique individu experience, and watch for bear, wapiti (elk), deer and Rock Mountain sheep just beyond the next turn.

BANFF NATIONAL PARK✦✦✦

ⓘ Parks Canada and Banff Visitor Centre *224 Banff Ave; tel: (403) 762-1550; web: www.parkscanada.pch.gc.ca/ banff Open late May–mid-Jun and Sep, 0800–1800; mid-Jun–early Sep, 0800–2000; late Sep–mid-May, 0900–1700.*

Banff/Lake Louise Tourism Bureau *tel: (403) 762-8431; web: www.banfflakelouise.com*

Canada's first national park, established in 1885, splashes scene around and between its two centres, Banff Townsite and Lake Louise.

Banff Park Museum National Historic Site✦✦ The 1903 'railroa pagoda' exterior and Douglas-fir interior, complete with balconi around an atrium, set off this fine Victorian-style collection of stuffe park birds, insects and animals.

Banff Springs Hotel✦✦ The 1888 tourist hotel was built by the CP to lure railway passengers to its Scottish-looking baronial manor, an some details remain. Stroll the grounds, but find the best pictur postcard views from Tunnel Mountain Road across the Bow River.

Buffalo Nations Luxton Museum✦✦✦ Plains First Nations peop who followed and hunted buffalo accurately portray tradition culture in a wooden stockade museum building. Walk by the diorama of tepee-dwellers and displays of peace pipes and elegant bead an porcupine quill clothing.

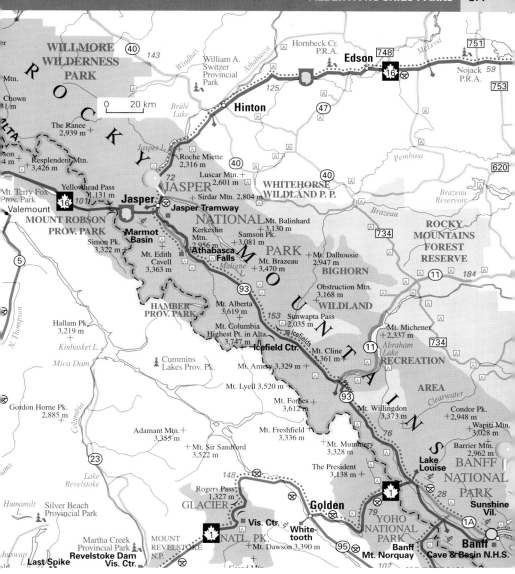

Tourism Canmore-Kananaskis tel: (403)
78-1295; web: www.
anmorekananaskis.com

Cave & Basin National Historic Site✲✲ Found by CPR workers in 1883,
the sulphuric hot springs were a gold mine for the Canadian
government and the CPR, who both wanted to develop the area as a
tourist stop. 'These springs will recuperate the patient and recoup the
treasury,' commented Prime Minister Sir John A Macdonald obligingly.
Banff's birthplace can be toured, but not bathed in. The free 0.6-km
Marsh Trail Loop✲✲✲ is fine for bird-, elk- and orchid-spotting.

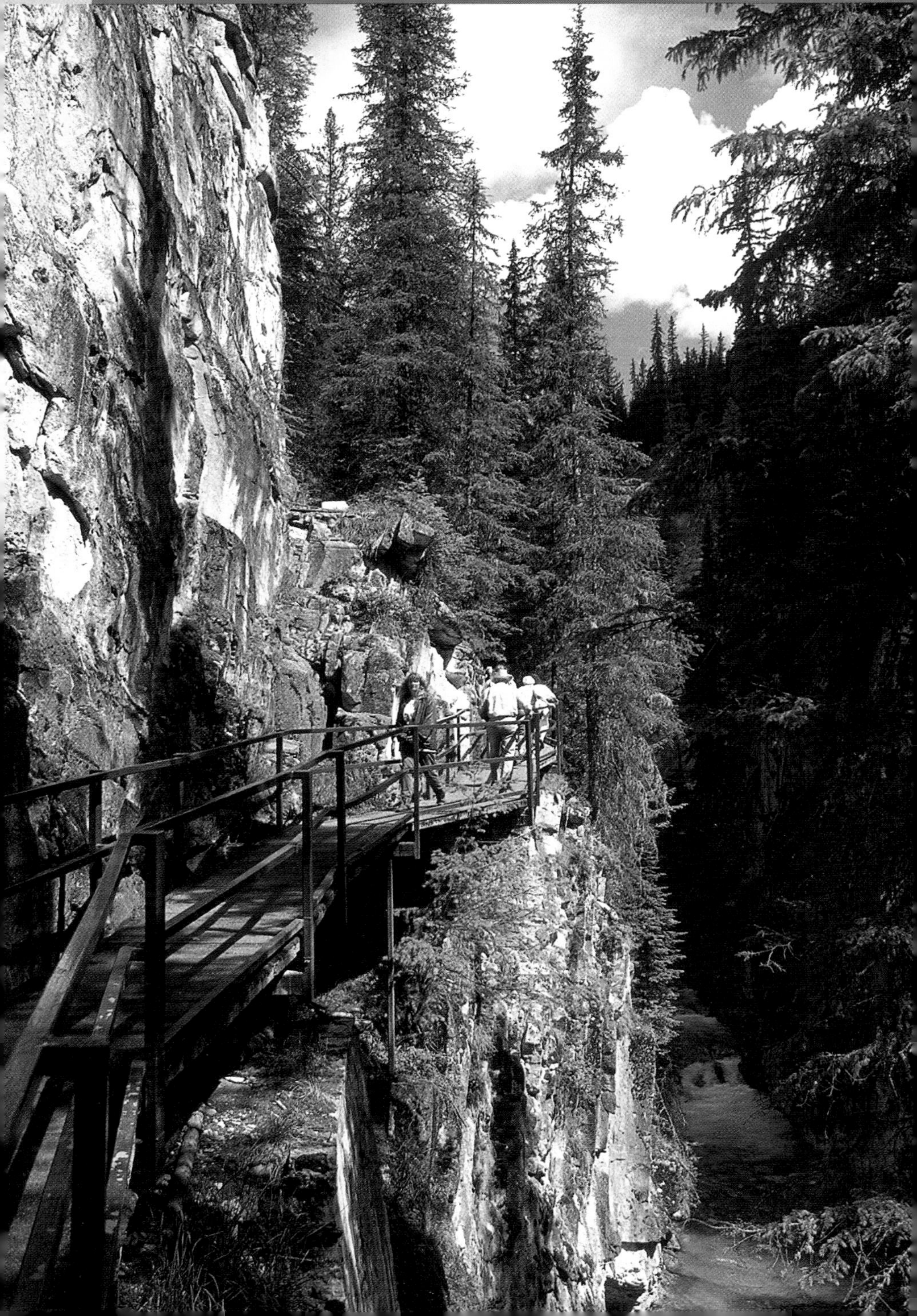

Lake Louise✦✦✦ Emerald water, white Victoria Glacier, red canoes, a rainbow of Icelandic poppies, a carved winter ice palace, tea-time elegance. The modernised, buff-coloured, château-style hotel stands at the east end of the lake like a sentinel. In summer, hikers take the **Lake Agnes Trail**✦✦ to one tea-house or follow the 10.5km return **Lakeshore Trail/Plain of the Six Glaciers Trail**✦✦✦ to another.

Moraine Lake✦✦✦ Ten craggy peaks surround this icy blue lake, with surreal beauty, beloved by summer canoeists. At the north end, the **Rockpile Trail**✦✦✦ boulders lead to a view of the peaks and moraine flow to the water.

Peyto Lake✦✦✦ Hike up Bow Summit through a flower carpet of Indian paintbrush and heather during July and August. Cloud patterns constantly change the colour of the lake, as it spreads long and blue before the wooden balcony viewpoint. Look left for a classic glacier flow into Peyto Lake.

Sulphur Mountain Gondola✦✦ The 8-minute ride up 2285-m Sulphur Mountain is lovely on a clear day, with unobstructed views of Banff Townsite. The short **Vista Trail Walkway** to Sanson's Peak Observatory provides a chance to stretch your legs with fabulous views.

Accommodation and food in Banff National Park

Banff Townsite and Lake Louise accommodation does not begin to serve the millions of visitors who arrive and want to stay the night. East of the park, **Canmore**, set amid stunning snow-capped peaks, provides an ever-increasing number of motels, posh lodges and bed and breakfasts. If you are arriving from Calgary *en route* to Banff National Park, stop at **Travel Alberta Visitor InfoCentre** *2801 Bow Valley Trail, Canmore; tel: (403) 678-5277 or (800) 661-8888.*

Banff Springs Hotel $$$ *405 Spray Ave, Banff; tel: (800) 441-1414 or (403) 762-2211; web: www.cphotels.ca,* is the castle-like, 770-room icon set against the forested mountains, jammed with guests and sightseers in summer. **Solace Spa** and the 27-hole **Banff Springs Golf Course** are enhanced by Bow Valley vistas. Intimate **Grapes Wine Bar** (mezzanine, open daily) serves delicious fondue. **Waldhaus Restaurant and Pub** (open 1800–2200), in a Bavarian-style building near the golf course, serves hearty dishes with lager and schnitzel. For Bow Valley views, have a sundowner in the piano bar **Rundle Lounge**.

Canmore Regency Suites $$ *1206 Bow Valley Trail, Canmore; tel: (800) 386-7248 or (403) 678-3788,* has large, clean accommodation, cheerful owners and helpful touring suggestions.

Chateau Lake Louise $$$ *at Lake Louise; tel: (403) 522-3511; web: www.cphotels.ca,* is a 489-room lakeside hotel with views across the lake to Victoria Glacier. In summertime, tea ($$$) is served 1200–1600

Moraine Lake $ *from Lake Louise Drive, turn south on Moraine Lake Road for 11km.*

Peyto Lake $ *West of Hwy 93, Icefields Parkway, 98km northwest of Banff; 40km northwest of Lake Louise.*

Sulphur Mountain Gondola $ *end of Mountain Ave; tel: (403) 762-5438; web: www.banffgondola.com Open daily late Jan–early Dec.*

Right
Banff Springs Hotel

in the aptly named **Lakeview Lounge**. The 24-hour **Chateau Deli** prepares delicious made-to-order sandwiches. The casual **Poppy Room** **$$** combines Lake Louise flower garden views with meals and a breakfast buffet.

The Crossing $$ *Saskatchewan River Crossing, Hwy 93 at Hwy 11; tel (403) 761-7000; web: www.canuckweb.com/crossing.* If you are driving between Banff and Jasper mid-Apr–mid-Nov, this is a convenient spot to stop and refresh with lodging, a cafeteria and a gift shop.

Deer Lodge $$$ *109 Lake Louise Dr, Lake Louise; tel: (403) 609-6199 or (800) 661-1595; web: www.crmr.com/dl/deer.html, open year-round,* has hand-hewn log décor for its 73 rooms, Victoria Glacier views from the rooftop hot-tub, and a fine restaurant serving Canadian wines with wild game, berries and local ingredients.

Moraine Lake Lodge $$ *end of Moraine Lake Rd at lakeside, 15km from Lake Louise; tel: (403) 522-3733 or (403) 760-2380.* While there can be snow even in summer, the 18 cabins and rooms in the lodge have spectacular mountain and lake views with complimentary tea-time pastries. Café snacks, lunches or fine dining are available in the glass roof **Atrium $$$** during summer season. Open June–Sept.

Panorama Restaurant $$ *at Sulphur Mountain Gondola; tel: (403) 762-5438; open Boxing Day–Nov,* is a high dining experience at 2285m serving breakfast and lunch buffets and dinner. The **Summit Restaurant $** serves light cafeteria fare.

JASPER NATIONAL PARK✧✧✧

Parks Canada Jasper InfoCentre
00 Connaught Dr; tel: (403) 852-6176; web: www.parkscanada.pch.gc.ca/jasper. Open daily.

Icefield InfoCentre
Icefields Parkway; tel: (780) 852-6288. Open May–mid-Oct, daily.

Jasper Tourism & Commerce 632 Connaught Dr; tel: (780) 852-3858; web: www.jaspercc@incentre.net Open daily.

Athabasca Falls $ Icefields Parkway, 30km south of Jasper.

Columbia Icefield $$ from Icefield Centre, Icefields Parkway; tel: (403) 762-6735; web: www.brewster.ca Weather-dependent Snocoach tours run mid-Apr–mid-Oct.

Icefields Parkway $ from 8km west of the Lake Louise exit, 230km north to Jasper Townsite.

Maligne Lake $ 48km from Jasper via Maligne Lake Rd.

Pyramid Lake $ end of Pyramid Lake Rd.

Jasper began in 1811 as a North West Company trading post outpost and was visited by Overlander gold prospectors in 1862. The park was designated in 1907 and Grand Trunk Pacific Railway passengers arrived *en masse* in 1911. Scenic attractions outweigh shopping and dining opportunities, but who cares when wildlife roams the streets and the edge of town is a 5-minute walk away?

Athabasca Falls✧✧ Misty and mysterious, the falls descend 23m through pure quartzite. Hold on to railings to walk the 2-minute path to various viewpoints. Nordic skiers find a frozen shaft of ice and rock in winter.

Columbia Icefield✧✧✧ A huge-tyred Snocoach hauls passengers over moraine gravel to the Continental-Divide-spanning icefield, for a 20-minute walk on a glacier and a sampling of glacial water. The InfoCentre has information on Athabasca Glacier Ice Walks.

Icefields Parkway✧✧✧ The 230-km drive along Hwy 93 between Lake Louise and Jasper offers glaciers, waterfalls, wildlife and awesome vistas for several hours' drive by car or narrated Brewster Coach Tours.

Maligne Lake✧✧✧ Though Jesuit missionary Fr Pierre de Smet lost horses and goods in the river he proclaimed 'wicked', the lake at river's end is quite lovely. Take a 90-minute narrated boat tour to Spirit Island in the middle of the lake, fish for trout or canoe and kayak at this day-use lakeside retreat. *En route* to the lake, hike (snowshoe or ice climb) Maligne Canyon, take a look at Roche Bonhomme, a horizontal mountain profile that plausibly resembles a Native chief laying in profile, search the shores of green Medicine Lake for sunning wapiti, or join rafters bouncing downstream over Maligne River rapids.

Pyramid Lake✧✧ A close 7km from Jasper Townsite, this large, crystalline lake reflects a pyramid-shaped mountain. Kayaks, canoes, sailboats and motorboats are for hire at Pyramid Lake Resort, while picnicking, horse-riding, fishing, and skating and Nordic skiing in winter are other options.

Accommodation and food in Jasper National Park

Athy B $ *Athabasca Hotel, 510 Patricia St; tel: (780) 852-3386*, is the drinking spot for locals.

The Glass House $$ *715 Miette Ave; tel: (780) 852-3861*, complete with a solarium, is a comfortable bed and breakfast serving home-made pastries, close to the town centre.

Jasper Park Lodge $$$ *tel: (780) 852-3301; web: www.cphotels.ca*, has 446 rooms in chalets and log cabins, and adds a fine 18-hole golf course favoured by wandering wapiti. Splendid floor-to-ceiling views

Below
Banff National Park

of Lac Beauvert are elegantly combined with rich meats, fish and wines in the adults-only **Edith Cavell Dining Room $$$**. For a panoply of Canadian décor and dishes such as buffalo skillet, there's the **Moose's Nook $$$**.

Rocky Mountain wildlife

Apart from iconic scenery, nothing draws people to the Rocky Mountains more seductively than the appearance of animals, most of them big and surprisingly active. The effect of 5 million visitors to Banff National Park and 2.2 million to Jasper National Park each year causes stress to the wildlife and frustrates drivers who park and line up in what park wardens refer to as 'animal jams' to get close to creatures while blocking the highways.

Yet the animals, such as bears and wapiti, which are close to Banff and Jasper Town sites, have adapted, looking for human food and, in the case of wapiti, getting protection from traditional predator wolves and cougars. They are wild animals, and when threatened retaliate with sharp teeth, horns, antlers, claws or hooves. Don't feed the animals, threaten their homes, food or young and force them to protect themselves. Such approaches usually end with the animal's death.

Though small, the Canadian and Parks Canada symbolic animal, the beaver, keeps streams, rivers and lakes healthy by damming. They were almost exterminated for their reddish pelts in the early 19th century.

There are probably no more than 300 straight-muzzle black bears and hump-shouldered grizzlies to be seen, grazing on berries and grass along roadsides. Fur colour can range from blond to red, brown or black for either species.

Bighorn sheep are easy to identify, front or back. Large, curling brown horns can crook 360 degrees on males. Brownish coats are accented by a large white patch on the rump, and all of them, young and old, love salt licks, especially in winter.

Listen at night around Banff and Jasper townsites for the plaintive, haunting howls of coyotes, those smart hunters who have avoided total decimation by those protecting cattle and sheep.

White-tail and mule deer are considerably smaller than elk, though both groups enjoy easy grazing near the Townsites. Mule deer have huge ears and white rumps; white-tail deer raise tails when they run, flashing the tail's white under-colouring.

Elk, or wapiti, are the size of horses, the males sporting many-pronged racks (antlers), and bellowing in combat with other males during the late autumn rut. They range in colour from light grey to light brown to ruddy, depending on season, and sport a cream-colour rump patch.

There are few moose in the two parks, but the elongated big nose and solid thick brown antlers on these 450kg animals are hard to mistake, even if half-hidden in a marsh.

Suggested tour

Total distance: 305km.

Time: Minimum 2 days, stopping at Lake Louise or Saskatchewan River Crossing.

Links: The **BC Rockies** (*see page 258*) at Castle Junction for Kootenay National Park, at the Hwy 1 fork to Yoho National Park, and Hwy 16 west from Jasper to Mount Robson Provincial Park.

Above
Lake Louise

Route: TransCanada Hwy 1 runs from **BANFF NATIONAL PARK** ◀
east gate by **Banff Townsite** to just north of the Lake Louise exit. Vee
right to take the Icefields Parkway, Hwy 93, 230km to Jasper.

Barriers along the roadside beyond Banff National Park's east gat
protect wildlife from vehicles, but also restrict the natural range of el
and other migrating animals through this section of the **Bow Valley**
For boating and bighorn sheep spotting, turn right to drive the loo
around **Lake Minnewanka**, 'Lake of the Water Spirits', or, in lat
spring to autumn, turn left on to Tunnel Mountain Road for views c
the **Hoodoos** and the **Bow River Valley**.

The main **Banff Townsite** turn-off is 1km further west on Hwy 1, across the highway from the winter-only **Mount Norquay Ski Area**. Take the Vermilion Lakes Drive immediately right for reflections in grassy-shore lakes of surrounding mountains filled with birds and wandering elk. In Banff, tour the Banff Springs Hotel, take pictures by **Bow Falls** below the hotel, canoe or play a round of golf. **Upper Hot Springs Pool**, near the parking area for the Sulphur Mountain Gondola, is the spot in Banff to soak up mountain views.

Banff's three museums and historic site cover history, natural history and First Nations. Banff's origins are exposed at **Cave & Basin National Historic Site**; the **Whyte Museum of the Canadian Rockies** covers mountain-climbing feats; the **Banff Park Museum** reveals the animals that lurked in the park in 1903, and the **Buffalo Nations Luxton Museum** shows the lives of First Nations Plains Indians. At the head of Banff Avenue, the main street, stroll around the Park Administration Building's flower-filled **Cascade Gardens**, with views across the **Bow River Bridge** and Banff Avenue to majestic **Cascade Mountain**.

Detour along Bow Valley Parkway: For 55-km, Hwy 1A parallels the TransCanada Hwy, but is considered the more scenic, if slower (60kph), route. Traffic flow may be restricted because of animal movement in some seasons, but driving one or both segments – Banff to Castle Junction or Castle Junction to Lake Louise – in either direction is the best way to spot wildlife, enjoy wild flowers and experience river canyons by getting off the generally straight TransCanada.

Pick up the Bow Valley Parkway 5.5km west of Banff Townsite. **Johnston Canyon**, at 23km, has a narrow 1km path, some of it boardwalk, along limestone wall and over a bright green river to the Lower Falls, above a blue pool. North, 2766m **Castle Mountain** acts as a landmark for those getting off at **Castle Junction** to go west to Kootenay National Park (*see page 258*). Drive towards Lake Louise through a forest of lodgepole pine, with occasional glimpses of trains, backed by mountains, travelling along the railway line at the base of the Bow Valley.

Side-leaning **Mount Rundle** dominates the view south (left) for many kilometres along the Bow River Valley. For winter skiing and snowboarding, turn left from Hwy 1 on to Sunshine Road to **Sunshine Meadows**.

Castle Mountain is the golden rock massif on the right side of Hwy 1. Turn left, 58km from Banff to Lake Louise. Lake Louise Village, with its Visitor InfoCentre, petrol station, stores, restaurants and services, is just off the highway; the lake and **Chateau Lake Louise** are 4km up a winding road, congested in summer. Turn left at Moraine Lake Road for left-hand side views of the **Valley of the 10 Peaks** before reaching **Moraine Lake**.

Follow signs right to the Icefields Parkway, Hwy 93. Mountains wi
appear higher and higher, less eroded. To the left is the **Crowfoo**
Glacier, where two pale-blue 'toes' hang on the cliff's edge. Crysta
blue **Bow Lake** is below, with **Bow Glacier** distant across the lake, an
red-roofed **Num-Ti-Jah Lodge** at the north end.

Trees thin out at 2088-m **Bow Summit**, with a wild flower-filled fores
trail up to the **Peyto Lake** viewpoint. **Mistaya Canyon**, 32km north
twists around its river a short hike away from Hwy 1. One of th
Rockies' most beautiful waterways, the **North Saskatchewan River**
rushes pale green at The Crossing, where David Thompson explore
the area from his base at Rocky Mountain House in 1807 (*see* **Shuswap**
Lakes *page 158*).

The **Weeping Wall** on the right, rivulets of water with spring run-off
is enjoyed by Rocky Mountain sheep and ice climbers when the roc
face freezes in winter. The **Big Bend** switchbacks wind up to Parke
Ridge.

Sunwapta Pass at 2035m marks **JASPER NATIONAL PARK ❷** and th
Columbia ₁Icefield. Take the 2km trail to **Sunwapta Falls**, best fo
photography in the afternoon. Hwy 93 moves north along th
Athabasca River, which creates a misty blanket over **Athabasca Falls**
frozen eerily in winter.

Mount Edith Cavell, standing regally to the west, is named for
brave British nurse executed in World War I for aiding prisoners. T
ski **Marmot Basin** from December to April, take the marked winding
road left from Hwy 93. Whistlers Road, named for the noisy hoar
marmots in the area, leads to the **Jasper Tramway** (Mar–Oct) fo
Jasper Townsite views and vistas of the Miette and Athabasca rivers.

Wapiti (elk) wander everywhere around **Jasper Townsite**, a relaxed
unpretentious tourist-catering community strung near the railway lin
along Connaught Drive. Drive out to Jasper Park Lodge for a lovely
series of water sports recreation lakes, epitomised by the lodge's own
Lac Beauvert. Pyramid Lake is north of town. The chilly **Athabasca**
and **Maligne rivers** offer challenging rafting and magnificent scenery.

Drive north of Jasper on Hwy 16, and turn right on to Maligne Lake
Road. The wildlife-rich road traverses **Maligne Canyon**, favoured by
ice climbers and snowshoers in winter, passes the conical-shaped
mountains around **Medicine Lake** before arriving at **Maligne Lake**.

Also worth exploring

Miette Hot Springs, at the edge of Jasper National Park (open mid-
May–mid-Oct), is one of three public soaks (along with Radium Hot
Springs, *see page 261,* and Banff Upper Hot Springs) in the Rockies

Parks. Look for wapiti and bighorn sheep along Hwy 16, the Yellowhead Hwy, for 43km northeast of Jasper. Turn right on to Fiddle Valley Road for 17km, past the ruined Jasper Park Collieries and coal tailings and 360-million-year-old **Ashlar Ridge**. There are ruined buildings at the old hot springs bathhouse. The modern resort has 53.9°C sulphuric waters, a motel and bungalows, café, restaurant and picnicking.

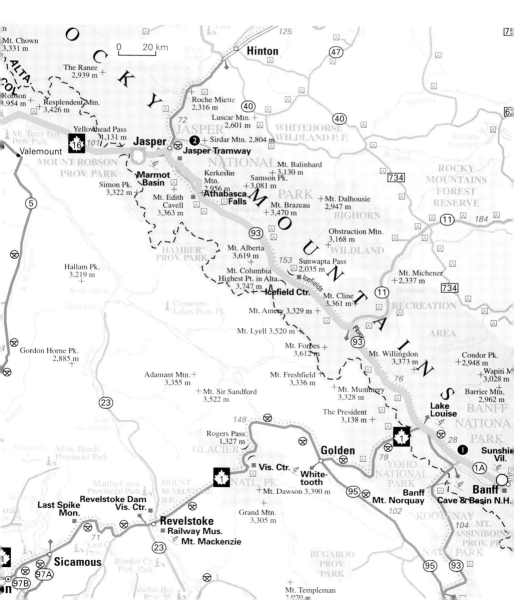

How to talk Canadian

Back bacon: known as Canadian bacon in the USA and as peameal bacon elsewhere.

Bannock: a deep-fried bread usually eaten with such trail 'delicacies' as moose stew.

Beaver fever: *giardiasis,* severe diarrhoea and fever from drinking untreated ground water infected with *Giardia lamblia.*

Big smoke: Vancouver.

Block heater: an electric engine heater attached to the other end of the plug dangling from the front bumper of most Canadian cars. The heater is plugged in on cold nights (-10ºC or colder) to prevent the engine coolant and oil from freezing and cracking the engine block.

Brew: a beer, either in a bottle or on draught.

Canuck: a Canadian or a member of the Vancouver Canucks ice hockey team.

Chinook: a warm wind from west of the Rockies that melts winter snows as it passes over the mountains, warming Calgary and southwest Alberta.

Cow pie: cattle droppings, a hazard to walkers on open grazing lands.

Cowtown: Calgary.

Donair, donner kebab, gyro, schwarma: a sandwich made of shaved meat (usually lamb) wrapped in pitta bread.

Downtown: city or town centre.

Flapjacks: pancakes.

Flat (of beer): a case of 24 bottles or cans of beer.

Fries: chips, usually, but not always, made of potatoes.

Galapagos of Canada: the Queen Charlotte Islands, also called Haida Gwaii.

Gas: petrol.

Goeduck: pronounced 'gooey duck'; a large clam with a long, thick neck, usually used for soup.

Gorbie: someone not from the area; a tourist, usually someone asking questions such as 'How much does that mountain weigh?'

Holiday: a public holiday, not a private holiday, which is more often a vacation.

Hoser: a teasing term used by men, implying the person being needled is none too bright.

Ice fog: fog composed of ice crystals instead of water vapour.

Loonie: $1 coin, named for the Canadian bird, the common loon, one of Canada's symbols.

Métis: a person of mixed aboriginal and white ancestry, constitutionally recognised as one of three First Nations entities.

Ogopogo: mythical beast similar to the Loch Ness monster, believed to lurk beneath the waters of Okanagan Lake.

Parkade: a parking garage.

Parking lot: a car park or parking garage.

Road apple: cattle or buffalo droppings on the road.

Road kill: literally animals killed by passing automobiles, but also used to describe bad restaurant food.

Sasquatch: Bigfoot, the legendary man-like hairy giant of the woods.

Shooter: a raw oyster, usually swallowed whole.

Shredding: snowboarding.

Sundog: ring around the sun formed by ice crystals in the upper atmosphere.

Talking stick: originally a carved staff used in First Nations gatherings to signify that the holder was entitled to speak to the group; now used in non-Native meetings to focus attention on the speaker.

Texas gate or cattle gate: a grate of widely separated metal pipes set in the roadway to keep cattle and horses at bay.

Toonie: the $2 bi-metal coin.

Toque: a winter hat, pronounced like 'spook'.

Vamping: van camping.

Wapiti: elk.

ndex

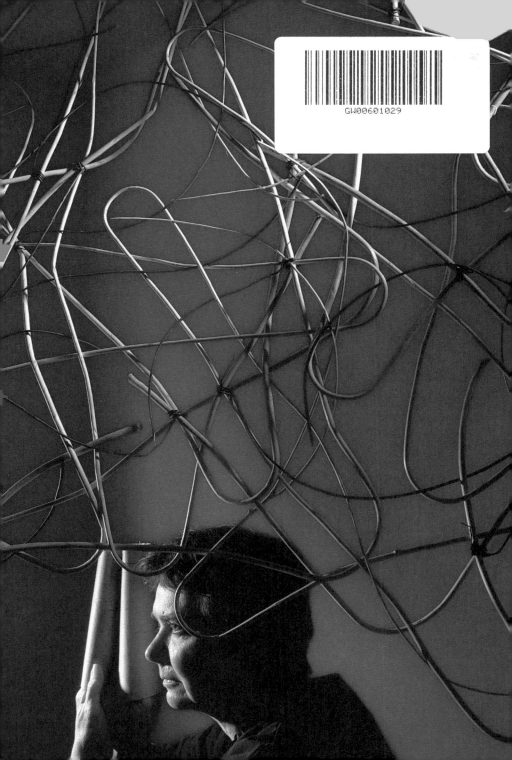

For *Alwyne Hawkins*, Basketmaker
Onno Boekhoudt, Jeweller

ACKNOWLEDGEMENTS

For their involvement in the exhibition 'BASKETRY CARTE BLANCHE', I would like to thank Tellervo Barnhoorn, Esmé Hofman and the team at Nationaal Vlechtmuseum, Noordwolde, Netherlands for all their help and encouragement. It has been a great pleasure working with them there and the link will continue. I would equally like to thank Sheena Watson and Lauren Sebastian of Kent Arts and Libraries. Thanks also to Lluis Grau, Carlos Fontales and Jesus Reguera for enabling the exhibition to travel to the Centro de Artesania y Disëno, Lugo, Galicia, Spain with student work from The City Lit Creative Basketmaking course, London.

Karen Wilks, Book Designer, has provided the ideas and creative flair which have made this catalogue the document it is. Lesley Jackson and Lottie Hoare, Writers and those at Perivan White Dove have equally put thought, imagination and energy into the project. I thank them all warmly. The Arts Council England, SouthEast funded a period of work before the exhibition as well as granting a major portion of publication costs: such time and support is invaluable. I thank them too. To the photographers: Barry Amos, Ed Barber, Marc Burden, Clifford Guttridge, Tim Johnson, David Manners, Shuna Rendel, Howard Rice, David Rowland, Nicholas Sinclair, Sÿtze Veldema, Mike Waterman, Simon Witham and to the Crafts Council Photostore for permission to use two photographs from their collection, thanks also.

I have been given assistance over many years by many people but for this project I would particularly like to thank Judy Barry, Embroiderer, Tim Johnson, Artist and Marian Gwiazda, Basketmaker. All have extended my picture of the world. I would also like to thank my family: Alice, Matthew and Andrew.

'BASKETRY CARTE BLANCHE': MARY BUTCHER', Nationaal Vlechtmuseum, Noordwolde, Netherlands May 24 - August 30, Ramsgate Library Gallery, Kent September 6 - October 11, Centro de Artesania y Disëno, Lugo, Galicia, Spain November 28 - January 7 2004.

Mary Butcher

'Basketry Carte Blanche'

Basketry Carte Blanche

TRADITIONALISTS IN THE BASKETMAKING WORLD DON'T QUITE KNOW WHAT TO MAKE OF Mary Butcher's recent work. Although schooled in traditional techniques, and highly respectful of the skills of others, over the last few years she has turned renegade. Neatness, precision and control have been transformed in favour of a looser, freer and more spontaneous approach. Her latest baskets have scars, loose ends and irregular, wayward forms. Some have so little structure that they hardly look finished at all. An acknowledged expert in the history of British basketmaking, Mary is also a leading international authority on basketry techniques from around the world. For someone with such a track record as a practitioner and academic to step aside determinedly from all that she has previously upheld, is unnerving for her fellow professionals, to say the least.

Whereas some artists reject convention as a way of achieving notoriety, Mary Butcher is simply not that sort. She wouldn't upset the close-knit basketmaking fraternity without good reason. In any case, she's left it rather late to become a rebel. Of all the crafts, basketmaking is one of the most prescriptive in purely technical terms. It is only because she has fully mastered the rules that Mary can flout them with impunity. What has prompted her change of direction has been a determination to push herself creatively and explore new realms. By opening up basketmaking to experimentation and cross-fertilisation with other disciplines, she has taken the lid off an area of practice that was in danger of stagnating. Hence the significance of the title of her latest exhibition, *Basketry Carte Blanche*.

Mary acquired her basketmaking skills during the late 1970s from an elderly artisan called Alwyne Hawkins, a meticulous craftsman who was anxious to pass on his knowledge to a receptive pupil. 'I quickly realised that basketmaking was a dying craft and that there weren't many basketmakers left. My interest in the history of the craft developed concurrently with my practical skills', Mary recalls. 'Personally I wouldn't want now to work in the old way, but I admire people who make beautiful functional things day after day'. Although her initial encounter with basketmaking came about by chance, she found herself immediately hooked. 'What appealed to me was the idea of starting out with a bundle of twigs and ending up with a structure. I also enjoyed manipulating materials, getting things to bend how you wanted. I like the concentration of making. It's absorbing and relaxing'.

A willow specialist, Mary spent many years producing everyday domestic items such as shopping baskets, log baskets, waste paper bins and cradles, mainly in traditional forms. Her other forte is seat-making for chairs. Her knowledge of these two subjects has been condensed into two technical manuals, Willow Work (1986) and Chair Seating (1989). In 1984 she began teaching on the City and Guilds Creative Basketry Course at the London College of Furniture (now at the City Literary Institute), becoming Course Organiser in 1989. Her high status within the profession is also indicated by her appointment as Chair of The Basketmakers' Association from 1993-1998 and as Trade Adviser to the Worshipful Company of Basketmakers.

Since the early 1990s the opportunity to travel abroad and study other forms of basketmaking has considerably broadened her horizons. A research trip to Poland to study traditional basketmaking at first hand was particularly important. 'I find travel invigorating. As a maker myself, I find it easier to communicate with other practitioners. What I've learnt has fed my own creative development'. However, the crucial turning point in her career was her appointment as Research Fellow in Basketmaking at Manchester Metropolitan University from 1994-1997. This experience completely changed her perspective and prompted a dramatic reassessment of her approach to her craft. 'I was based in the embroidery studio in the textile department, but active across the whole Faculty of Art and Design. I was exposed to lots of new things, and I found it very exciting. I did a lot of research on makers and in museums. I also did a lot of communicating'. Her Fellowship culminated in a groundbreaking group exhibition called *Beyond the Bounds*, exploring the relationship between textiles and basketmaking. The exhibition, which she co-curated, acted as a showcase for her recent radical experiments, which were completely different from the traditional baskets for which she was known. 'Because of my background, people expected me to make something thick and structural, but instead I made three huge willow cones, which were open and non-traditional structures'.

What Mary has been trying to do ever since is to break away from her reliance on technique. She sees this as a 'quiet rebellion', not only against her own training and professional indoctrination, but against the 'constraining expectations' of her parents during her youth. Teaching is very important to her in this respect. She sees it as a way of giving people the freedom to express themselves — women in particular, many of whom are still burdened by anxieties even in our supposedly liberated age. 'Teaching is not about control, but about giving people a voice and building their self-confidence. You have to impart enough information, and offer just enough suggestions along the way to help them move forward'. She is proud that the work produced by her students is so varied and individual, so un-tutor-led. Today, when she conducts specialist workshops, she encourages participants to use minimal technique in the hope of making their work more free.

In 1999 Mary joined forces with another 'reformist' basketmaker, Lois Walpole, to co-curate the extremely successful touring exhibition, *Contemporary International Basketmaking*. She also wrote the accompanying best-selling book. Her desire to avoid offending other leading basketmakers whose work was not selected, prompted the decision to exclude her own work from this high-profile show. This perhaps explains why the radical new departures in her output over the last six years have yet to receive the attention they deserve. Public response to recent exhibitions and installations has been extremely positive, though, which gives her great encouragement. Having found her own voice at last, she is now developing it with growing confidence. *Basketry Carte Blanche* has enabled her to take stock and draw together many different strands.

Mary still loves willow and regularly incorporates it in her work, but it is no longer the be-all and end-all of her creative existence. She now draws on a much wider range of materials, both natural and synthetic. These materials feed her imagination in a very immediate and tangible way, suggesting the forms, structures and textures of the pieces she now creates. Her belated conversion to synthetic materials came about during her time at Manchester, where she was able to help herself to a weird and wonderful array of manufacturers' remnants from big bins in the textile studios. She also raided a nearby recycling centre. This exposure to new materials has 'opened doors', and had a liberating effect on her work. Over the years she has become an inveterate hunter-gatherer. Today her converted garage studio in Canterbury is piled high with boxes of miscellaneous 'treasures', picked up locally and internationally on her travels – anything from mulberry bark, pine needles and seaweed, to metal wire, linen yarn and plastic washing line. She particularly enjoys devising uses for unlikely odds and ends. Small pine cones, bark curls and seed pods were all co-opted in a recent series of NATURAL NECKLACES.

Mary's attraction to natural materials, such as fibrous date palm cloth and magnolia pods, is easy to appreciate. It is also very much in tune with prevailing concerns about sustainability, although as an erstwhile ecologist these are issues she has been aware of since the 1960s. However, her fondness for shiny plastics and glittery metals is perhaps more difficult to comprehend. 'I work instinctively using a variety of materials, often by serendipity. It's natural for me to cross over from organic materials to synthetics', she explains. 'I like the mobility and lustre of plastic washing line in the same way as I love the dull sheen and mellowness of willow, the way it catches the light when you bend it in particular ways'. Harnessing the intrinsic qualities of a particular material lies at the heart of her current work. Finnish birch bark, which is golden brown on the inside and silvery grey on the outside with a patchy lichen patina, provides a good example of this. 'The nature of birch bark, with its two surfaces, is very fascinating', she says, adding that she particularly likes the texture of lichen and its knobbly quality. She has used this material to make two simple bags in complementary colourways called GOLDEN BAG WITH HIDDEN SILVER and SILVER BAG WITH HIDDEN GOLD. On the latter the fringe curves inwards, and on the former it spills outwards. The lichen forms an intrinsic part of the decoration.

Speaking of a piece called RUCHED RUSH BAG ON THE CURVE, Mary explains that the curvature of the bag and the wandering lines of the stitching reflect the rhythms of her work pattern on the day she made it. Mid-way through, she was forced to break off. On resuming, the tension with which the soft damp rushes were strung together was subtly different. 'I don't have preconceptions about how a piece will turn out. I've learnt to relax and make it a pleasure. Basketmaking is a problem-solving exercise. I never give up on a piece. Altering, changing, adding, subtracting – there's always something that can be done'. When discussing her work, Mary frequently refers to intense sensory experiences – not only the impact of particular colours and tonal contrasts, but the varied tactile qualities of materials when wet and dry, their distinctive sounds when handled, and even their vivid smells. She compares the feel of moist rushes to 'soft suede or peach skin'. When the rushes have dried out, she enjoys their 'hard fleshy feel' and their 'natural colours'. Of a bag made of polyolefin tubing she remarks that she likes 'the translucence, flexibility and the noise of the plastic as it is handled', while with plastic washing line she likes the way it droops and drapes. Speaking of a piece called SCENTED BARK POCKET, made of western red cedar bark, she exclaims, 'Scented is an understatement. I was almost asphyxiated while making it'!

Originally trained as a zoologist and botanist, Mary is unusually sensitive to the physical structure of plants and animals. For her MA during the late 1960s she studied the habitat of the remote Fenlands of Wisconsin in the United States, a project that involved the intensive gathering, handling, analysis and classification of flora and fauna. In her RUSH BAGS she deliberately leaves the thick cut ends of the rushes exposed to reveal the spongy quality of the plant. 'It's the air that makes them stand up', she points out. But synthetic materials are sometimes equally effective at evoking natural phenomena. A basket made of red washing line was given the title RED SEA ANEMONE, because its vibrant colouring and upright fringe conjured up the tentacles of this underwater polyp. 'My interest in the structure of animals, particularly their internal structure and behaviour, in an odd way has come to be part of the basketmaking that I do', she observes. This is particularly evident in the fluid, squid-like forms of her SEA CREATURES, made from streamlined bundles of materials such as plastic washing line, willow, poelute cane and electric flex. Their linear structures also suggest animal skeletons. Another series of pieces with indirect animal associations are her FLYING TRAPS, huge suspended cone-shaped mobiles measuring up to two metres long, alluding to traditional fish traps. Made of willow and poelute cane, bound by string and wire, these loose spiralling forms look as though they have just burst open. Her primary concerns are aesthetic – the moiré effects of the spaced criss-crossing rods producing zingy optical patterns as the object rotates, the internal spaces within the cones and the shadows cast on ceilings and walls.

Mary's scientific background, her activities as a historian and collector of baskets, and her close on-going relationship with museums, make the use of the term 'artefact' seem particularly apt as a description of her work. Certainly she is more at ease with this than with the word 'art'. The term 'artefact' is pertinent not only for its implicit allusion to craftsmanship, but because of its secondary associations with social history and anthropology (a career she admits she might have chosen in another life). In purely visual terms, many of Mary's artefacts evoke a quasi-ethnographic context. For example, her CYCAD WEAVINGS, made from interlaced Cycad leaves ('an ancient plant from dinosaur times'), suggest tribal neckpieces. It's not that these objects aspire to any specific function, or presume to any ritual or mystical significance, but they reflect an unusually high level of unselfconsciousness in the making process, a decidedly non-Western characteristic. They also embody a heightened sensitivity to materials, suggesting that the maker is in tune with the physical world at a more basic elemental level than most Western city dwellers. 'I'm happy for my work to be seen in an ethnographic context, although this isn't something I've been conscious of until now', Mary admits. 'I love museums. They're a great source of stimulation for me. I also appreciate the fact that they take what I'm doing seriously in terms of information-gathering'. In fact, several of her recent pieces relate directly to ethnic artefacts. An African stringed musical instrument inspired the shape of one of her BARK WEAVINGS, made of willow, willow bark, bay twigs, Kniphofia leaves and linen thread. Similarly, the unusual structure of her BUD BURST AND THORN series derives from a Native American system associated with the First People of California. Each piece consists of an oval willow hoop, across which twigs of ash, oak, maple, or wild rose are laid. The twigs were collected from an English hedgerow on a bright spring day on the eve of the Iraq war, which makes the objects especially portentous. They are held in place with string, wire and black plastic cable ties, emphasising their spikiness and the associations with barbed wire.

With their strange, imperfect beauty, Mary's artefacts challenge the negative attitudes within Western society towards ephemeral objects made of 'worthless' materials and 'humble' manual activities. Intriguing objects such as SKEIN NET – a horseshoe-shaped willow frame interlaced with fine knotted willow skein – have an obvious magnetism, yet within the conventional categories of art and craft, they are impossible to define. So unique is her current work that even her profession becomes difficult to categorise. No longer a traditional basketmaker, she is uncomfortable with alternative tags such as willow artist, fibre artist, environmental artist, artist basketmaker, which all seem spurious in various ways. Even the term basketmaker is wide of the mark, given how far she has moved away from creating recognisable basket forms. That just leaves 'maker', perhaps the only term simple and open enough to encompass her present and future activities.

Some of the most significant developments in Mary's recent work have arisen by responding to happy accidents, as in the series of free-flowing willow sculptures variously described as Ripples, Scribbles and Dazzles. The first of these came about after she was left with a pile of pre-bent willow rods, having been commissioned to make a seat for a chair that proved technically impossible and had to be dismantled. Noticing the pleasing appearance of the rods lying at random on the studio floor, she began to play about with them, arrange them in an interlaced pattern and tie them together. 'There was just this heap on the floor with lots of crossovers and junctions', she recalls. 'I liked this discarded material because there were lovely loops at the end, and zig zags and wavy lines in the weaving. It reminded me of my own hand-writing and the calligraphy that I've enjoyed so much'. Subsequently, during her residency at Cambridge University Botanic Gardens as part of the Year of the Artist, she developed these ideas further, creating an irregular, frenetic, snaking mesh called WILLOW SCRIBBLE TRACING, suspended dramatically against a dark Thuja hedge. Since then she has created a series of variations using specially prepared willow rods with bends, kinks and bulges in different places. Full of whiplash lines and dancing rhythms, these sculptures recall the dynamism of Jackson Pollock's action paintings. Although the technique is entirely different, the spontaneity and the intensity are the same. Some recent pieces have incorporated rods of different coloured willow. Their character also alters dramatically depending on the colour and texture of the surface behind. 'Materials have their own properties. They sometimes do unexpected things', Mary observes. 'You have to notice oddities. You have to stretch them to the limit. There's something sensually pleasing about this'.

Mary also pushes her audience to the limits by challenging their preconceptions. Some of her recent pieces are openly mischievous, such as CHOCOLATE BELLIED BASKET WITH SPLASHES OF CREAM, in which an otherwise 'normal' basket is blemished by 'slashes' in a contrasting colour, which throw the weaving off beam. In fact the careful positioning of the 'cuts' at intervals around the basket ensures that it all balances out in the end, but the immediate response of most people is to assume that they have spotted a mistake. WILLOW LINE DRAWING is another teasing piece. A basketmaker's in-joke, it's an installation composed entirely of the knotted willow ties used to hold bundles of willow rods together. It was prompted by Mary's admiration for the beautiful springy shapes of the ties after they had been cut open and their contents released.

Many of the pieces Mary makes are deliberately open-ended — open to interpretation as well as literally open to the air. They are not containers in the conventional sense, they are partial forms, often with holes and slits in unexpected places. Some pieces look as though they have exploded — alarming to some, but exhilarating to her. 'I don't like enclosed things very much. You can create something that looks balanced, even if it's pleasantly irregular. The rhythms are the crucial thing, the rhythms and the lines'. This sense of her pieces not being finished — physically as well as metaphorically — is a central feature of her current work. 'Unfinished is not a problem for me, although it unsettles other people. I used to make things as near perfect as you could make them, but that doesn't interest me anymore. I'm not a perfectionist. These days I'm quite pragmatic. I tie knots and cobble things together. When I'm making pieces for an exhibition, I'll just stop at a certain point and send things off. I don't see anything as actually finished. It's just one step towards something else'.

Having served her time as a jobbing basketmaker, her main aim now is to satisfy herself. She has reached the stage where she would rather risk isolation than compromise on creative matters. At present she is only able to spend about a quarter of her time in her studio, but she hopes to increase this in the future by cutting down on travel and teaching commitments. From an aesthetic point of view, her chief aspiration is to refine the rhythms of her work. 'Rhythmic qualities are more important to me than form. The forms of my pieces are often quite crude. It's because the lines are different that each piece looks unique. Each piece takes on an individual character from its particular rhythms and lines'. As to how her work might develop in future years, she is both philosophical and optimistic. 'You can't stop evolving. It's all part of a continuum. As soon as I start doing something, the next idea is there'.

Lesley Jackson
Freelance writer and curator

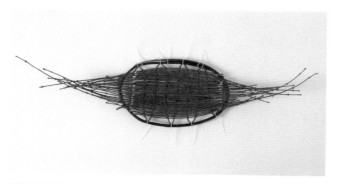

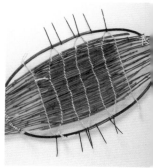

BUD BURST AND THORN
Willow, field maple, jute string, plastic, cable ties
36 x 93 x 23cm

BUD BURST AND THORN
Willow, ash, sisal string, plastic, cable ties
68 x 156 x 7cm

'The day war was declared on Iraq, a beautiful blue-skied day, I spent several hours collecting branches from an English hedgerow for these pieces'.

BUD BURST AND THORN
Willow, wild rose, plastic covered wire, plastic, cable ties
56 x 86 x 4cm

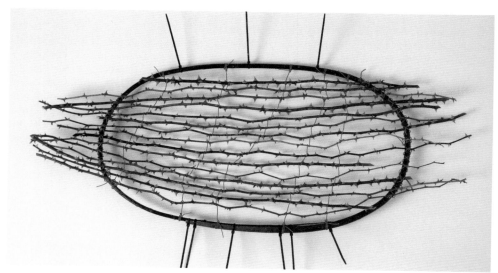

BARK WEAVING
Willow, willow bark, chestnut
50 x 80 x 6cm

BARK WEAVING
*Willow, willow bark, bay, Kniphofia,
linen thread*
44 x 140 x 4cm

'I don't like enclosed things very much. You can create something that looks balanced, even if it's pleasantly irregular. The rhythms are the crucial thing, the rhythms and the lines'

RUSH NET
Dutch salt rush, wild Clematis
62 x 66 x 16cm

  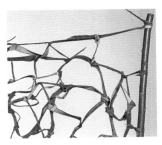

BARK NET details *Willow, willow bark, wire* 63 x 65 x 14cm

SKEIN NET *Willow, skeined willow, wire* 40 x 55 x 5cm

PLEASURE TO PIN LEAVES
WITH THORNS IN A STIFF
BREEZE detail
Cycad leaves and thorns
36 x 34 x 4cm

CYCAD WEAVING
Cycad leaf
64 x 54 x 18cm

CYCAD WEAVINGS
Cycad leaves
90 x 98 x 7cm

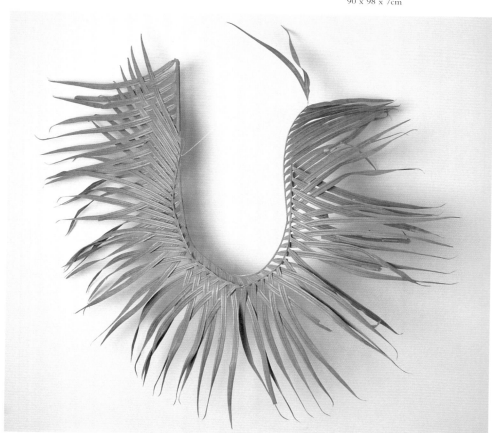

BAMBOO PURSE
Bamboo leaves, bay, ginger
20 x 18 x 2cm

'I'm happy for my work to be seen in an ethnographic context, although this isn't something I've been conscious of until now'

SCENTED BARK POCKET
Western red cedar bark, ginger
19 x 24 x 8cm

SCENTED BARK POCKET detail
Western red cedar bark, ginger

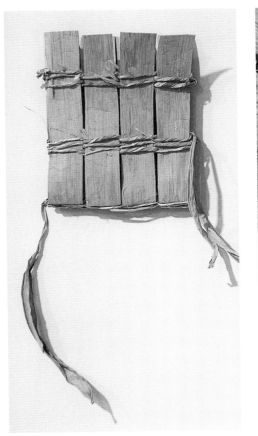

SEA CREATURE
Plastic covered washing line, wire,
willow
60 x 180 x 60cm

'My interest in the structure of animals, particularly their internal structure and behaviour, in an odd way has come to be part of the basketmaking that I do'

SEA CREATURE
Plastic, poelute cane, plastic covered
wire, copper foil, willow bark, bay
10 x 37 x 12cm

SEA CREATURE
Plastic covered washing line, poelute
cane, plastic covered wire, linen thread
17 x 78 x 17cm

WILLOW BURST
Split willow, poelute cane, hemp
string, wire, willow bark
63 x 32 x 36cm

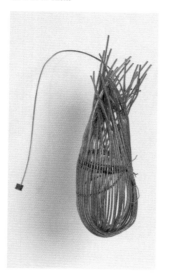

'Rhythmic qualities are more important to me than form. The forms of my pieces are often quite crude. It's because the lines are different that each piece looks unique. Each piece takes on an individual character from its particular rhythms and lines'

FLYING TRAP
White and brown willow, poelute cane, plastic covered wire
65 x 195 x 30cm

CONICLE detail
Willow, poelute cane, hemp string
8 x 141 x 29cm

WILLOW CONE detail
Buff and white willow, poelute cane
270 x 150 x 160cm

DARK BOWL WITH FLYING
TIPS
Brown and white willow
100 x 36 x 110cm

THREE WILLOW CONES
uff and white willow, poelute cane
70 x 150 x 160cm approx

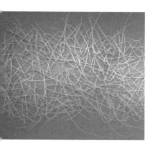

WILLOW LINE detail
White and steamed willow

WILLOW DAZZLES 2
White and steamed willow
150 x 140 x 25cm

Poster for Crafts Council
Exhibition 'OUT THERE '

'Materials have their own properties. They sometimes do unexpected things'

Installation left:
WILLOW DAZZLES 1
White and steamed willow
120 x 170 x 26cm
and FLYING TRAP
Willow, poelute cane, plastic covered wire
140 x 120 x 130cm

WILLOW SCRIBBLE TRACING
White and brown willow
390 x 190 x 25cm

Line 1: RUSH BAG WITH CROSSINGS *Dutch seating rush;* BARK BOX *Willow bark, paper string;* FLYING TRAP *White and brown willow, poelute cane, plastic covered wire.*

Line 2: RED SEA ANENOME *Plastic washing line, plastic covered wire;* FLYING TRAP *plastic covered washing line, poelute cane, plastic covered wire, linen thread;* CHOCOLATE POT WITH DASHES OF CREAM *White and steamed willow.*

Line 3: SKEIN NET *Willow, wire;* BARK WEAVING *Willow, willow bark;* BARK NET *Willow bark.*

Line 4: MARY'S TOOL BOX; PLEASURE TO PIN LEAVES WITH THORNS IN A STIFF BREEZE *Cycad leaves;* TRANSLUCENT BAG *Polyolefin tubing, cotton string, electric flex, wooden beads.*

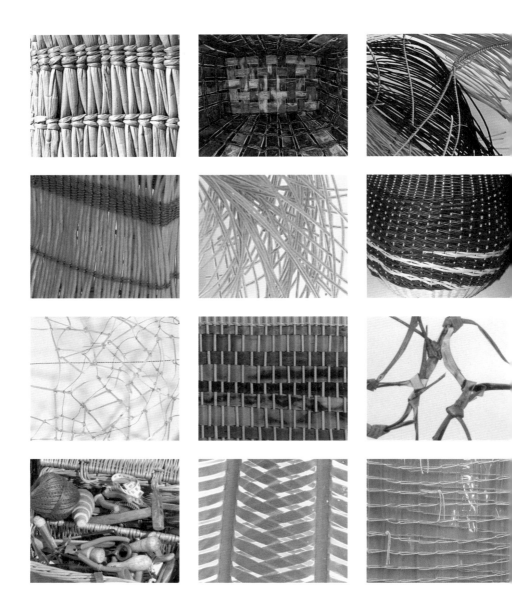

Line 1: WILLOW DISH *buff willow, willow skein*; SILVER BAG WITH HIDDEN GOLD *Birch bark, linen thread, leather;*
ANDS.

Line 2: SEA CREATURE *Washing line, poelute cane, plastic covered wire, copper foil, willow bark, bay*; BARK WEAVING
Willow, willow bark, bay, Kniphofia, linen thread; RUCHED RUSH BAG *Rush, linen thread.*

Line 3: ELEVEN WINGS *Willow, plastic, acetate, wire, film*; PLEASURE TO PIN LEAVES WITH THORNS IN A STIFF
BREEZE *Cycad leaves*, BUD BURST AND THORN *Wild rose, plastic covered wire, willow, cable ties.*

Line 4: RIB *Construction*; WILLOW TIE LINES *Willow*; RUSH BAG WITH BLUE LIGHTS *English rush, wire, beads.*

COLLABORATIONS
with Tim Johnson

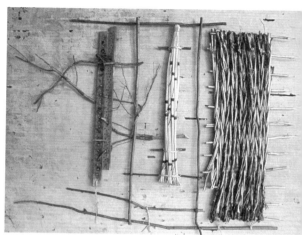

TRAVELLING
Vissingaard Museum, Denmark. Permanent Installation
White and brown willow, hazel, hemp string, stones, wood, pine root, plaster, wire mesh

FISH WEIR WALK
Wildlife and Wetland Centre, Arundel
Willow, hazel, sack ties

BILLOW
Painters cloths, willow, washing line
Robert Phillips Gallery, Walton-on-Thames
Temporary Exhibition

Mary Butcher: Basketmaker

'It's beautiful to sit and yarn while you weave together. I like weaving with old people because they yarn about things, the past, which is the future for their children. Sometimes I tell secrets, it' good to share and exchange'.
Ellen Treverrow, Aboriginal basket maker.

Orsman Road is a bleak street full of warehouses, close to the Regents Canal in East London. It i. the kind of street where roof tiles fall off old buildings from a height, at speed. Temporary barrier are put up and signs appear in chalk warning occasional passers by but this is Hackney so nobody clears the broken tiles from the pavement. Hurrying through debris I had never really thought abou what lay beyond the facades of these warehouses until Mary Butcher described her trip to the British Museum store at the far end of the road:

'Each level in the store belongs to a different continent or section of one, and each curator had brought out sufficient basketry items to show the extraordinary wealth and diversity of form, from the classical vessel to the bizarre, from many natural shades to the optically dazzling and vivid. ... A we went from floor to floor, seeing so much richness, and in such contrast to the cage-like lift, the darkness of the building and the metal shelves, it became clear that none of us had quite grasped the abundance of information available, simply from those baskets'.[1]

Her account brought to mind a market place offering intoxicating range of choice. But this store i. not a market and nothing is to be taken home. These are precious examples of different materials techniques, skills, patterns, all there to be preserved. Without this exercise in conservation we may forget something that a basketmaker somewhere once knew. And yet baskets were not made to las forever.

Mary Butcher accepts that baskets themselves cannot be preserved indefinitely. It is not in their nature. She take pleasure in the temporary nature of an installation such as her own WILLOW SCRIBBLES that were designed to be ephemeral. She welcomes the effect of the weather on the structure – 'the willow becomes a muted coffee colour before decaying and returning to the compos heap'.[2] And it is not just in her own work that we find this acceptance of the power of nature through creative work. Describing exhibits at the University of Liverpool's Ness Gardens:

'David Drew, our best known basket maker, and Annette Holdensen, a Danish artist, produced thi fascinating series of triangles, carefully planned so that the microclimates under the triangles produce tall green grass and the walkway between becomes trampled and brown. In time these triangles were used as seats and began to sag delightfully and finally disintegrated along with the other pieces.'[3]

So as makers and curators we cannot make time stand still. Nor can we anticipate precisely the pace at which things will unravel. Yet in both Mary Butcher's conversation and in her writings there is an urgency not to let a knowledge and understanding of basketmaking slip beyond our reach. It is not that the objects themselves must always be hoarded but that the skills of the makers must be recorded and disseminated.

In 1991 Mary Butcher made a trip to Poland. She chose Poland because she respected the high standard of craftsmanship within the long-established basket making industry which has continually adapted to political climates and the needs of local people and foreign buyers. There was no official archive in Poland which explained how and where people had learned to make baskets. Many of the basketmakers were women and they were surprised to hear of the British view of the basketmaking industry as traditionally male. Mary Butcher's own grasp of the Polish language was slim but she was struck by how the basketmakers and their families were untroubled by the language barrier. A shared appreciation of work seemed sufficient to draw her into family life which included swims in the lake, roast sausages, apples round a fire and singing in the dark.

Collaboration in the here and now was celebrated in Poland but when she visited museums she found none of the British Museum style categorising of material that had made an impact back in Orsman road:

'...Finally to a locked 18th century store in Warsaw's lovely Lazienki Park, led me to a collection of spectacular baskets and other objects which had been made in the 1940s and early 1950s. These were basket structures made of wide pieces of cleaved willow bound with skeins. They were made by one or two people who worked in Art Colleges in Kazimierz and then Warsaw but no one knows how or where they learnt to use the basket making materials. Wladyslaw Wolkowski made many of them in his own style and he also specialised in making hangings from willow threads although I never saw any of these. He was very secretive about his techniques and never taught anyone. He died in 1985 and the curator at the store, Halina, told me that she thought that the skills were lost. However, at the Basket School in Kwidzyn I discovered more baskets in the same style, made by the first Director of the school. These predated Wolkowski's and it seems possible that this director taught Wolkowski.'[4]

Despite the absence of any written archive, or cataloguing system, Mary Butcher could recognise the secrets in Wolkowski's work by looking at the surviving material and remembering the patterns sufficiently to enable her to identify them in the work of others. The baskets needed to have been preserved thus far in order for experts to see and at least half-understand the secrets woven into them.

Looking at the baskets of the past provided Mary Butcher with some clues. She also enjoyed watching contemporary basketmakers produce objects during her research trips to Poland, Hungary,

Latvia and of course Britain. She might watch a basket take shape over 10 hours. Such close observation inspired the onlooker as both maker and teacher. Without teachers willing to share the codes they have uncovered perhaps a material understanding could disappear between one generation and the next: 'to provide a strong surge forward to contemporary basket making it is not necessary to be a historian but it is necessary to know something of the past that is in every basket'.[5]

When I first listened to Mary Butcher's enthusiasm for both research into basketmaking communities and her own teaching I did not understand how she could maintain the space for her own creative work. Surely it would be crowded out by innumerable influences, traditions and styles vying for space in her mind's eye. What I had not understood was the potential energy and direction that is bound up in the materials themselves. This is more powerful than any haunting memories of decorative and functional form.

Anthropologists consider "Do different peoples in different places come to the same conclusions about the best way of doing things ?" Mary Butcher's own research into international basketmaking has shown that although the basket forms created are diverse, the ways of working with willow, and various other woods, have evolved in very similar ways amongst basketmaking communities which have had no contact. This is because the natural materials behave in a certain way and therefore they teach the maker how to work safely and how to manipulate and weave. Hungarian gypsies prepare black maple for splitting by roasting on a fire in the same way as Slovak peoples and Cumbrians in the North West of England prepare their oak as the materials respond in the same way. Again similar tools have evolved the world over. When Mary Butcher discussed the tools used by Chilean basketmakers she discovered that they use a device with three angled edges, identical to the English basketmakers cleave.

If natural materials are our best guide, in a sense then, every basket in the world could disintegrate over time; every transcript of every interview with crafts people discussing their methods, techniques, secrets even, could be mislaid and in time people would re-learn from the possibilities and the limitations of the materials themselves. The vital thing then must be the cultivation of healthy crops and the knowledge of how to rear the best plants for a given purpose. To this end Mary Butcher was fascinated by the writings of the basketmaker and willow cultivator William Scaling in the early nineteenth century, who published detailed studies of the growth and uses of different varieties of willow species. Arguably our most important archive is the knowledge of how to secure a stable ecology in which plants can be reared.

However, part of our concern for ecology is represented by accommodating other found materials from the modern world into the craft of basketmaking. Traditionally Zulu women wove coiled baskets known as imbenge from grasses and Ilala palm. These saucer-shaped baskets formed a tight lid over clay pots for beer brewing. In the 1980s many Zulus had moved to the cities and they continued to make imbenge out of locally available materials, often out of telephone wire brightly coated with plastic. Ecological changes here resulted in the innovative use of new materials while retaining form but not function.

Basketmaking appears to be a craft where traditions are not exactly lost but concealed for certain periods of time. The nature of basketmaking requires materials to be held together with a closeness that is man-made and often more tightly bound than the natural world dictates. Mary Butcher's work plays with materials and coaxes them into a form which looks natural and yet, as with her weaving of Cycad leaves, great patience and skill is required in order to give the materials a final form which makes them look at ease.

Mary Butcher compares the metaphor of essential oppositions that belongs to basketmaking: 'as an elegy – a song of lament, at once individual and spiritual, but also social, historical and political.'[6] Mary Butcher's own basketwork suggests a kind of tribute, a kind of grieving that is re-building with every movement that which is required to make an object. But once the object is created it is not as important as the process of its own making, the interaction with both the natural materials and the stories that have been woven together across time. I am reminded of the psychoanalyst Anna Freud's practice of weaving while she listened to her clients. There is an attention that comes from being focused on one task and open to another. There is also a tremendous strength embodied in Mary Butcher's work; the strength that is reflected when looking at her workshop floor awash with branches as if the building had been at sea all night, and remarking with a commanding sincerity: 'It will only take a few hours to tidy up and work again.'

Lottie Hoare

1   Mary Butcher, 'Opening Up the Store' from draft essay on 'Beyond Contemporary Basketmaking: Forces for Change in the Second Millennium.' Delivered at the Crafts Council 1999
2   Diana Woolf, 'Outside Insight', p7, in the Crafts Council 'Out There' gallery guide, July/August 2003.
3   Mary Butcher, notes for a lecture, Copenhagen October 1997.
4   Mary Butcher, draft of a lecture 'The Life and Death of the Polish Basketmaking Industry' for The South East Association of Churchill Fellows, November, 1999
5   Mary Butcher, 'Opening Up the Store' from draft essay on 'Beyond Contemporary Basketmaking: Forces for Change in the Second Millennium.'
6   Mary Butcher, 'Introduction' from draft essay on 'Beyond Contemporary Basketmaking: Forces for Change in the Second Millennium.'

EXHIBITIONS

Inaugural Exhibition What is Craft?, The Hub, Sleaford: October 2003 – January 2004
Fletchen, Gallerie Handwerk, Munich, Germany: September 5th – October 4th 2003
Willows in the Wind with Tim Johnson, The Robert Phillips Gallery, Walton-on-Thames: September 3rd – 28th 2003
Out There Crafts Council, London: June – July 2003
Basketry Carte Blanche: Mary Butcher, National Vlechtmuseum, Noordewolde, The Netherlands: May 24 – August 30 2003, Ramsgate Library Gallery, Ramsgate, Kent: September 6 – October 11 2003
Irish Basketmaking: Tradition today co-curator with Joe Hogan, Crafts Council of Ireland: 2003 & tour
Strands, Oxfordshire Basketmakers and the Guild of Weavers, Spinners & Dyers, Oxford: November 2002
Plant [Weave], Royal Edinburgh Botanic Garden: installation *Bag Reflections and Contradictions:* August – October 2002
New Basketry, Courtyard Gallery, Hertfordshire: July 2002
Christmas at the Lillie, Lillie Art Gallery, Glasgow: November – December 2001
Thirteen Hands, Fort William, Scotland and Tour, in collaboration with Tim Johnson, Vincent Large, Sue Paraskeva: November 2001– 2004
Inaugural Art Exhibition, Friends of the Pitt Rivers Museum: October 2001
Mary Butcher Collection, Decorative Art Museum, Trondheim, Norway: April 2001, Vissinggaard: Denmark 2002
Travelling with Tim Johnson, Cambridge University Botanic Garden: August 2001
Form and Function with Helen Yardley, Riverhouse, Robert Phillips Gallery, Walton-on-Thames, Surrey: January 2001
All in the Making: Basketry Explored, co-curator and sole exhibitor alongside an ethnographic collection from the Powell Cotton Museum, Ramsgate Library Art Gallery: November 1999 – January 2000
Mary Butcher Baskets, Hove Museum and Art Gallery: solo exhibition: September – October 1999
Vessels, Portsmouth Cathedral for Hampshire Sculpture Trust 1999
Craft in the Bay: Cardiff, August 1999
Contemporary International Basketmaking, co-curator with Lois Walpole for The Crafts Council: major touring exhibition of over sixty artists: 1997 – 1999
The Medici Gallery, Dover Street, London: October 1998
Works in Wood, The Star Gallery, Lewes, West Sussex: Summer 1997
Beyond the Bounds co-curator and exhibitor, Manchester Metropolitan University; Milton Keynes Summer Show; Maidstone Museum & Art Gallery: 1996.

PUBLICATIONS

Willow Work, Batsford 1986, fourth reprint 2001
essay for catalogue *Cross Over,* Bury St Edmunds Art Gallery 2001
Chair Seating with O. Elton Barratt, K. Johnson, Batsford 1989, reprint 2001
Basketmaking by Polly Pollock: major contributor 1997
Contemporary International Basketmaking, Crafts Council & Merrill Holberton 1999: 120 page,
definitive book on basketmaking today, to accompany Crafts Council Exhibition
article in *Ideas in the Making,* editor Pam Johnson, Crafts Council 1998
essay in *Obscure Objects of Desire,* editor Tanya Harrod, Crafts Council 1997
Many short articles in the *Basketmakers' Association Newsletter* and elsewhere

RESIDENCIES

Research Associate, Norwich School of Art & Design: construction of database after research on
textile and basketry artists and crafts people in Norfolk and Suffolk 2000 – 2002
YOTA Millenium project *Art in the Environment* with Tim Johnson, Cambridge University Botanic
Garden: art works using materials from the Garden for exhibition outside and in the Tropical House
March 2001
Year of the Artist (YOTA Millennium project) with Tim Johnson: *Fish Weir Walk* at The Wildlife and
Wetland Centre, Arundel, West Sussex June 2000
Bridgewater Hall Manchester for *Grand Piano* 2000: to weave a grove of small grand pianos with
help from Big Issue vendors February 2000
Willow residency, Congleton Borough Council: teaching; commissioned sculpture, *Two,* in
collaboration with Tim Johnson; willow piece *Mystical Wings* for Bereton Heath Country Park
February and March 1998

CONFERENCES

Oxford Brookes University Japanese Culture conference: *Japanese Traditional & Contemporary
Basketmaking* April 2002
British Museum and Crafts Council joint conference *Art and Artefact in the 21st Century:* major
speaker *Translating Stake and Strand,* published on the web February 2002
Ideas in the Making, University of East Anglia 1998
Obscure Objects of Desire, University of East Anglia 1997